FUTURE MAN
MAN
SUPER APE
APE
YAY!
尾田栄一郎

Should we think about "Evolution" today? Or should we not? Yes, let's take a look.

The ape became a man, just like in the drawing above. You can probably see how the ape's body starts to straighten up, little by little. Now then, let's look at the next man. As his body continues to straighten, let's have him flip backwards. And from then on, mankind will float a little in space. I'M SURE OF IT.

-Eiichiro Oda, 2000

Eiichiro Oda began his manga career at the age of 17, when his one-shot cowboy manga **Wanted!** won second place in the coveted Tezuka manga awards. Oda went on to work as an assistant to some of the biggest manga artists in the industry, including Nobuhiro Watsuki, before winning the Hop Step Award for new artists. His pirate adventure **One Piece**, which debuted in **Weekly Shonen Jump** in 1997, quickly became one of the most popular manga in Japan.

ONE PIECE VOL. 12
EAST BLUE PART 12 &
BAROQUE WORKS PART 1

SHONEN JUMP Manga Edition

This volume contains material that was originally
published in English in **SHONEN JUMP** #42–44.

STORY AND ART BY EIICHIRO ODA

English Adaptation/Lance Caselman
Translation/JN Productions
Touch-up Art & Lettering/Vanessa Satone
Additional Touch-up/Josh Simpson
Design/Sean Lee
Editor/Yuki Takagaki

ONE PIECE © 1997 by Eiichiro Oda. All rights reserved.
First published in Japan in 1997 by SHUEISHA Inc., Tokyo.
English translation rights arranged by SHUEISHA Inc.

The stories, characters and incidents mentioned in this
publication are entirely fictional.

Printed in the U.S.A.

Published by VIZ Media, LLC
P.O. Box 77010
San Francisco, CA 94107

19
First printing, October 2006
Nineteenth printing, November 2023

viz.com

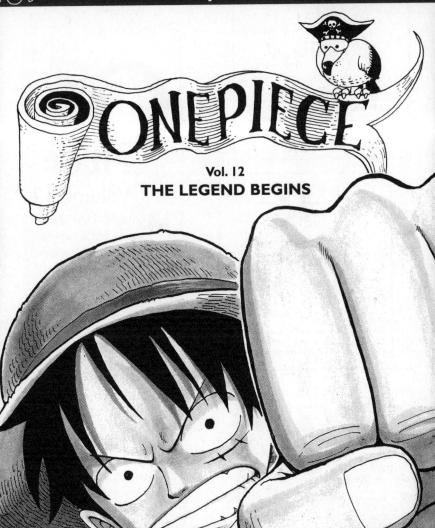

ONE PIECE

Vol. 12
THE LEGEND BEGINS

STORY AND ART BY
EIICHIRO ODA

THE STORY OF ONE PIECE

Volume 12

Monkey D. Luffy started out as just a kid with a dream—and that dream was to become the greatest pirate in history! Stirred by the tales of pirate "Red-Haired" Shanks, Luffy vowed to become a pirate himself. That was before the enchanted Devil Fruit gave Luffy the power to stretch like rubber, at the cost of being unable to swim—a serious handicap for an aspiring sea dog. Undeterred, Luffy set out to sea and recruited some crewmates: master swordsman Zolo, treasure-hunting thief Nami, lying sharpshooter Usopp, and Sanji, the high-kicking chef.

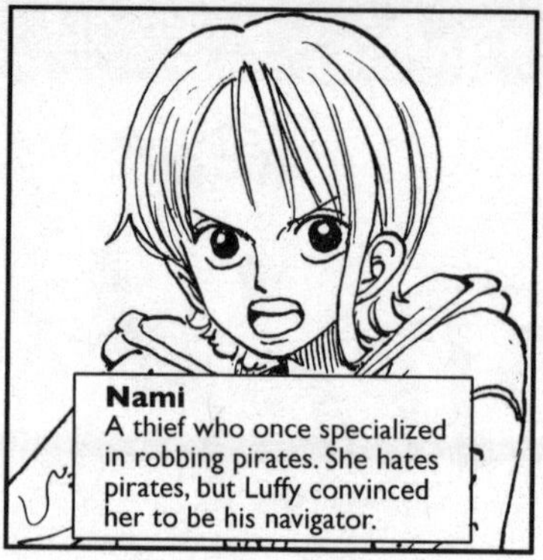

Nami
A thief who once specialized in robbing pirates. She hates pirates, but Luffy convinced her to be his navigator.

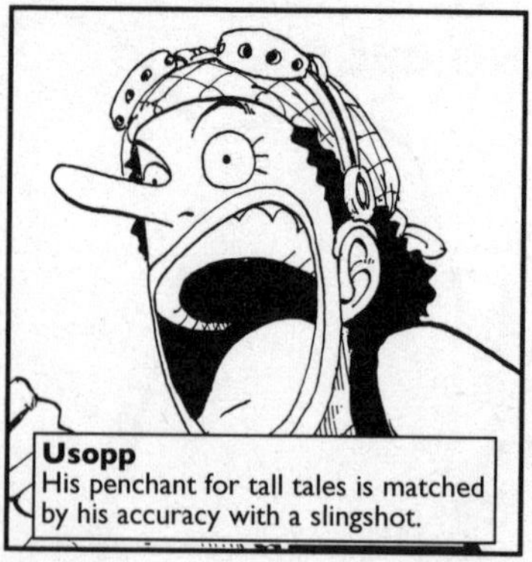

Usopp
His penchant for tall tales is matched by his accuracy with a slingshot.

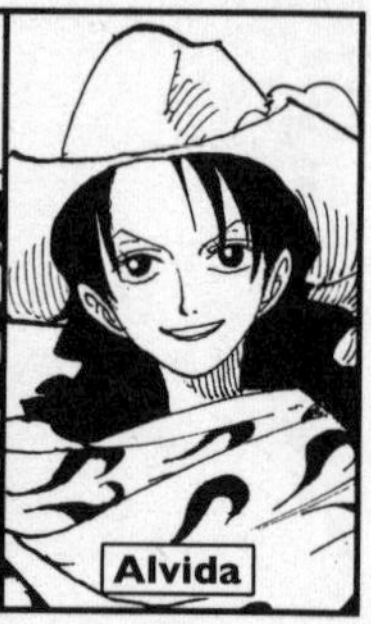

Alvida

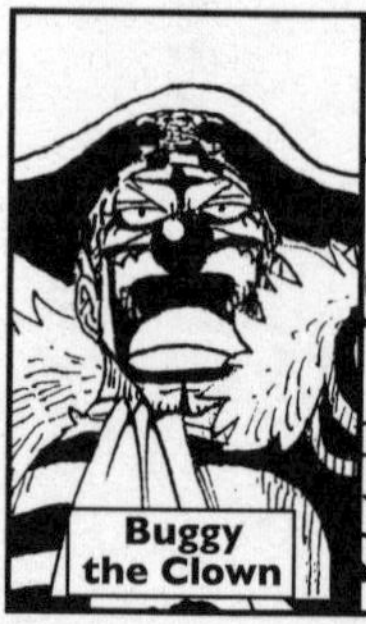

Buggy the Clown

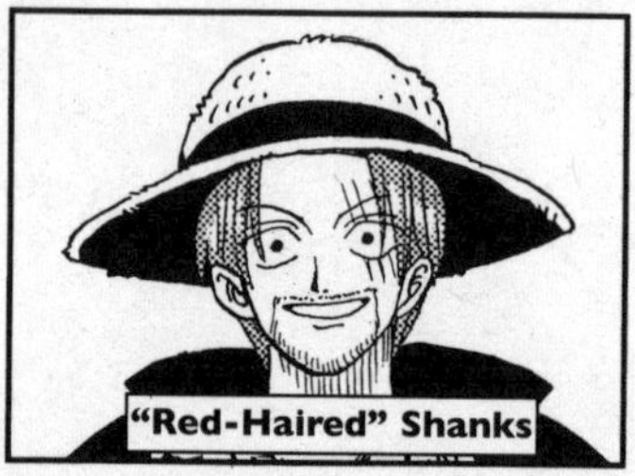

"Red-Haired" Shanks

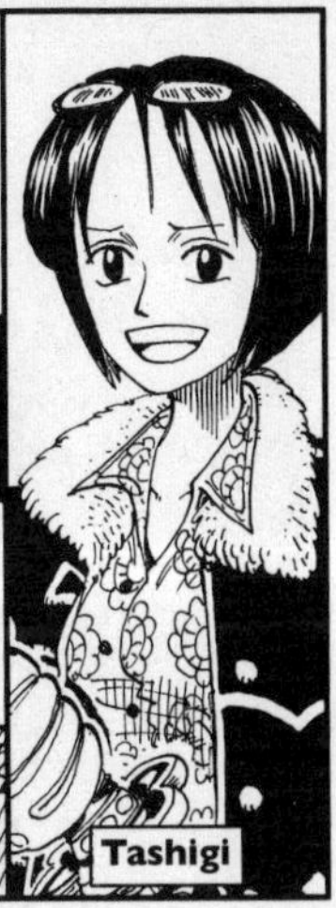

Tashigi

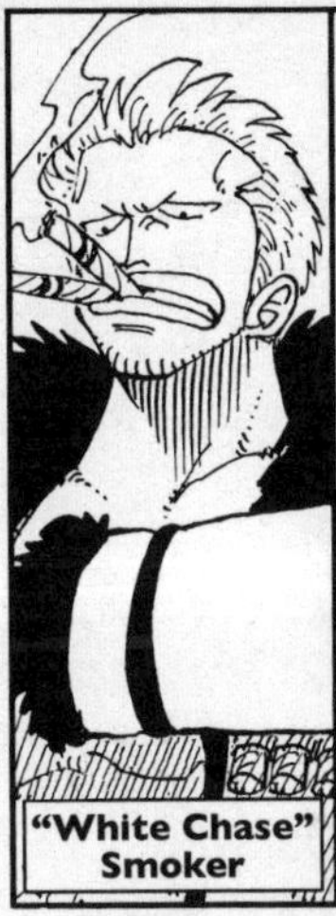

"White Chase" Smoker

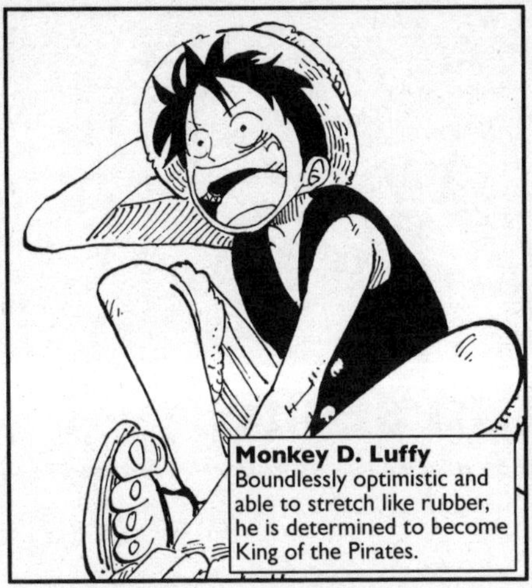

Monkey D. Luffy
Boundlessly optimistic and able to stretch like rubber, he is determined to become King of the Pirates.

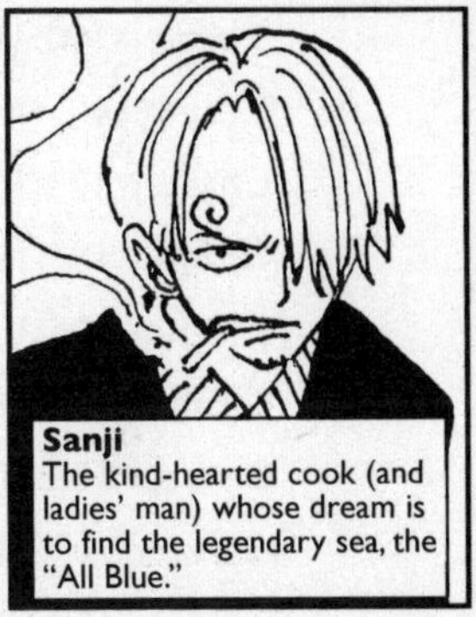

Sanji
The kind-hearted cook (and ladies' man) whose dream is to find the legendary sea, the "All Blue."

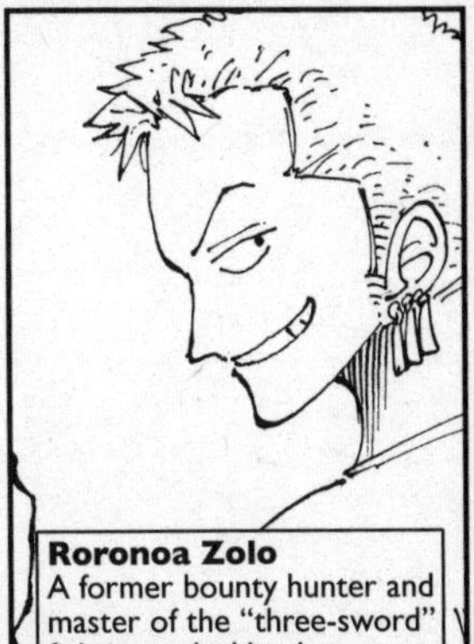

Roronoa Zolo
A former bounty hunter and master of the "three-sword" fighting style. He plans to become the world's greatest swordsman!

In order to make Nami smile again, Luffy challenges Arlong to a climactic battle. His furious attack destroys Arlong Park and frees Nami and the people of Coco Village.

Having defeated the monstrous Arlong, Luffy and his crew set sail. Luffy is overjoyed to discover that he is known the world over as a wanted pirate, with a bounty on his head. As they near the Grand Line, they stop at Roguetown where the pirate king, Gold Roger, met his fate. Luffy climbs onto the execution scaffold to see Gold Roger's final view, when the beautifully transformed Alvida and Buggy the Clown appear. They capture Luffy and prepare to execute him publicly. But in the instant before what seems to be certain death, Luffy laughs, just as Gold Roger had before he died.

BAROQUE WORKS

ONE PIECE

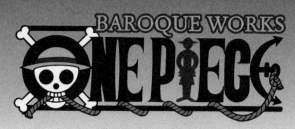

Vol. 12
THE LEGEND BEGINS

CONTENTS

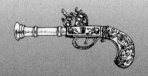

Chapter 100: THE LEGEND BEGINS

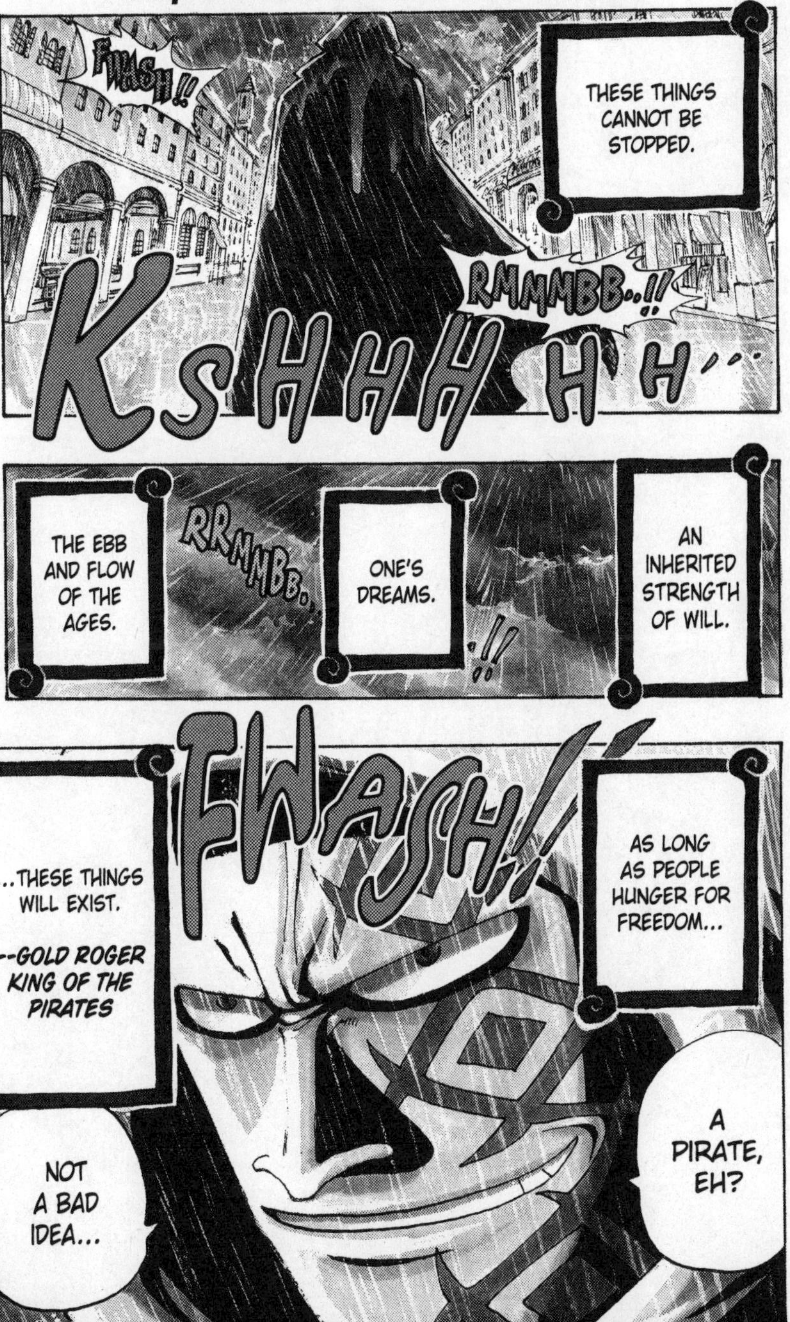
THESE THINGS CANNOT BE STOPPED.
FWASH!!
RMMMBB..!!
KSHHHHH...
AN INHERITED STRENGTH OF WILL.
ONE'S DREAMS.
RRMMBB..!!
THE EBB AND FLOW OF THE AGES.
AS LONG AS PEOPLE HUNGER FOR FREEDOM...
FWASH!
...THESE THINGS WILL EXIST.
--GOLD ROGER KING OF THE PIRATES
A PIRATE, EH?
NOT A BAD IDEA...

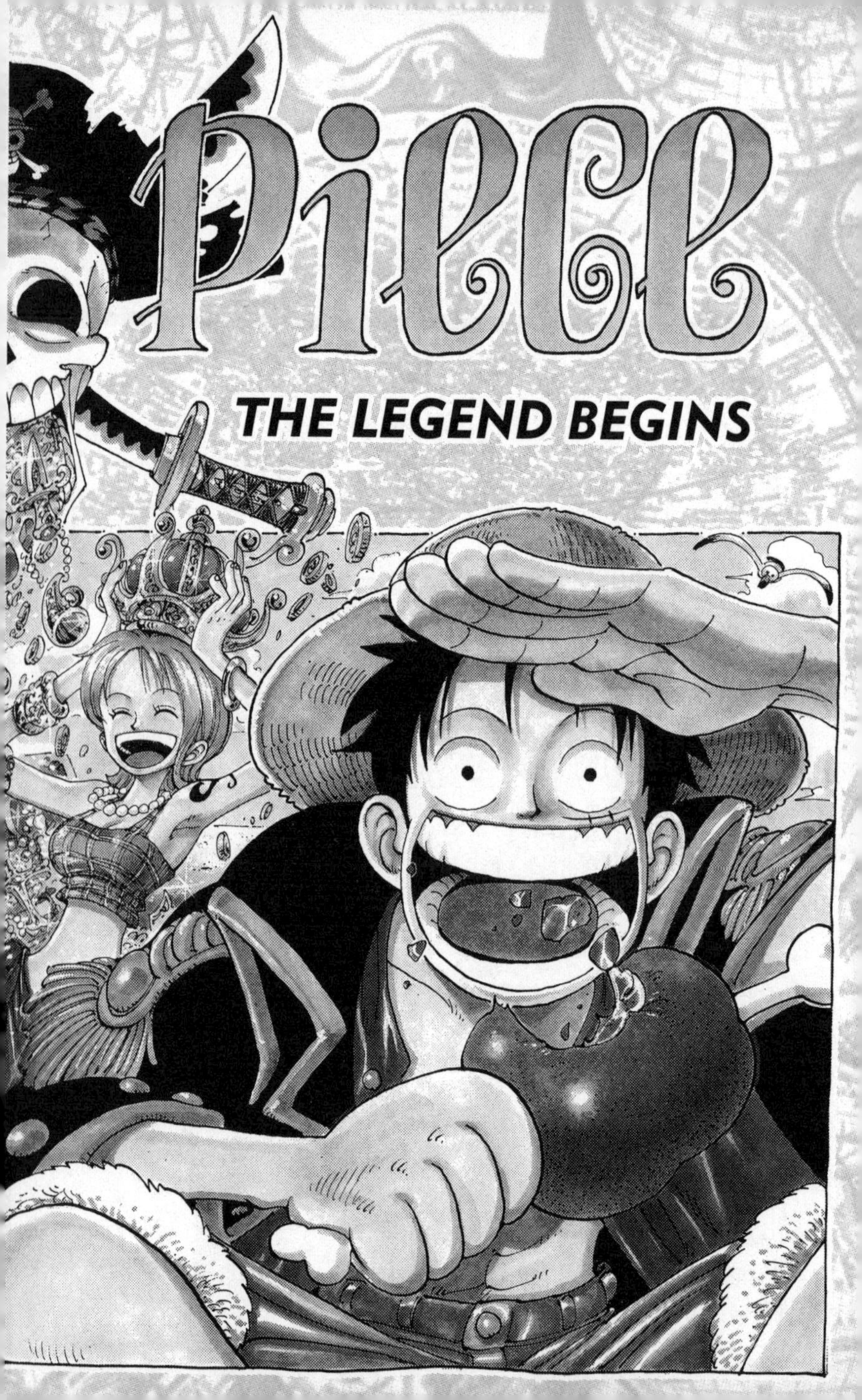
Piece
THE LEGEND BEGINS

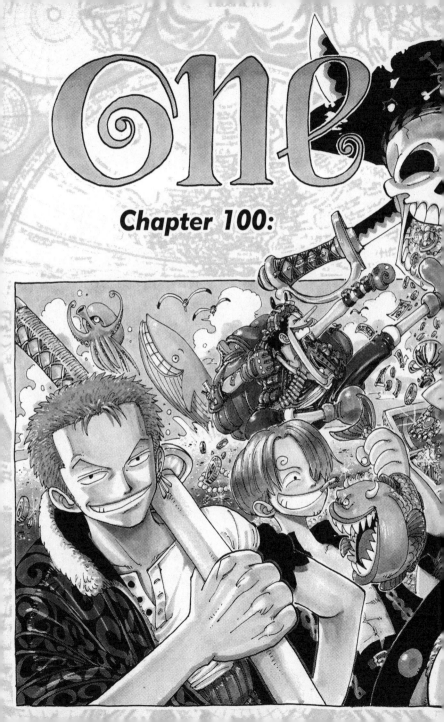

one

Chapter 100:

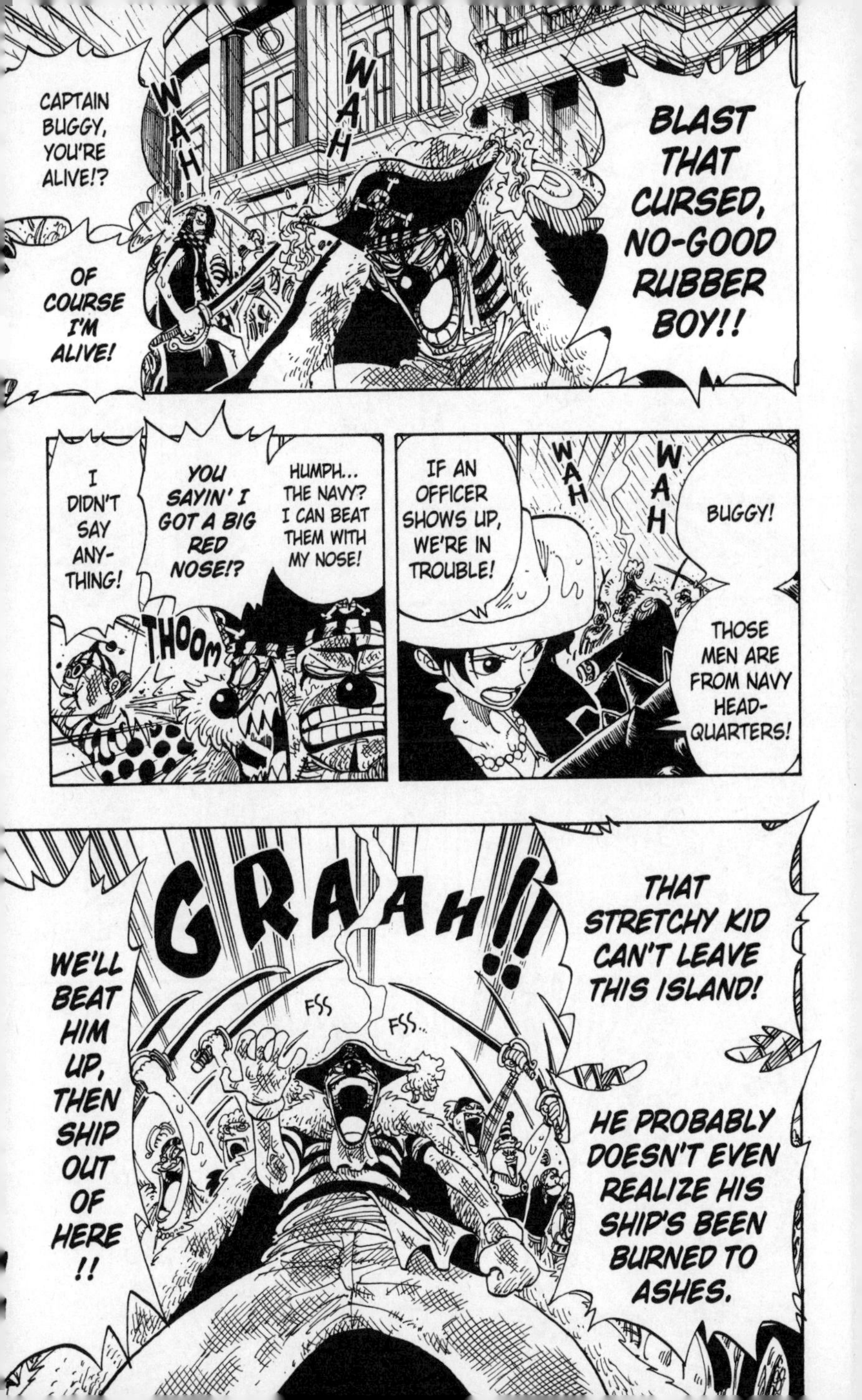
BLAST THAT CURSED, NO-GOOD RUBBER BOY!!
WAH
WAH
CAPTAIN BUGGY, YOU'RE ALIVE!?
OF COURSE I'M ALIVE!
BUGGY!
WAH
WAH
THOSE MEN ARE FROM NAVY HEAD-QUARTERS!
IF AN OFFICER SHOWS UP, WE'RE IN TROUBLE!
HUMPH... THE NAVY? I CAN BEAT THEM WITH MY NOSE!
YOU SAYIN' I GOT A BIG RED NOSE!?
THOOM
I DIDN'T SAY ANY-THING!
THAT STRETCHY KID CAN'T LEAVE THIS ISLAND!
GRAAAH!!
HE PROBABLY DOESN'T EVEN REALIZE HIS SHIP'S BEEN BURNED TO ASHES.
FSS
FSS...
WE'LL BEAT HIM UP, THEN SHIP OUT OF HERE!!

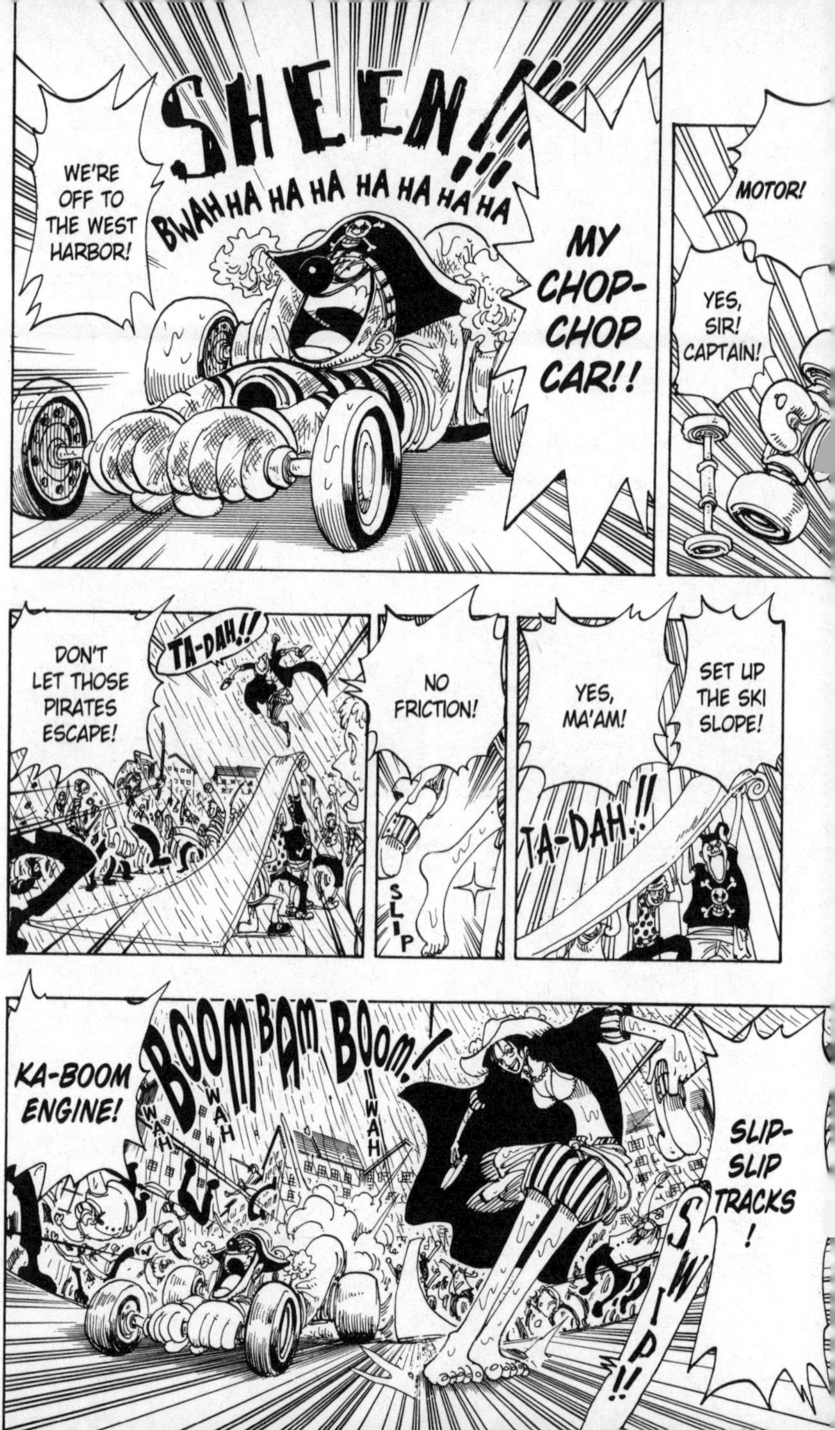
MOTOR!
YES, SIR! CAPTAIN!
WE'RE OFF TO THE WEST HARBOR!
SHEEN!!!
BWAHHA HA HA HA HA HA HA HA
MY CHOP-CHOP CAR!!
SET UP THE SKI SLOPE!
YES, MA'AM!
TA-DAH!!
NO FRICTION!
SLIP
DON'T LET THOSE PIRATES ESCAPE!
TA-DAH!!
SLIP-SLIP TRACKS!
SWIP!!
BOOM BAM BOOM!
WAH
WAH
WAH
KA-BOOM ENGINE!

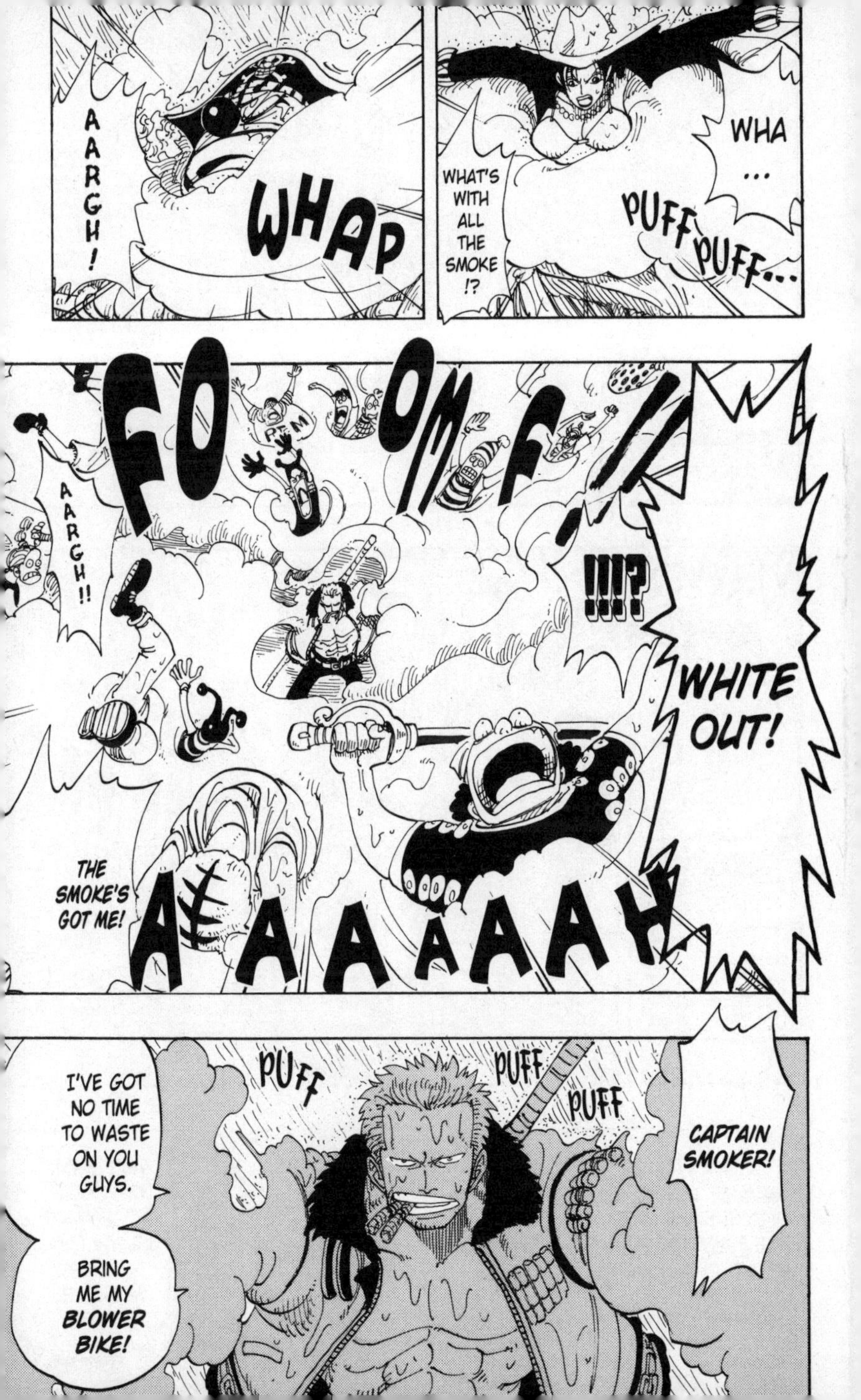
WHA ...
PUFF PUFF...
WHAT'S WITH ALL THE SMOKE !?
AARGH!
WHAP
FOOMF!!
!!!?
WHITE OUT!
AARGH!!
AAAAAAH
THE SMOKE'S GOT ME!
CAPTAIN SMOKER!
PUFF PUFF PUFF
I'VE GOT NO TIME TO WASTE ON YOU GUYS.
BRING ME MY *BLOWER BIKE!*

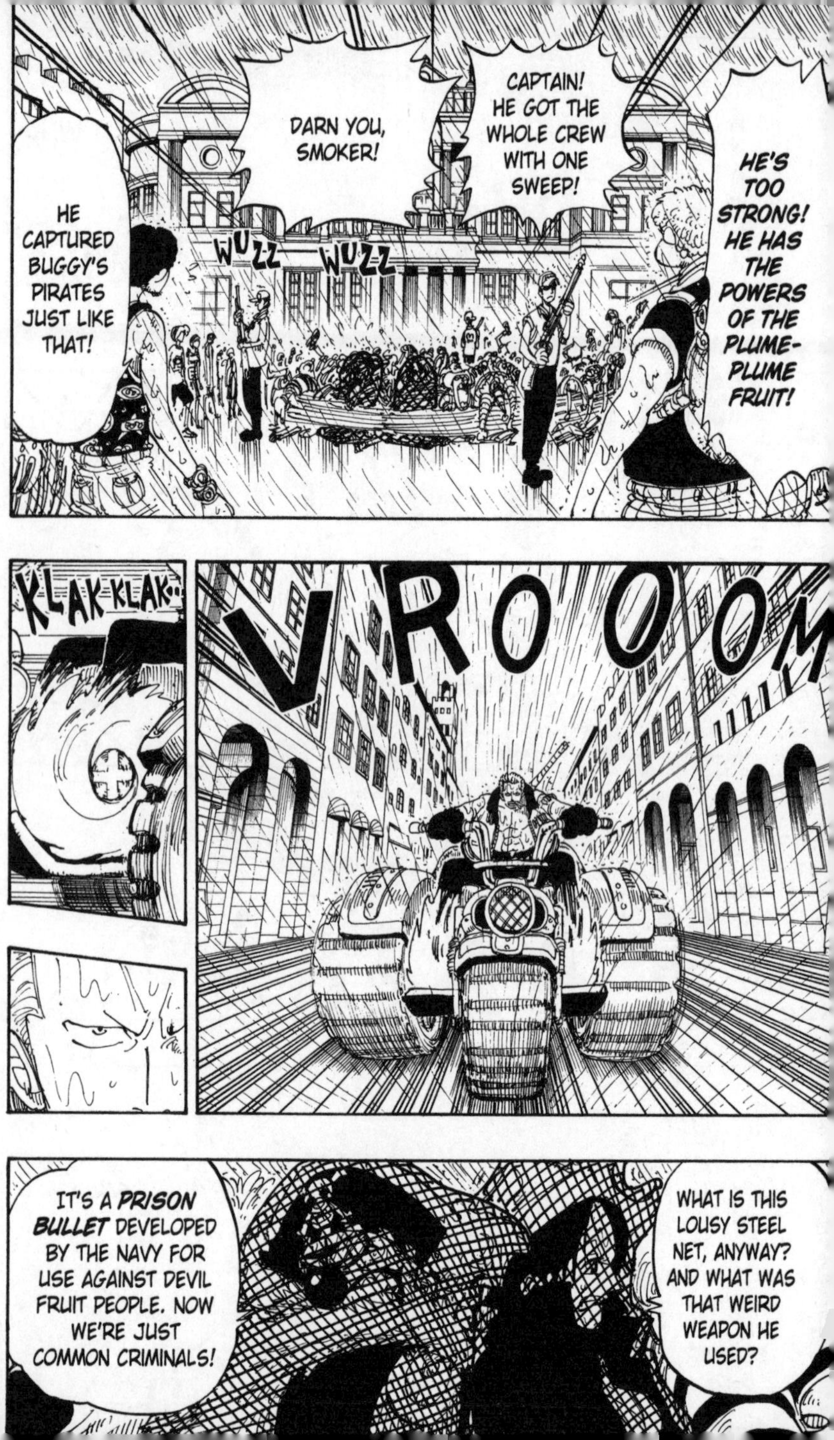
CAPTAIN! HE GOT THE WHOLE CREW WITH ONE SWEEP!
HE'S TOO STRONG! HE HAS THE POWERS OF THE PLUME-PLUME FRUIT!
DARN YOU, SMOKER!
HE CAPTURED BUGGY'S PIRATES JUST LIKE THAT!
WUZZ
WUZZ
VROOOOM
KLAK KLAK..
WHAT IS THIS LOUSY STEEL NET, ANYWAY? AND WHAT WAS THAT WEIRD WEAPON HE USED?
IT'S A *PRISON BULLET* DEVELOPED BY THE NAVY FOR USE AGAINST DEVIL FRUIT PEOPLE. NOW WE'RE JUST COMMON CRIMINALS!

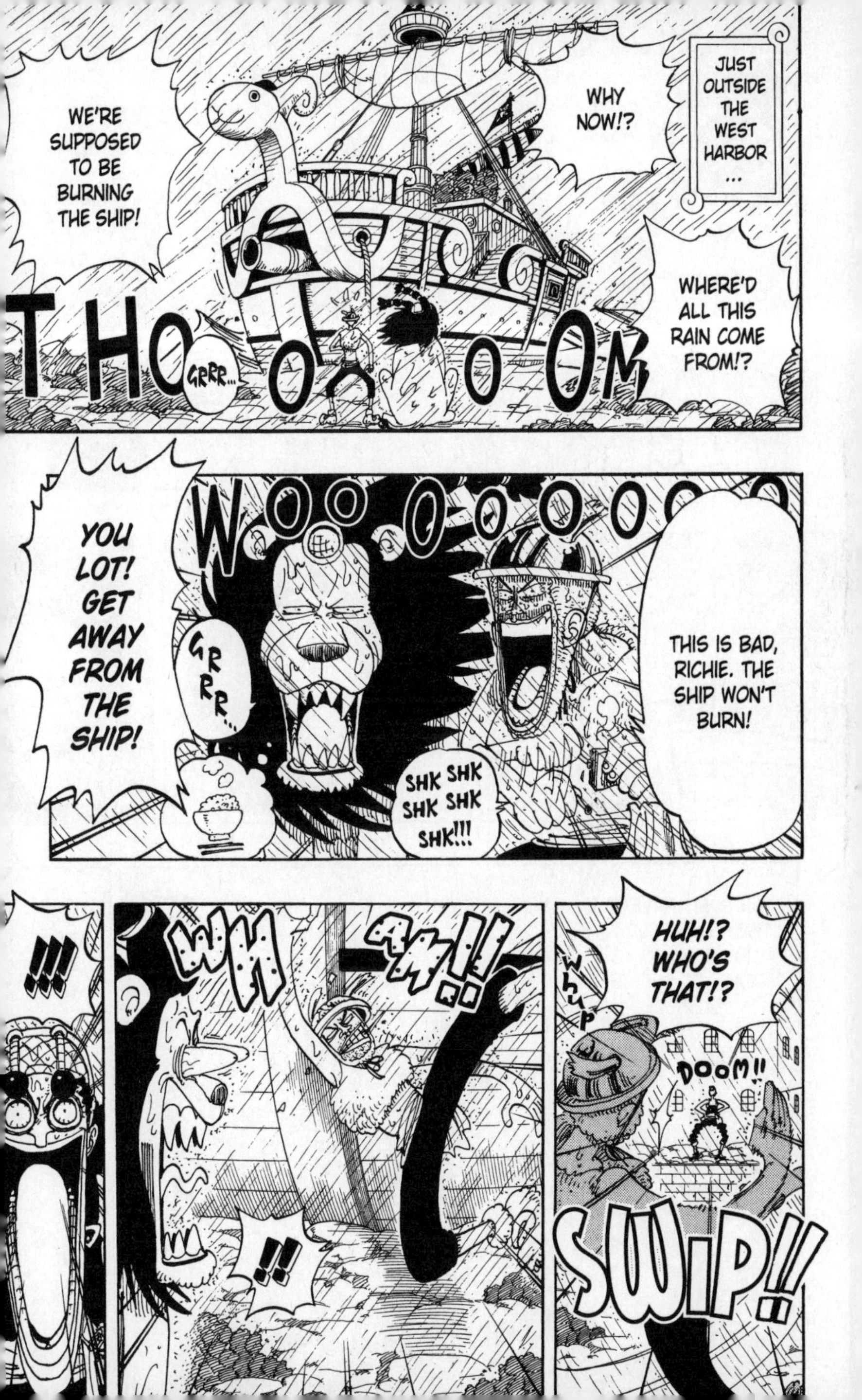
JUST OUTSIDE THE WEST HARBOR ...
WHY NOW!?
WE'RE SUPPOSED TO BE BURNING THE SHIP!
WHERE'D ALL THIS RAIN COME FROM!?
THOOOOOOM
GRRR...
THIS IS BAD, RICHIE. THE SHIP WON'T BURN!
WOOOOOOOOOO
SHK SHK SHK SHK SHK!!!
GRRR...
YOU LOT! GET AWAY FROM THE SHIP!
HUH!? WHO'S THAT!?
WHUP
DOOM!!
SWIP!!
WH-AW!!
!!
!!!

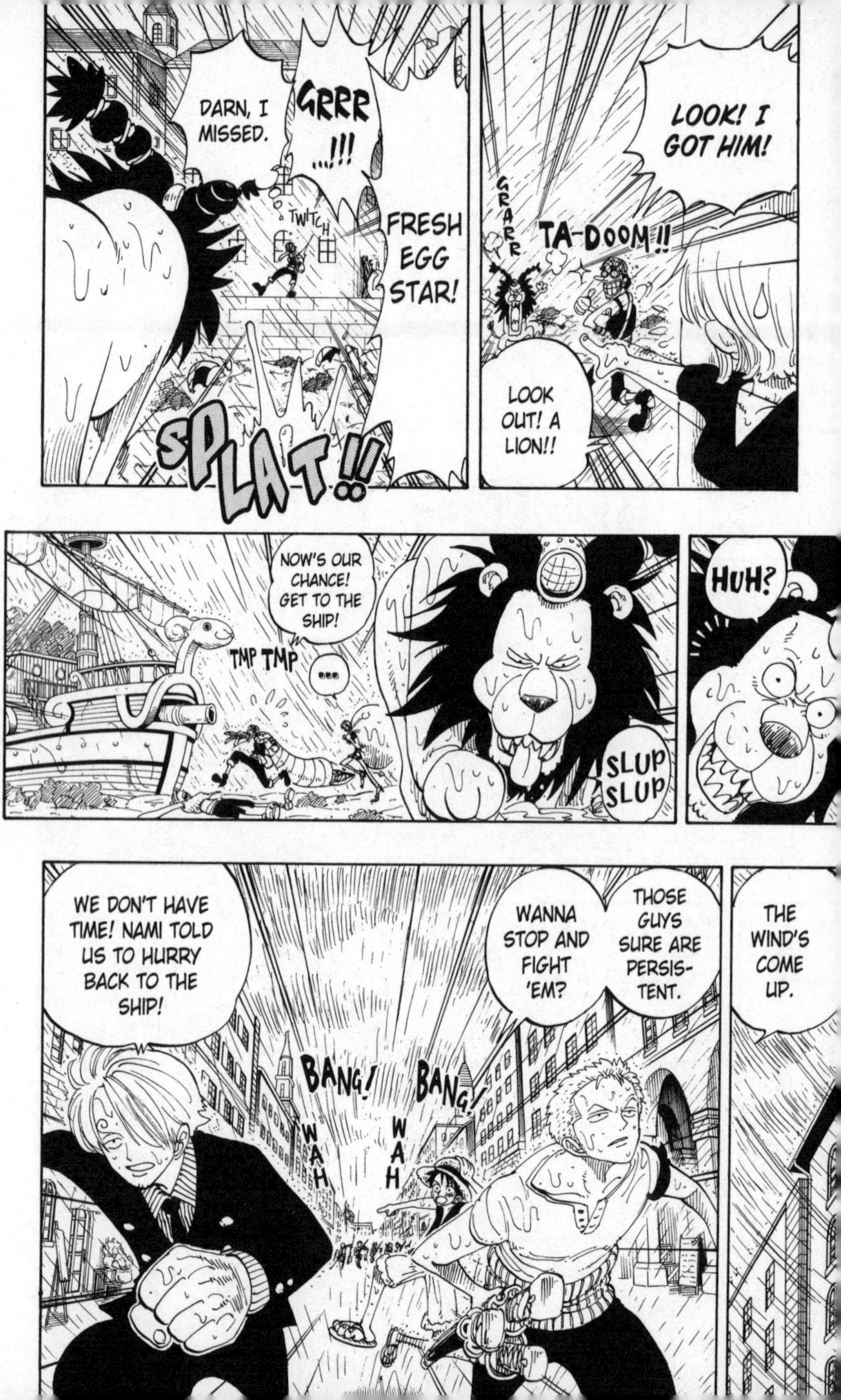
LOOK! I GOT HIM!
GRARR
TA-DOOM!!
LOOK OUT! A LION!!
GRRR ...!!!
DARN, I MISSED.
FRESH EGG STAR!
TWITCH
SPLAT!!
HUH?
SLUP SLUP
NOW'S OUR CHANCE! GET TO THE SHIP!
TMP TMP
...
THE WIND'S COME UP.
THOSE GUYS SURE ARE PERSIS-TENT.
WANNA STOP AND FIGHT 'EM?
WE DON'T HAVE TIME! NAMI TOLD US TO HURRY BACK TO THE SHIP!
BANG!
BANG!
WAH
WAH

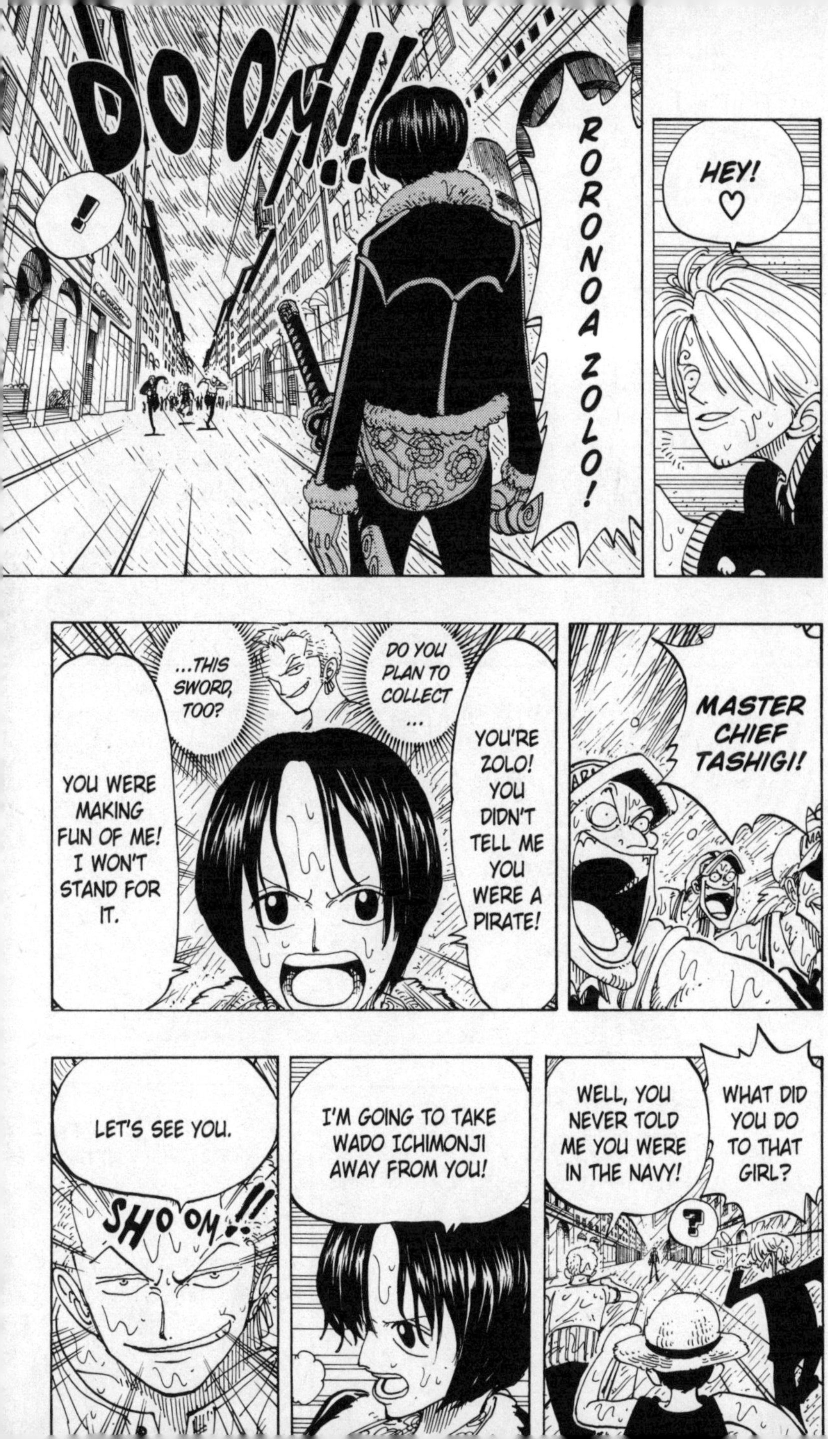
HEY! ♡
RORONOA ZOLO!
DOOM!!
!
MASTER CHIEF TASHIGI!
YOU'RE ZOLO! YOU DIDN'T TELL ME YOU WERE A PIRATE!
DO YOU PLAN TO COLLECT ...
...THIS SWORD, TOO?
YOU WERE MAKING FUN OF ME! I WON'T STAND FOR IT.
WHAT DID YOU DO TO THAT GIRL?
WELL, YOU NEVER TOLD ME YOU WERE IN THE NAVY!
?
I'M GOING TO TAKE WADO ICHIMONJI AWAY FROM YOU!
LET'S SEE YOU.
SHOOM!!

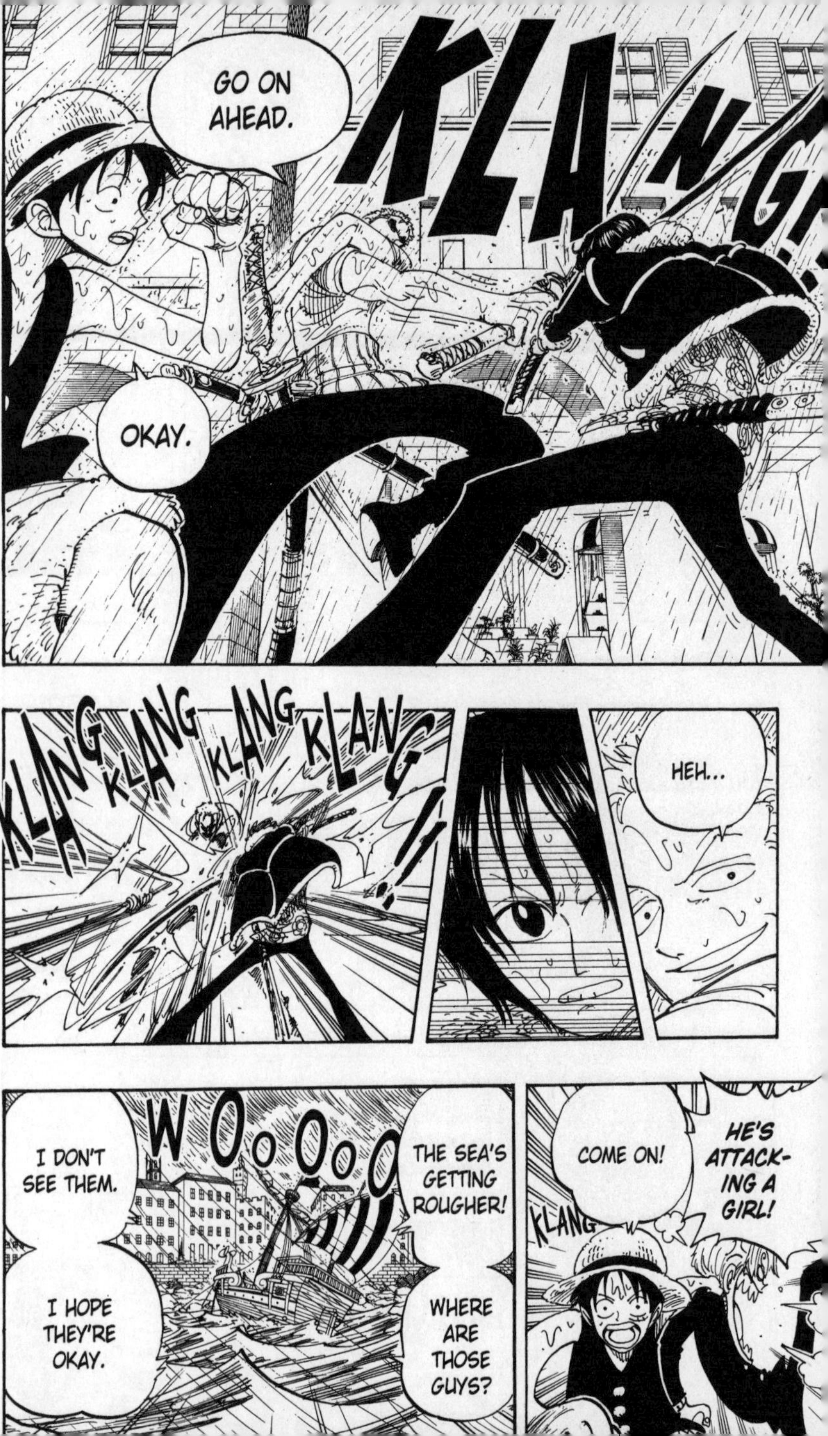
KLANG!!
GO ON AHEAD.
OKAY.
HEH...
KLANG KLANG KLANG KLANG!!
HE'S ATTACKING A GIRL!
COME ON!
KLANG
THE SEA'S GETTING ROUGHER!
WOOOOO
I DON'T SEE THEM.
WHERE ARE THOSE GUYS?
I HOPE THEY'RE OKAY.

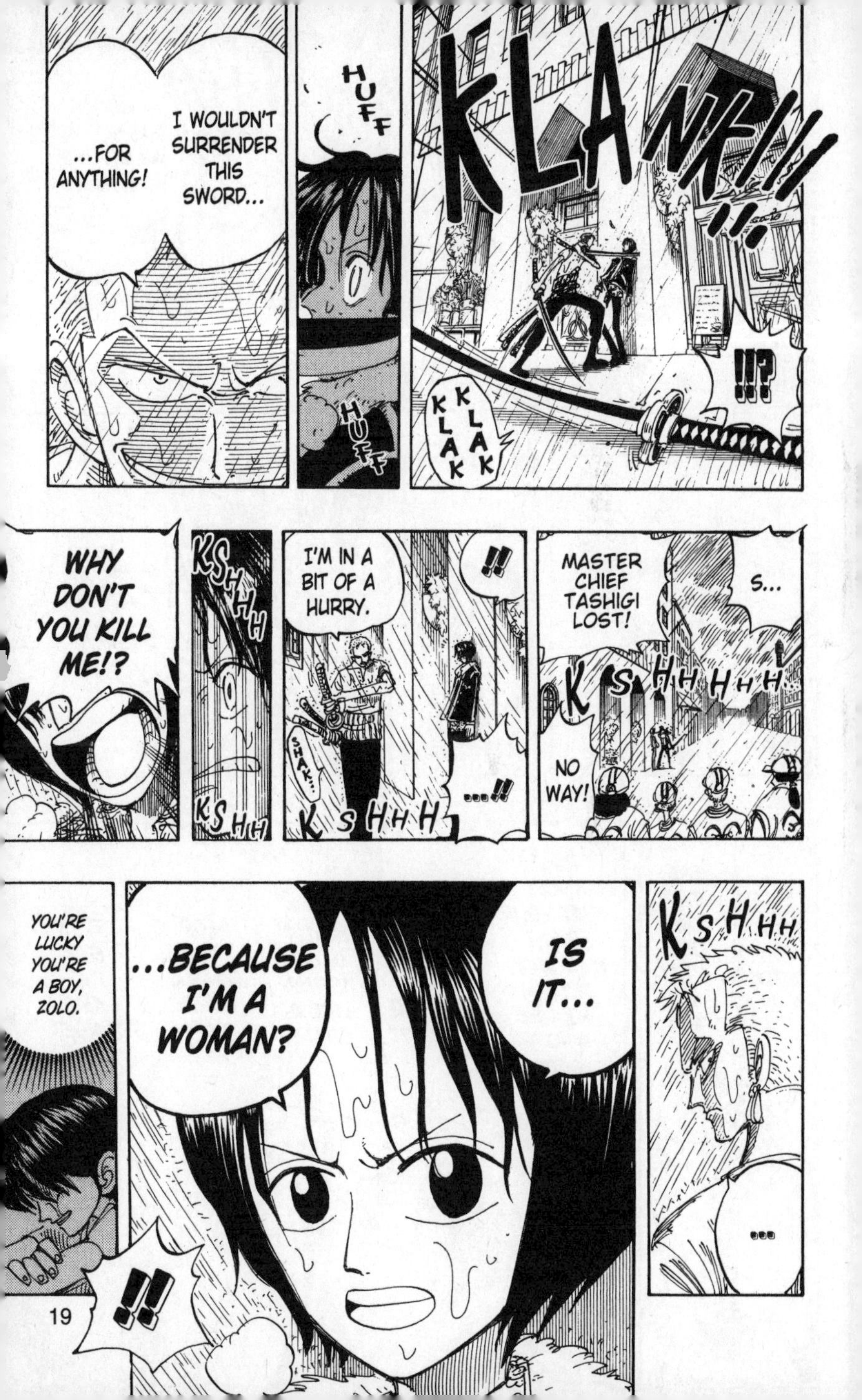
KLANK!!!
KLAK KLAK
!!?
HUFF
HUFF
I WOULDN'T SURRENDER THIS SWORD...
...FOR ANYTHING!
S...
MASTER CHIEF TASHIGI LOST!
KSHHHHH...
NO WAY!
!!
I'M IN A BIT OF A HURRY.
SHAK...
...!!
KSHHH
KSHHH
KSHH
WHY DON'T YOU KILL ME!?
KSHHHH
...
IS IT...
...BECAUSE I'M A WOMAN?
!!
YOU'RE LUCKY YOU'RE A BOY, ZOLO.

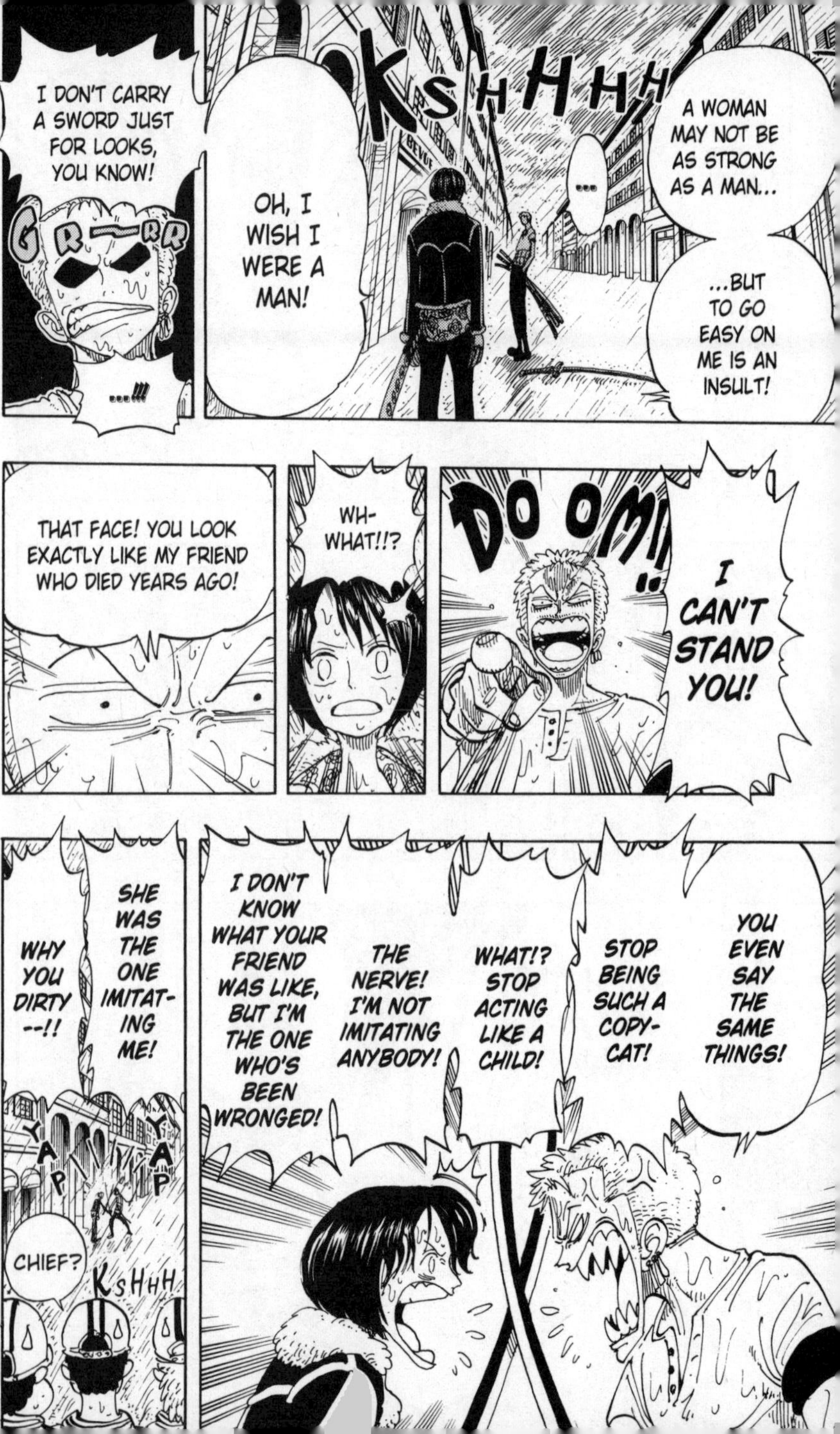
KSHHHH
A WOMAN MAY NOT BE AS STRONG AS A MAN...
...BUT TO GO EASY ON ME IS AN INSULT!
...
OH, I WISH I WERE A MAN!
I DON'T CARRY A SWORD JUST FOR LOOKS, YOU KNOW!
GR—RR
...!!!
DOOM!!
I CAN'T STAND YOU!
WH- WHAT!!?
THAT FACE! YOU LOOK EXACTLY LIKE MY FRIEND WHO DIED YEARS AGO!
YOU EVEN SAY THE SAME THINGS!
STOP BEING SUCH A COPY-CAT!
WHAT!? STOP ACTING LIKE A CHILD!
THE NERVE! I'M NOT IMITATING ANYBODY!
I DON'T KNOW WHAT YOUR FRIEND WAS LIKE, BUT I'M THE ONE WHO'S BEEN WRONGED!
SHE WAS THE ONE IMITATING ME!
WHY YOU DIRTY --!!
YAP YAP
CHIEF?
KSHHH

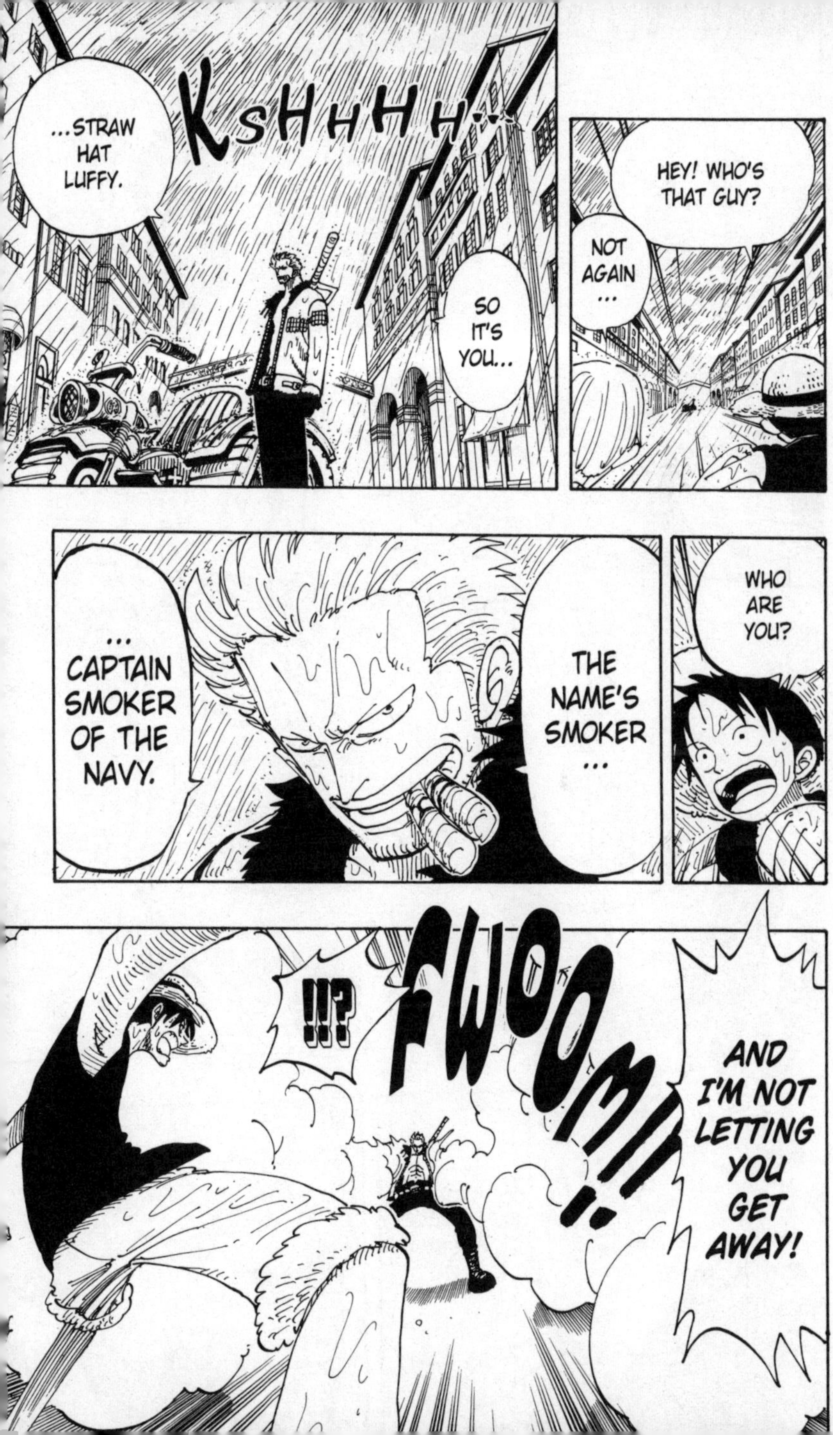
HEY! WHO'S THAT GUY?
NOT AGAIN ...
KSHHHH...
SO IT'S YOU...
...STRAW HAT LUFFY.
WHO ARE YOU?
THE NAME'S SMOKER ...
... CAPTAIN SMOKER OF THE NAVY.
AND I'M NOT LETTING YOU GET AWAY!
FWOOM!!
!!?

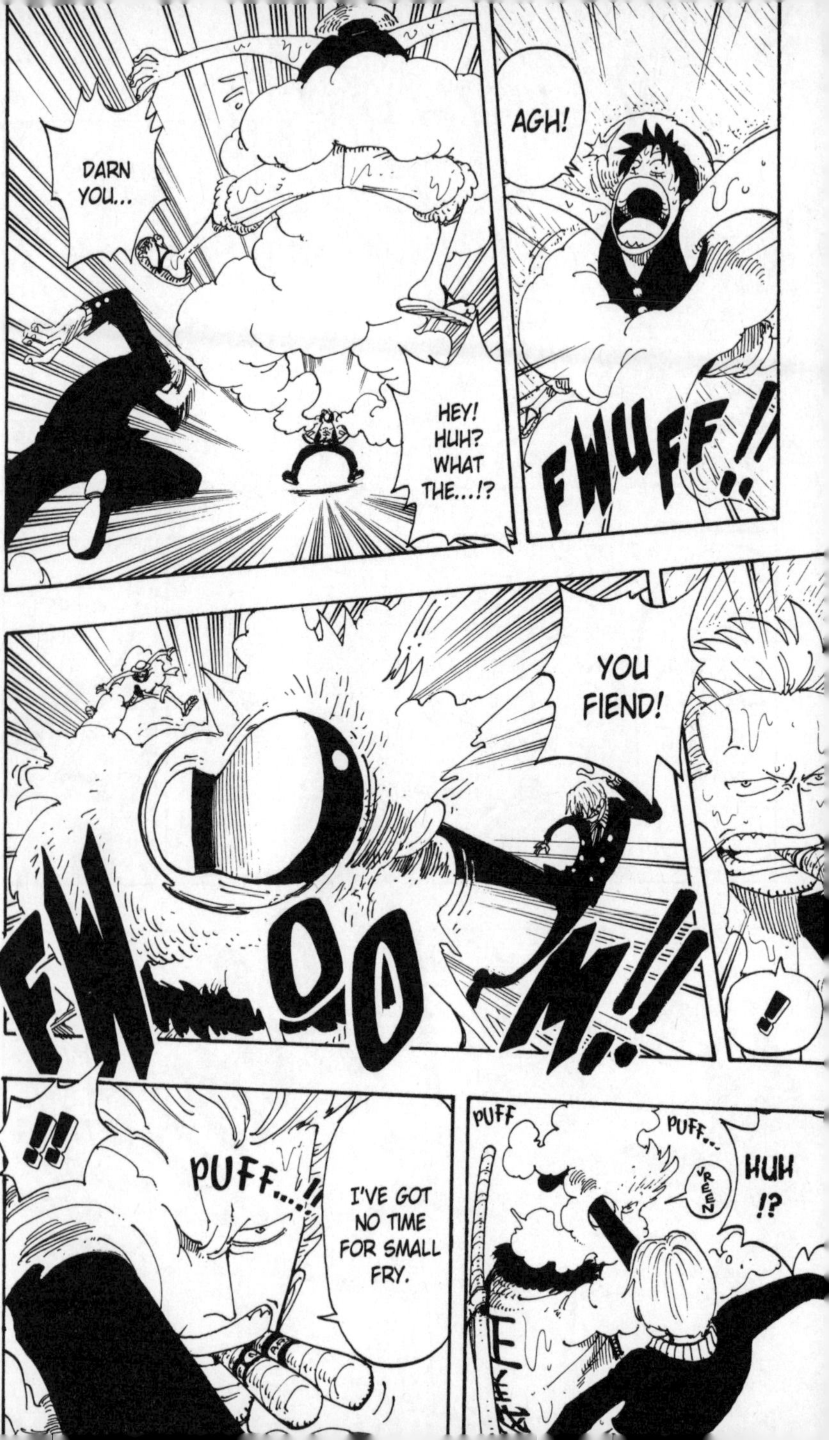
AGH!
FWUFF!!
DARN YOU...
HEY! HUH? WHAT THE...!?
!
YOU FIEND!
FWOOM!!
HUH !?
PUFF...
VREEN
PUFF
I'VE GOT NO TIME FOR SMALL FRY.
PUFF...!!
!!

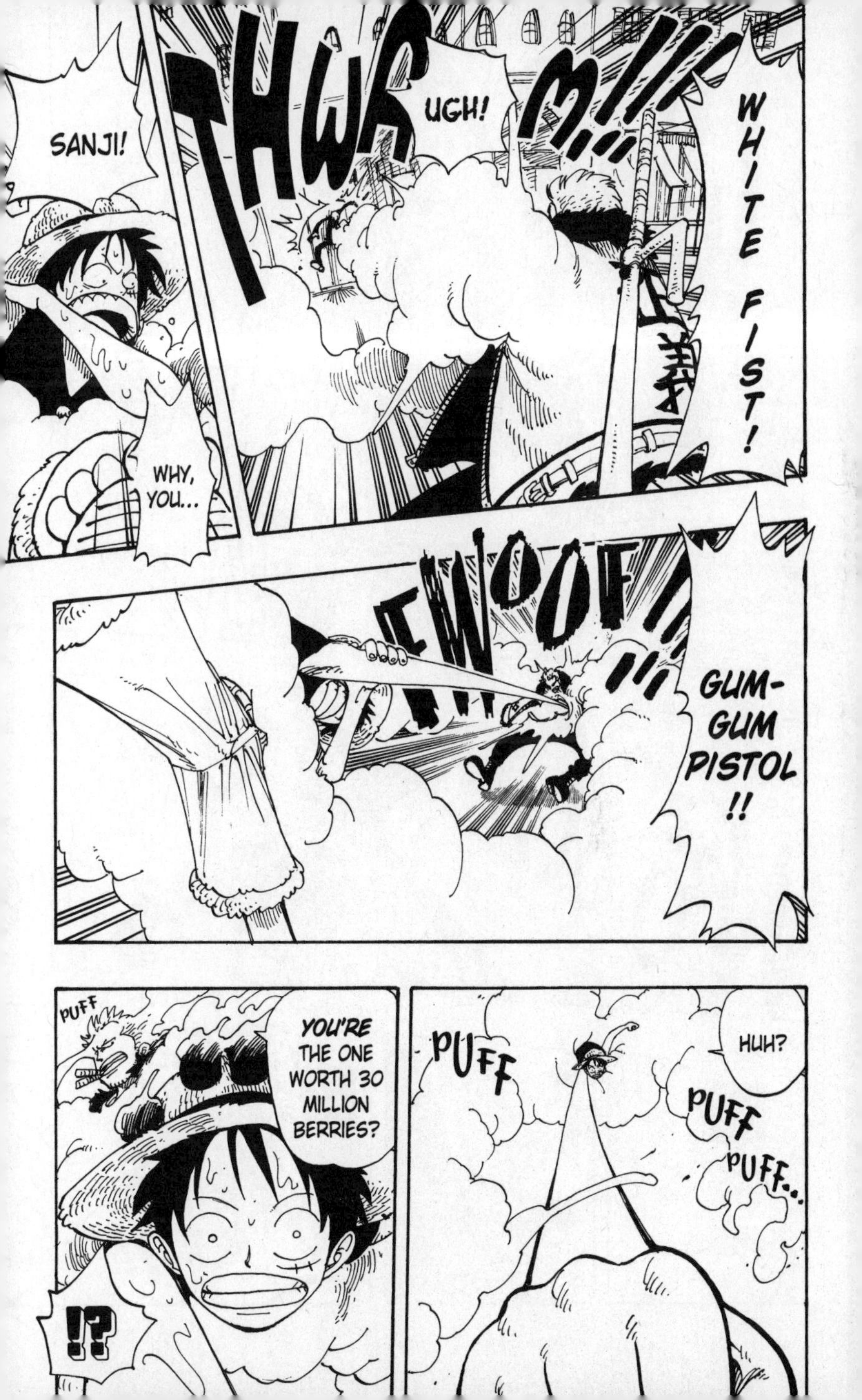
WHITE FIST!
THWAM!!!
UGH!
SANJI!
WHY, YOU...
FWOOF!!!
GUM-GUM PISTOL!!
HUH?
PUFF
PUFF
PUFF...
PUFF
YOU'RE THE ONE WORTH 30 MILLION BERRIES?
!?

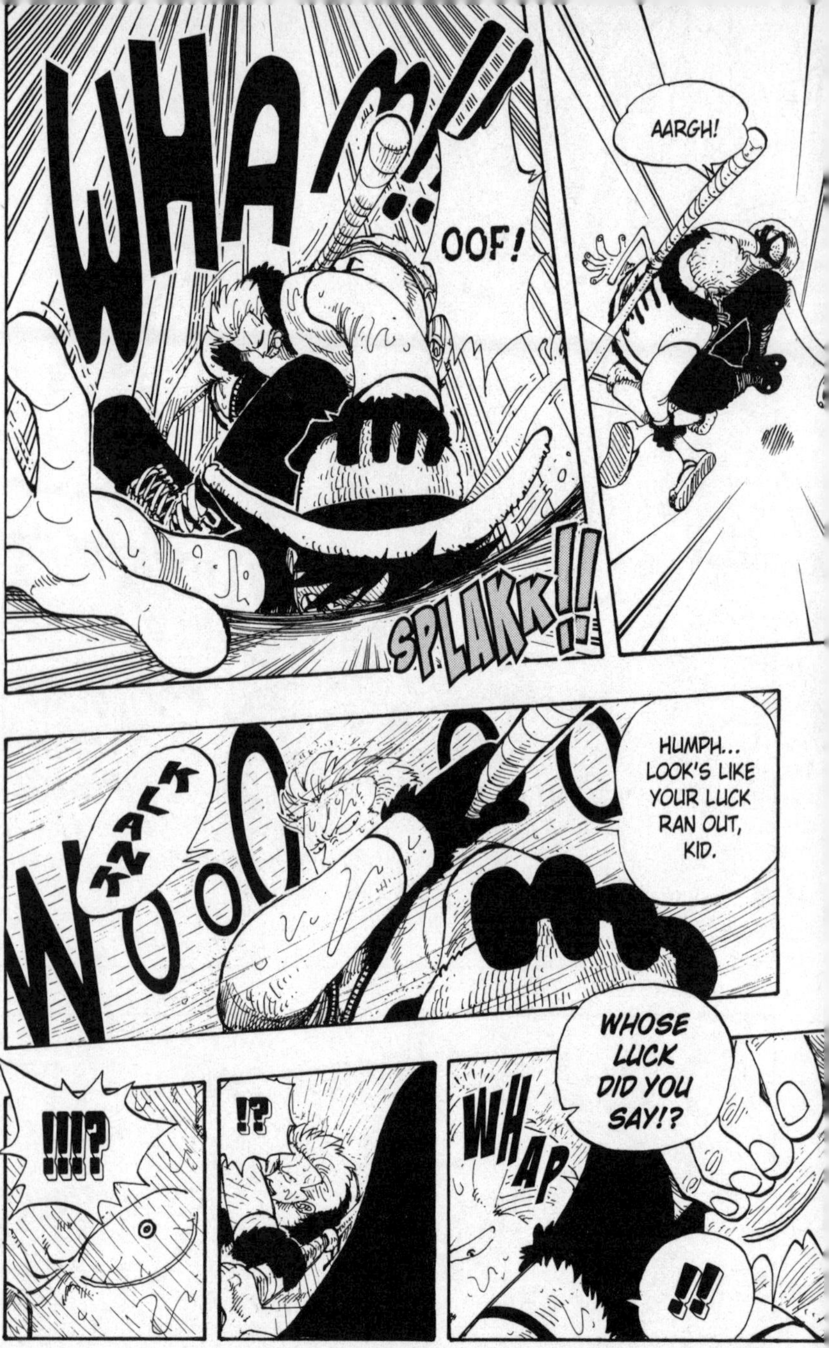
AARGH!
WHAM!!
OOF!
SPLAKK!!
HUMPH... LOOK'S LIKE YOUR LUCK RAN OUT, KID.
KLANK
WHOSE LUCK DID YOU SAY!?
WHAP
!!
!?
!!!?

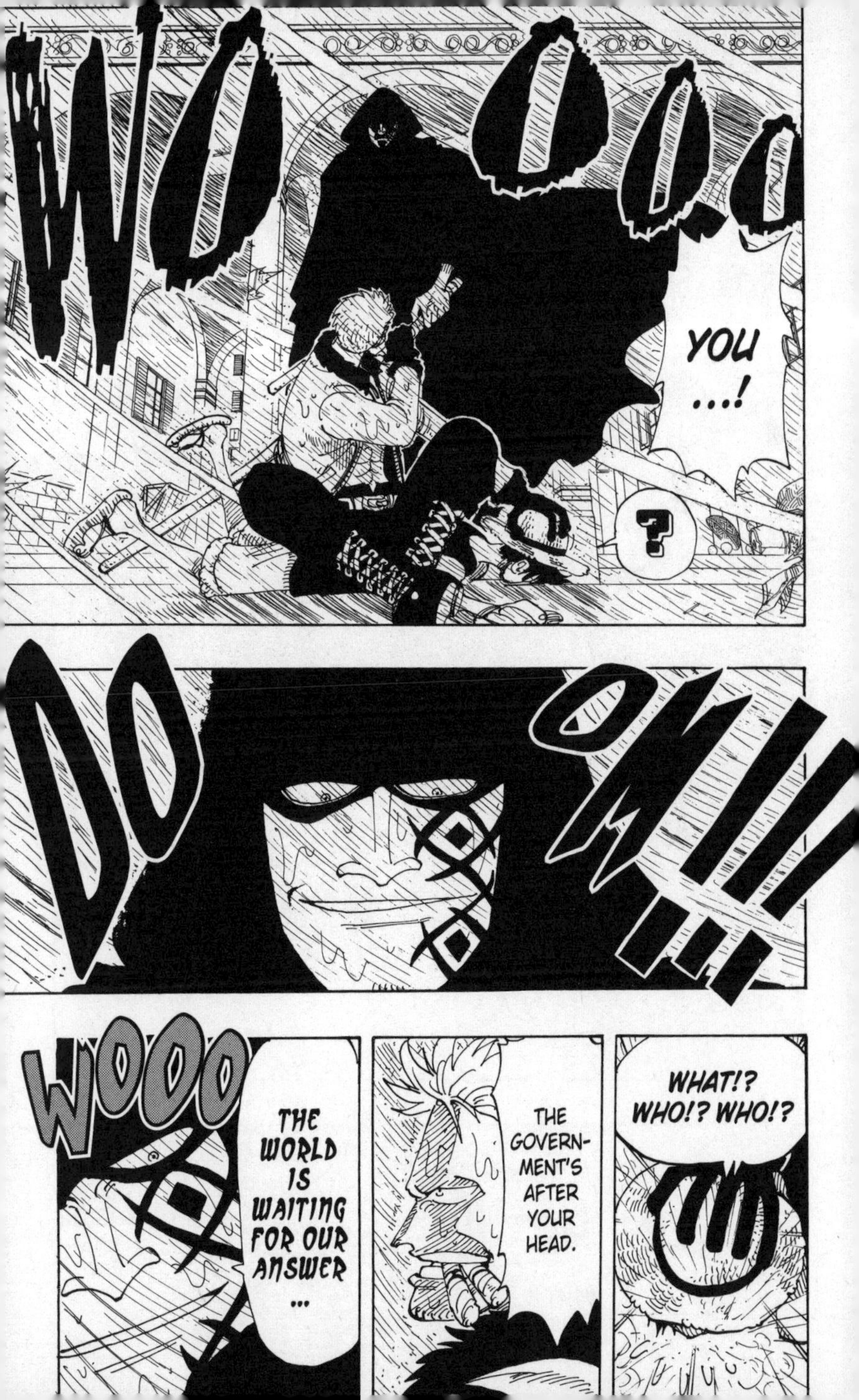
WOOOO
YOU ...!
?
DOON!!!
WHAT!? WHO!? WHO!?
THE GOVERNMENT'S AFTER YOUR HEAD.
WOOO
THE WORLD IS WAITING FOR OUR ANSWER ...

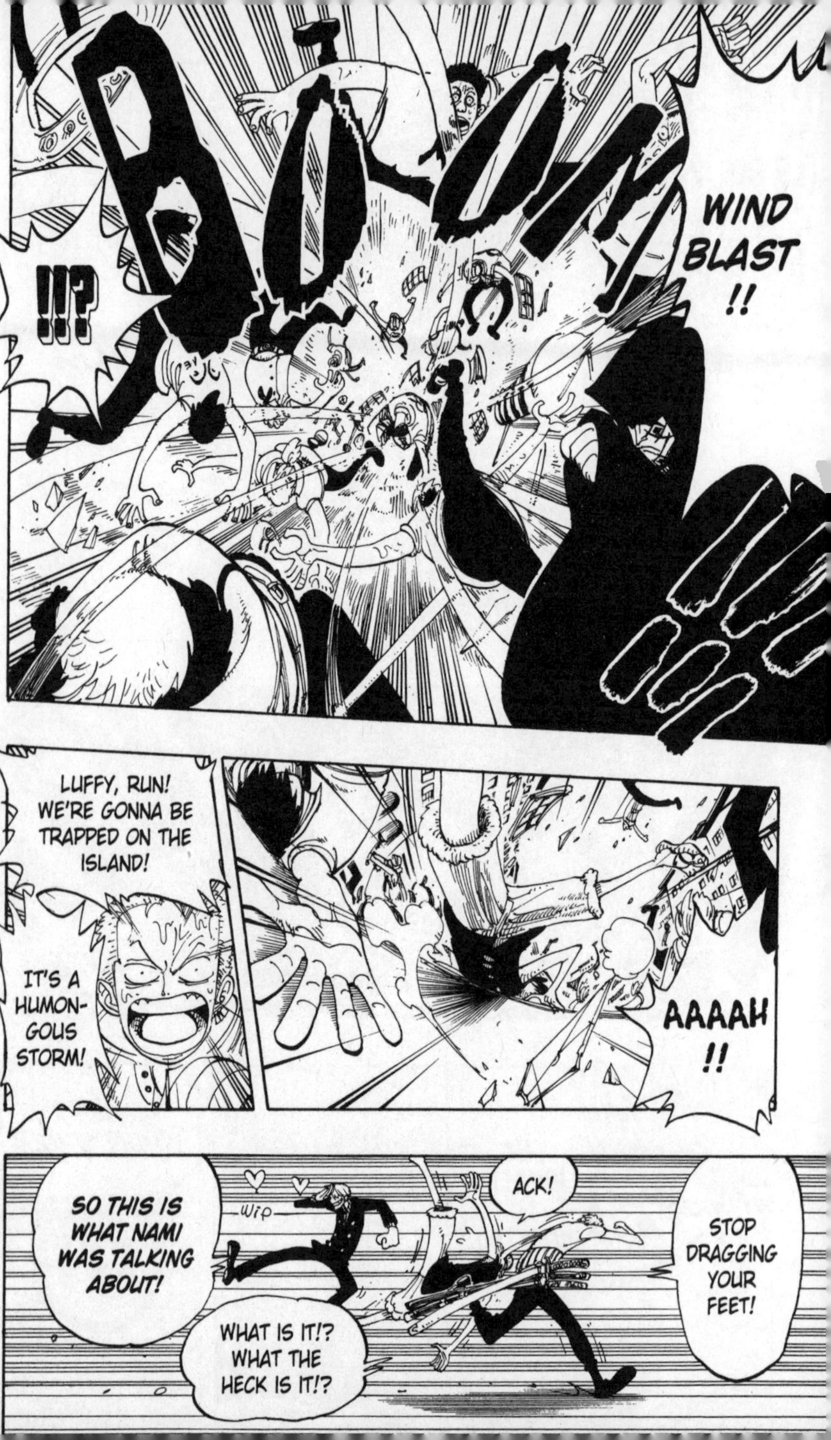

WIND BLAST !!
BOOM
!!?
AAAAH !!
LUFFY, RUN! WE'RE GONNA BE TRAPPED ON THE ISLAND!
IT'S A HUMON-GOUS STORM!
STOP DRAGGING YOUR FEET!
ACK!
WHAT IS IT!? WHAT THE HECK IS IT!?
SO THIS IS WHAT NAMI WAS TALKING ABOUT!

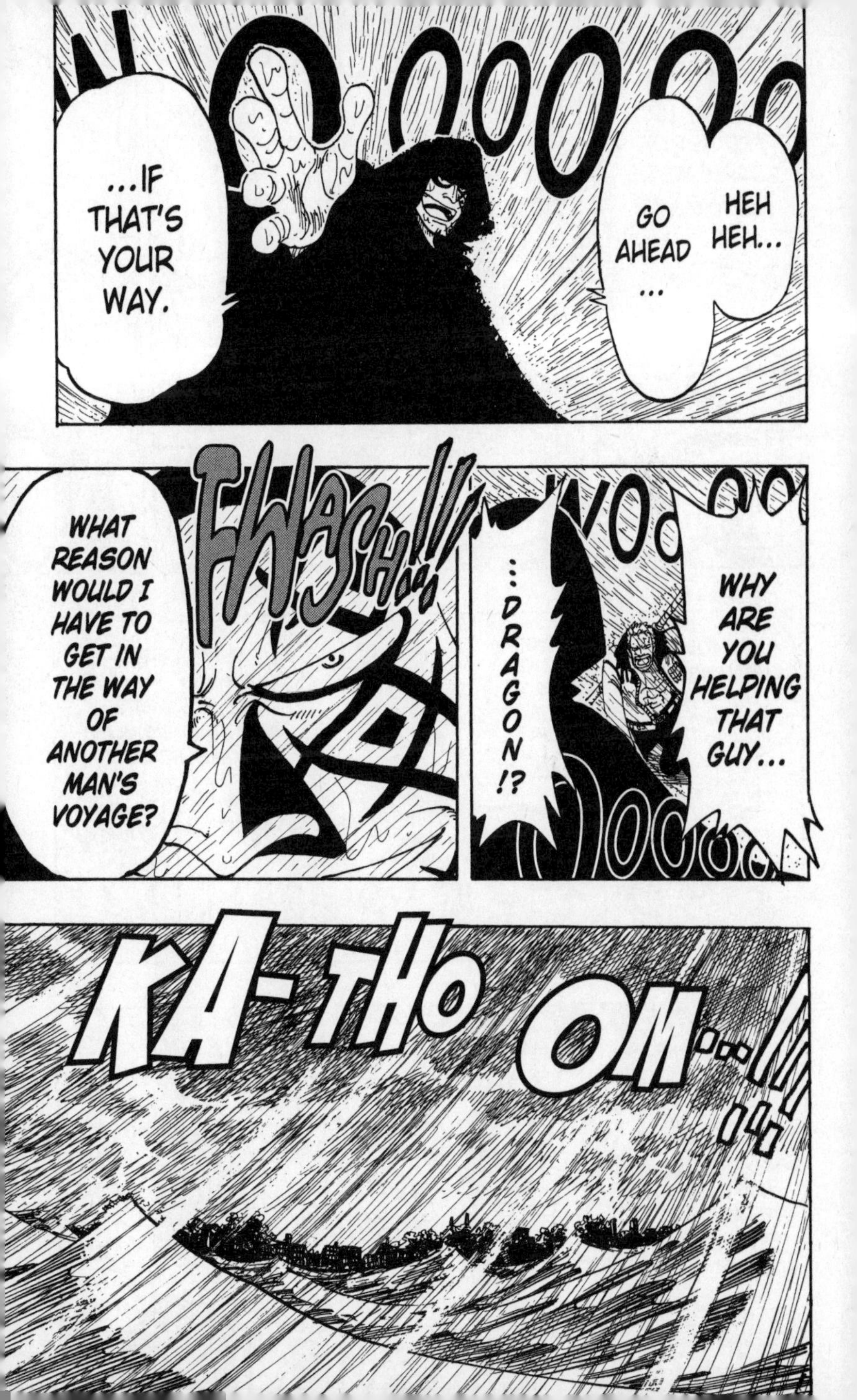
HEH HEH... GO AHEAD...
...IF THAT'S YOUR WAY.
WHY ARE YOU HELPING THAT GUY...
...DRAGON!?
FWASH!!
WHAT REASON WOULD I HAVE TO GET IN THE WAY OF ANOTHER MAN'S VOYAGE?
KA-THOOM...!!

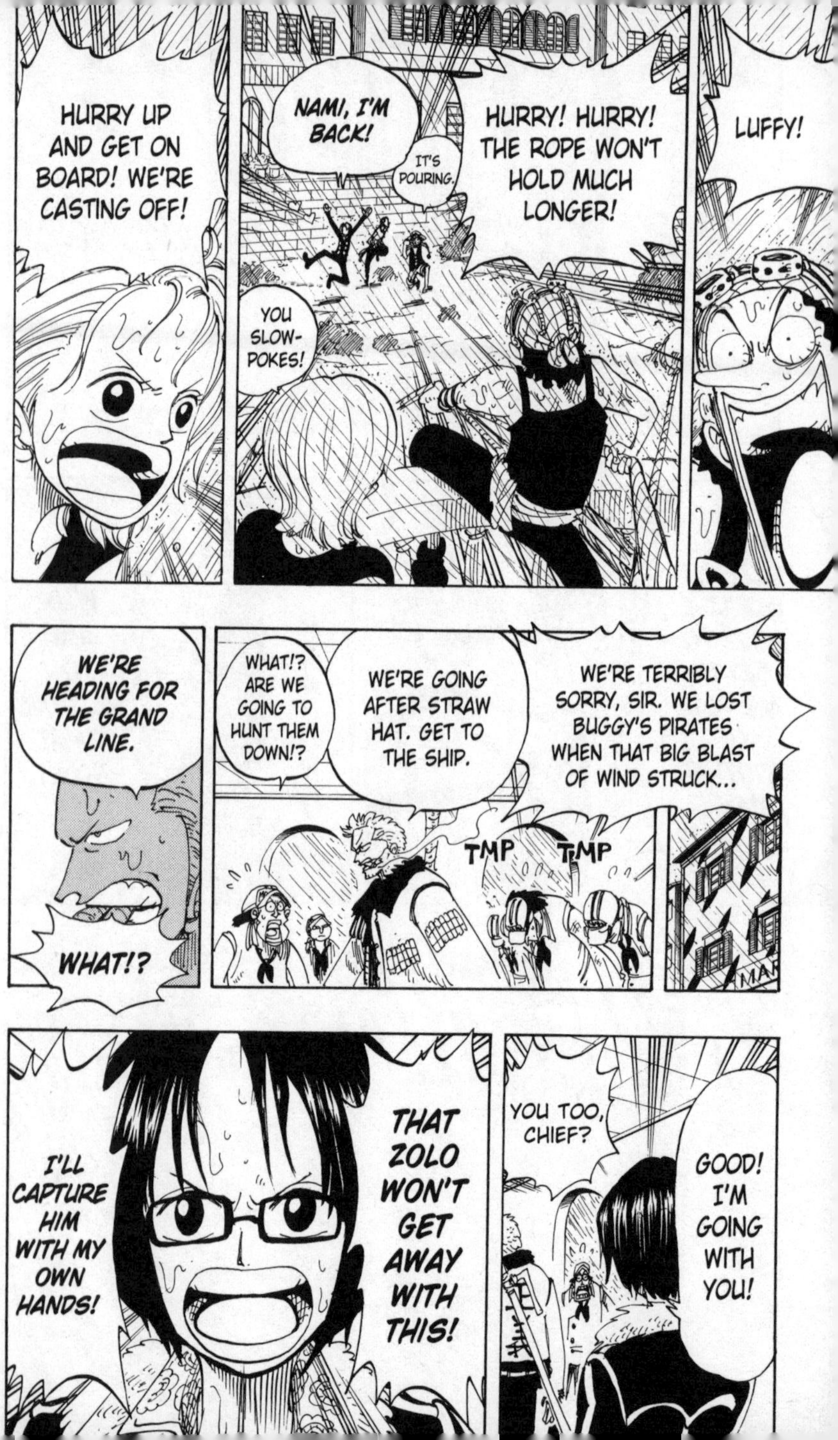
LUFFY!
HURRY! HURRY! THE ROPE WON'T HOLD MUCH LONGER!
NAMI, I'M BACK!
IT'S POURING.
YOU SLOW-POKES!
HURRY UP AND GET ON BOARD! WE'RE CASTING OFF!
WE'RE TERRIBLY SORRY, SIR. WE LOST BUGGY'S PIRATES WHEN THAT BIG BLAST OF WIND STRUCK...
TMP TMP
WE'RE GOING AFTER STRAW HAT. GET TO THE SHIP.
WHAT!? ARE WE GOING TO HUNT THEM DOWN!?
WE'RE HEADING FOR THE GRAND LINE.
WHAT!?
GOOD! I'M GOING WITH YOU!
YOU TOO, CHIEF?
THAT ZOLO WON'T GET AWAY WITH THIS!
I'LL CAPTURE HIM WITH MY OWN HANDS!

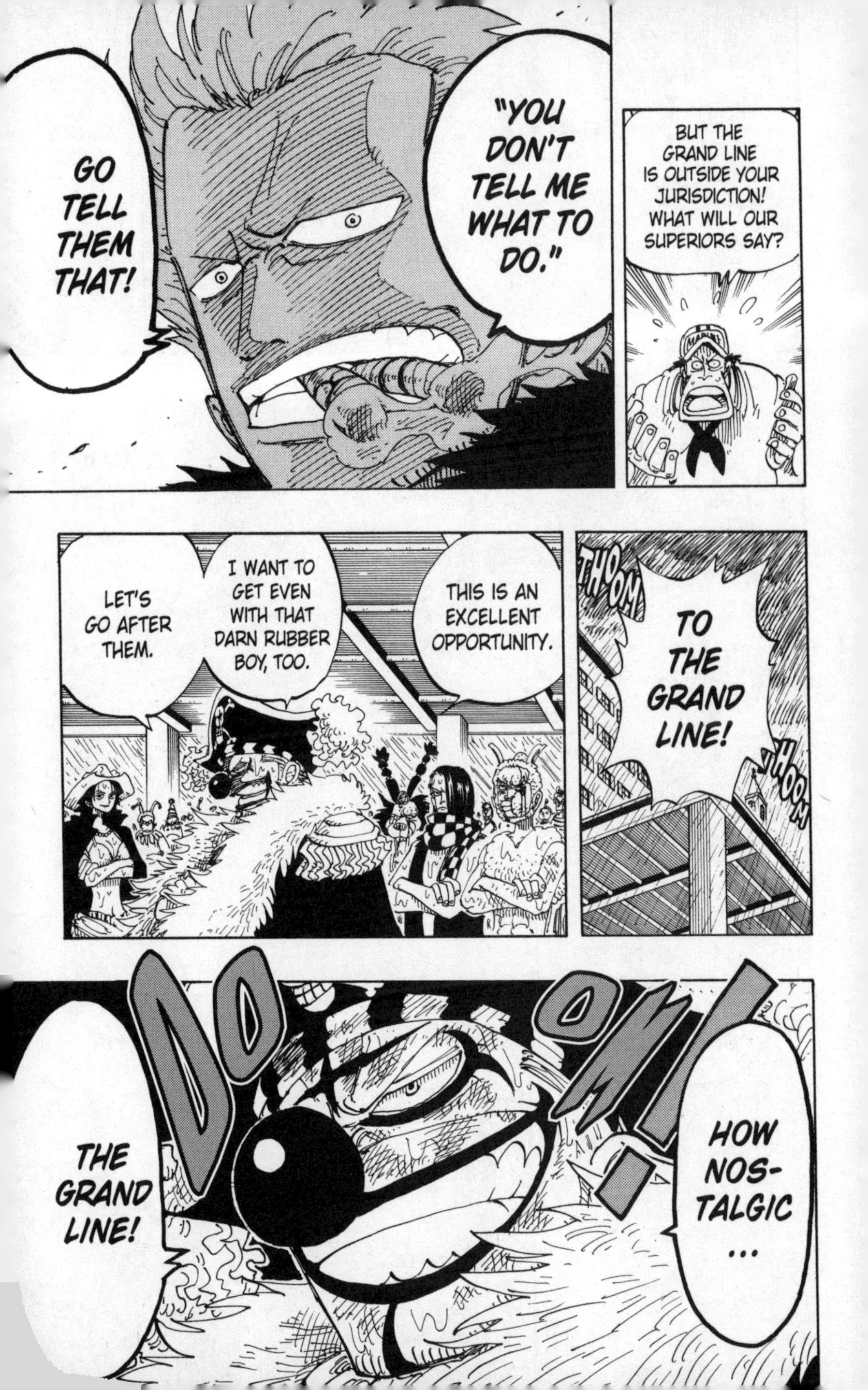
BUT THE GRAND LINE IS OUTSIDE YOUR JURISDICTION! WHAT WILL OUR SUPERIORS SAY?
"YOU DON'T TELL ME WHAT TO DO."
GO TELL THEM THAT!
THOOM
TO THE GRAND LINE!
THOOM
THIS IS AN EXCELLENT OPPORTUNITY.
I WANT TO GET EVEN WITH THAT DARN RUBBER BOY, TOO.
LET'S GO AFTER THEM.
HOW NOS-TALGIC...
DOOM!
THE GRAND LINE!

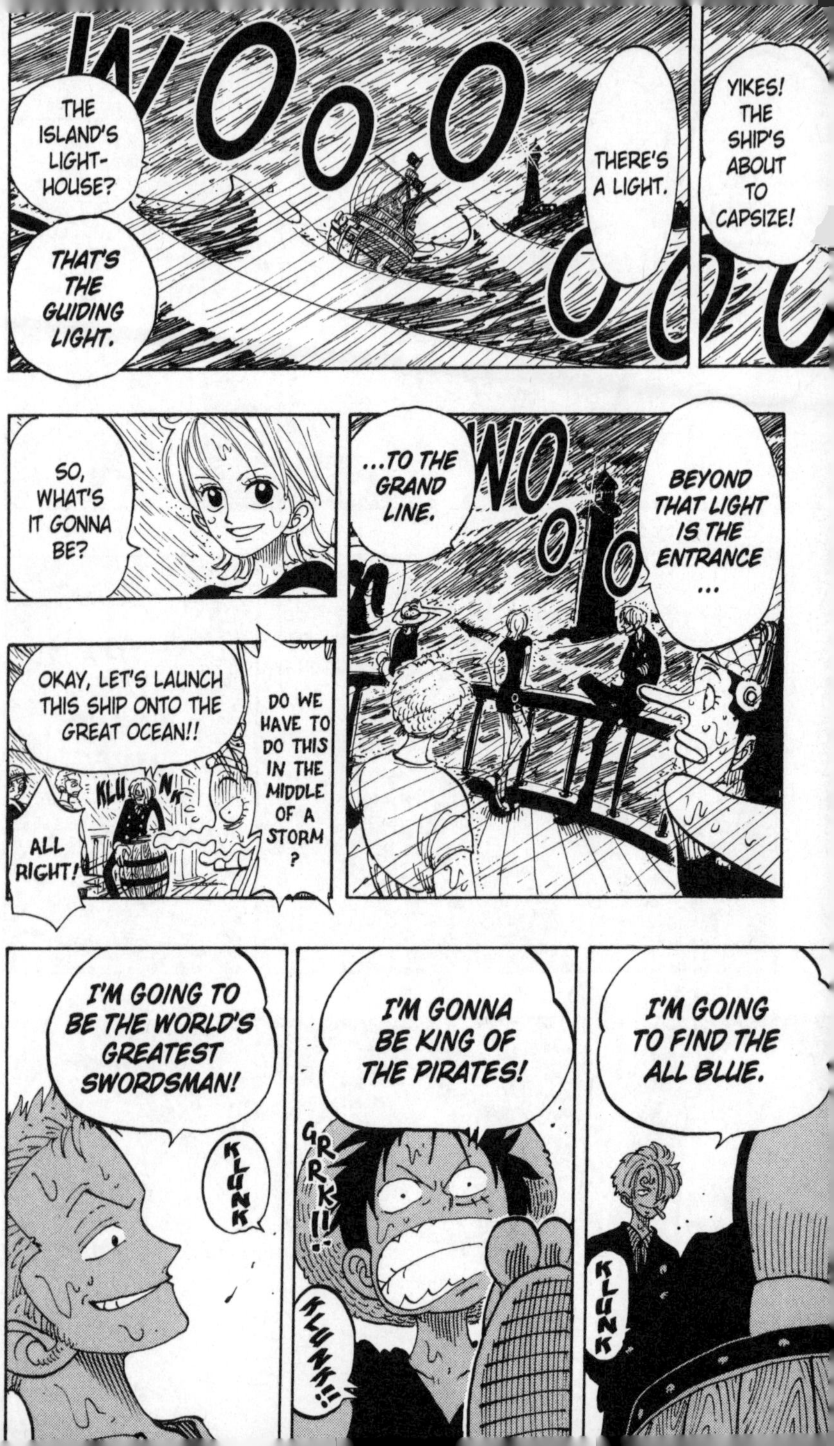
YIKES! THE SHIP'S ABOUT TO CAPSIZE!
THERE'S A LIGHT.
WOOOOOOOOO
THE ISLAND'S LIGHTHOUSE?
THAT'S THE GUIDING LIGHT.
BEYOND THAT LIGHT IS THE ENTRANCE ...
...TO THE GRAND LINE.
WOOOO
SO, WHAT'S IT GONNA BE?
DO WE HAVE TO DO THIS IN THE MIDDLE OF A STORM?
OKAY, LET'S LAUNCH THIS SHIP ONTO THE GREAT OCEAN!!
KLUNK
ALL RIGHT!
I'M GOING TO FIND THE ALL BLUE.
KLUNK
I'M GONNA BE KING OF THE PIRATES!
GRRK!!
KLUNK!!
I'M GOING TO BE THE WORLD'S GREATEST SWORDSMAN!
KLUNK

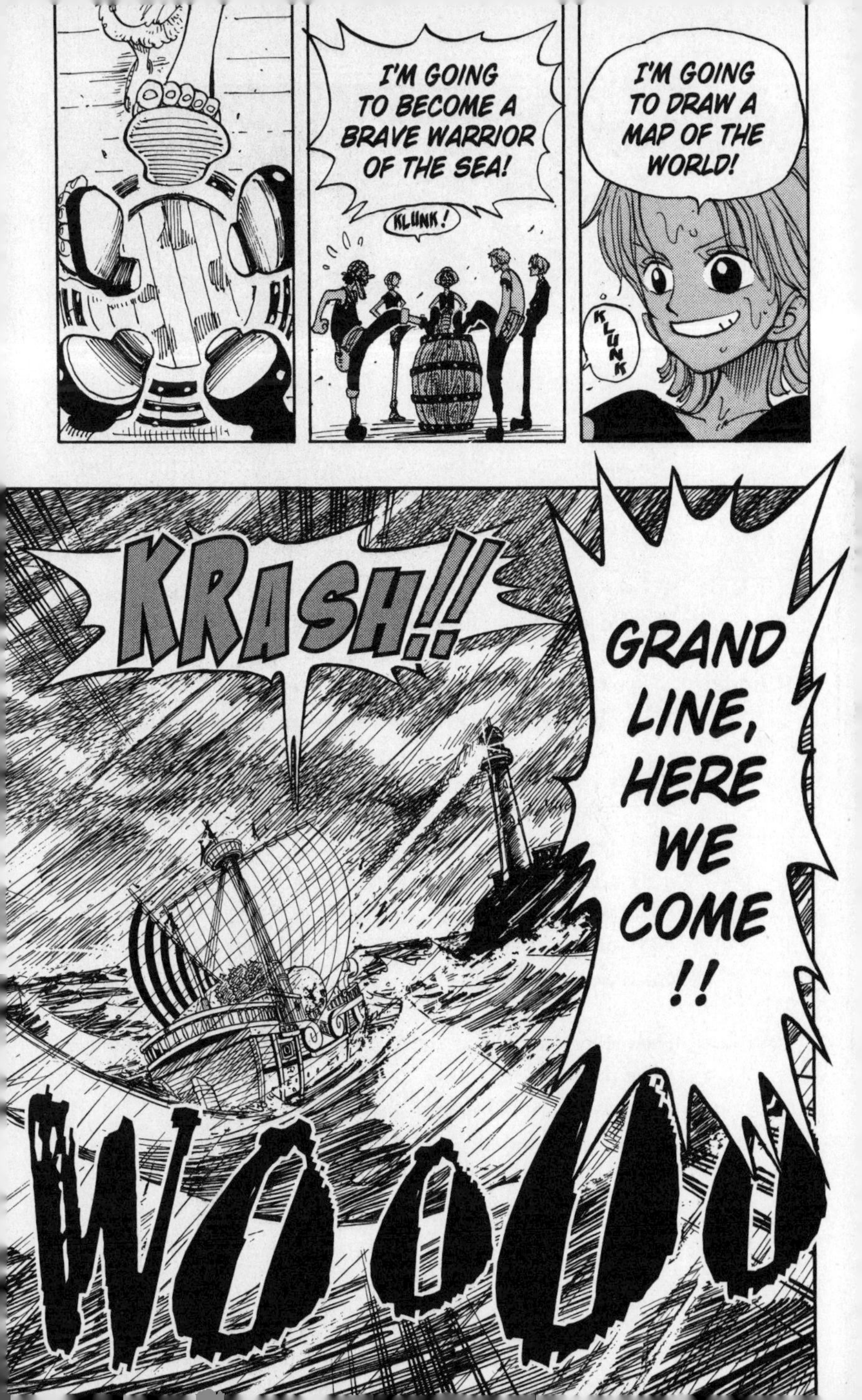
I'M GOING TO DRAW A MAP OF THE WORLD!
KLUNK
I'M GOING TO BECOME A BRAVE WARRIOR OF THE SEA!
KLUNK!
GRAND LINE, HERE WE COME!!
KRASH!!

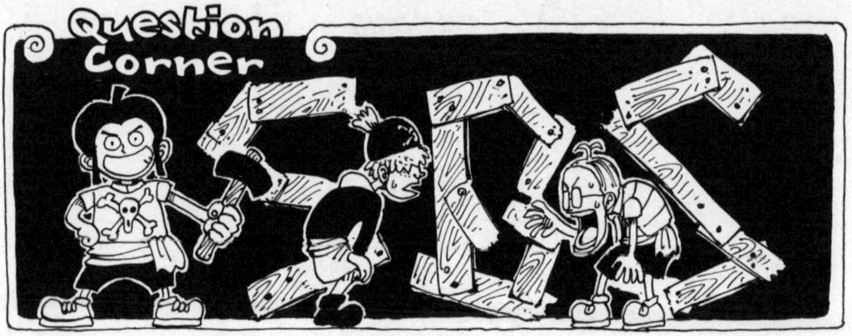
Question Corner
SBS

Reader: Timmy Ueda of the SBS Takeover Gang, please make me, Martha Shimoda, one of your cohorts! I'll do anything! First off, I'll begin the SBS! Yeah! How do you like that, Timmy? I've started it! ♡

Oda: ...!! Aaaah! He's done it again!! Darn you, Timmy! And darn you, Timmy's new cohort! Darn!

Reader: Hello, Oda Sensei. Today I trained hard once more at kendo. If I continue to practice, will I be as strong as Sanji someday?

Oda: Darn that Timmy! Are you one of his cohorts, too? Are you!? You're not? Oh! Sorry. I'm sorry you got caught up in my tirade. Let's see. Will you become as strong as Sanji if you practice hard at kendo? Of course not! He's got nothing to do with kendo! Oh no, I've lost my cool again! BE COOL. BE COOL.

Reader: How do you do? I like Luffy the best. I like Sanji second best. I like the way Sanji talks:

Darn old man ⇒ Crap-geezer
Darn guys ⇒ Crap-heads
Darn tasty ⇒ Crap-good
He's so vulgar. Can I change Sanji's ranking?

Oda: I guess it can't be helped.
Right, it can't be helped.

Chapter 101:
REVERSE MOUNTAIN

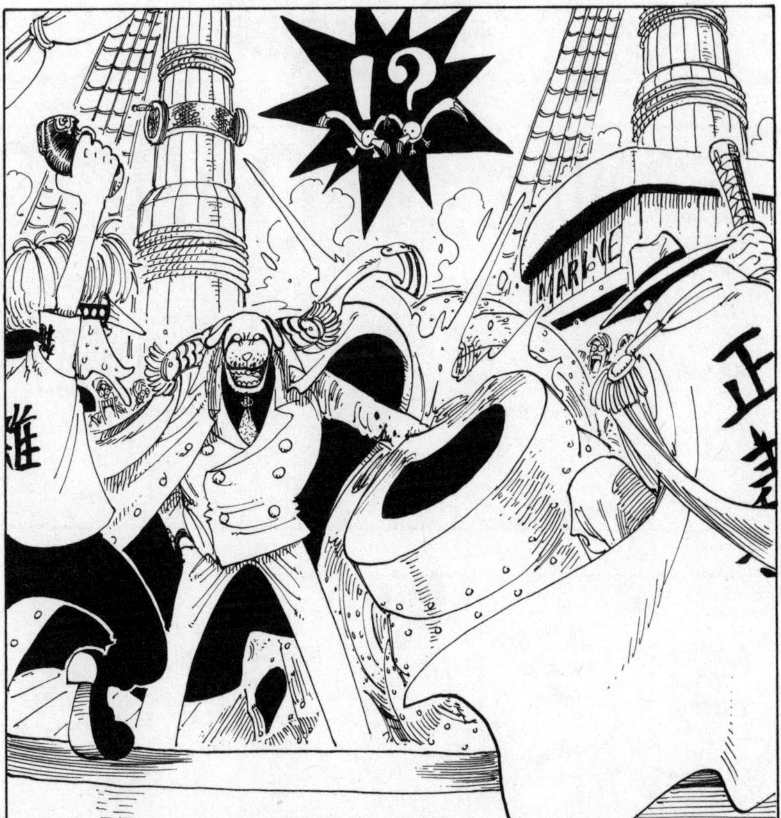
!?

THE TRAVAILS OF KOBY AND HELMEPPO, VOL. 16: "HINDERING A HINDRANCE TO THE HINDRANCE OF THE ARTILLERY ATTACK"

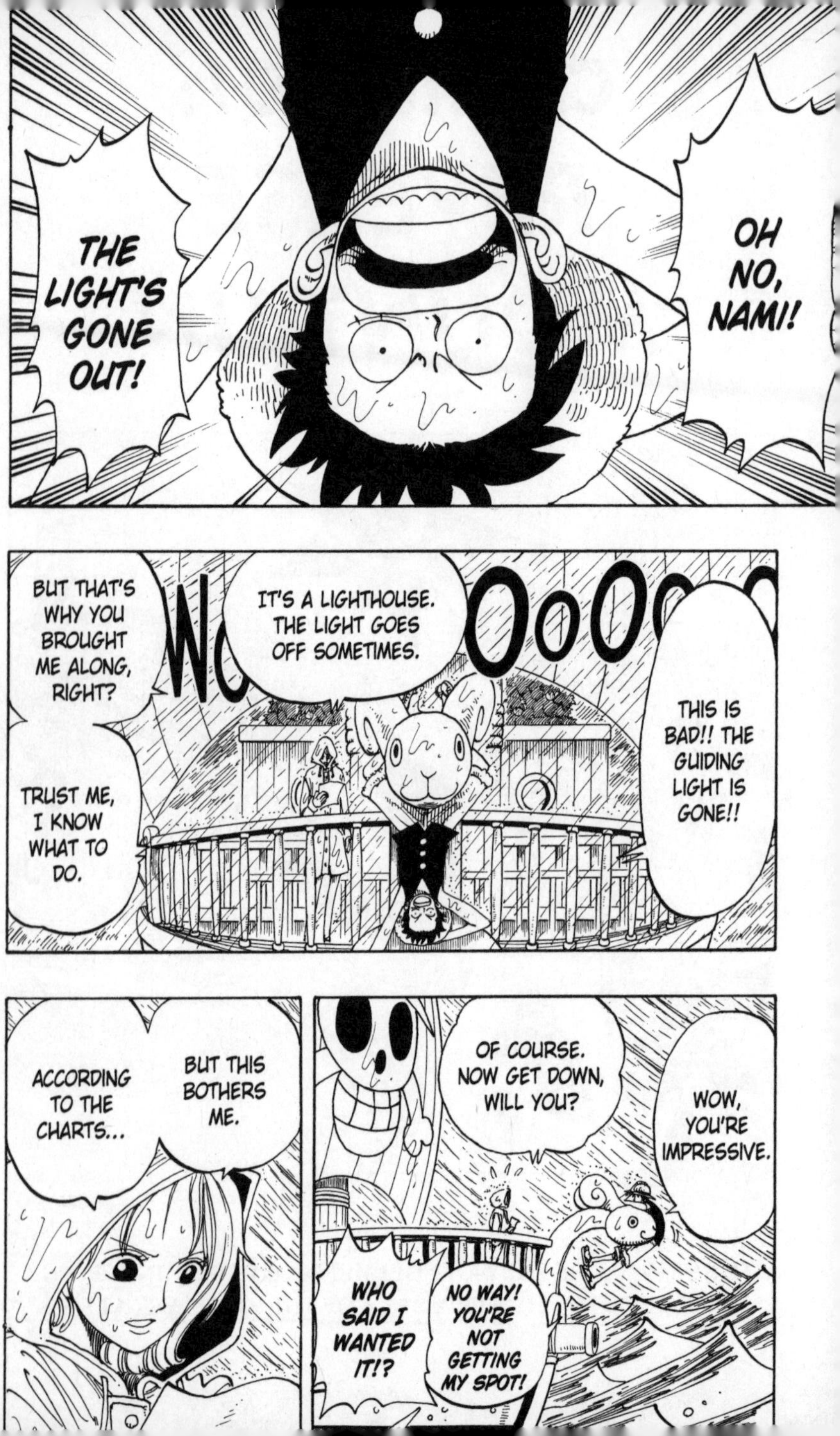
OH NO, NAMI!
THE LIGHT'S GONE OUT!
THIS IS BAD!! THE GUIDING LIGHT IS GONE!!
IT'S A LIGHTHOUSE. THE LIGHT GOES OFF SOMETIMES.
BUT THAT'S WHY YOU BROUGHT ME ALONG, RIGHT?
TRUST ME, I KNOW WHAT TO DO.
WOW, YOU'RE IMPRESSIVE.
OF COURSE. NOW GET DOWN, WILL YOU?
NO WAY! YOU'RE NOT GETTING MY SPOT!
WHO SAID I WANTED IT!?
BUT THIS BOTHERS ME.
ACCORDING TO THE CHARTS...

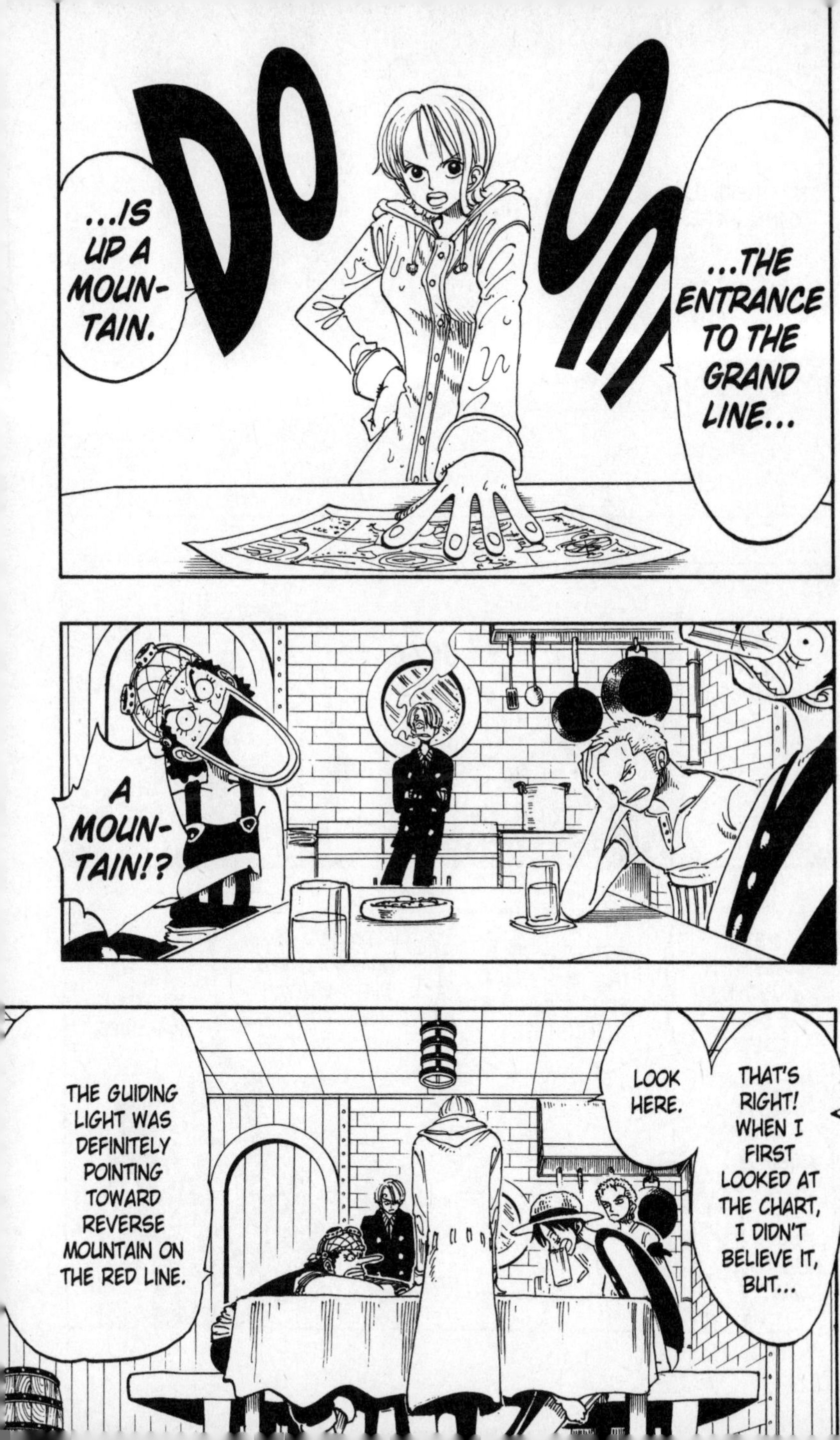
...THE ENTRANCE TO THE GRAND LINE...
DOS
...IS UP A MOUNTAIN.
A MOUNTAIN!?
THAT'S RIGHT! WHEN I FIRST LOOKED AT THE CHART, I DIDN'T BELIEVE IT, BUT...
LOOK HERE.
THE GUIDING LIGHT WAS DEFINITELY POINTING TOWARD REVERSE MOUNTAIN ON THE RED LINE.

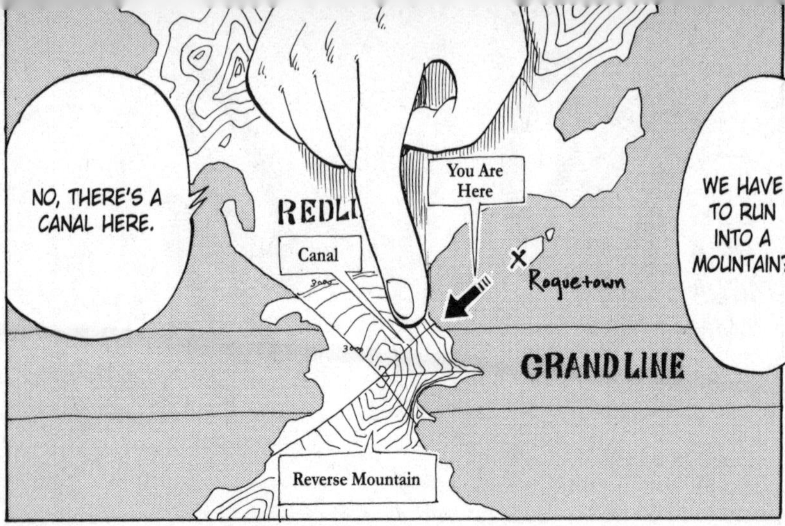
WE HAVE TO RUN INTO A MOUNTAIN?
You Are Here
REDLI
Roquetown
Canal
GRAND LINE
Reverse Mountain
NO, THERE'S A CANAL HERE.

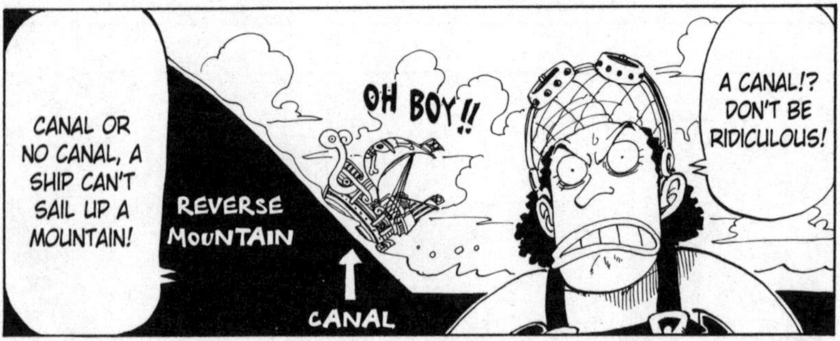
A CANAL!? DON'T BE RIDICULOUS!
OH BOY!!
REVERSE MOUNTAIN
CANAL
CANAL OR NO CANAL, A SHIP CAN'T SAIL UP A MOUNTAIN!

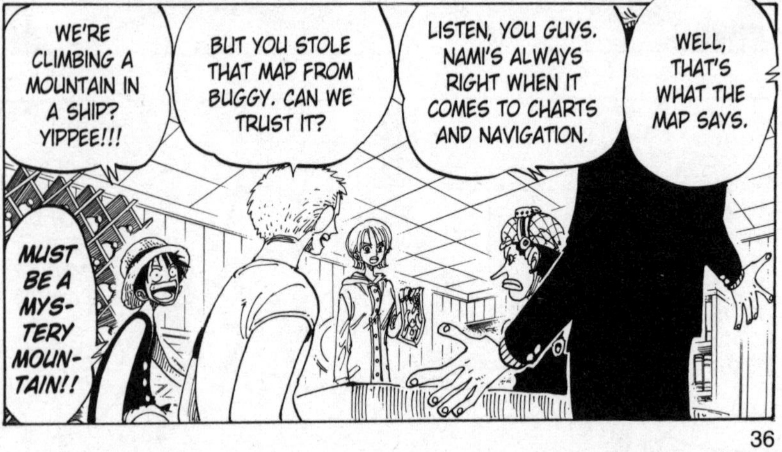
WELL, THAT'S WHAT THE MAP SAYS.
LISTEN, YOU GUYS. NAMI'S ALWAYS RIGHT WHEN IT COMES TO CHARTS AND NAVIGATION.
BUT YOU STOLE THAT MAP FROM BUGGY. CAN WE TRUST IT?
WE'RE CLIMBING A MOUNTAIN IN A SHIP? YIPPEE!!!
MUST BE A MYS-TERY MOUN-TAIN!!

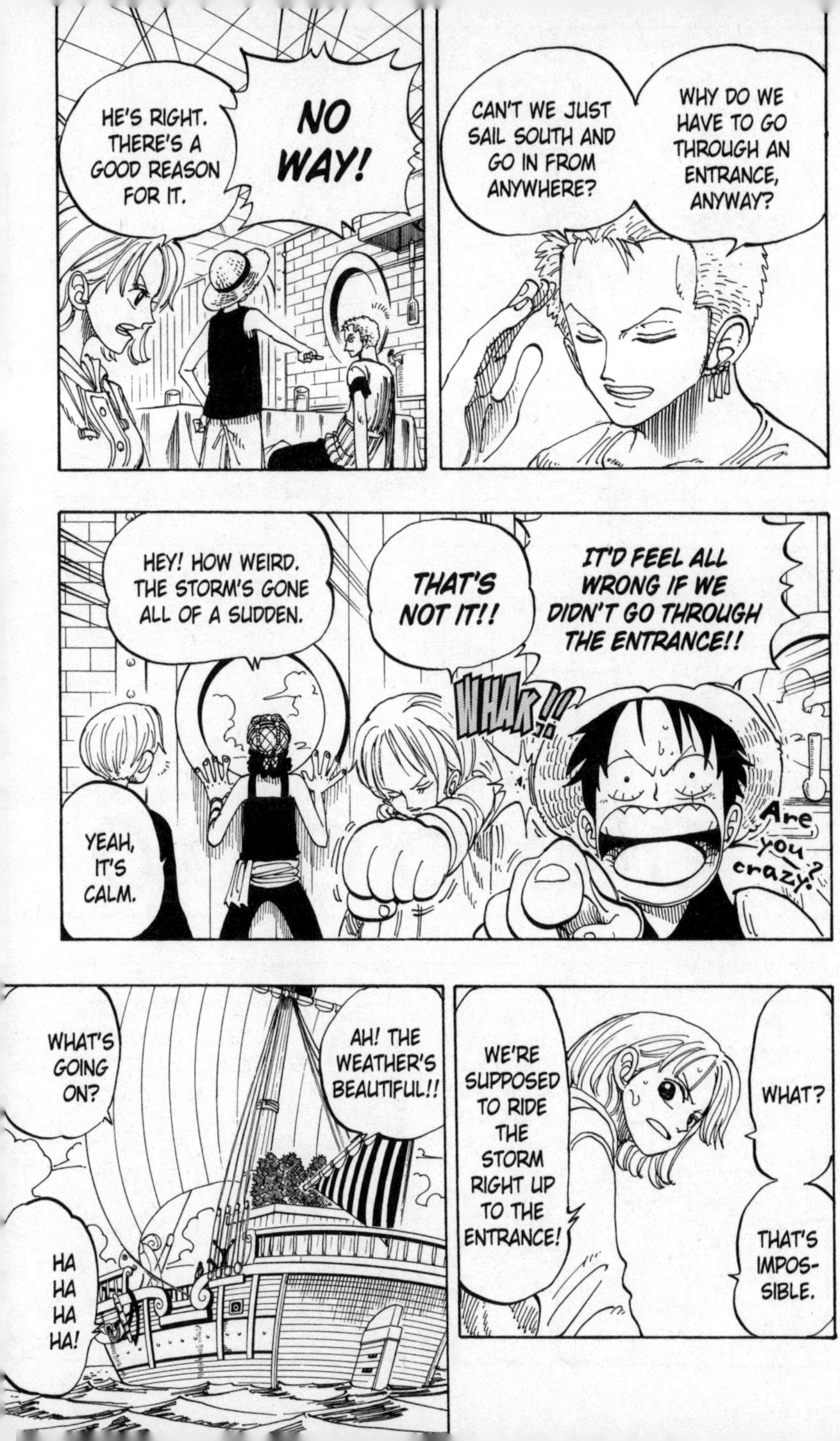
WHY DO WE HAVE TO GO THROUGH AN ENTRANCE, ANYWAY?
CAN'T WE JUST SAIL SOUTH AND GO IN FROM ANYWHERE?
NO WAY!
HE'S RIGHT. THERE'S A GOOD REASON FOR IT.
IT'D FEEL ALL WRONG IF WE DIDN'T GO THROUGH THE ENTRANCE!!
Are you crazy?
THAT'S NOT IT!!
WHAK!!
HEY! HOW WEIRD. THE STORM'S GONE ALL OF A SUDDEN.
YEAH, IT'S CALM.
WHAT?
THAT'S IMPOSSIBLE.
WE'RE SUPPOSED TO RIDE THE STORM RIGHT UP TO THE ENTRANCE!
AH! THE WEATHER'S BEAUTIFUL!!
WHAT'S GOING ON?
HA HA HA HA!

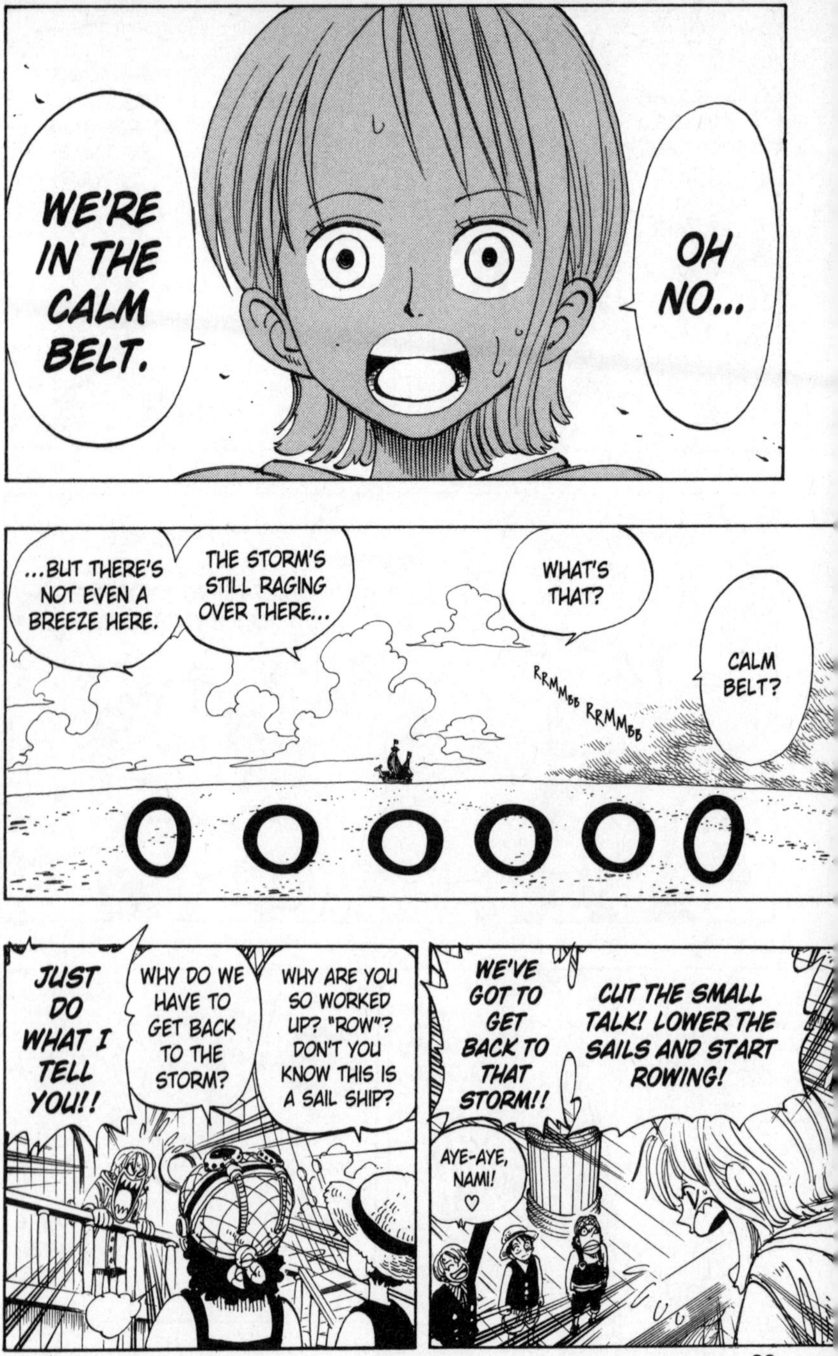
OH NO...
WE'RE IN THE CALM BELT.
CALM BELT?
WHAT'S THAT?
RRMMBB RRMMBB
THE STORM'S STILL RAGING OVER THERE...
...BUT THERE'S NOT EVEN A BREEZE HERE.
OOOOOO
CUT THE SMALL TALK! LOWER THE SAILS AND START ROWING!
WE'VE GOT TO GET BACK TO THAT STORM!!
AYE-AYE, NAMI! ♥
WHY ARE YOU SO WORKED UP? "ROW"? DON'T YOU KNOW THIS IS A SAIL SHIP?
WHY DO WE HAVE TO GET BACK TO THE STORM?
JUST DO WHAT I TELL YOU!!

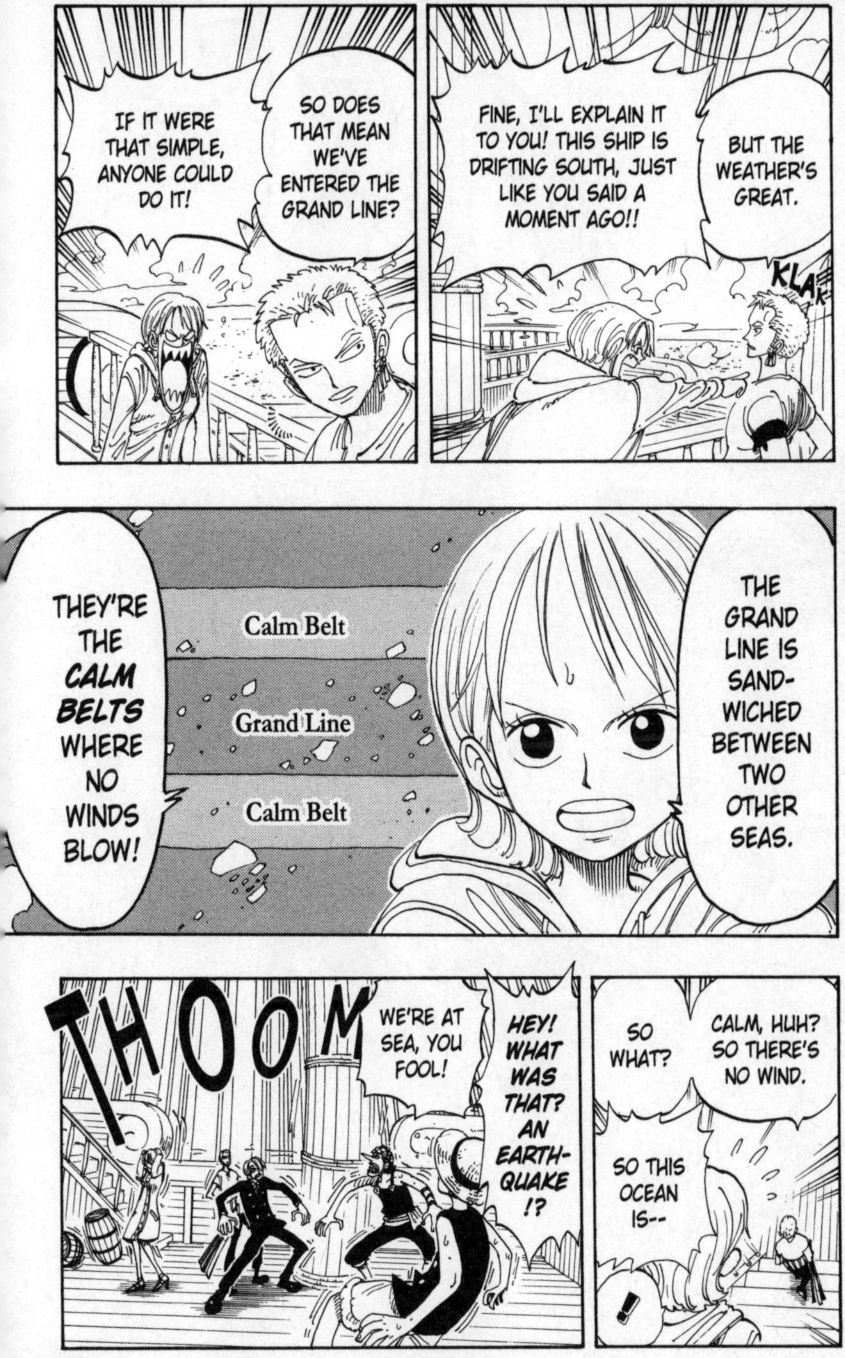
BUT THE WEATHER'S GREAT.
FINE, I'LL EXPLAIN IT TO YOU! THIS SHIP IS DRIFTING SOUTH, JUST LIKE YOU SAID A MOMENT AGO!!
KLAK
SO DOES THAT MEAN WE'VE ENTERED THE GRAND LINE?
IF IT WERE THAT SIMPLE, ANYONE COULD DO IT!
THE GRAND LINE IS SAND-WICHED BETWEEN TWO OTHER SEAS.
Calm Belt
Grand Line
Calm Belt
THEY'RE THE *CALM BELTS* WHERE NO WINDS BLOW!
CALM, HUH? SO THERE'S NO WIND.
SO WHAT?
SO THIS OCEAN IS--
!
THOOM
HEY! WHAT WAS THAT? AN EARTH-QUAKE!?
WE'RE AT SEA, YOU FOOL!

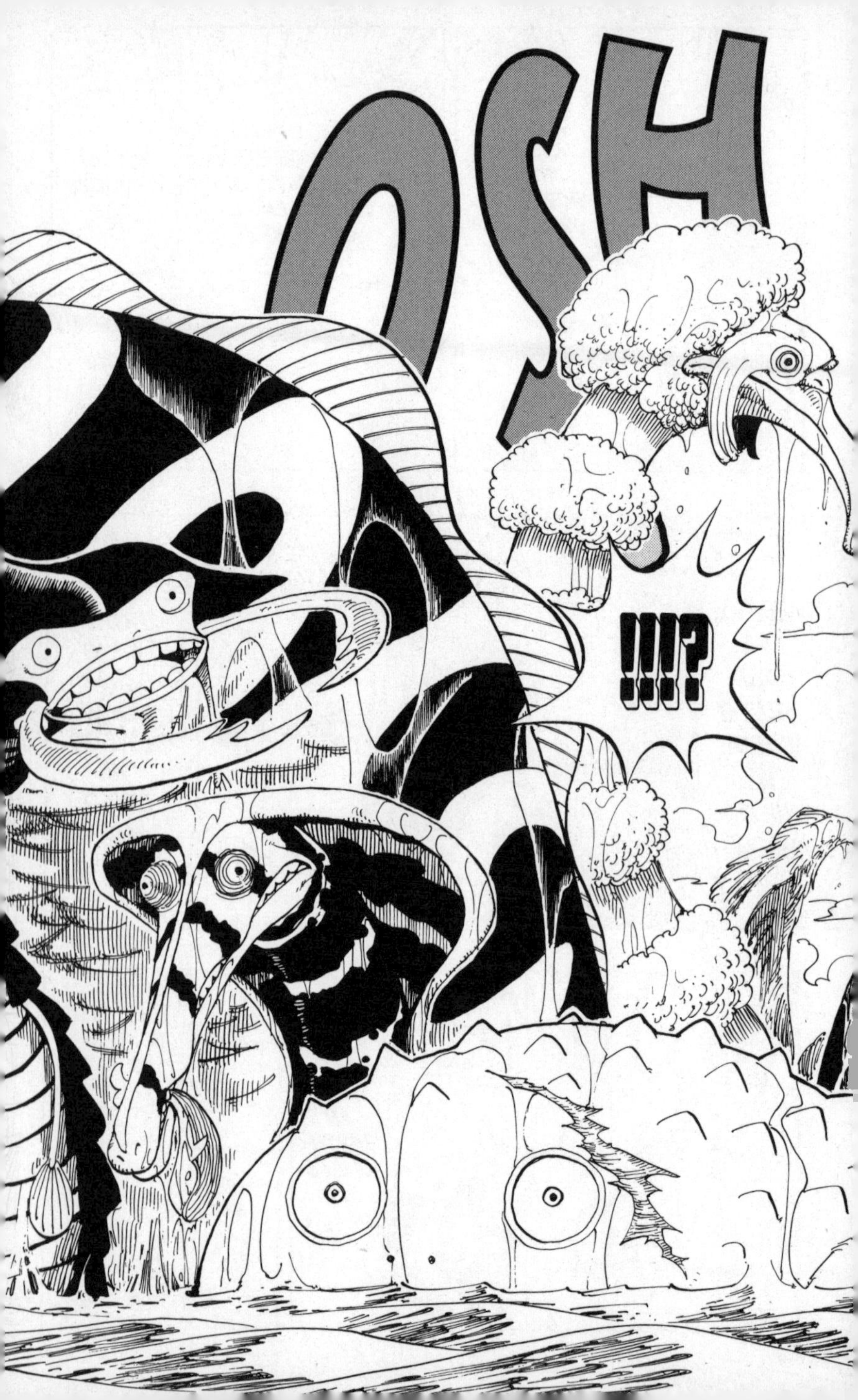
OSH
!!!?

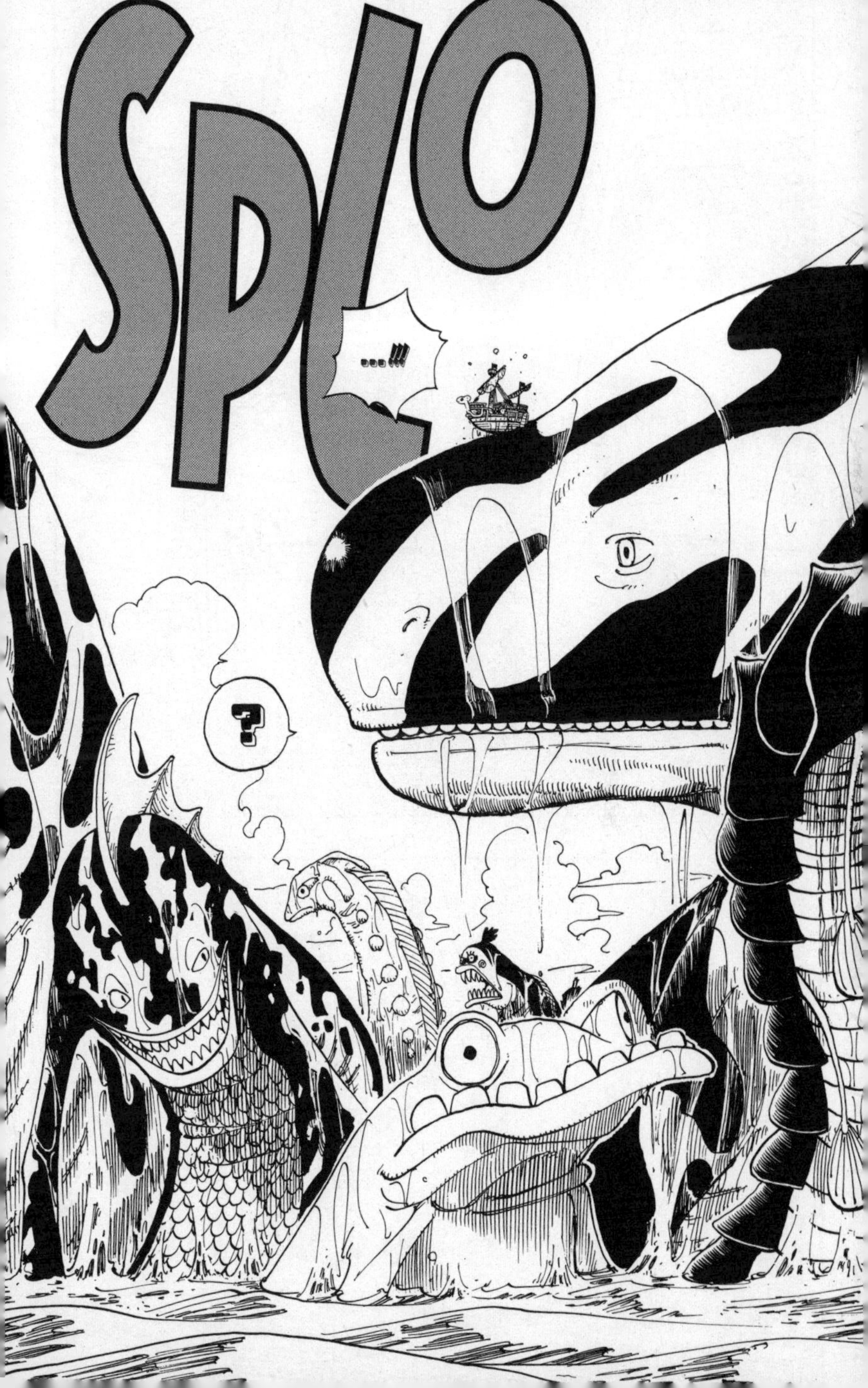
SPLO
...!!!
?

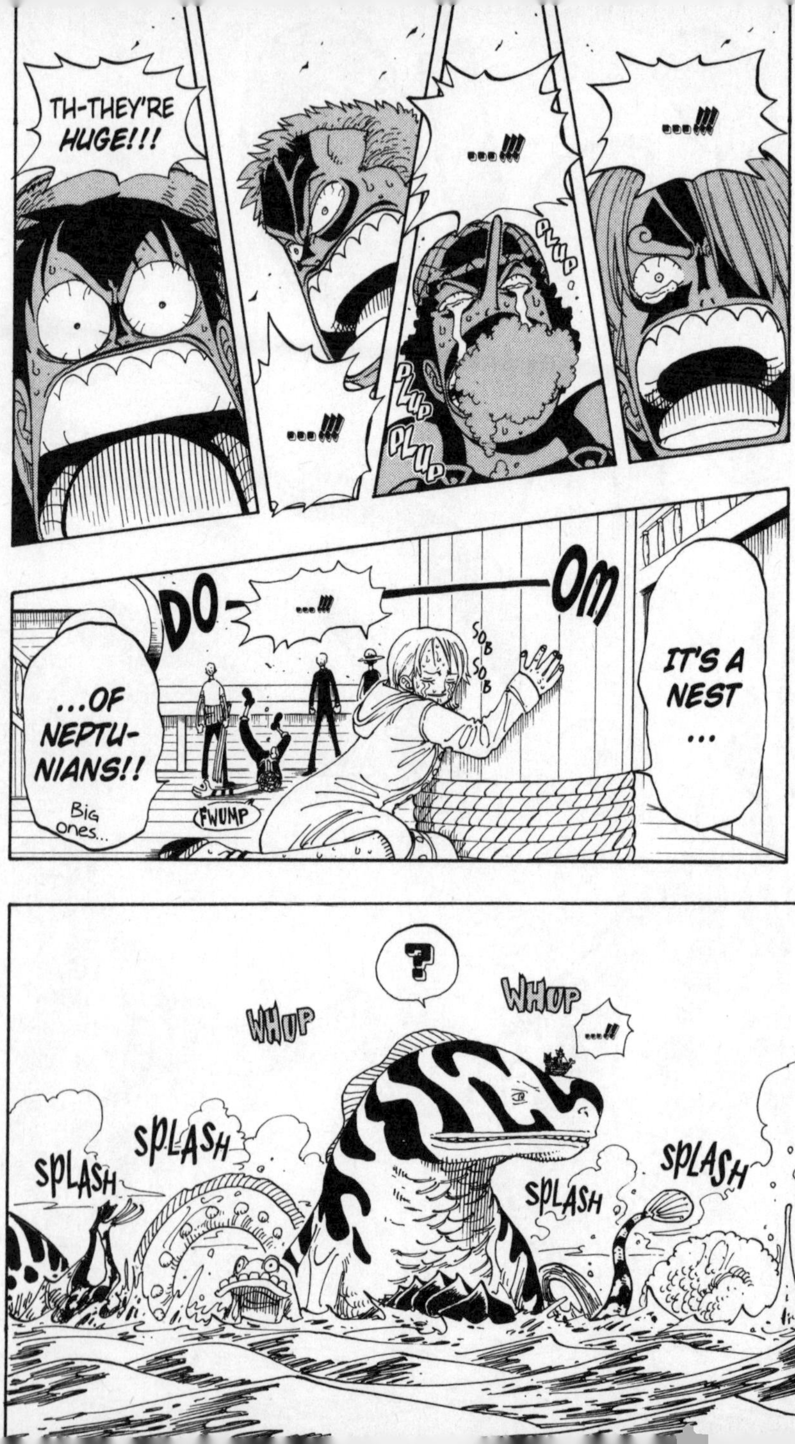
...!!!
...!!!
PLUP
PLUP
PLUP
PLUP
...!!!
TH-THEY'RE HUGE!!!
IT'S A NEST ...
DO——OM
SOB SOB
...!!!
...OF NEPTUNIANS!!
Big ones...
FWUMP
...!!
SPLASH
WHUP
?
SPLASH
WHUP
SPLASH
SPLASH

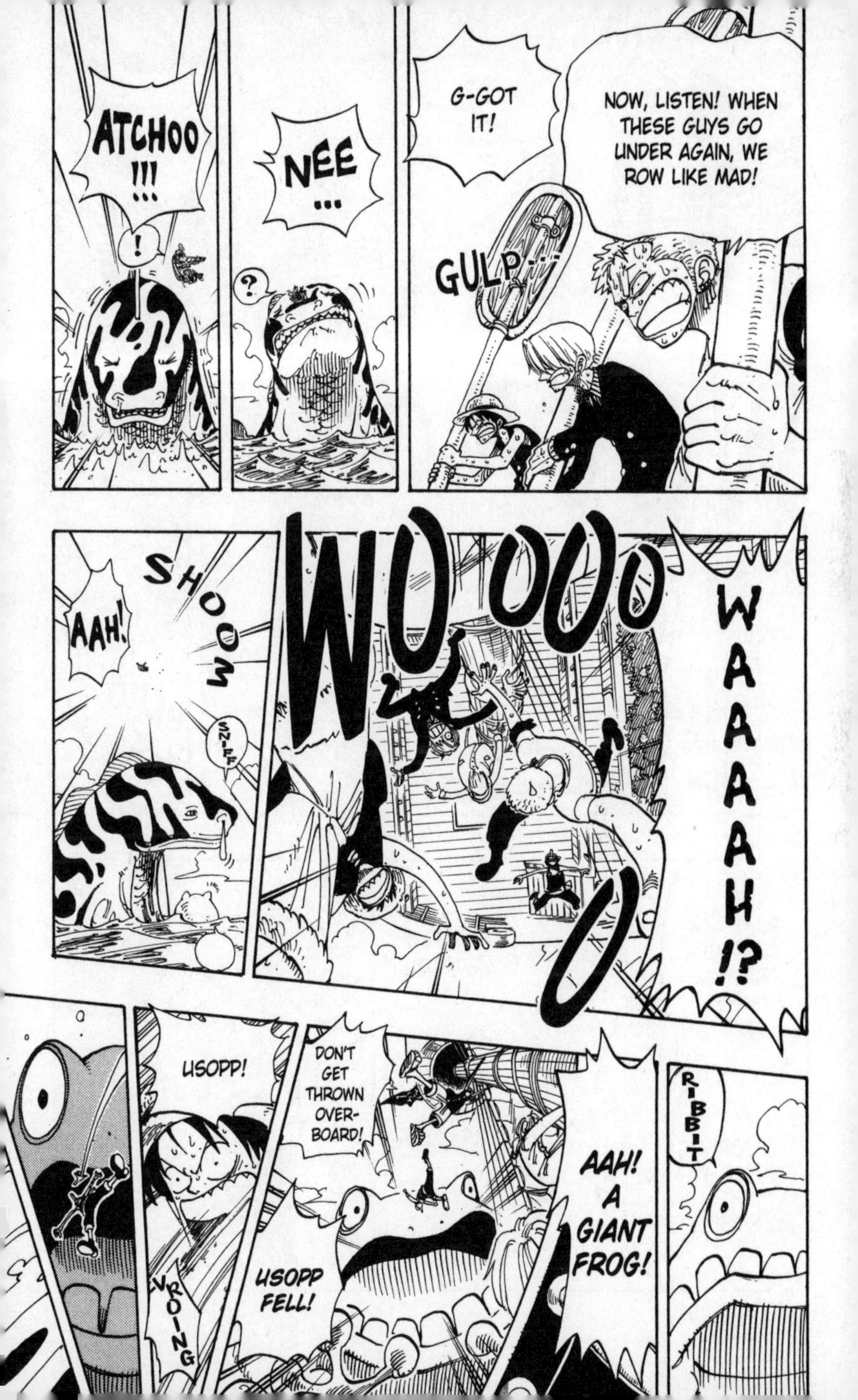
NOW, LISTEN! WHEN THESE GUYS GO UNDER AGAIN, WE ROW LIKE MAD!
G-GOT IT!
GULP...
NEE ...
?
ATCHOO !!!
!
WAAAAAH!?
WOOOOOO
SHOOM
AAH!
SNIFF
RIBBIT
AAH! A GIANT FROG!
DON'T GET THROWN OVER-BOARD!
USOPP FELL!
USOPP!
VROING

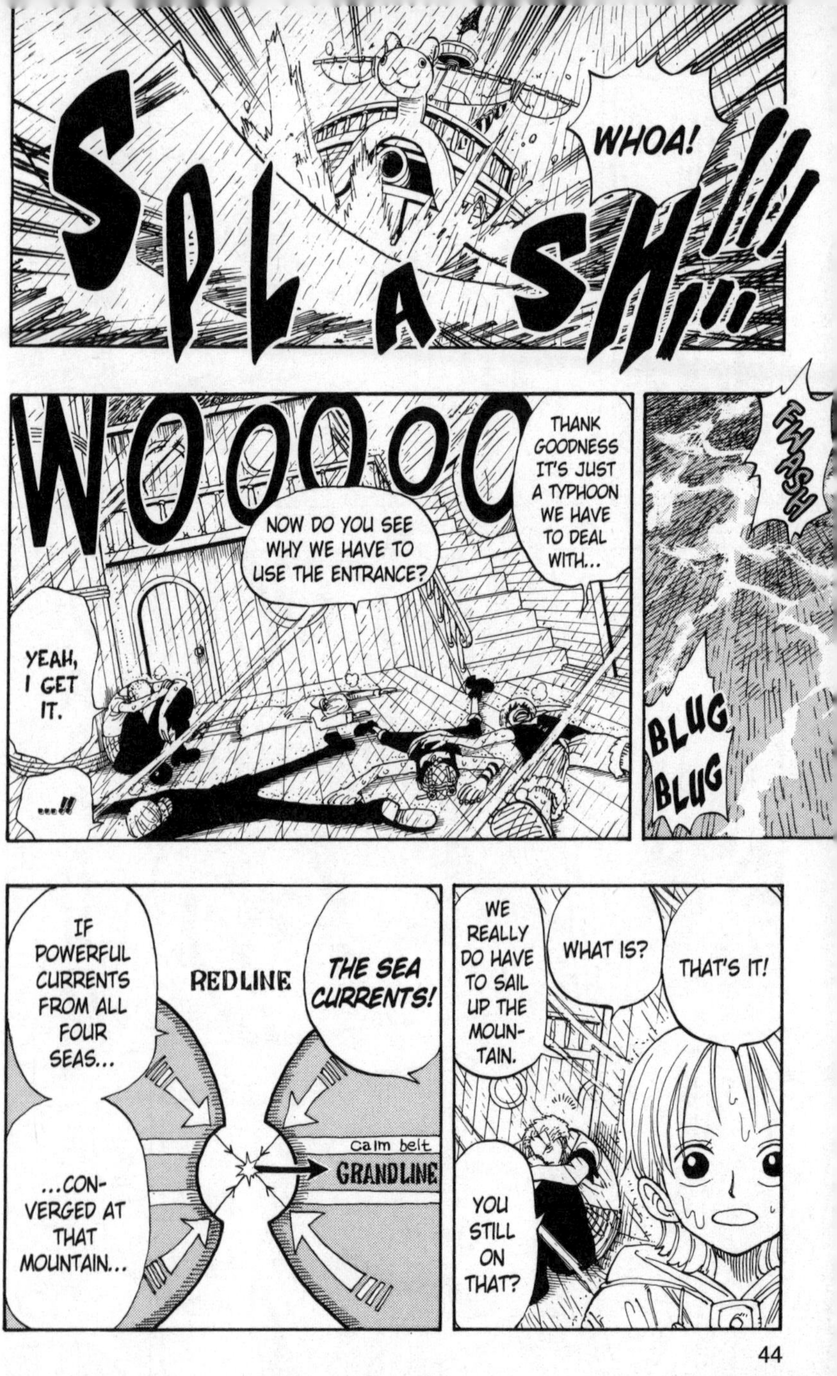
WHOA!
SPLASH!!!!
FWASH
BLUG BLUG
THANK GOODNESS IT'S JUST A TYPHOON WE HAVE TO DEAL WITH...
WOOOOO
NOW DO YOU SEE WHY WE HAVE TO USE THE ENTRANCE?
YEAH, I GET IT.
...!!
THAT'S IT!
WHAT IS?
WE REALLY DO HAVE TO SAIL UP THE MOUN-TAIN.
YOU STILL ON THAT?
THE SEA CURRENTS!
REDLINE
IF POWERFUL CURRENTS FROM ALL FOUR SEAS...
Calm belt
GRANDLINE
...CON-VERGED AT THAT MOUNTAIN...

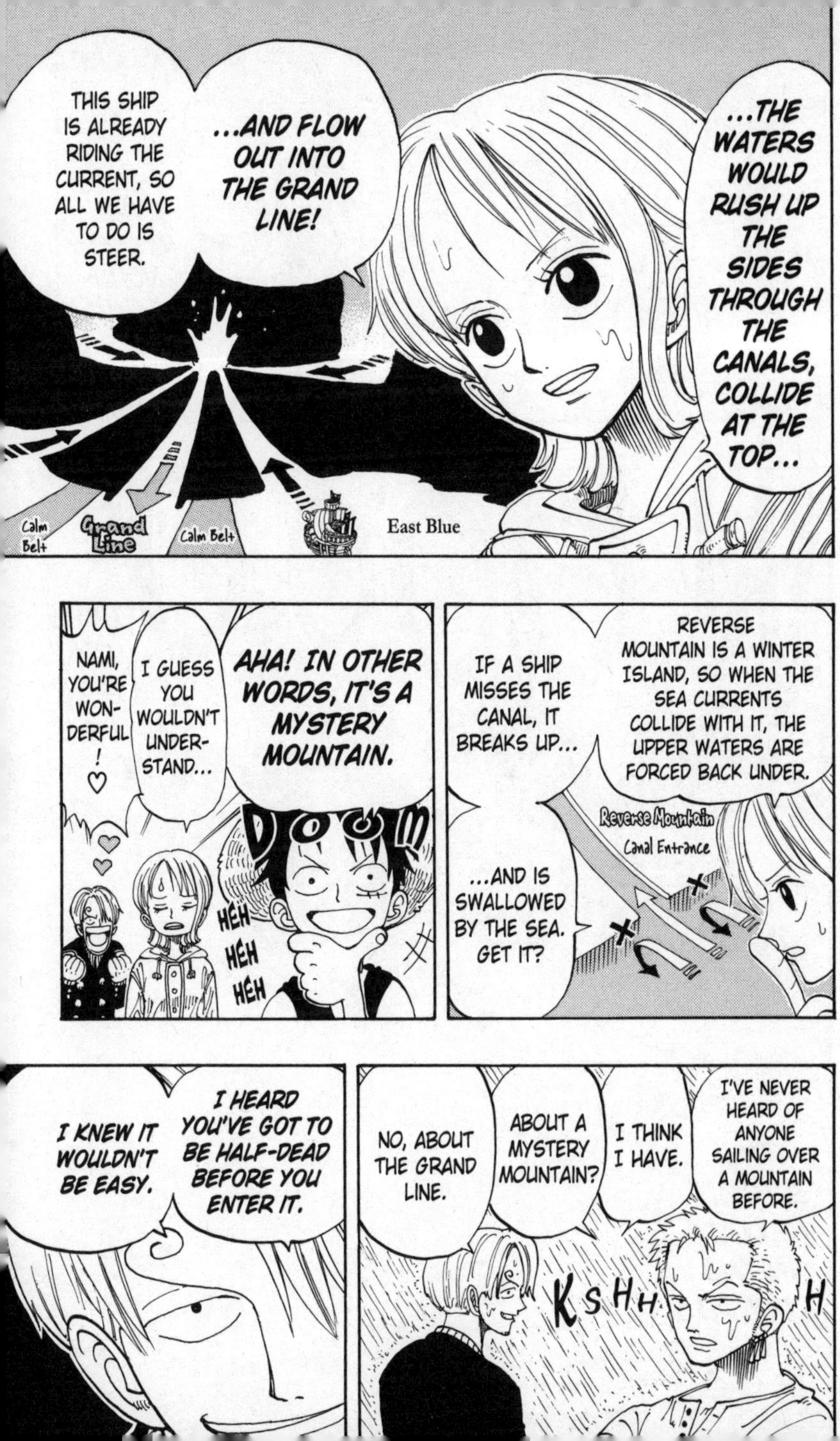
...THE WATERS WOULD RUSH UP THE SIDES THROUGH THE CANALS, COLLIDE AT THE TOP...
...AND FLOW OUT INTO THE GRAND LINE!
THIS SHIP IS ALREADY RIDING THE CURRENT, SO ALL WE HAVE TO DO IS STEER.
East Blue
Calm Belt
Grand Line
Calm Belt
REVERSE MOUNTAIN IS A WINTER ISLAND, SO WHEN THE SEA CURRENTS COLLIDE WITH IT, THE UPPER WATERS ARE FORCED BACK UNDER.
IF A SHIP MISSES THE CANAL, IT BREAKS UP...
Reverse Mountain
Canal Entrance
...AND IS SWALLOWED BY THE SEA. GET IT?
AHA! IN OTHER WORDS, IT'S A MYSTERY MOUNTAIN.
I GUESS YOU WOULDN'T UNDERSTAND...
NAMI, YOU'RE WONDERFUL! ♡
DOOM
HEH HEH HEH
I'VE NEVER HEARD OF ANYONE SAILING OVER A MOUNTAIN BEFORE.
I THINK I HAVE.
ABOUT A MYSTERY MOUNTAIN?
NO, ABOUT THE GRAND LINE.
KSHHH
I HEARD YOU'VE GOT TO BE HALF-DEAD BEFORE YOU ENTER IT.
I KNEW IT WOULDN'T BE EASY.

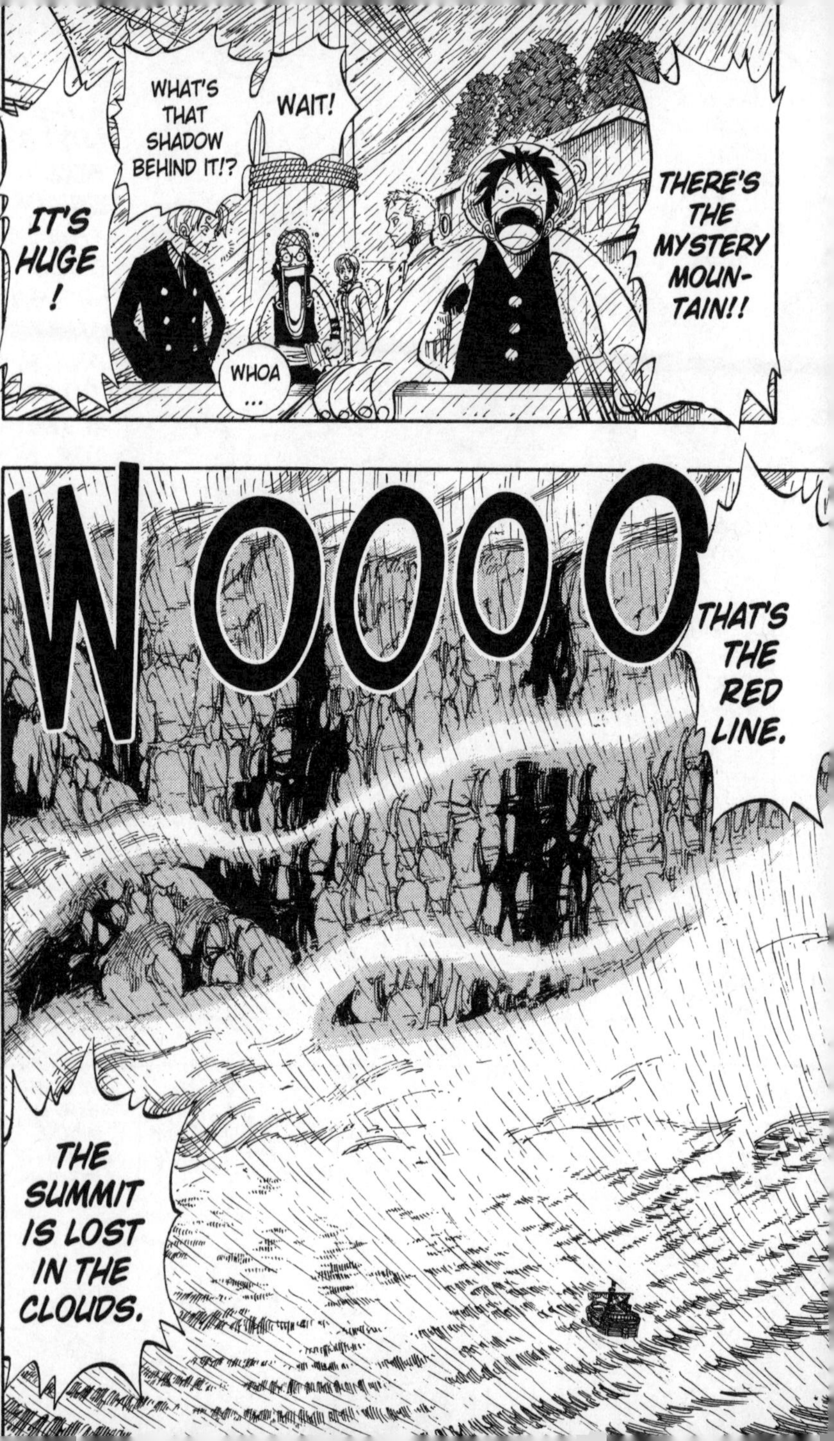
THERE'S THE MYSTERY MOUN- TAIN!!
WAIT!
WHAT'S THAT SHADOW BEHIND IT!?
IT'S HUGE!
WHOA ...
WOOOO
THAT'S THE RED LINE.
THE SUMMIT IS LOST IN THE CLOUDS.

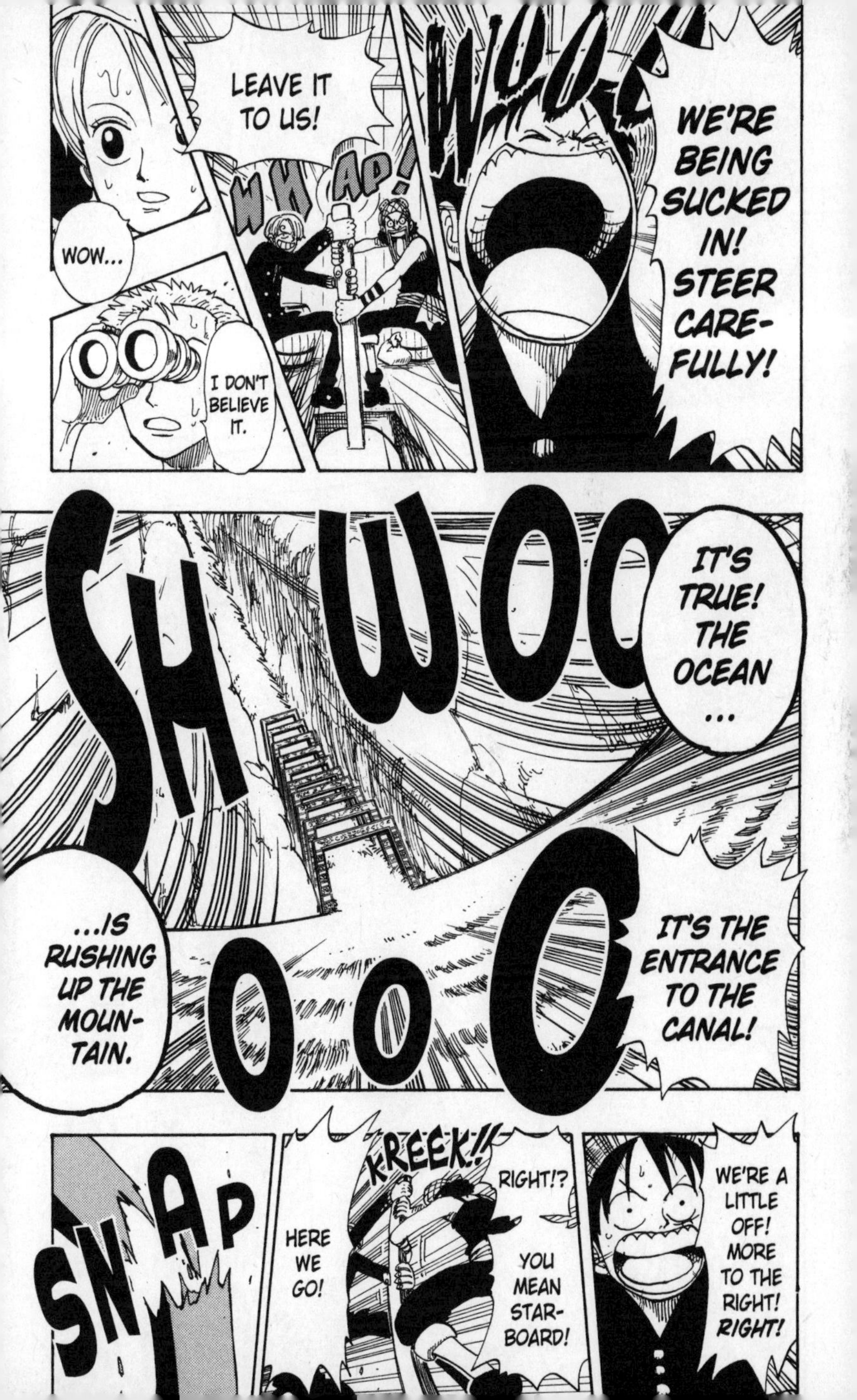
WOO
WE'RE BEING SUCKED IN! STEER CARE-FULLY!
WHAP!
LEAVE IT TO US!
WOW...
I DON'T BELIEVE IT.
SHWOOOOO
IT'S TRUE! THE OCEAN ...
...IS RUSHING UP THE MOUN-TAIN.
IT'S THE ENTRANCE TO THE CANAL!
WE'RE A LITTLE OFF! MORE TO THE RIGHT! RIGHT!
RIGHT!?
YOU MEAN STAR-BOARD!
KREEK!!
HERE WE GO!
SNAP

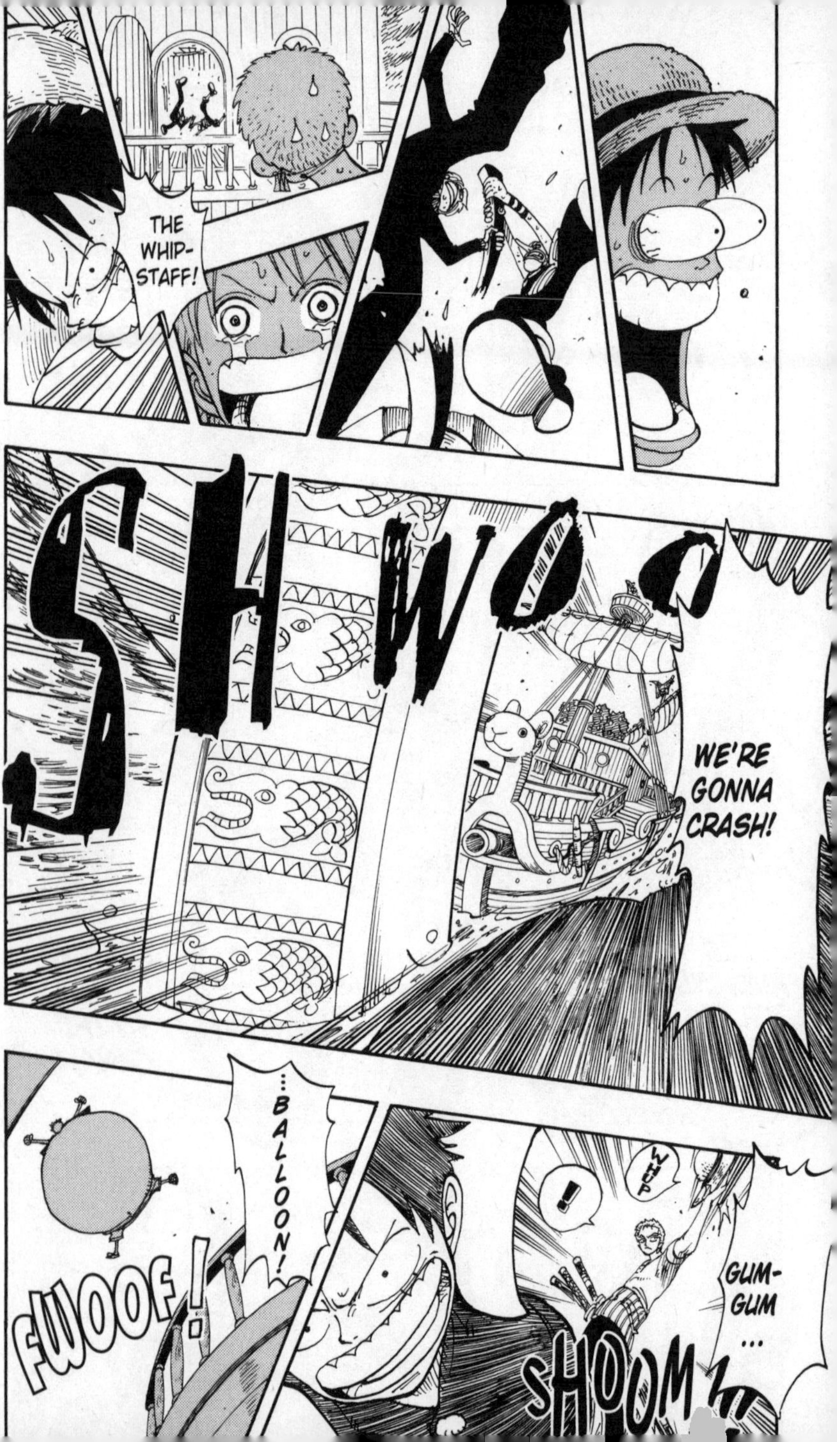
THE WHIP-STAFF!
SHWOO
WE'RE GONNA CRASH!
GUM-GUM ...
WHUP
!
SHOOM!!
...BALLOON!
FWOOF!

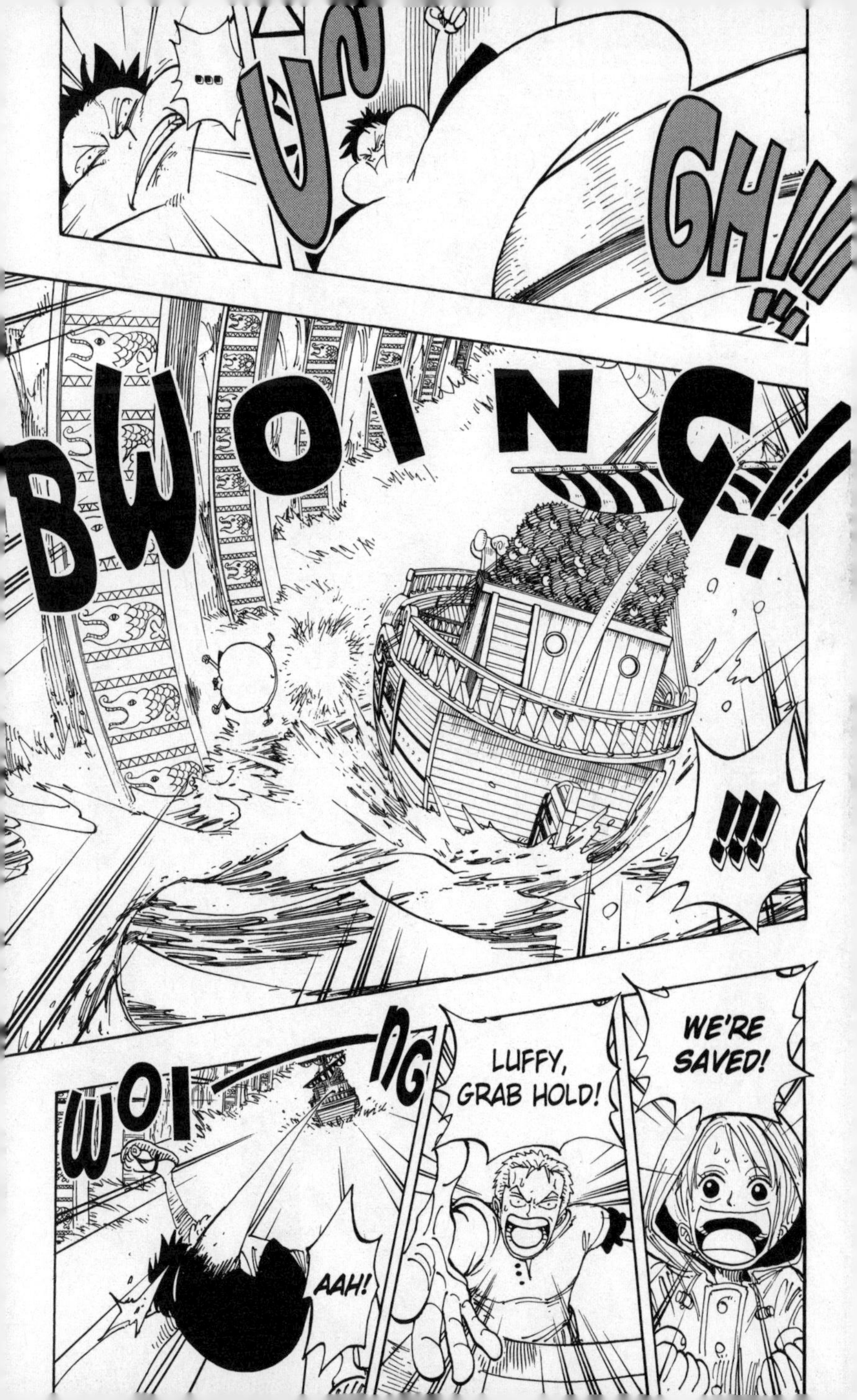
...
UN
GH!!!
BWOING!!
!!!
WOI
NG
WE'RE SAVED!
LUFFY, GRAB HOLD!
AAH!

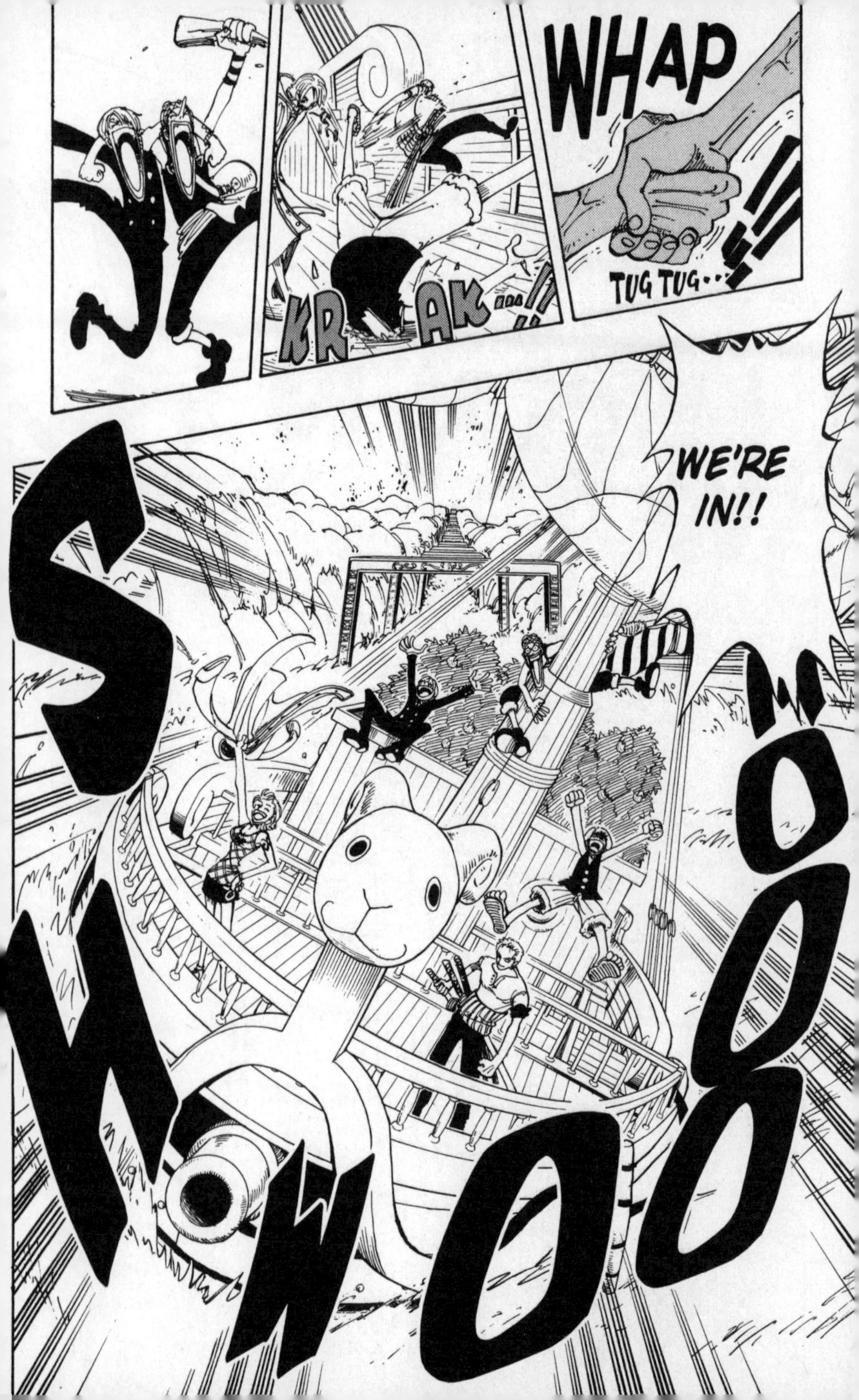
WHAP
TUG TUG...
KRAK...!!
WE'RE IN!!
SHWOOOO

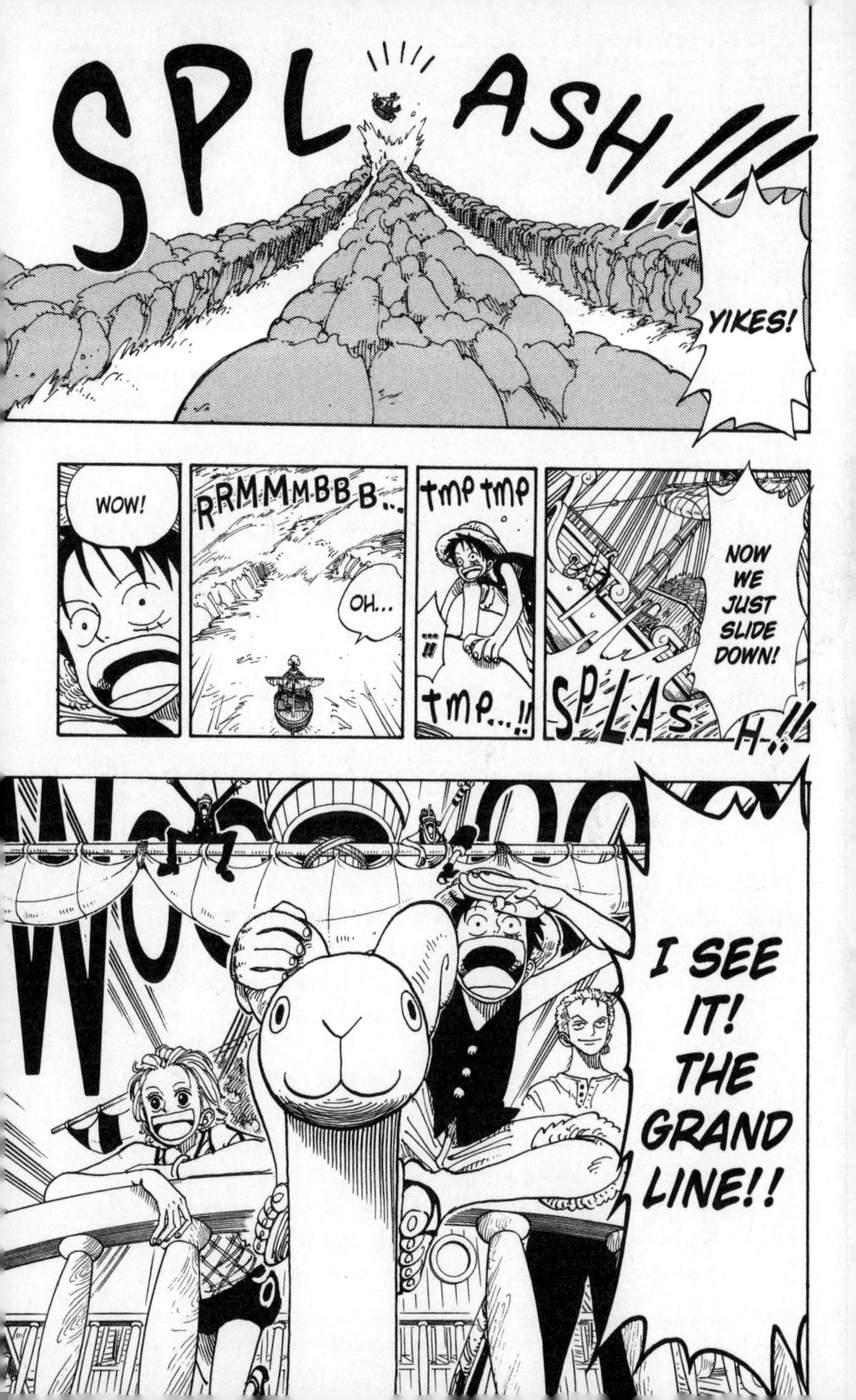
SPLASH!!
YIKES!
NOW WE JUST SLIDE DOWN!
SPLASH!!
tmp tmp
...!!
tmp...!!
RRMMMBBB...
OH...
WOW!
WOOO
I SEE IT! THE GRAND LINE!!

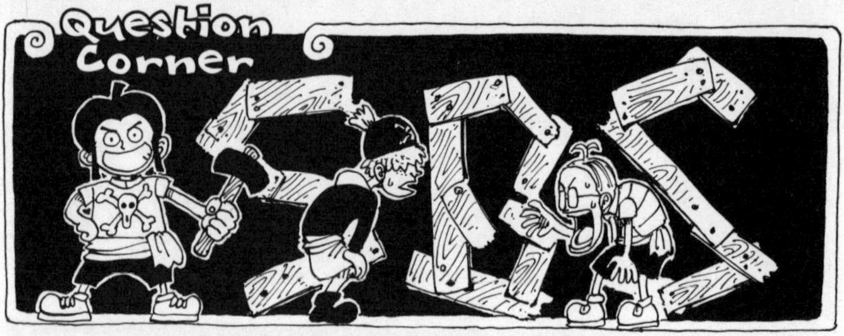
Question Corner
SBS

Q: Here's a question for Oda Sensei. Zolo, Sanji, and Nami look too young to be drinking alcohol. Should they be doing that?

A: No.

Q: I don't usually do things like this, but I just had to send this to you. Here's a challenge for you. Try saying these words three times: akatakoashikiken, kitakoashikiken, chatakoashikiken.* (Please print this in the SBS.)

A: Oh, a tongue twister, eh? This one's easy. Ready and...

AchakaBatasaBadarappa!!!

Okay, next.

Q: Oda Sensei, I've always wanted to ask you this. At the end of the Japanese volume, it says that photocopying without permission from the author is an infringement of copyright, but is it okay to photocopy things like the class schedule? Please tell me. From Koby's cheerful friend no. 3.

A: The illustrations on that page are rather complicated, but I've already gotten permission from the various parties, so it's okay. As far as the class schedule is concerned, I got word from people saying, "At our school, we have eight periods." Please, give me a break. I'm sorry. I guess your studies must keep you very busy...

*These three tongue twisters play on the name of Hachi's Tentacle-Sword Overload (takoashi kiken) attack, which itself is a play on the Japanese term for the dangers of plugging too many appliances into an outlet. --Ed.

Chapter 102:
AND NOW, THE GRAND LINE

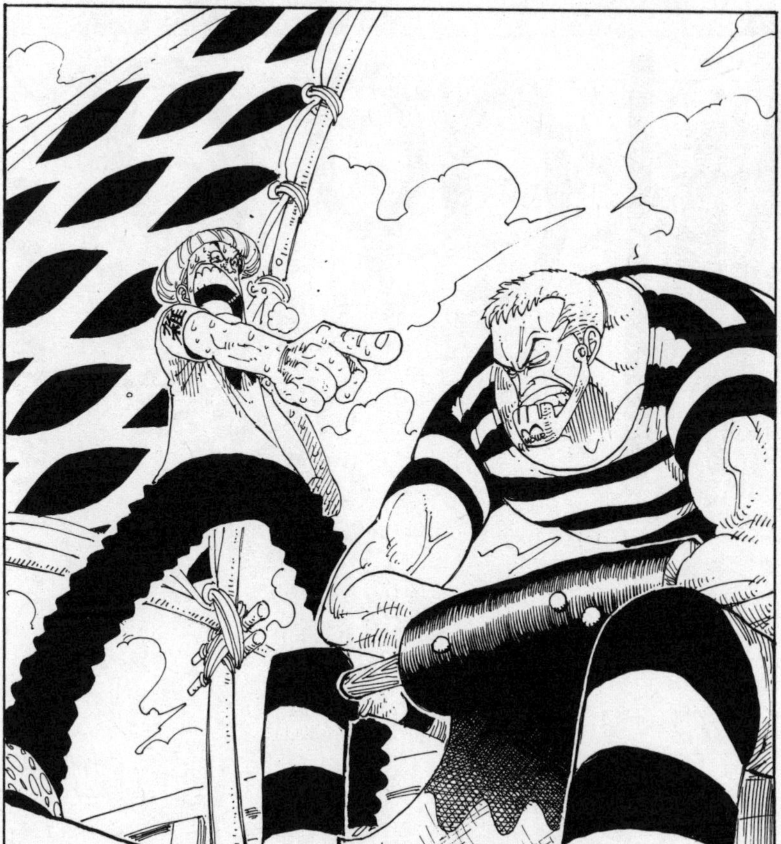
THE TRAVAILS OF KOBY AND HELMEPPO, VOL. 17:
"HELMEPPO'S BIG DECISION"

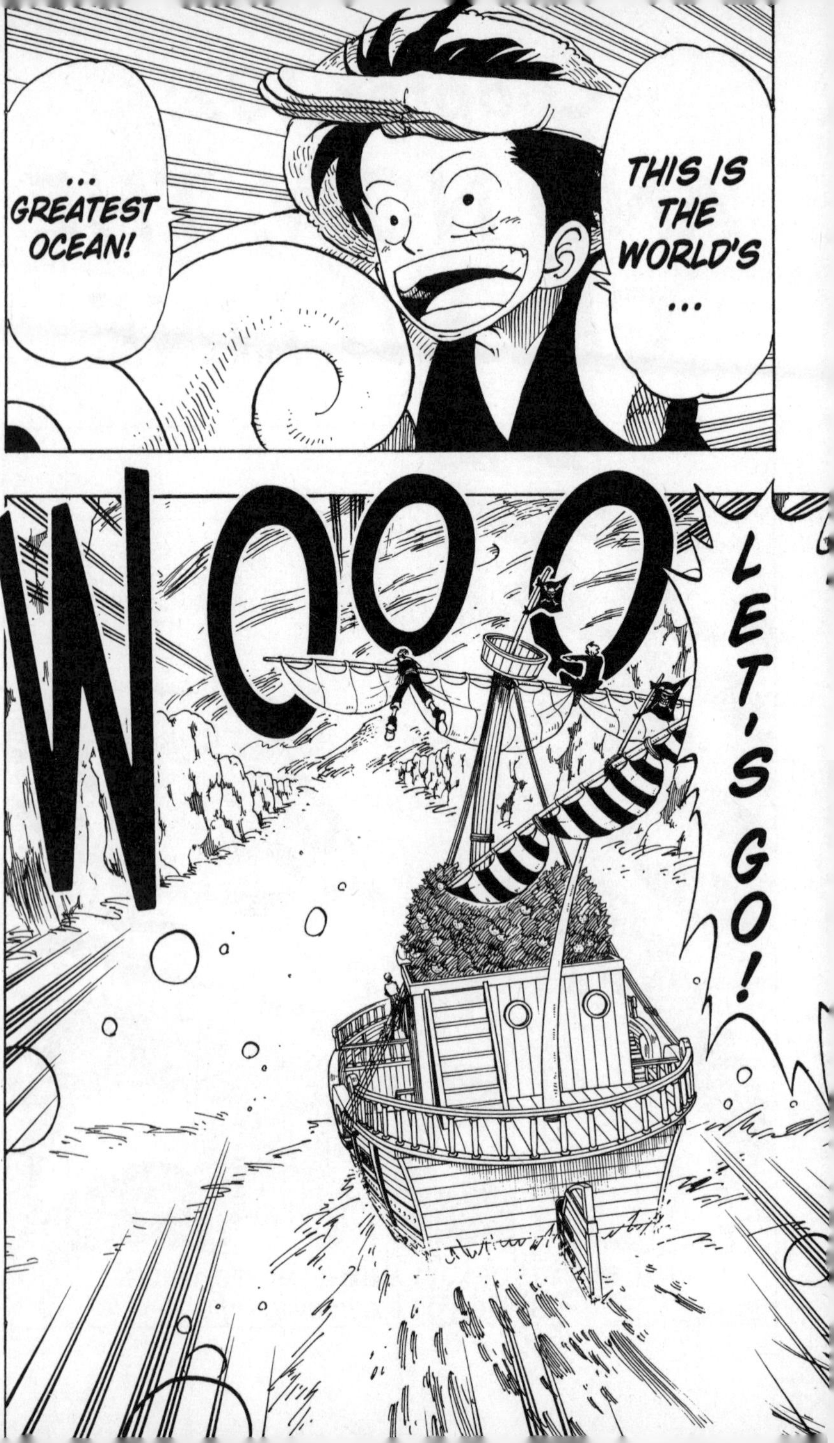
THIS IS THE WORLD'S ...
... GREATEST OCEAN!
LET'S GO!
WOOO

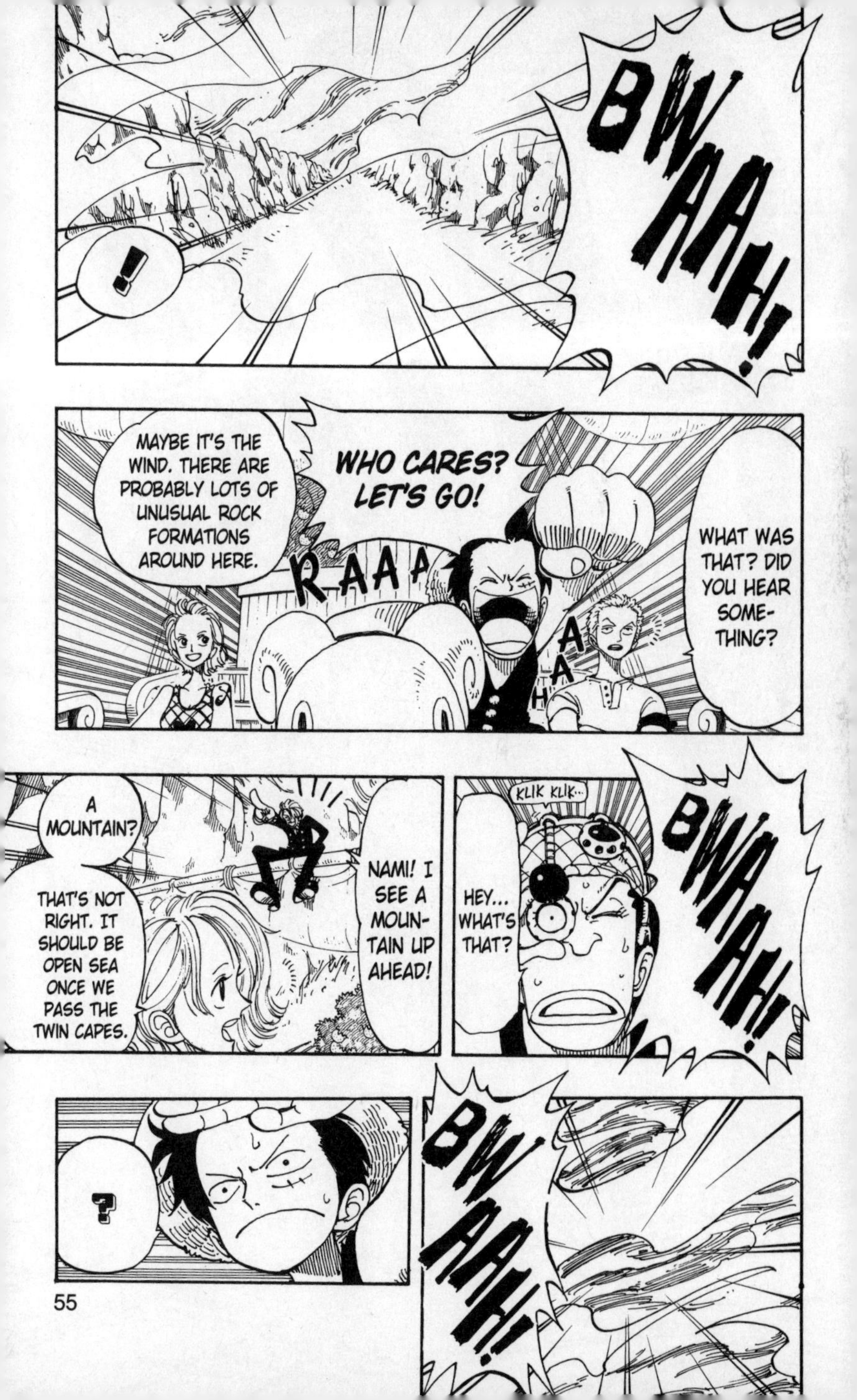
BWAAAH!!
!
WHAT WAS THAT? DID YOU HEAR SOMETHING?
WHO CARES? LET'S GO!
MAYBE IT'S THE WIND. THERE ARE PROBABLY LOTS OF UNUSUAL ROCK FORMATIONS AROUND HERE.
RAAAA
AAH
BWAAAH!!
KLIK KLIK...
HEY... WHAT'S THAT?
NAMI! I SEE A MOUNTAIN UP AHEAD!
A MOUNTAIN?
THAT'S NOT RIGHT. IT SHOULD BE OPEN SEA ONCE WE PASS THE TWIN CAPES.
BWAAAH!!
?

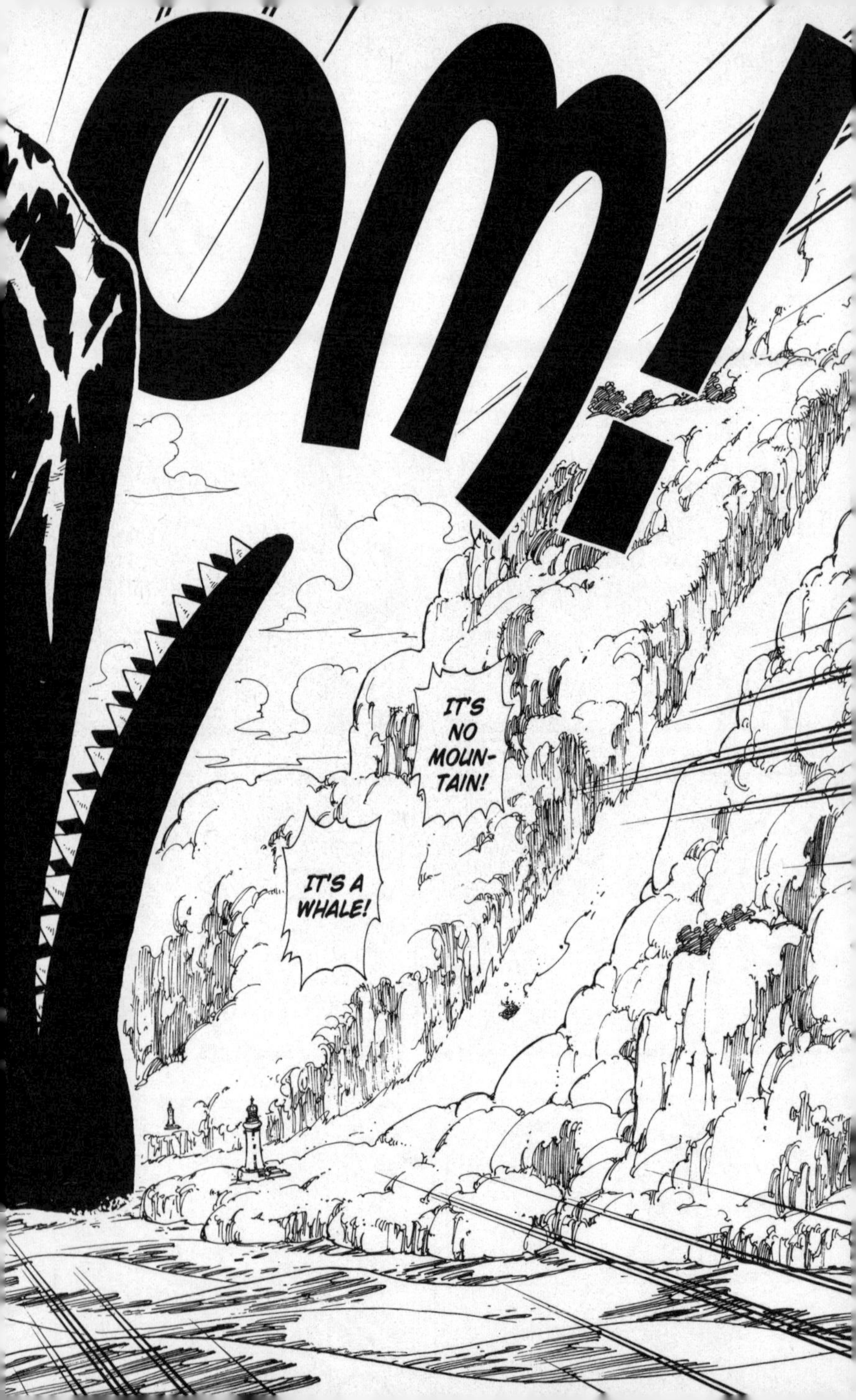
OM!!
IT'S NO MOUNTAIN!
IT'S A WHALE!

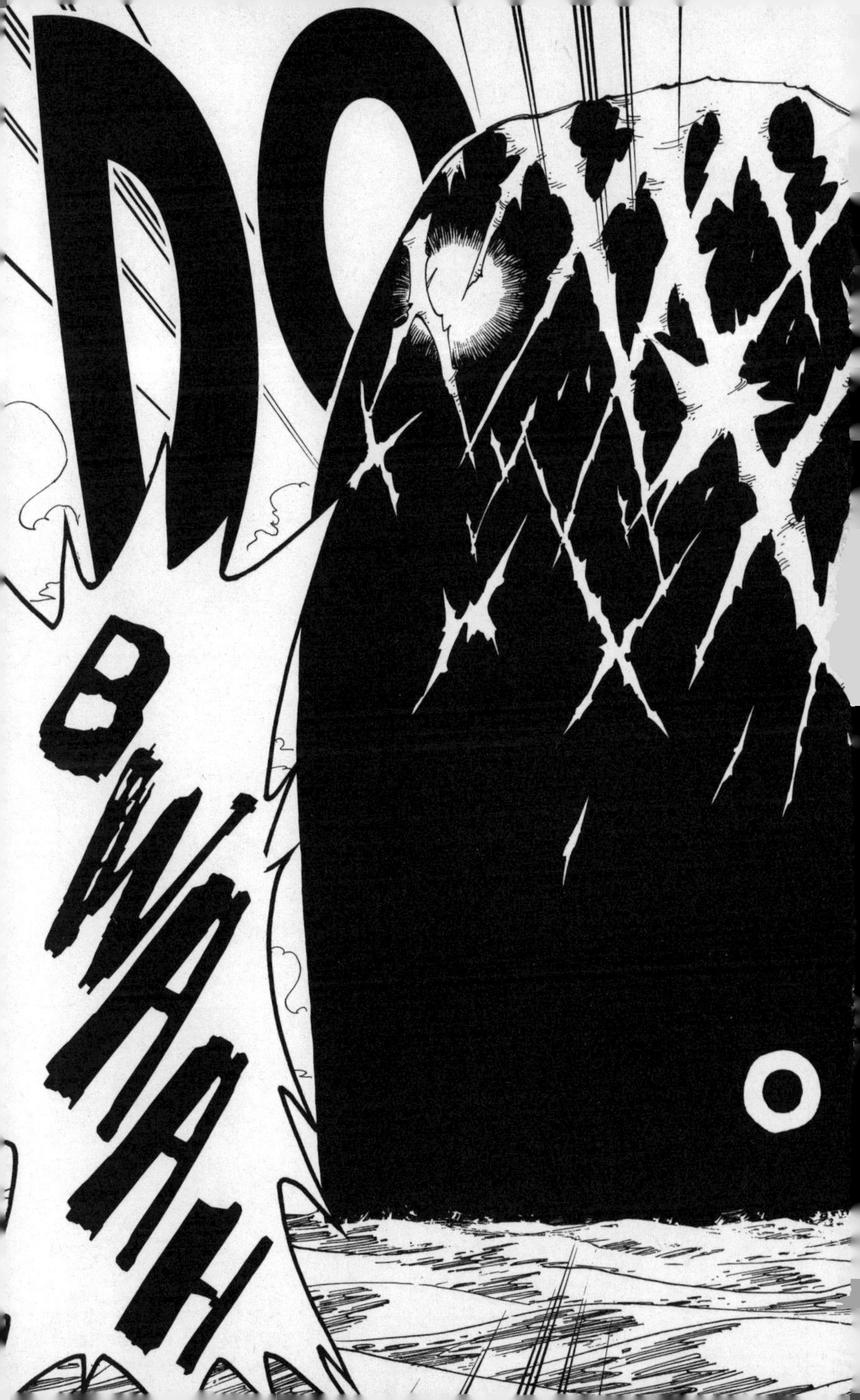
DO
BWAAH

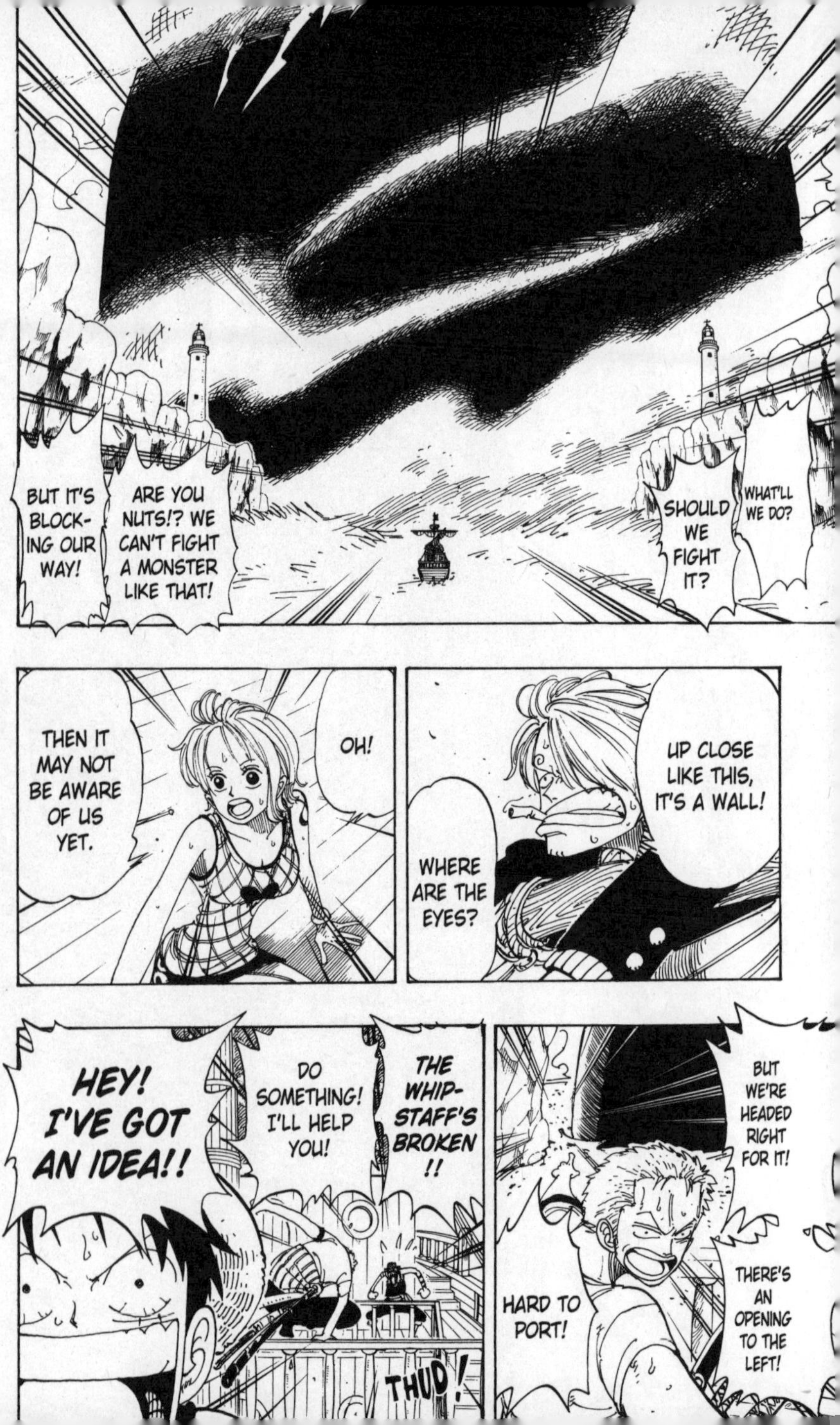
WHAT'LL WE DO?
SHOULD WE FIGHT IT?
ARE YOU NUTS!? WE CAN'T FIGHT A MONSTER LIKE THAT!
BUT IT'S BLOCKING OUR WAY!
UP CLOSE LIKE THIS, IT'S A WALL!
WHERE ARE THE EYES?
OH!
THEN IT MAY NOT BE AWARE OF US YET.
BUT WE'RE HEADED RIGHT FOR IT!
THERE'S AN OPENING TO THE LEFT!
HARD TO PORT!
THE WHIP-STAFF'S BROKEN!!
DO SOMETHING! I'LL HELP YOU!
THUD!
HEY! I'VE GOT AN IDEA!!

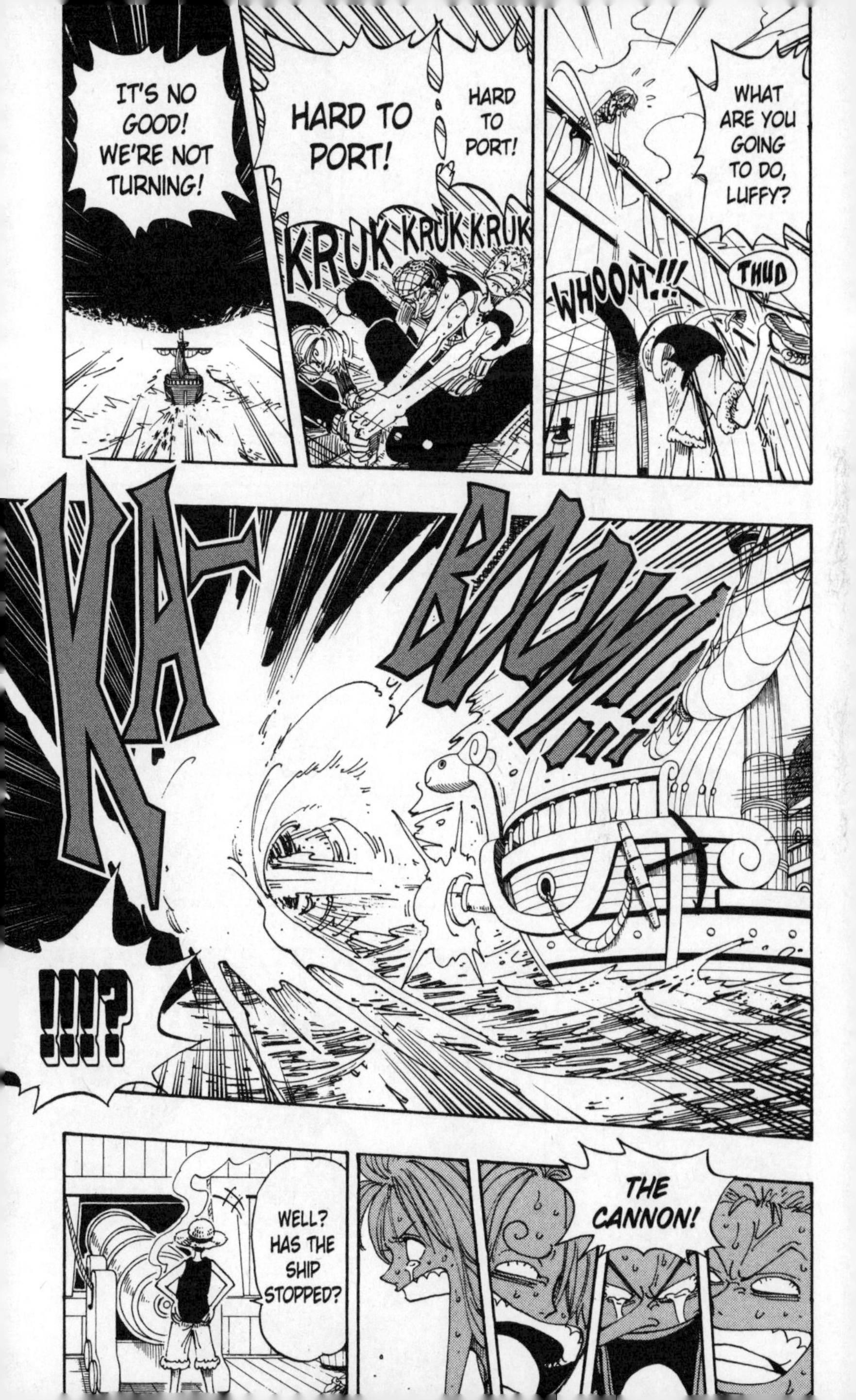
WHAT ARE YOU GOING TO DO, LUFFY?
THUD
WHOOM!!!
HARD TO PORT!
HARD TO PORT!
KRUK KRUK KRUK
IT'S NO GOOD! WE'RE NOT TURNING!
KA-BOOM!!!
!!!?
THE CANNON!
WELL? HAS THE SHIP STOPPED?

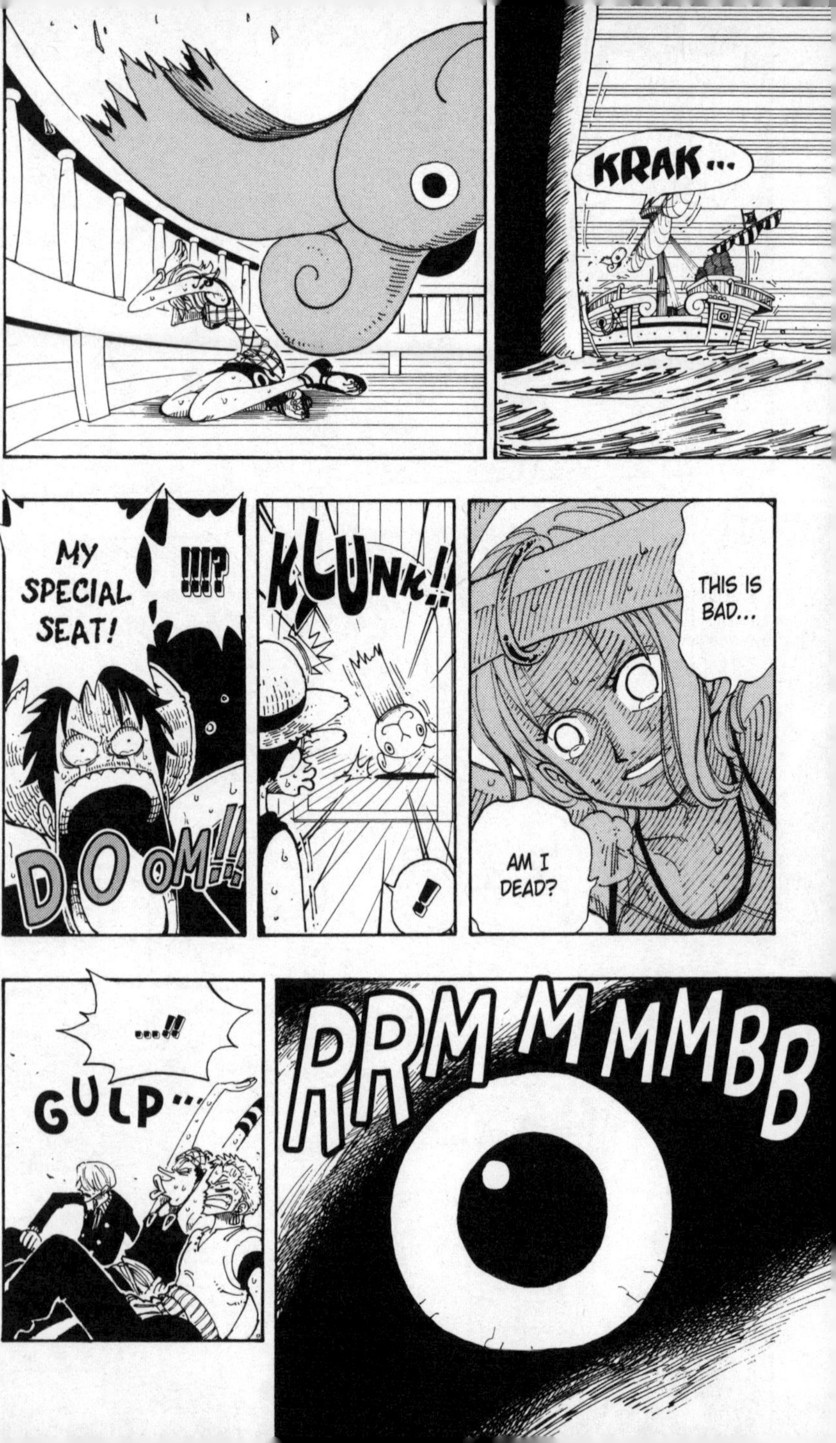
KRAK...
THIS IS BAD...
AM I DEAD?
KLUNK!!
!
MY SPECIAL SEAT!
!!!?
DOOM!!
RRM M MMBB
...!!
GULP...

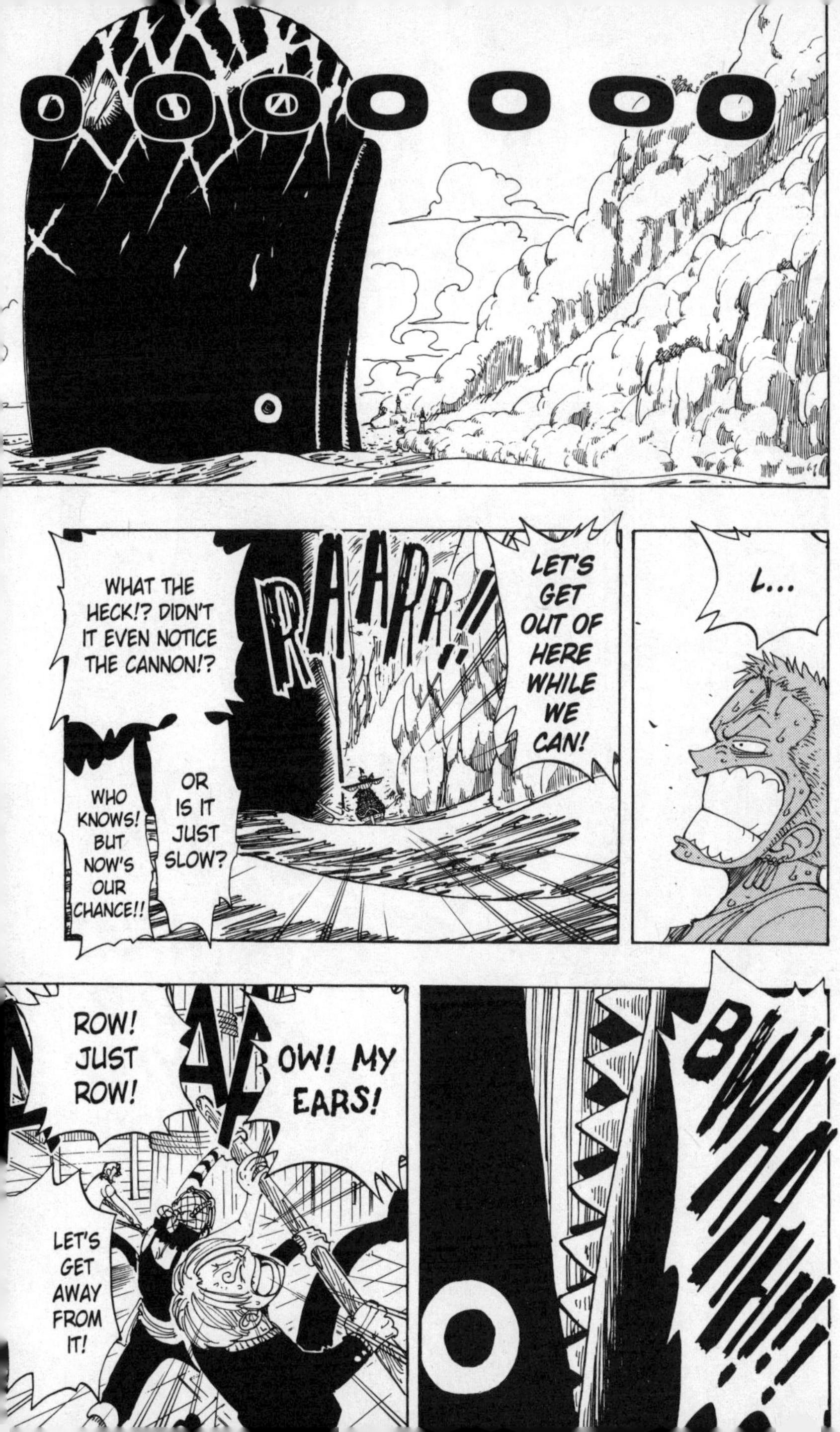
OOOOOOO
I...
RAARR!!
LET'S GET OUT OF HERE WHILE WE CAN!
WHAT THE HECK!? DIDN'T IT EVEN NOTICE THE CANNON!?
OR IS IT JUST SLOW?
WHO KNOWS! BUT NOW'S OUR CHANCE!!
OW! MY EARS!
ROW! JUST ROW!
LET'S GET AWAY FROM IT!

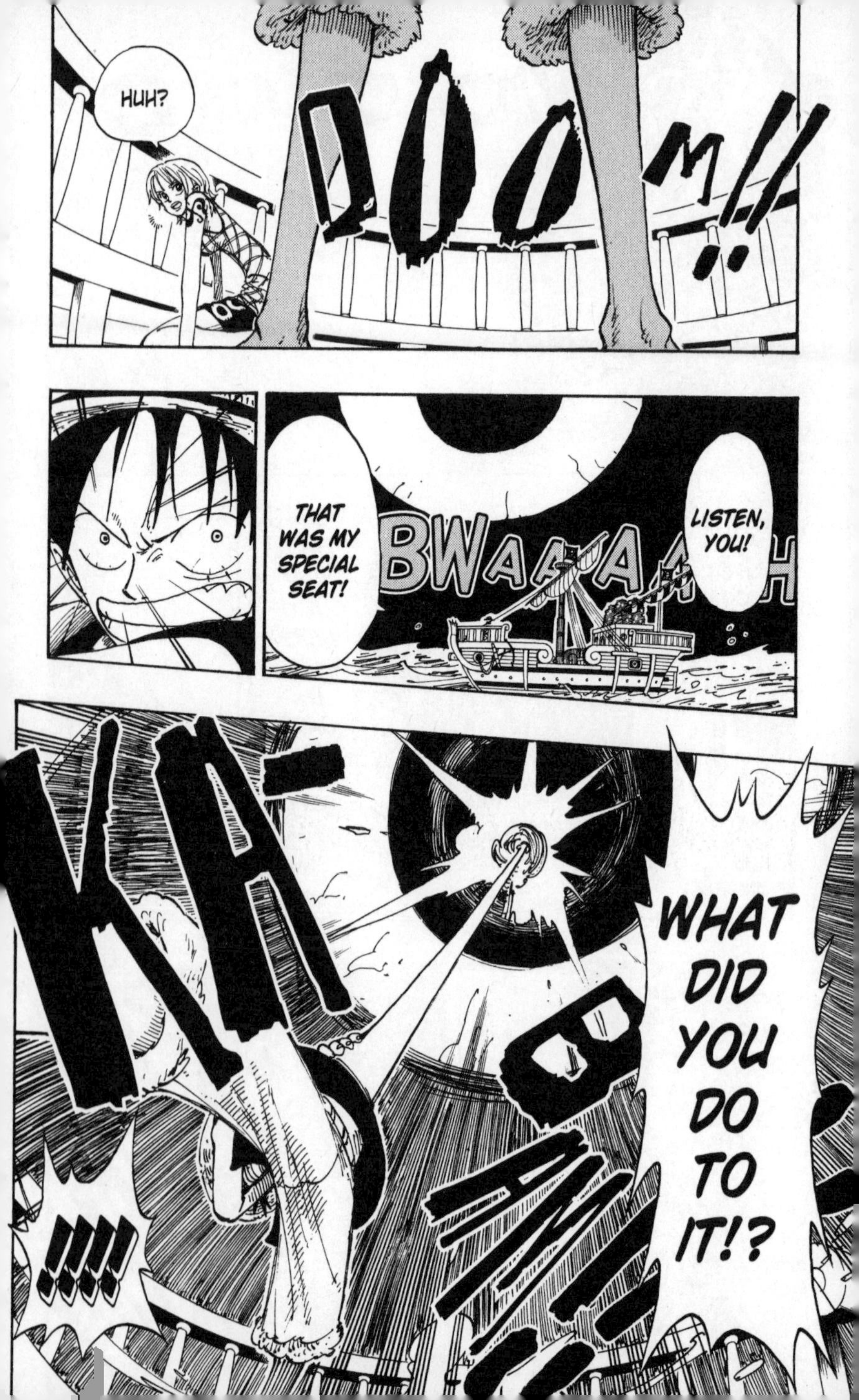
DOOM!!
HUH?
LISTEN, YOU!
BWAAAAH
THAT WAS MY SPECIAL SEAT!
WHAT DID YOU DO TO IT!?
KA-BAM
!!!!

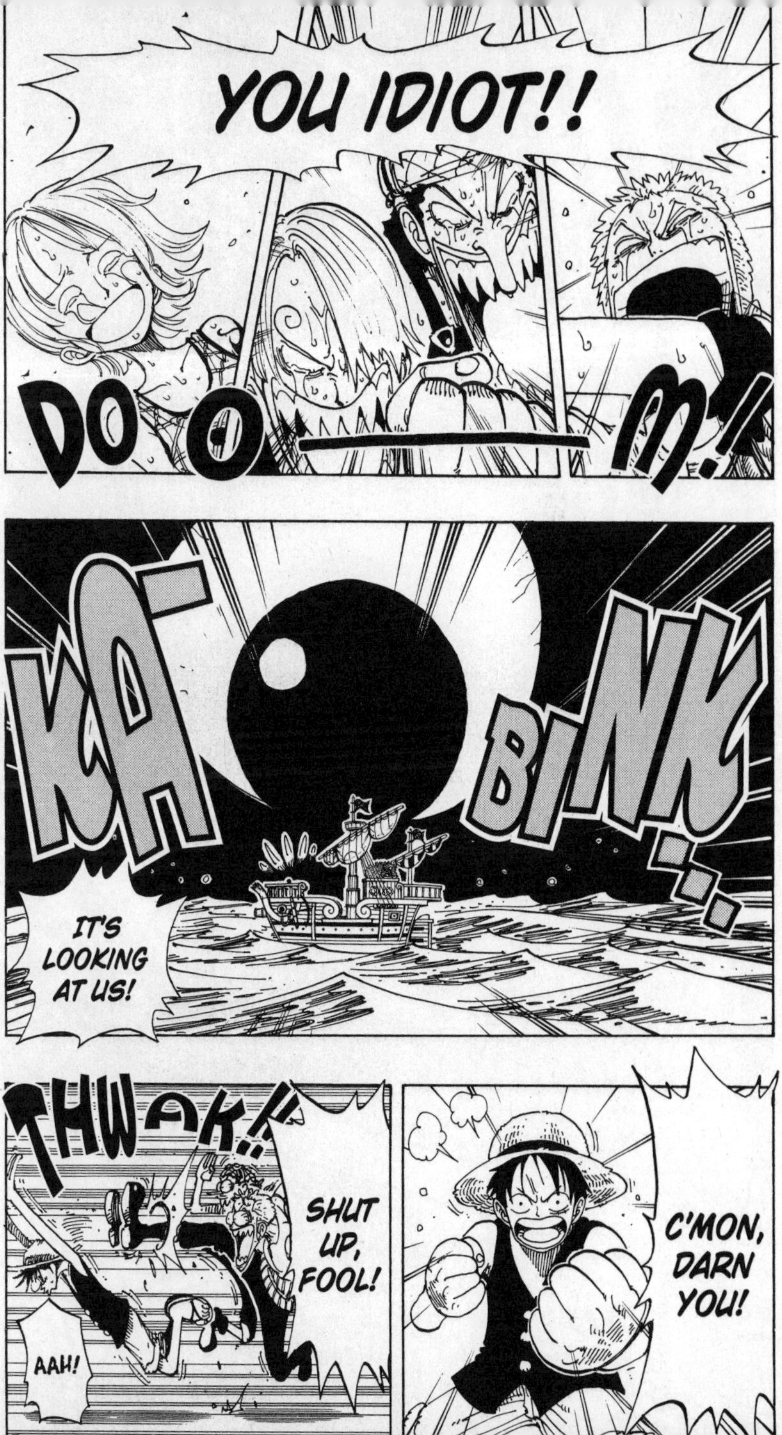
YOU IDIOT!!
DOO—M!!
KA BINK..
IT'S LOOKING AT US!
C'MON, DARN YOU!
THWAK!!
SHUT UP, FOOL!
AAH!

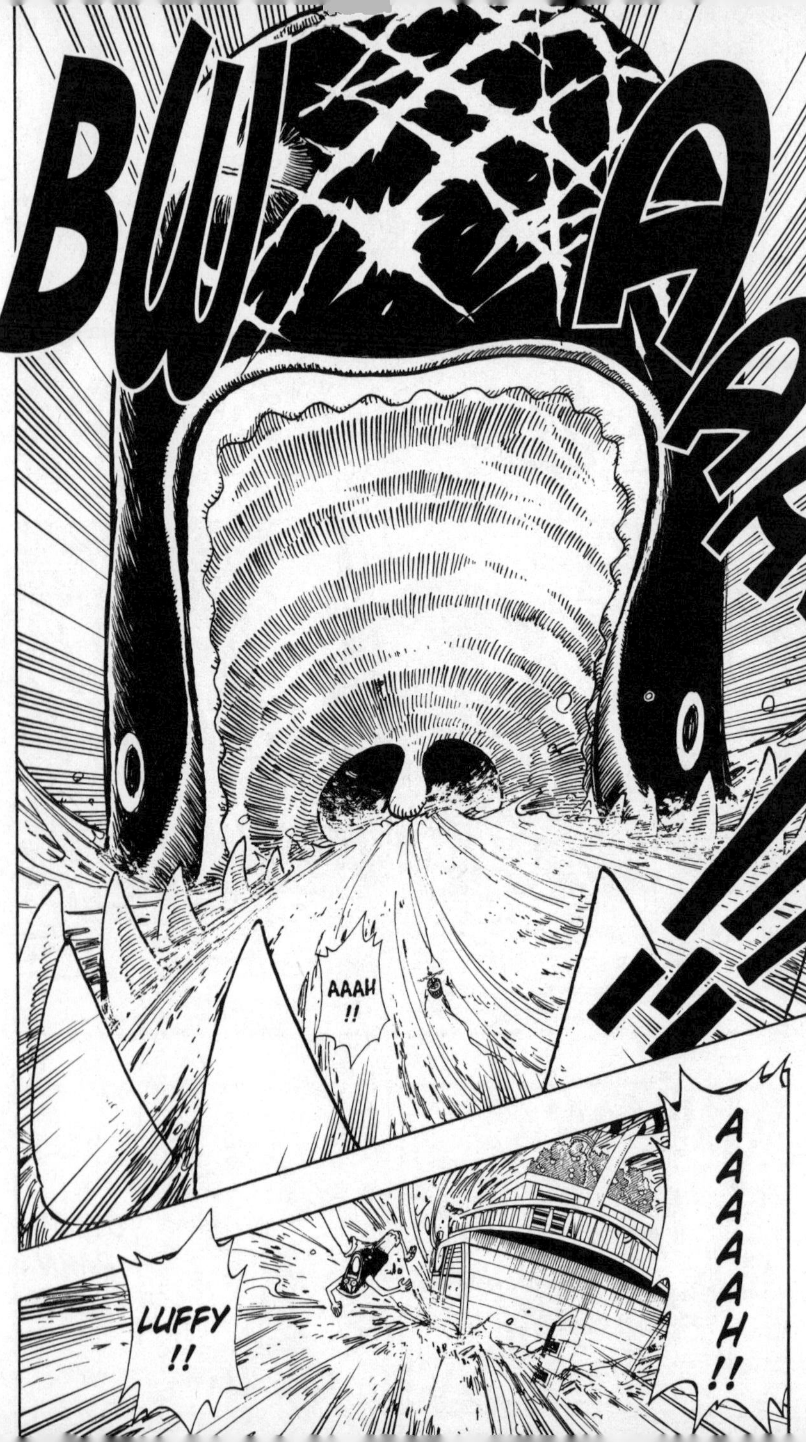
BUAAH...!!!
AAAH!!
AAAAAH!!
LUFFY!!

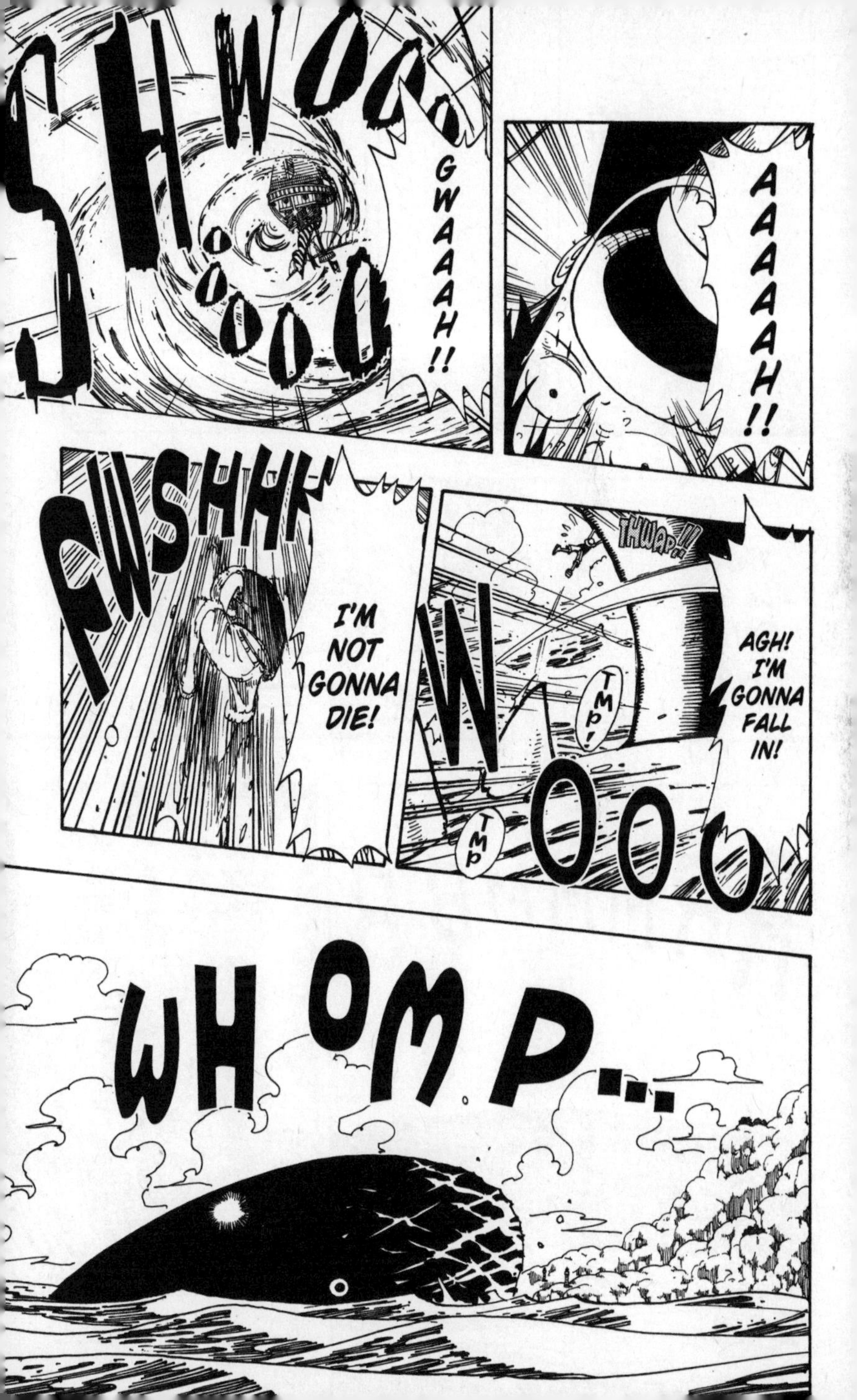
AAAAAH!!
SHWOOOOOO
GWAAAAH!!
THWAP!!
AGH! I'M GONNA FALL IN!
TMP!
WOOO
TMP
FWSHHH
I'M NOT GONNA DIE!
WHOMP...

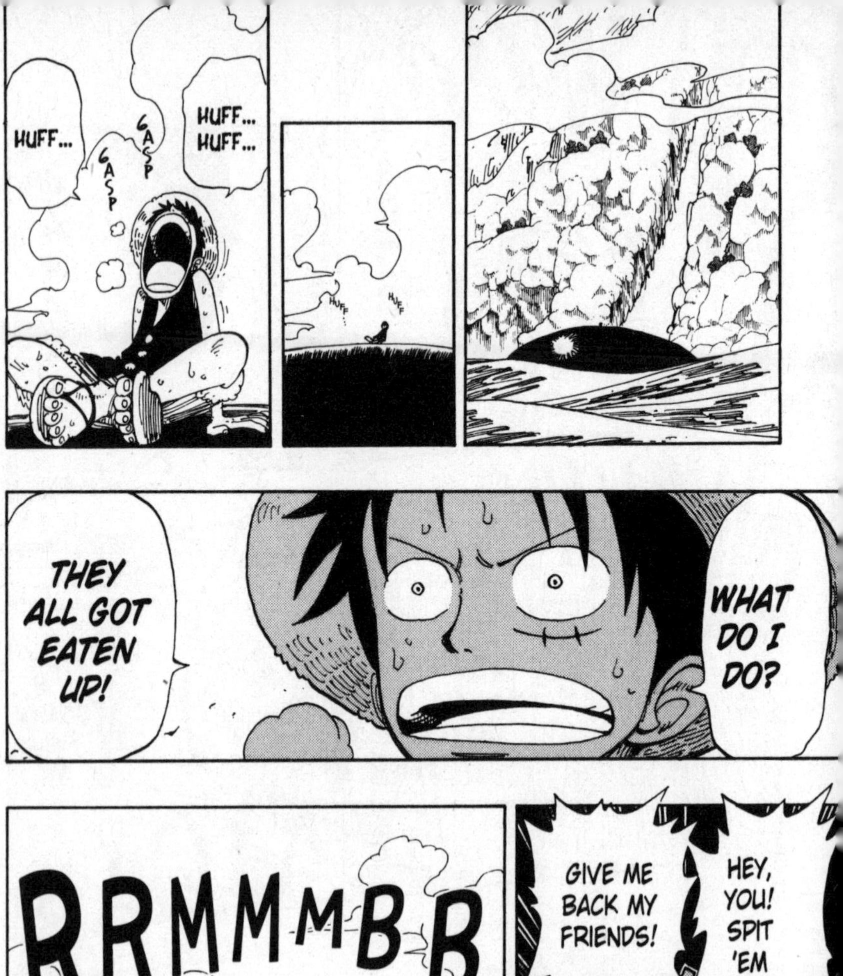
HUFF
HUFF
HUFF... HUFF...
GASP
GASP
HUFF...
WHAT DO I DO?
THEY ALL GOT EATEN UP!
HEY, YOU! SPIT 'EM OUT!
GIVE ME BACK MY FRIENDS!
WHAM!!
SPIT 'EM OUT!
RRMMMBB
!

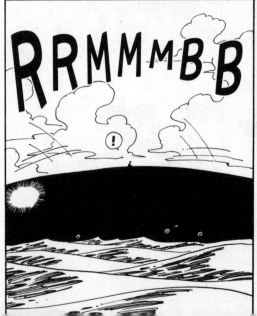

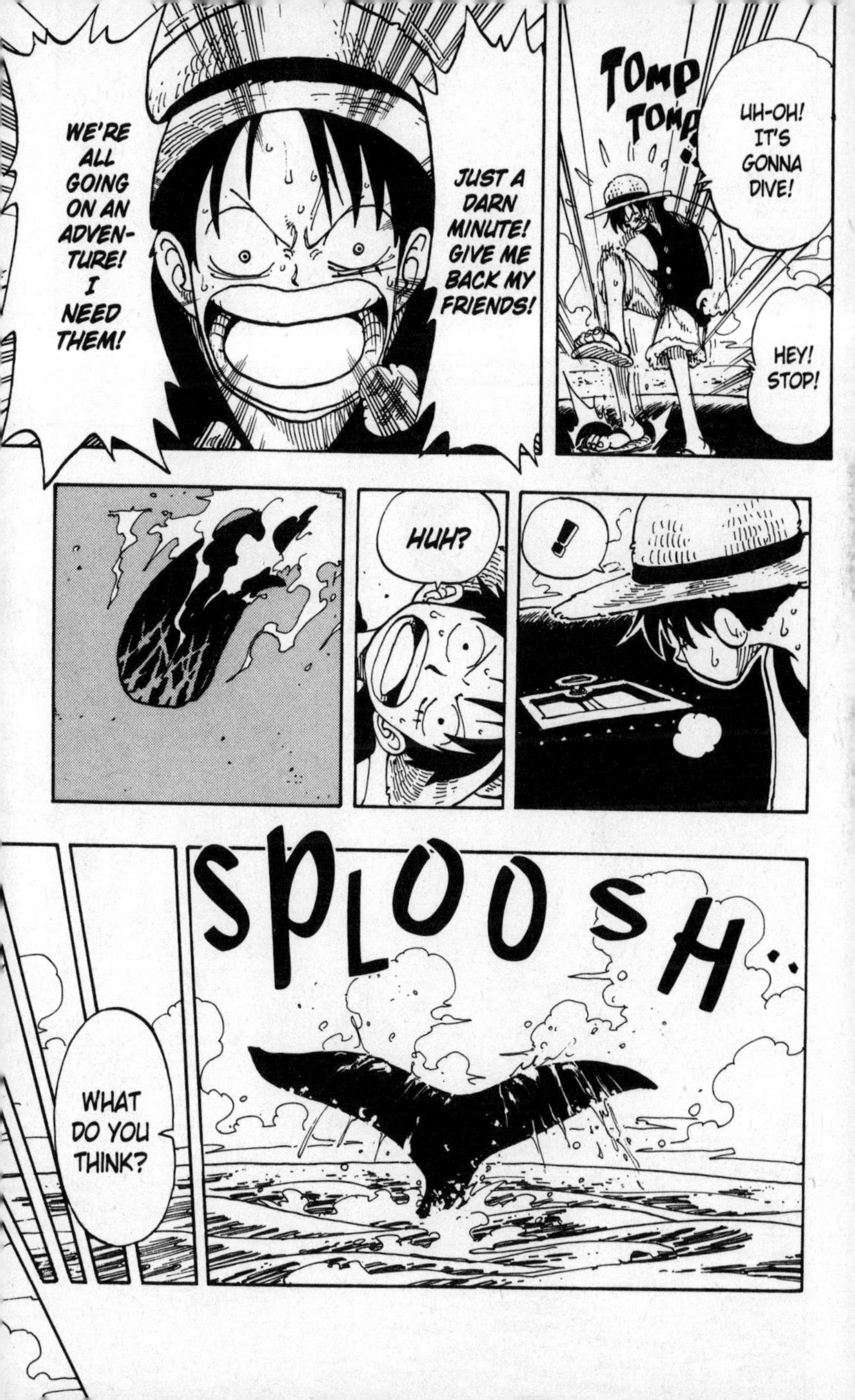
TOMP TOMP
UH-OH! IT'S GONNA DIVE!
HEY! STOP!
JUST A DARN MINUTE! GIVE ME BACK MY FRIENDS!
WE'RE ALL GOING ON AN ADVENTURE! I NEED THEM!
!
HUH?
SPLOOSH
WHAT DO YOU THINK?

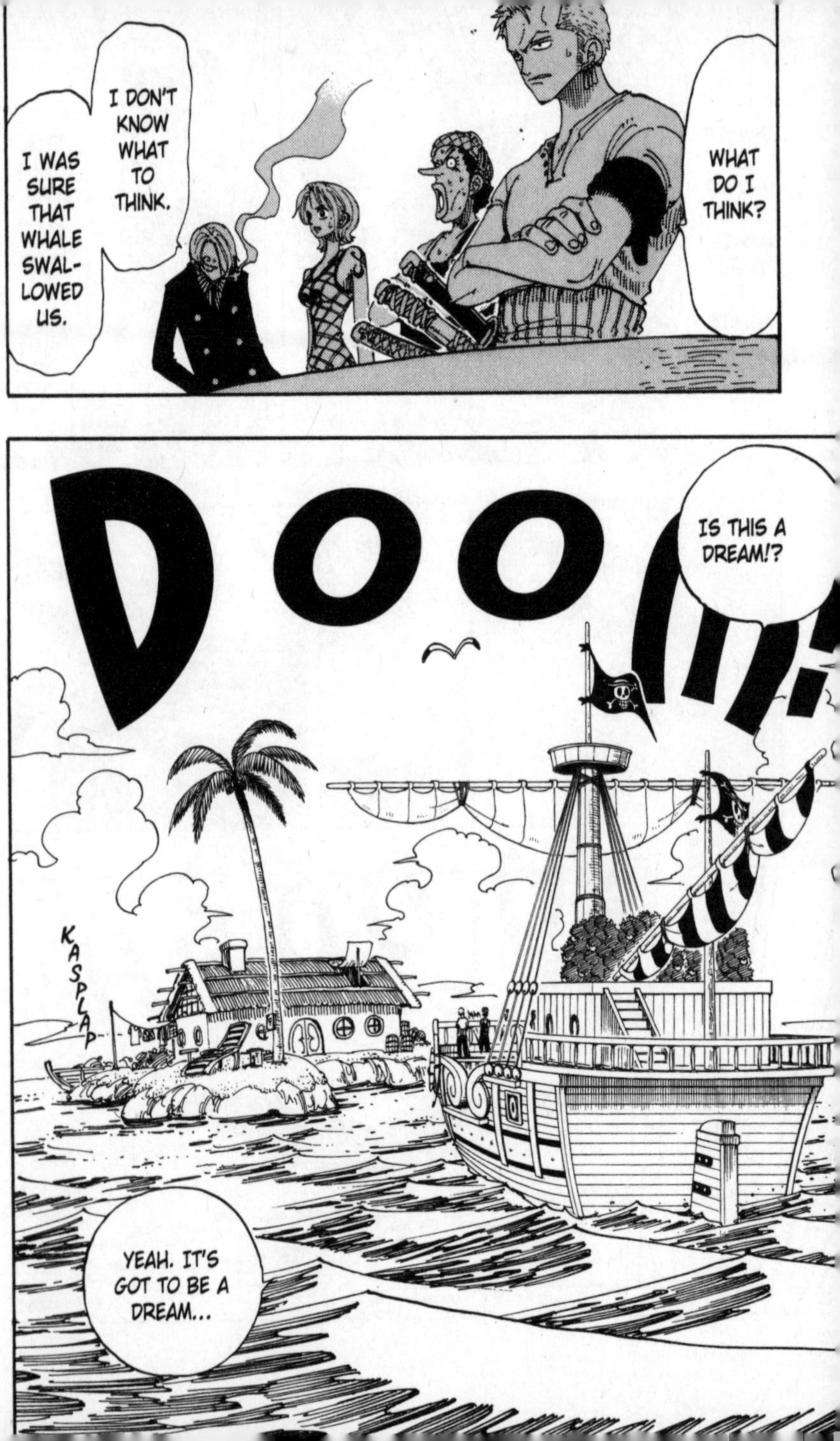
WHAT DO I THINK?
I DON'T KNOW WHAT TO THINK.
I WAS SURE THAT WHALE SWAL-LOWED US.
DOOM!!
IS THIS A DREAM!?
KASPLAP
YEAH. IT'S GOT TO BE A DREAM...

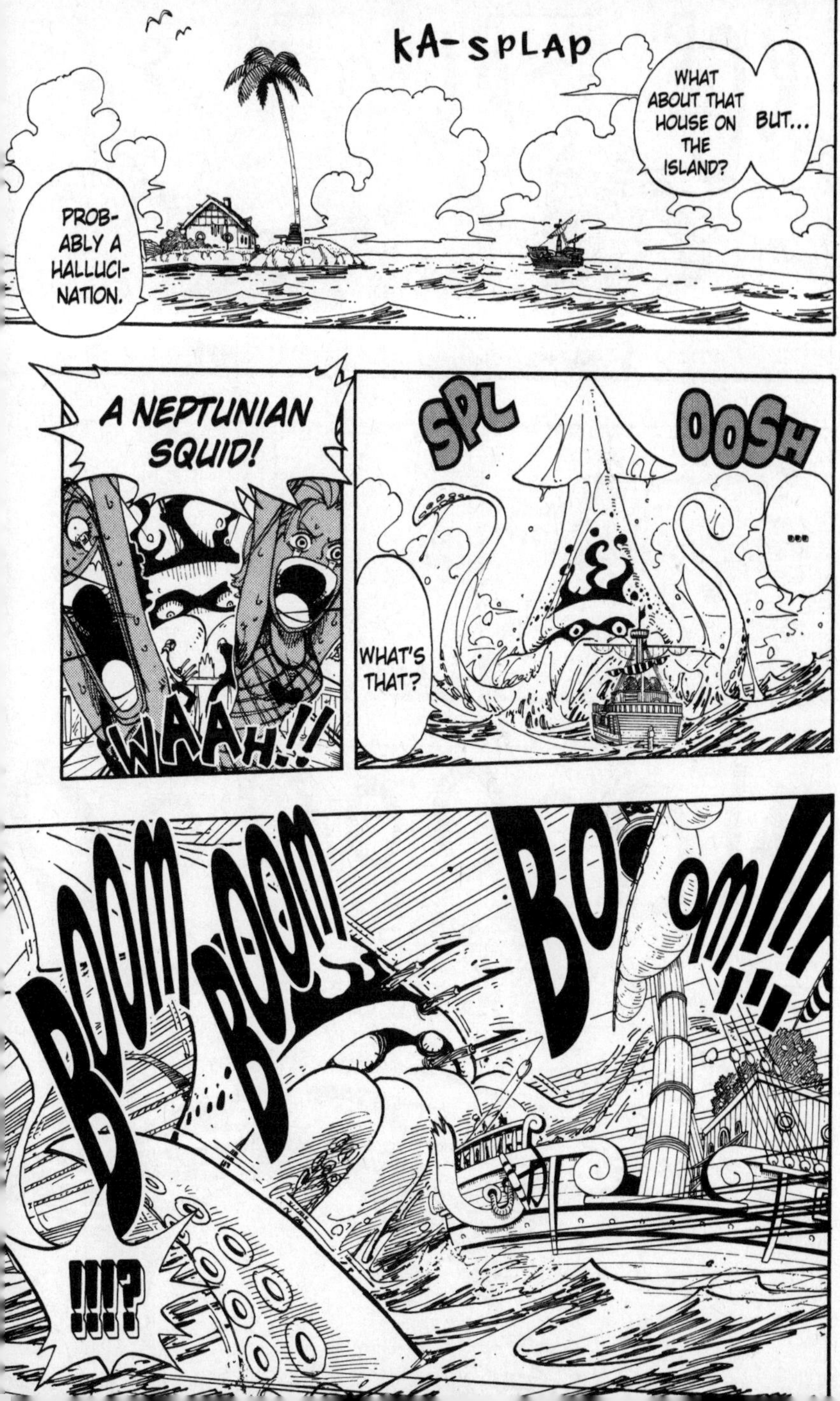
KA-SPLAP
BUT...
WHAT ABOUT THAT HOUSE ON THE ISLAND?
PROB-ABLY A HALLUCI-NATION.
SPL OOSH
...
WHAT'S THAT?
A NEPTUNIAN SQUID!
WAAH!!
BOOM
BOOM
BOOM!!
!!!?

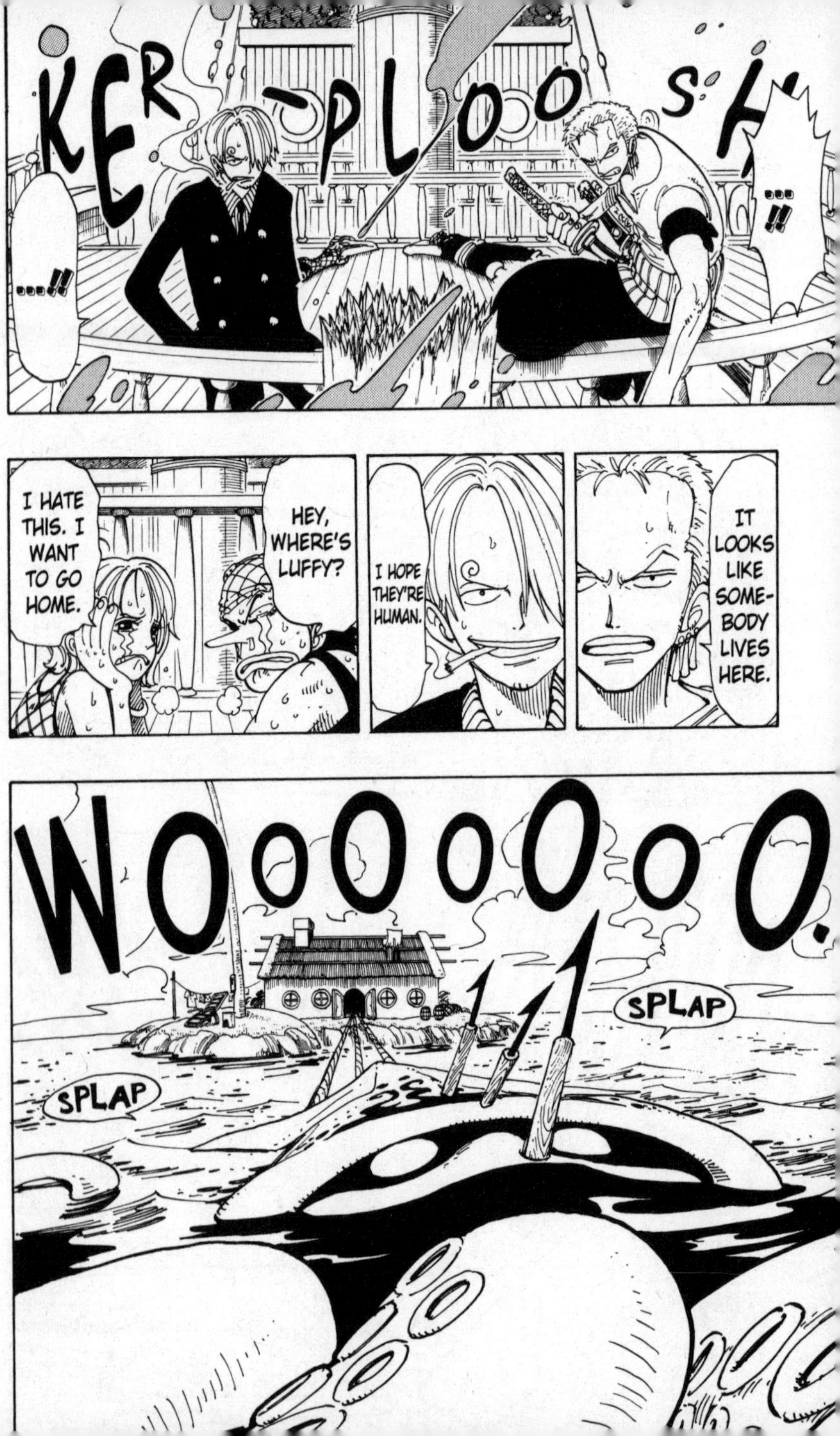
KER-PLOOOSH
...!!
...!!
IT LOOKS LIKE SOME-BODY LIVES HERE.
I HOPE THEY'RE HUMAN.
HEY, WHERE'S LUFFY?
I HATE THIS. I WANT TO GO HOME.
WOOOOOOO.
SPLAP
SPLAP

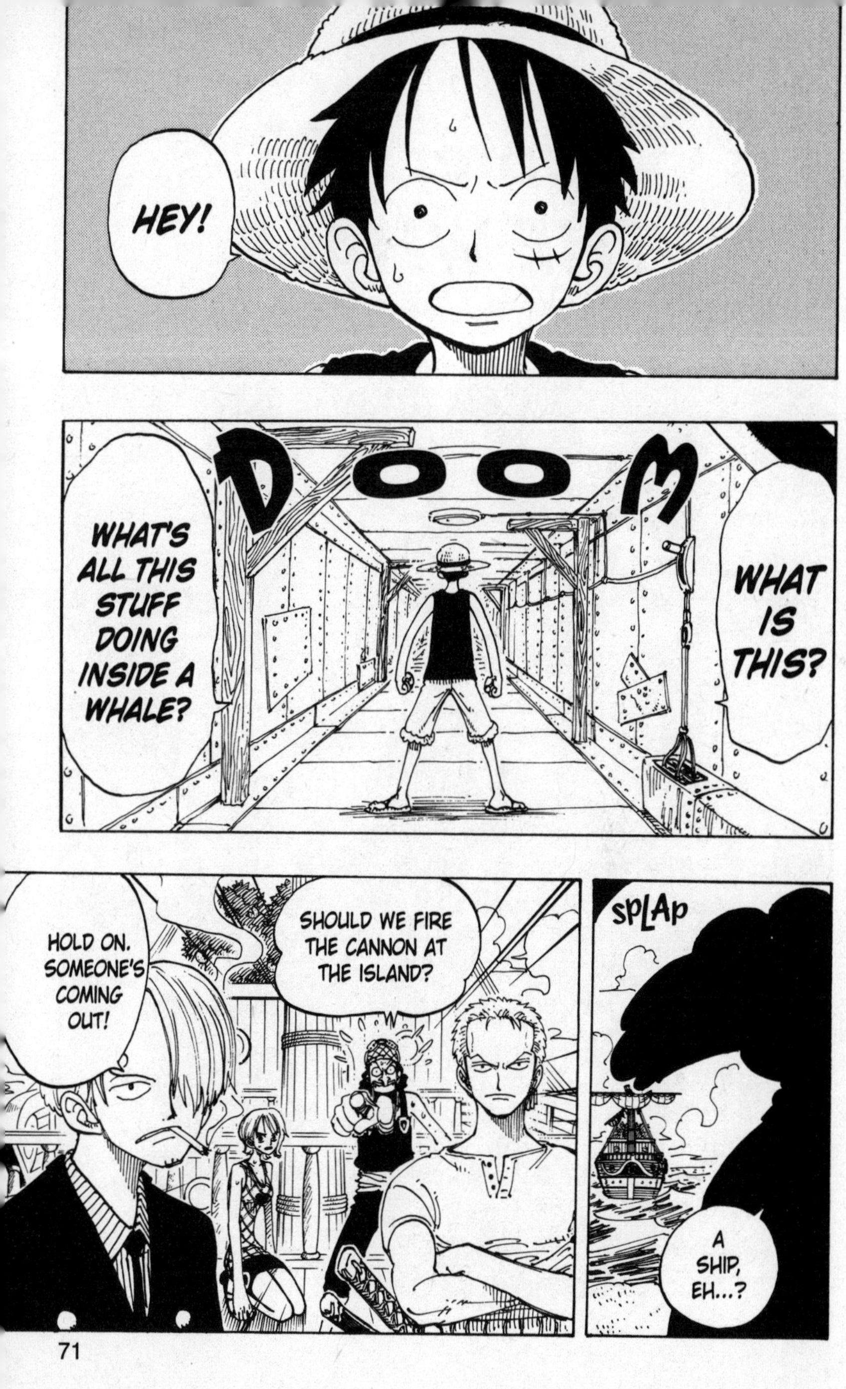
HEY!
WHAT IS THIS?
DOOM
WHAT'S ALL THIS STUFF DOING INSIDE A WHALE?
SPLAP
A SHIP, EH...?
SHOULD WE FIRE THE CANNON AT THE ISLAND?
HOLD ON. SOMEONE'S COMING OUT!

Chapter 103: THE WHALE

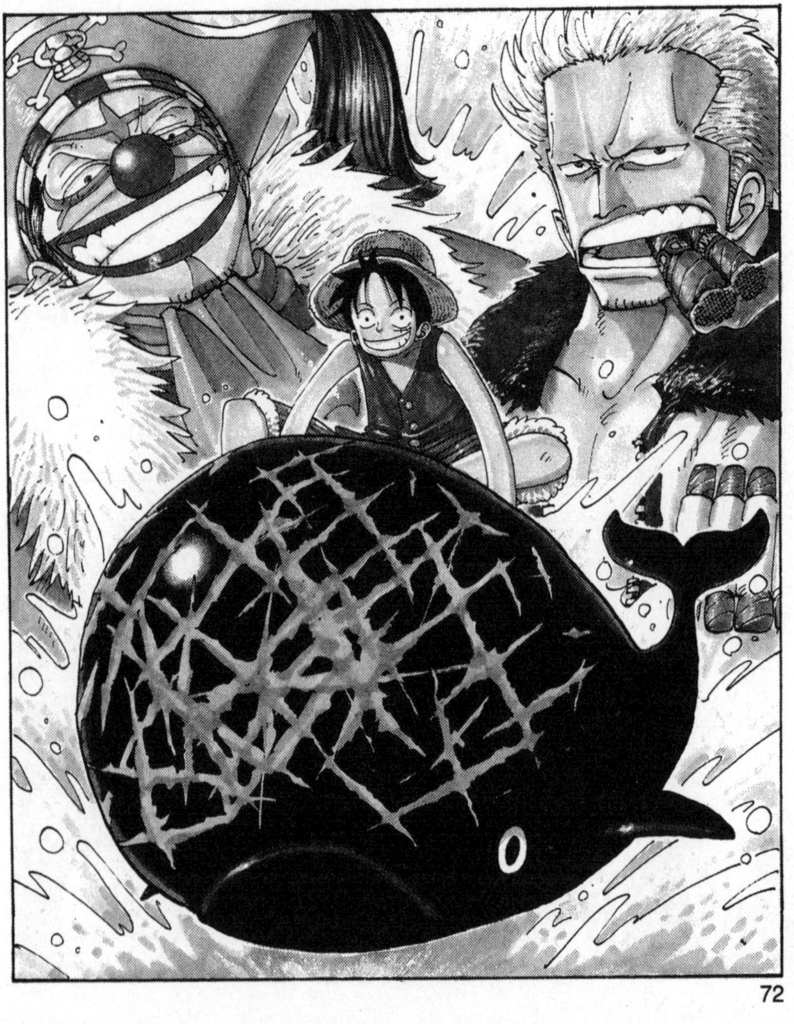

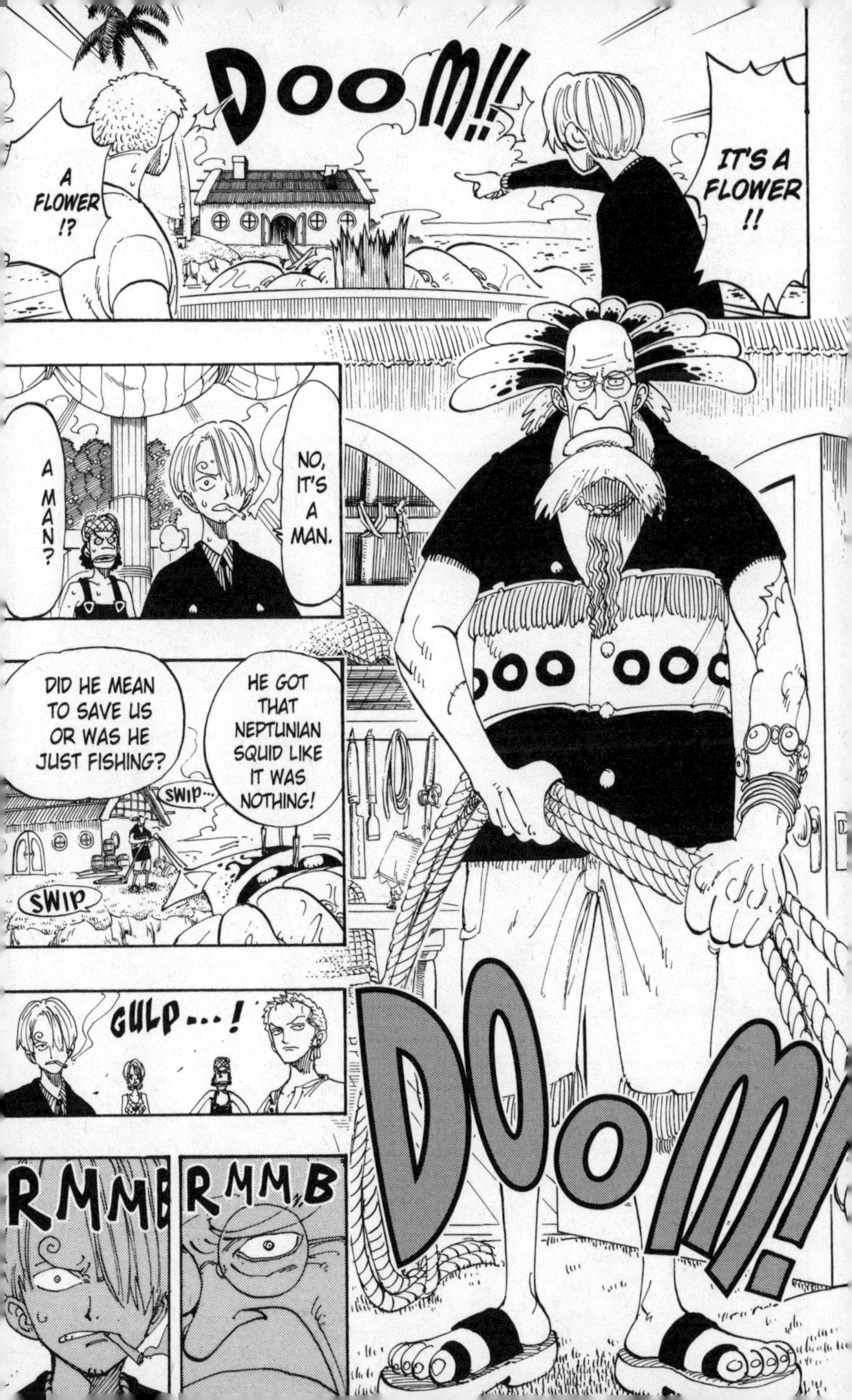
DOOM!!
IT'S A FLOWER !!
A FLOWER !?
DOOM!
NO, IT'S A MAN.
A MAN?
HE GOT THAT NEPTUNIAN SQUID LIKE IT WAS NOTHING!
DID HE MEAN TO SAVE US OR WAS HE JUST FISHING?
SWIP...
SWIP
GULP...!
RMMB
RMMB

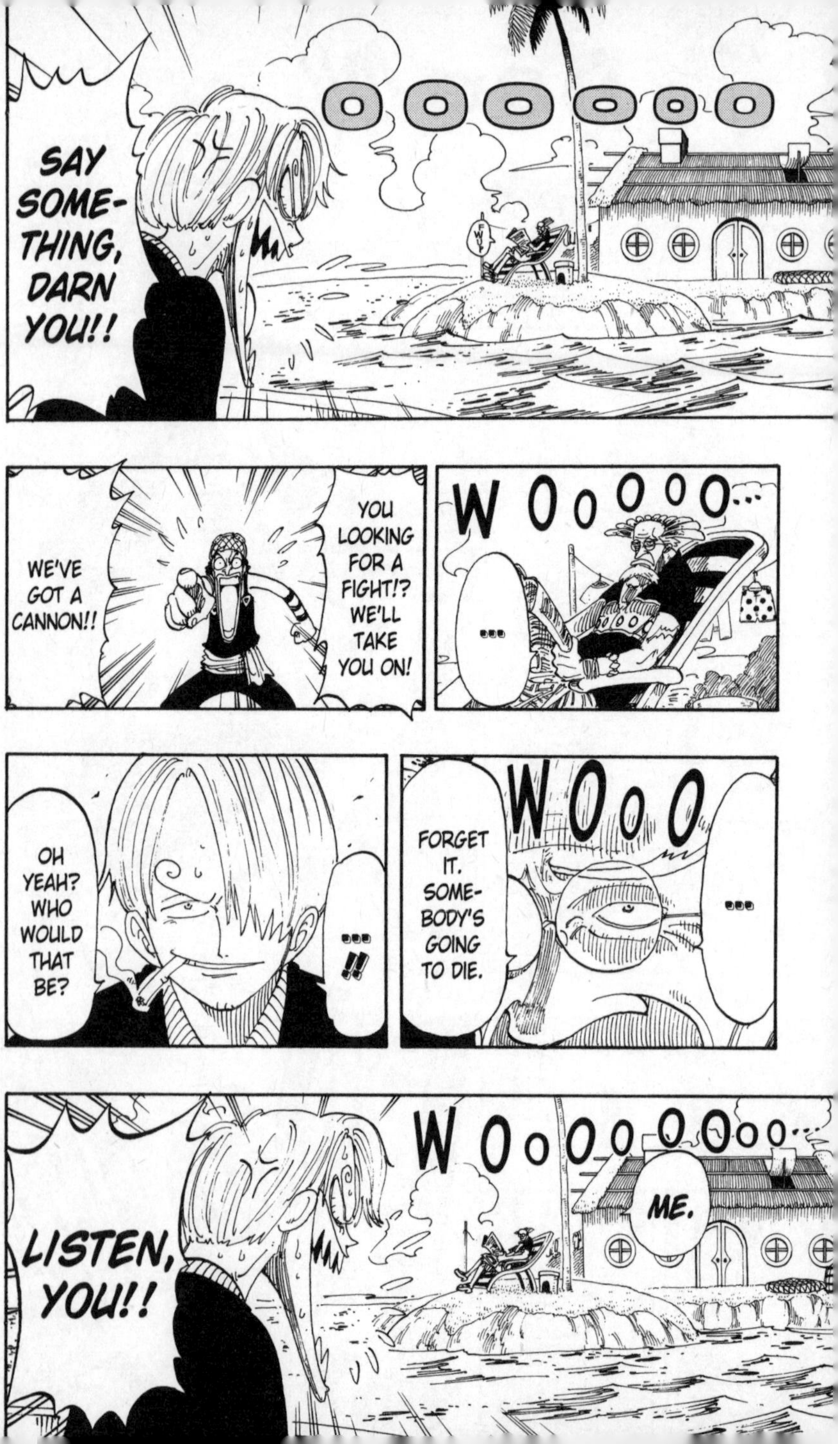
OOOOOO
SAY SOME-THING, DARN YOU!!
WOOOOO...
...
YOU LOOKING FOR A FIGHT!? WE'LL TAKE YOU ON!
WE'VE GOT A CANNON!!
WOOO
...
FORGET IT. SOME-BODY'S GOING TO DIE.
...!!
OH YEAH? WHO WOULD THAT BE?
WOOOOOOOOO...
ME.
LISTEN, YOU!!

READ THIS WAY

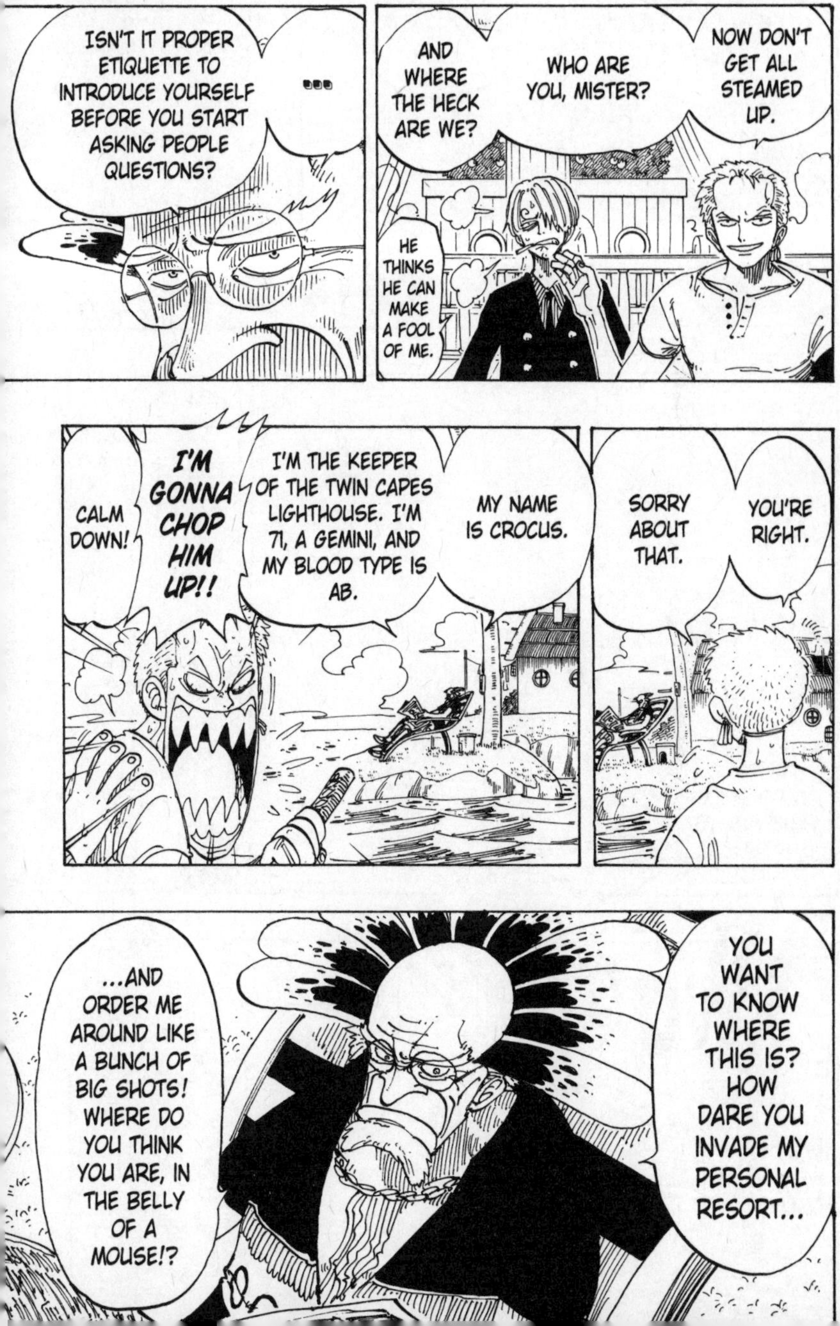
NOW DON'T GET ALL STEAMED UP.
WHO ARE YOU, MISTER?
AND WHERE THE HECK ARE WE?
HE THINKS HE CAN MAKE A FOOL OF ME.
...
ISN'T IT PROPER ETIQUETTE TO INTRODUCE YOURSELF BEFORE YOU START ASKING PEOPLE QUESTIONS?
YOU'RE RIGHT.
SORRY ABOUT THAT.
MY NAME IS CROCUS.
I'M THE KEEPER OF THE TWIN CAPES LIGHTHOUSE. I'M 71, A GEMINI, AND MY BLOOD TYPE IS AB.
I'M GONNA CHOP HIM UP!!
CALM DOWN!
YOU WANT TO KNOW WHERE THIS IS? HOW DARE YOU INVADE MY PERSONAL RESORT...
...AND ORDER ME AROUND LIKE A BUNCH OF BIG SHOTS! WHERE DO YOU THINK YOU ARE, IN THE BELLY OF A MOUSE!?

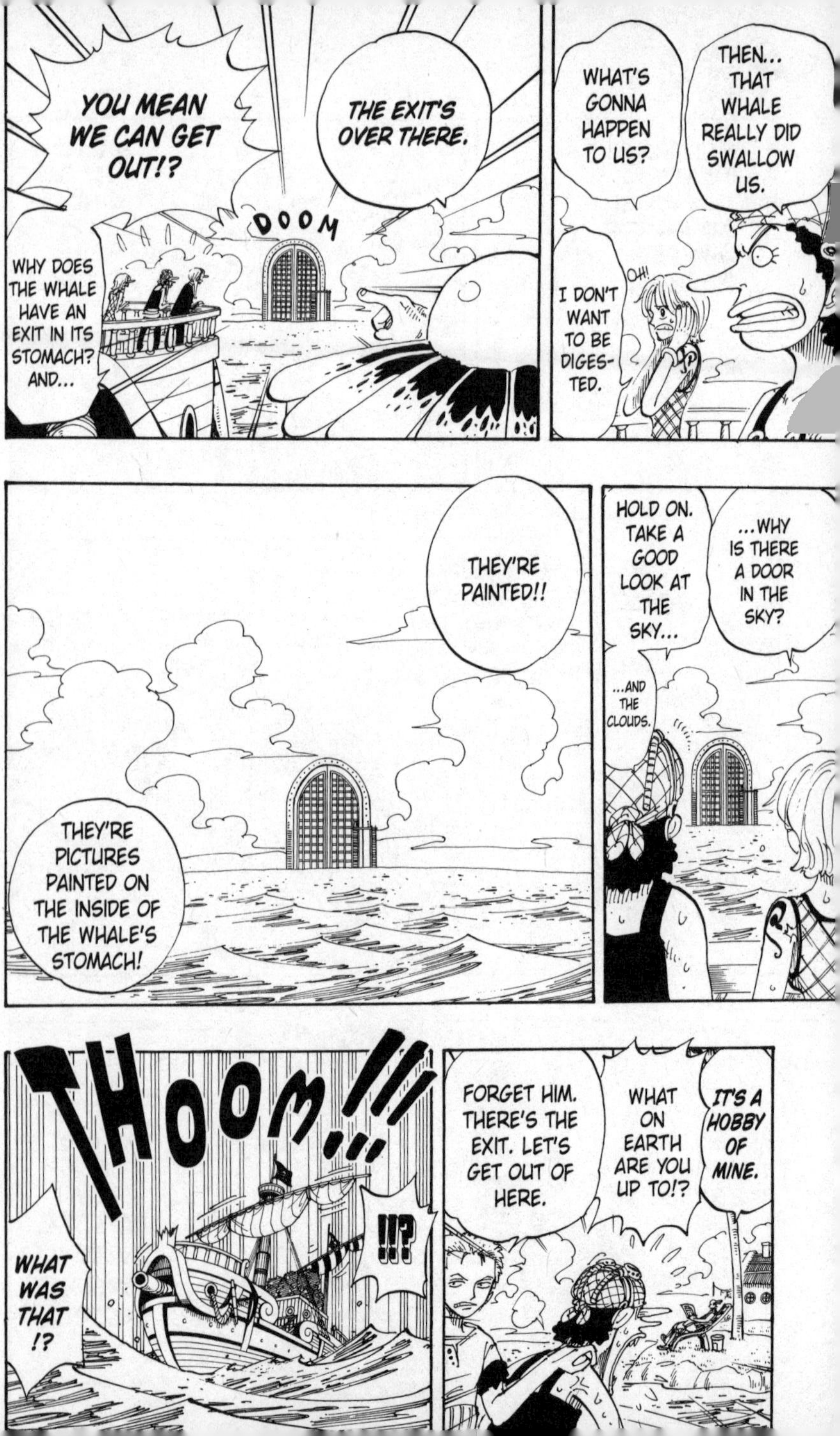
THEN... THAT WHALE REALLY DID SWALLOW US.
WHAT'S GONNA HAPPEN TO US?
OH!
I DON'T WANT TO BE DIGES-TED.
THE EXIT'S OVER THERE.
YOU MEAN WE CAN GET OUT!?
DOOM
WHY DOES THE WHALE HAVE AN EXIT IN ITS STOMACH? AND...
...WHY IS THERE A DOOR IN THE SKY?
HOLD ON. TAKE A GOOD LOOK AT THE SKY...
...AND THE CLOUDS.
THEY'RE PAINTED!!
THEY'RE PICTURES PAINTED ON THE INSIDE OF THE WHALE'S STOMACH!
IT'S A HOBBY OF MINE.
WHAT ON EARTH ARE YOU UP TO!?
FORGET HIM. THERE'S THE EXIT. LET'S GET OUT OF HERE.
THOOM!!!
!!?
WHAT WAS THAT !?

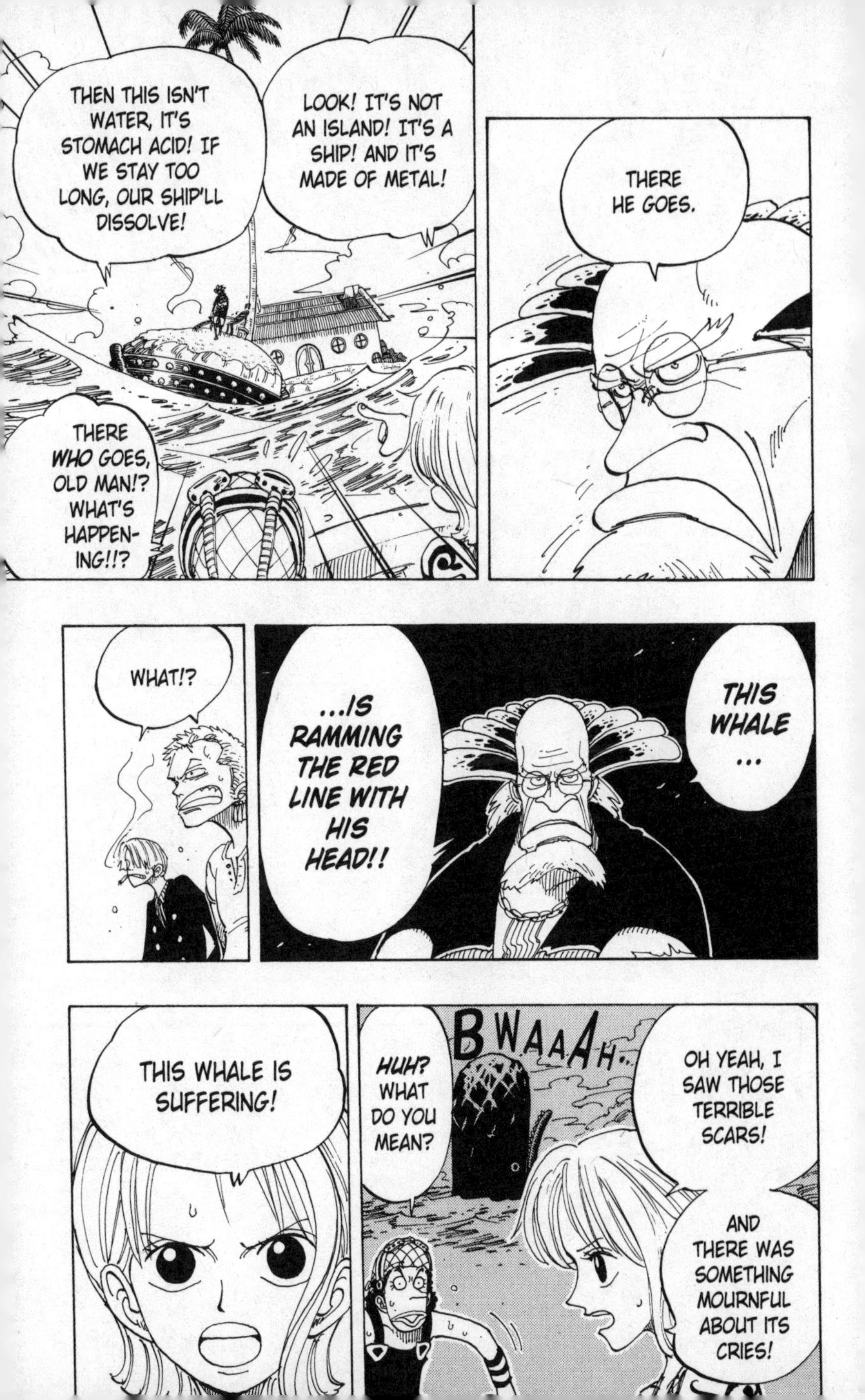
THERE HE GOES.
LOOK! IT'S NOT AN ISLAND! IT'S A SHIP! AND IT'S MADE OF METAL!
THEN THIS ISN'T WATER, IT'S STOMACH ACID! IF WE STAY TOO LONG, OUR SHIP'LL DISSOLVE!
THERE *WHO* GOES, OLD MAN!? WHAT'S HAPPENING!!?
THIS WHALE ...
...IS RAMMING THE RED LINE WITH HIS HEAD!!
WHAT!?
OH YEAH, I SAW THOSE TERRIBLE SCARS!
BWAAAH..
HUH? WHAT DO YOU MEAN?
AND THERE WAS SOMETHING MOURNFUL ABOUT ITS CRIES!
THIS WHALE IS SUFFERING!

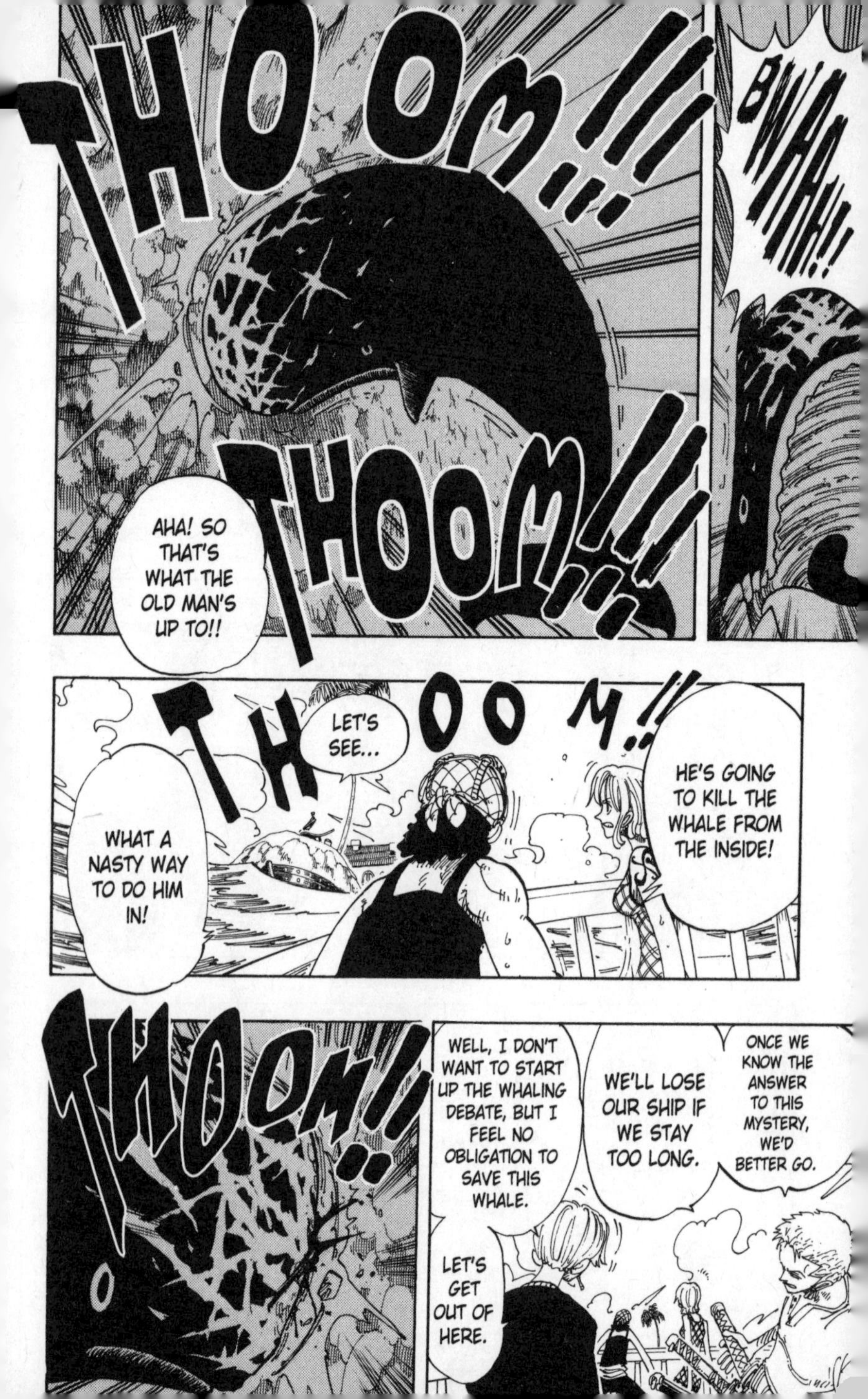
BWAAH!!
THOOM!!
THOOM!!
AHA! SO THAT'S WHAT THE OLD MAN'S UP TO!!
HE'S GOING TO KILL THE WHALE FROM THE INSIDE!
THOOM!!
LET'S SEE...
WHAT A NASTY WAY TO DO HIM IN!
ONCE WE KNOW THE ANSWER TO THIS MYSTERY, WE'D BETTER GO.
WE'LL LOSE OUR SHIP IF WE STAY TOO LONG.
WELL, I DON'T WANT TO START UP THE WHALING DEBATE, BUT I FEEL NO OBLIGATION TO SAVE THIS WHALE.
LET'S GET OUT OF HERE.
THOOM!!

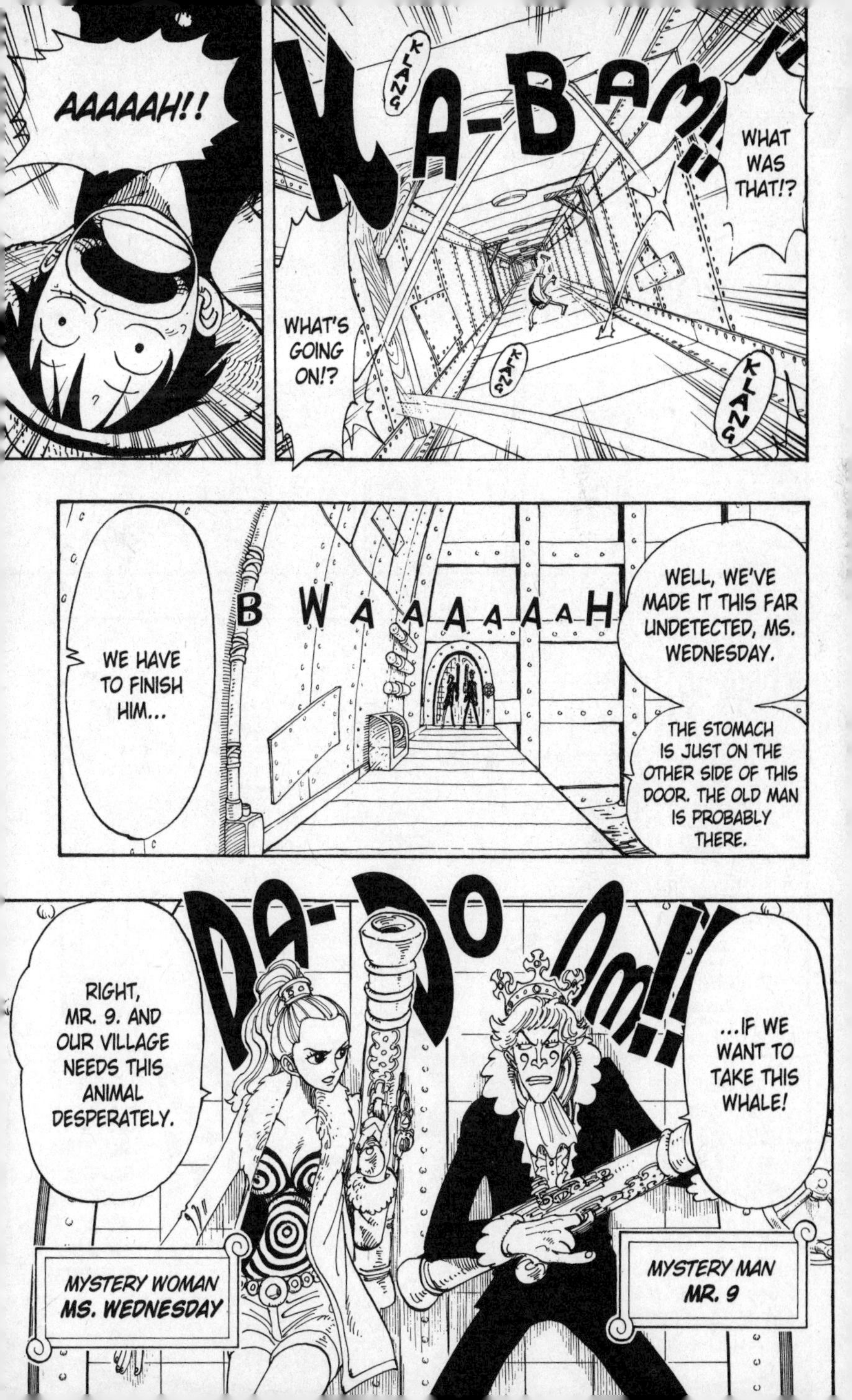
KA-BAM!!
KLANG
WHAT WAS THAT!?
WHAT'S GOING ON!?
KLANG
KLANG
AAAAAH!!
WELL, WE'VE MADE IT THIS FAR UNDETECTED, MS. WEDNESDAY.
THE STOMACH IS JUST ON THE OTHER SIDE OF THIS DOOR. THE OLD MAN IS PROBABLY THERE.
BWAAAAAH
WE HAVE TO FINISH HIM...
...IF WE WANT TO TAKE THIS WHALE!
DA-DOOM!!
RIGHT, MR. 9. AND OUR VILLAGE NEEDS THIS ANIMAL DESPERATELY.
MYSTERY MAN MR. 9
MYSTERY WOMAN MS. WEDNESDAY

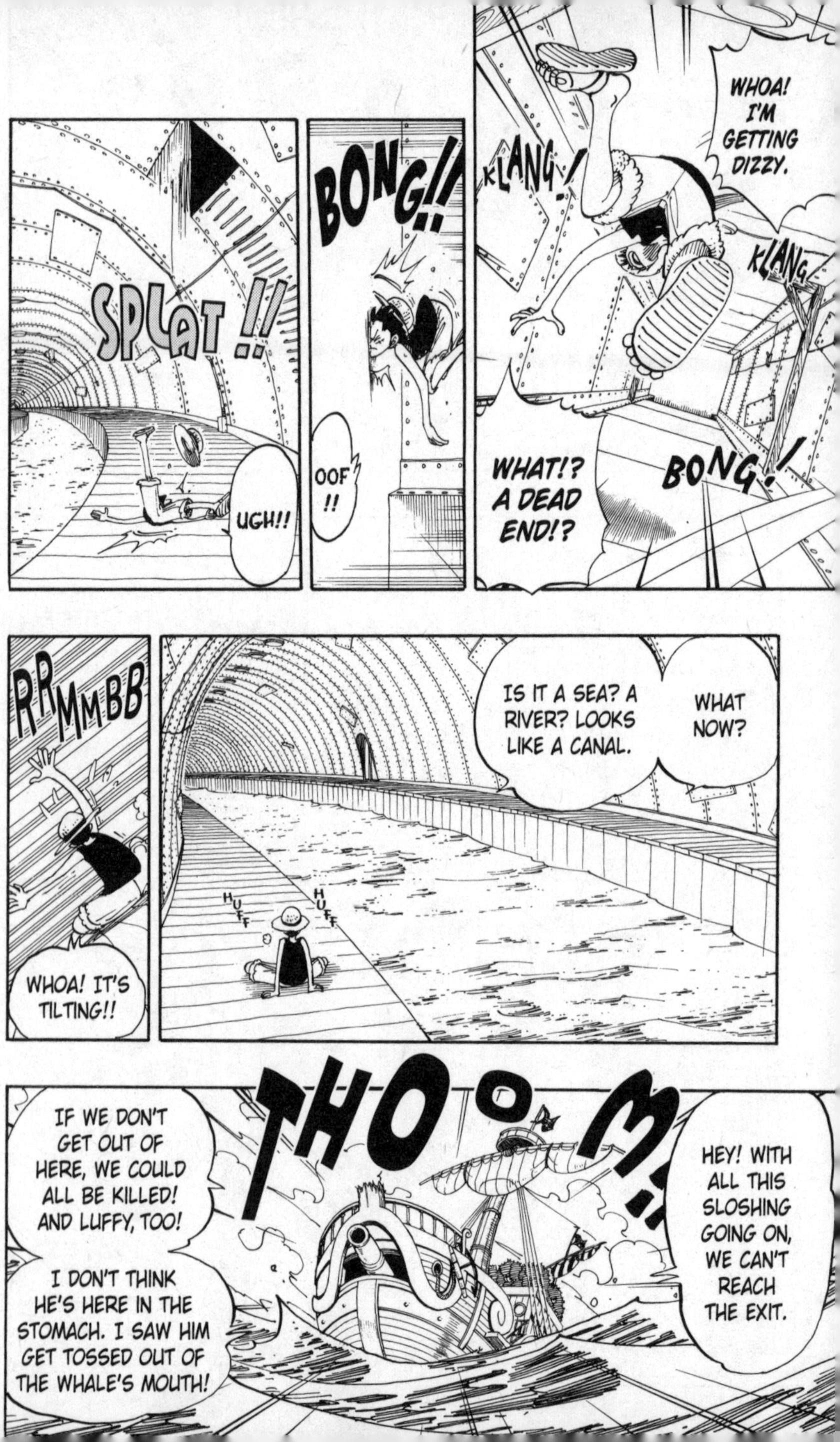
WHOA! I'M GETTING DIZZY.
KLANG!
KLANG!
BONG!
WHAT!? A DEAD END!?
BONG!!
OOF!!
SPLAT!!
UGH!!
WHAT NOW?
IS IT A SEA? A RIVER? LOOKS LIKE A CANAL.
HUFF
HUFF
RRMMBB
WHOA! IT'S TILTING!!
HEY! WITH ALL THIS SLOSHING GOING ON, WE CAN'T REACH THE EXIT.
THOOM!!
IF WE DON'T GET OUT OF HERE, WE COULD ALL BE KILLED! AND LUFFY, TOO!
I DON'T THINK HE'S HERE IN THE STOMACH. I SAW HIM GET TOSSED OUT OF THE WHALE'S MOUTH!

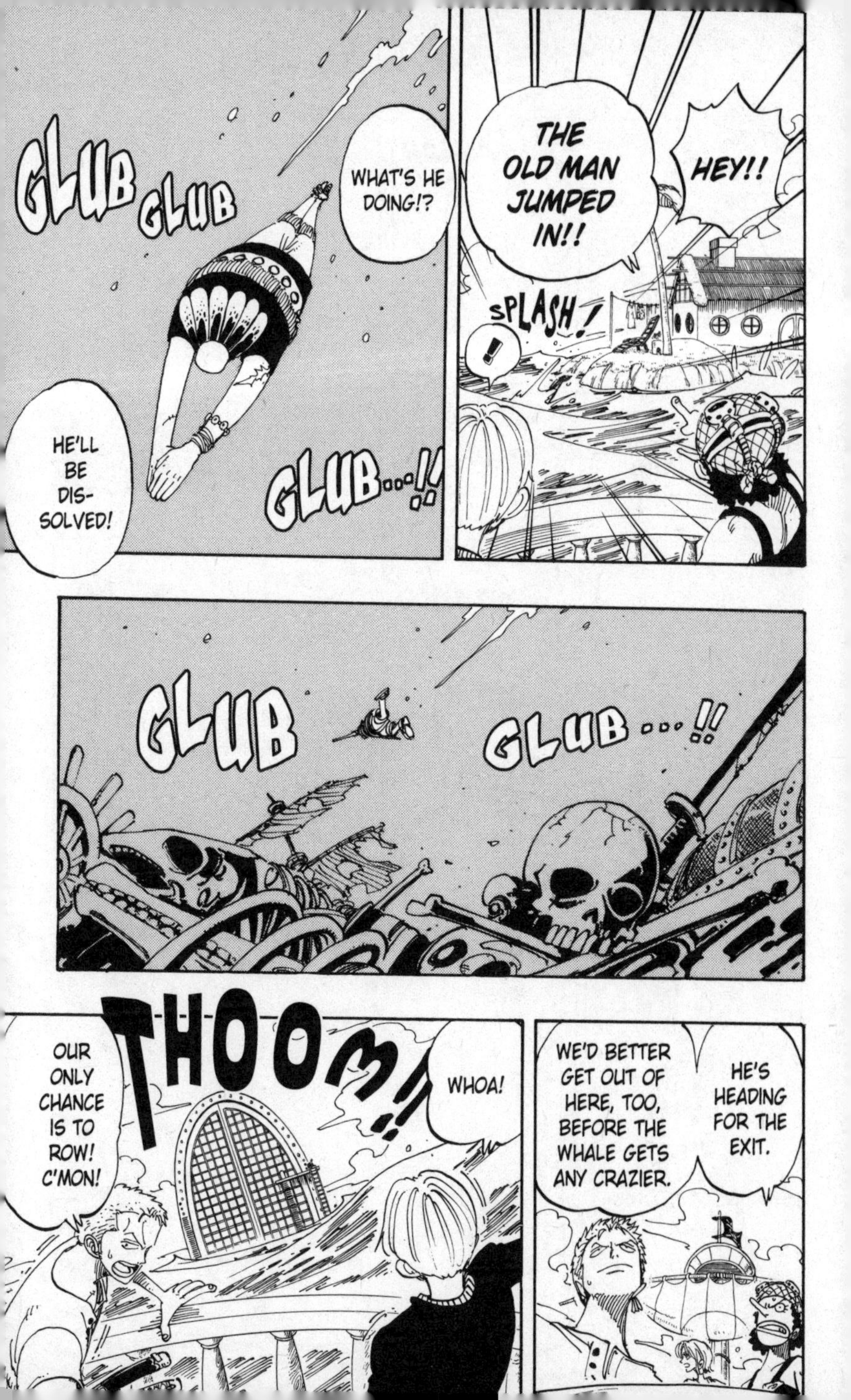
HEY!!
THE OLD MAN JUMPED IN!!
SPLASH!
!
WHAT'S HE DOING!?
GLUB GLUB
HE'LL BE DIS-SOLVED!
GLUB...!!
GLUB GLUB...!!
HE'S HEADING FOR THE EXIT.
WE'D BETTER GET OUT OF HERE, TOO, BEFORE THE WHALE GETS ANY CRAZIER.
WHOA!
THOOM!!
OUR ONLY CHANCE IS TO ROW! C'MON!

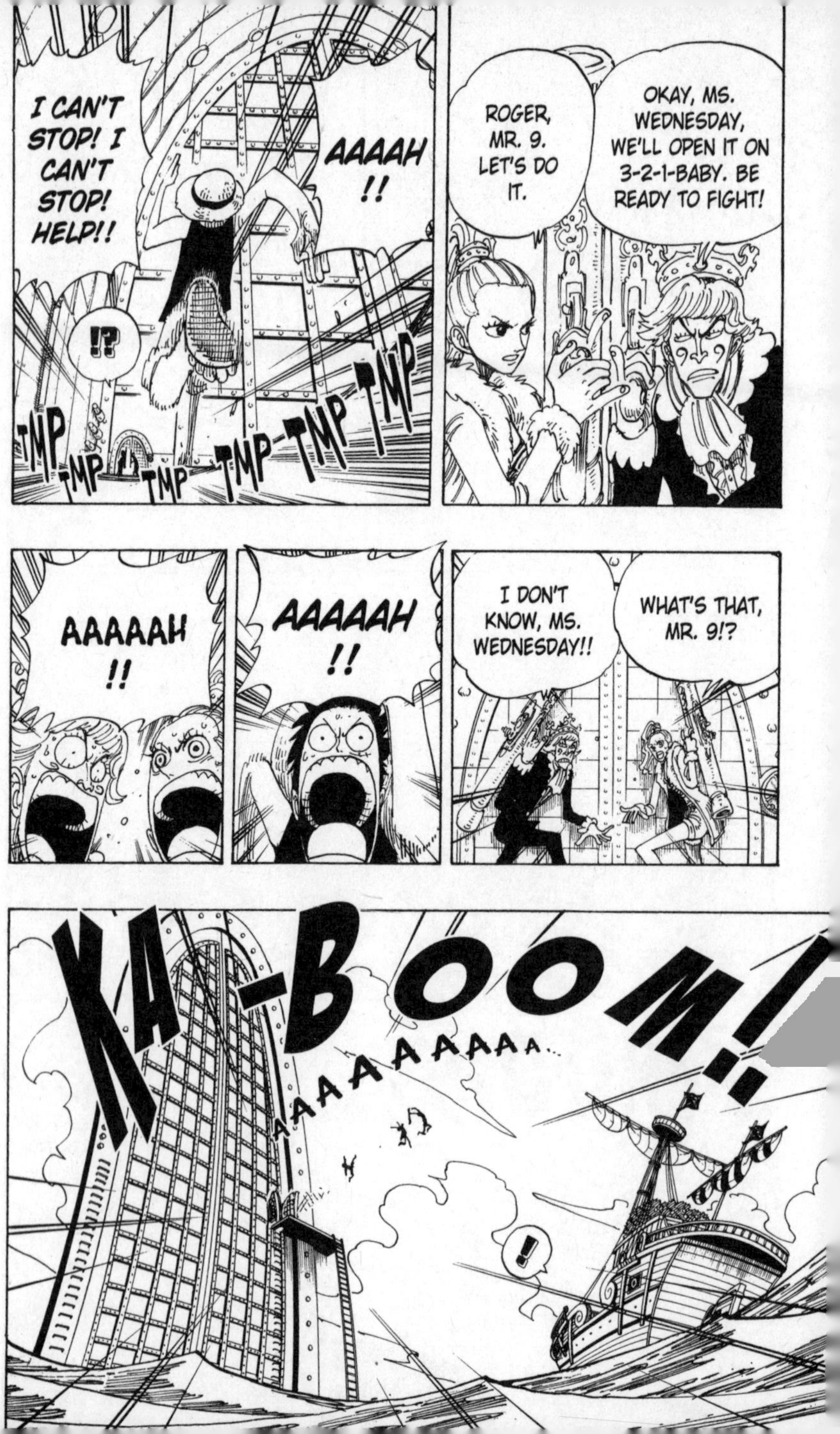
OKAY, MS. WEDNESDAY, WE'LL OPEN IT ON 3-2-1-BABY. BE READY TO FIGHT!
ROGER, MR. 9. LET'S DO IT.
AAAAH!!
I CAN'T STOP! I CAN'T STOP! HELP!!
!?
TMP TMP TMP TMP-TMP-TMP TMP
WHAT'S THAT, MR. 9!?
I DON'T KNOW, MS. WEDNESDAY!!
AAAAAH!!
AAAAAH!!
KA-BOOM!!
AAAAAAAAAA...
!

READ THIS WAY

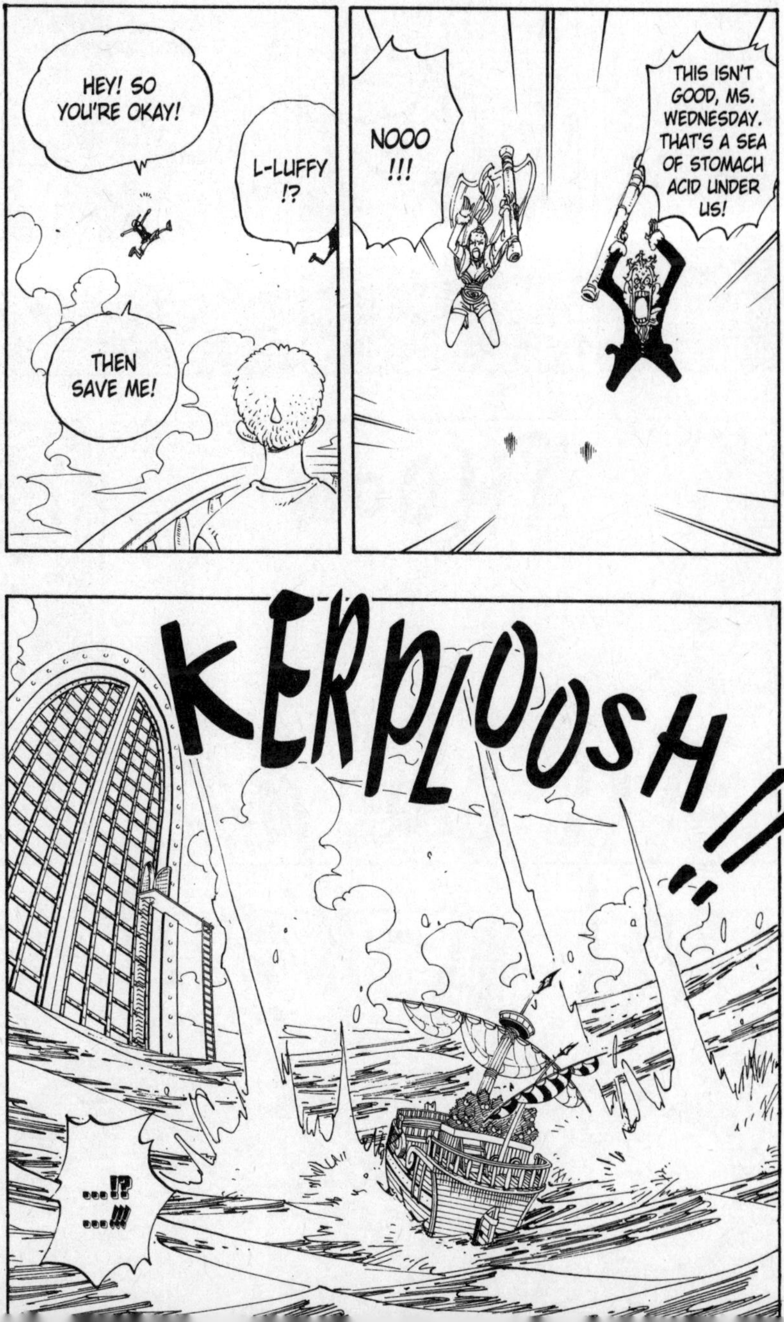
THIS ISN'T GOOD, MS. WEDNESDAY. THAT'S A SEA OF STOMACH ACID UNDER US!
NOOO !!!
HEY! SO YOU'RE OKAY!
L-LUFFY !?
THEN SAVE ME!
KERPLOOSH!!
...!? ...!!!

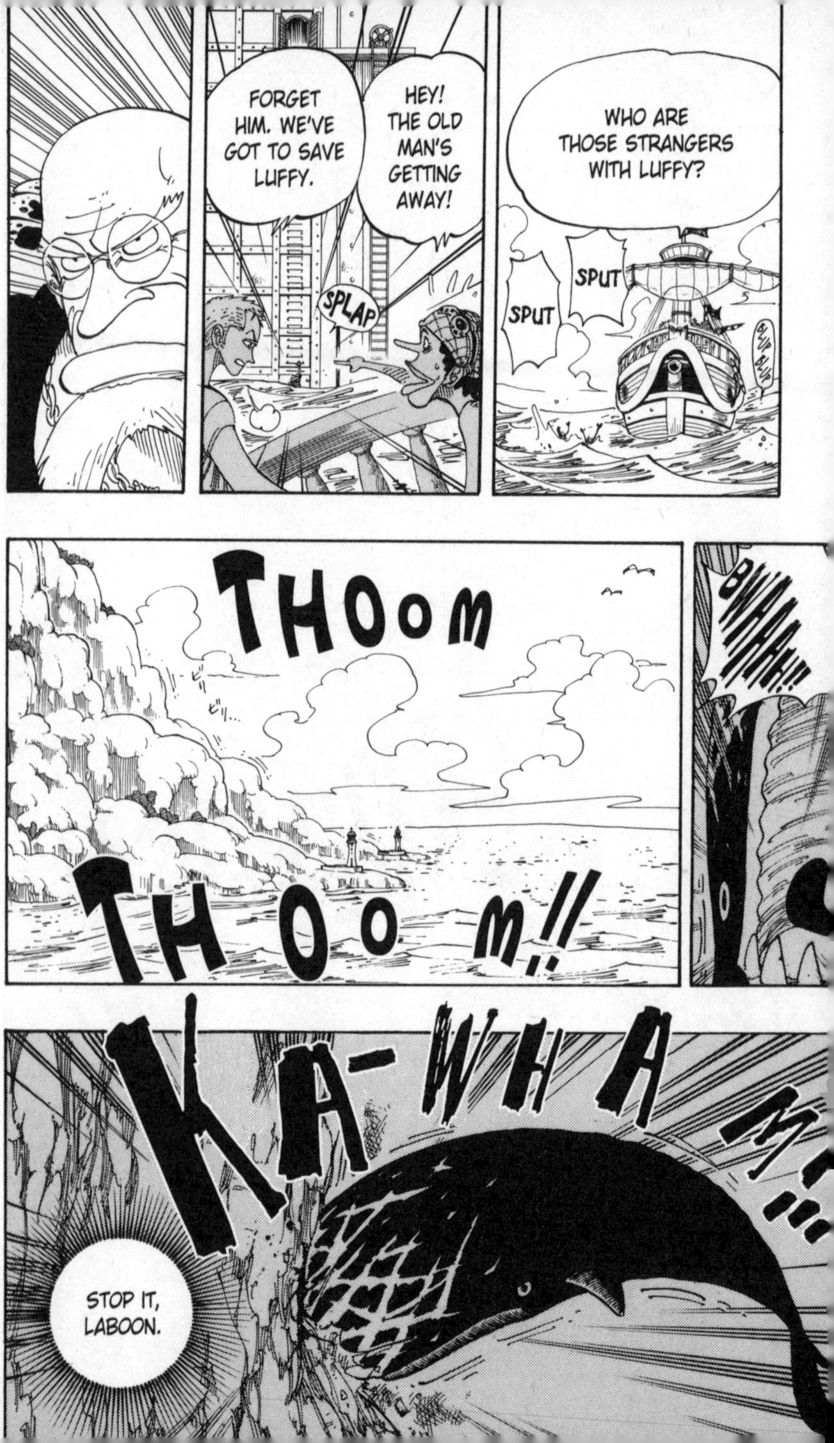
WHO ARE THOSE STRANGERS WITH LUFFY?
SPUT
SPUT
BLUP BLUP
HEY! THE OLD MAN'S GETTING AWAY!
FORGET HIM. WE'VE GOT TO SAVE LUFFY.
SPLAP
BWAAAH!!
THOOM
THOOM!!
KA-WHAM!!
STOP IT, LABOON.

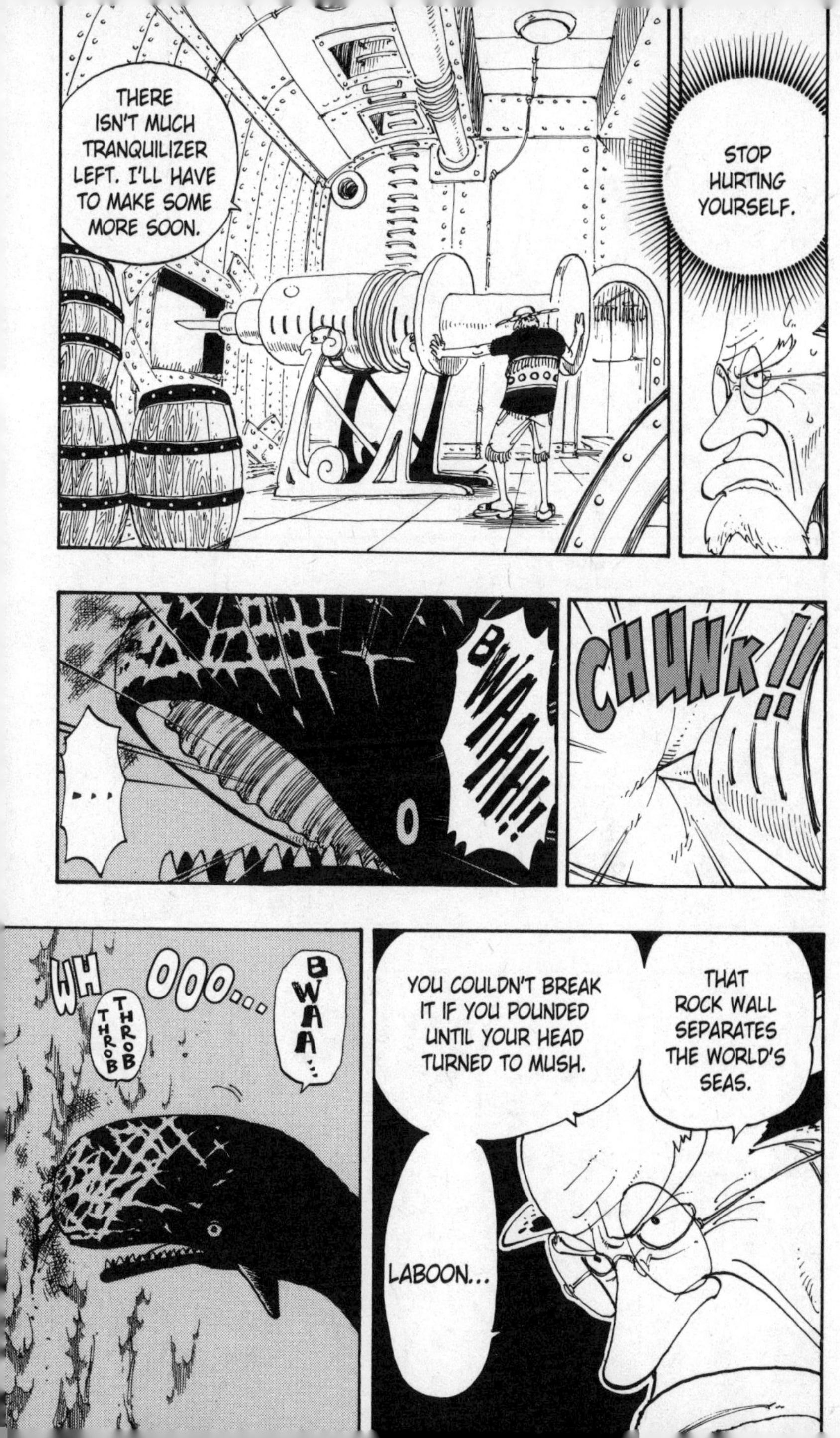
STOP HURTING YOURSELF.
THERE ISN'T MUCH TRANQUILIZER LEFT. I'LL HAVE TO MAKE SOME MORE SOON.
CHUNK!!
BWAAAH!!
...
THAT ROCK WALL SEPARATES THE WORLD'S SEAS.
YOU COULDN'T BREAK IT IF YOU POUNDED UNTIL YOUR HEAD TURNED TO MUSH.
LABOON...
BWAA...
WH OOO...
THROB THROB

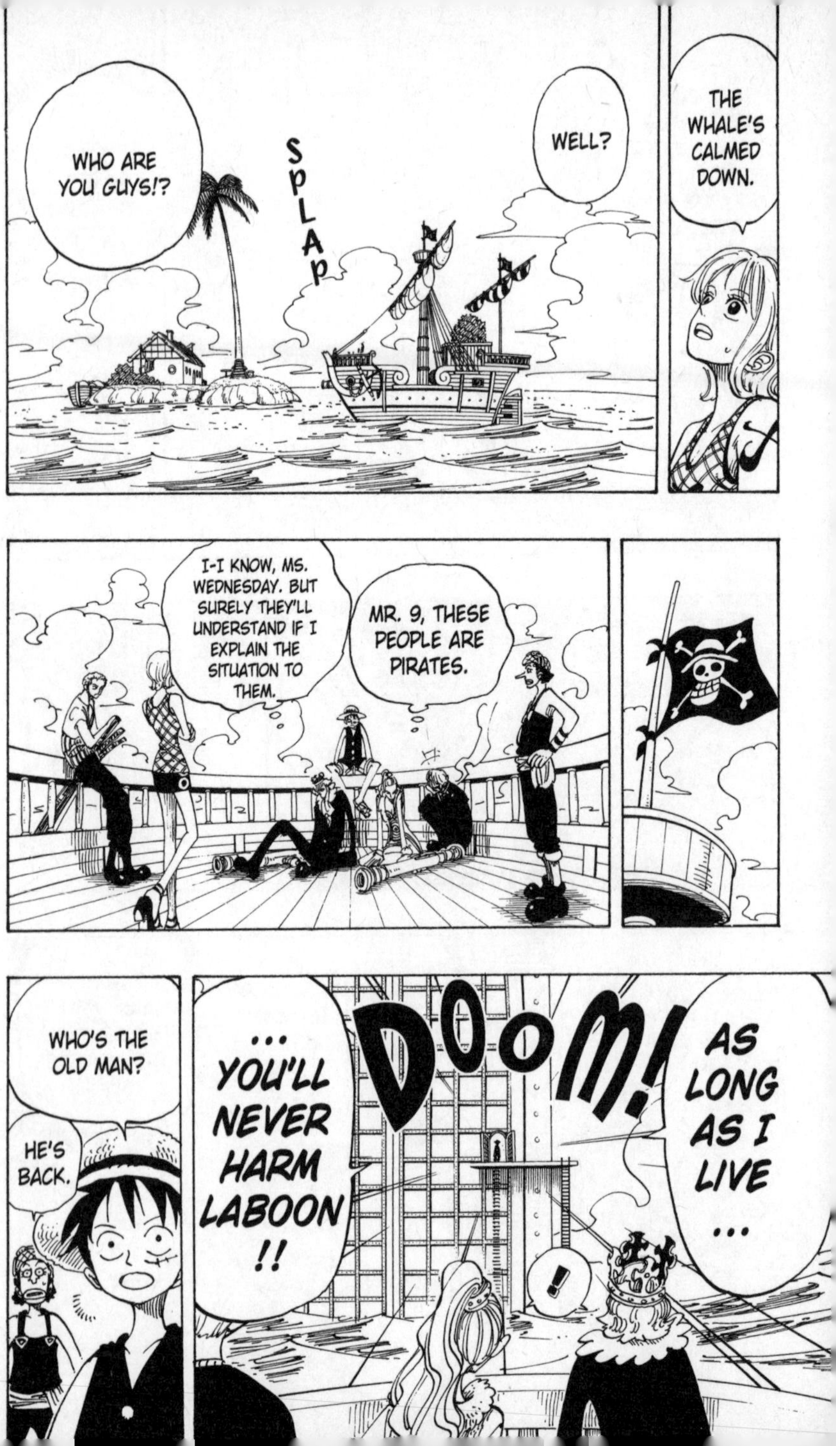
THE WHALE'S CALMED DOWN.
WELL?
SPLAP
WHO ARE YOU GUYS!?
MR. 9, THESE PEOPLE ARE PIRATES.
I-I KNOW, MS. WEDNESDAY. BUT SURELY THEY'LL UNDERSTAND IF I EXPLAIN THE SITUATION TO THEM.
AS LONG AS I LIVE...
DOOM!
...YOU'LL NEVER HARM LABOON!!
!
WHO'S THE OLD MAN?
HE'S BACK.

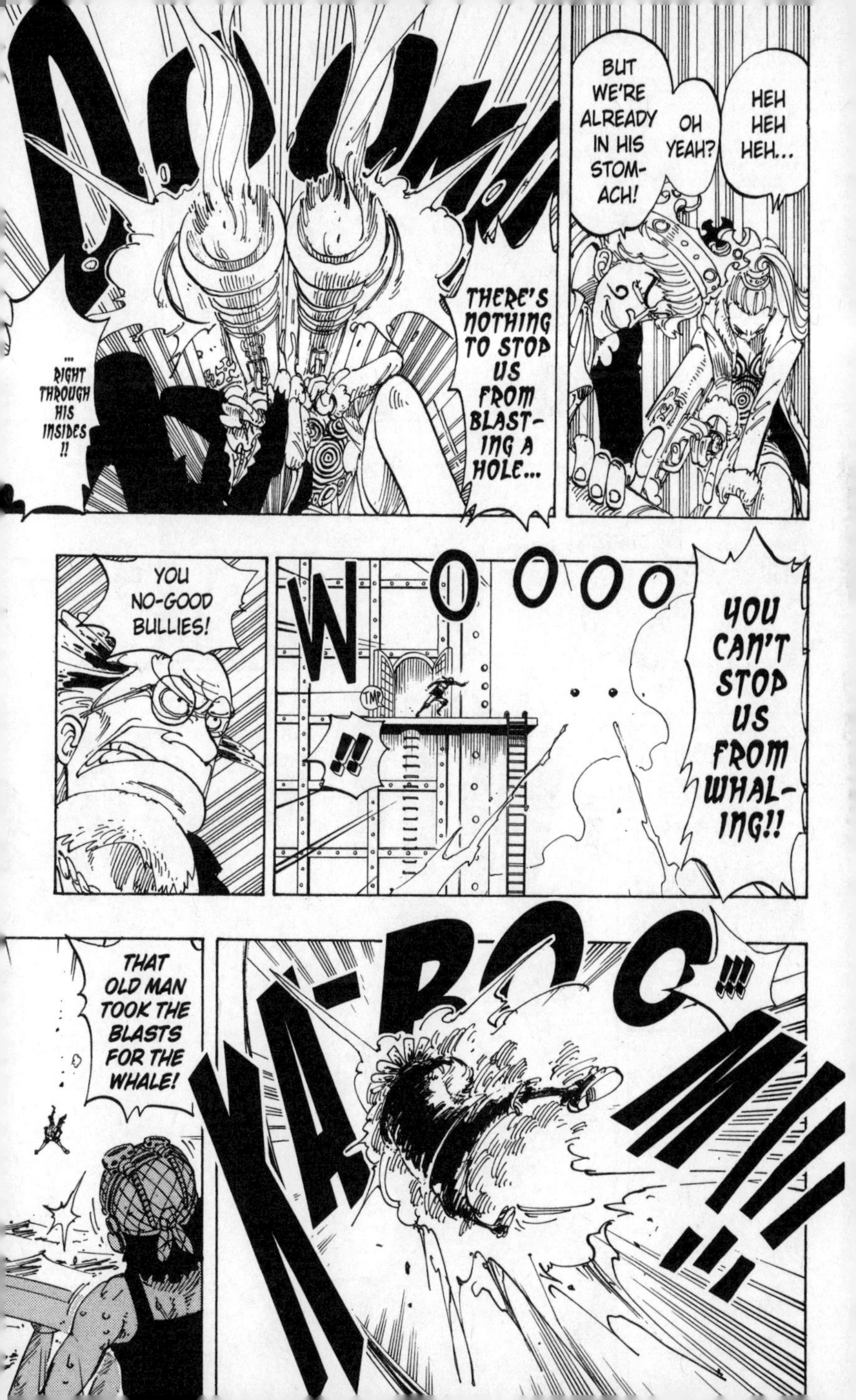
HEH HEH HEH...
OH YEAH?
BUT WE'RE ALREADY IN HIS STOMACH!
THERE'S NOTHING TO STOP US FROM BLASTING A HOLE...
...RIGHT THROUGH HIS INSIDES!!
WOOOO
YOU CAN'T STOP US FROM WHALING!!
TMP
!!
YOU NO-GOOD BULLIES!
KA-BOOM!!!
THAT OLD MAN TOOK THE BLASTS FOR THE WHALE!

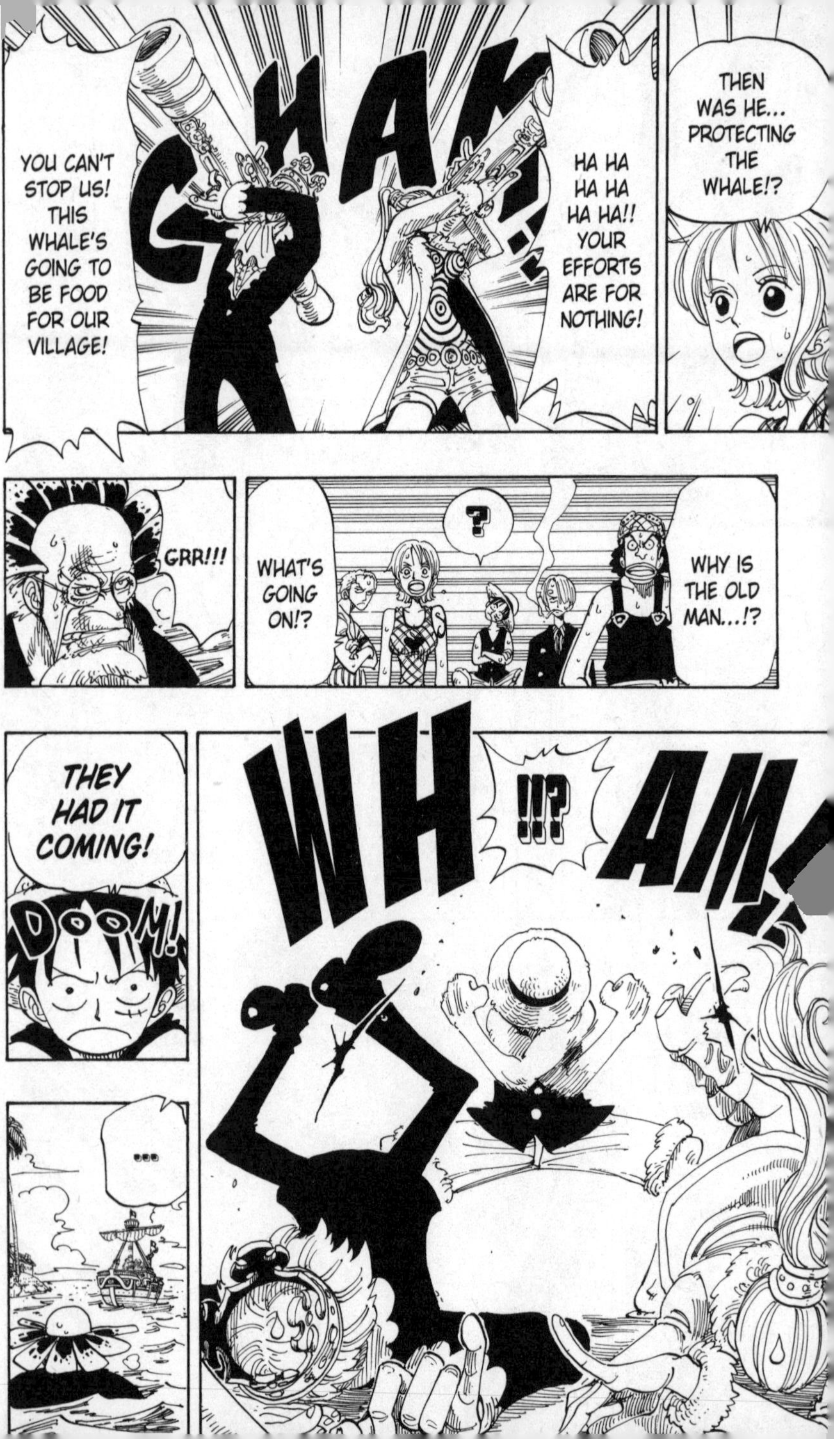
THEN WAS HE... PROTECTING THE WHALE!?
HA HA HA HA HA HA!! YOUR EFFORTS ARE FOR NOTHING!
YOU CAN'T STOP US! THIS WHALE'S GOING TO BE FOOD FOR OUR VILLAGE!
WHY IS THE OLD MAN...!?
?
WHAT'S GOING ON!?
GRR!!!
WH
!!?
AM
THEY HAD IT COMING!
DOOM!
...

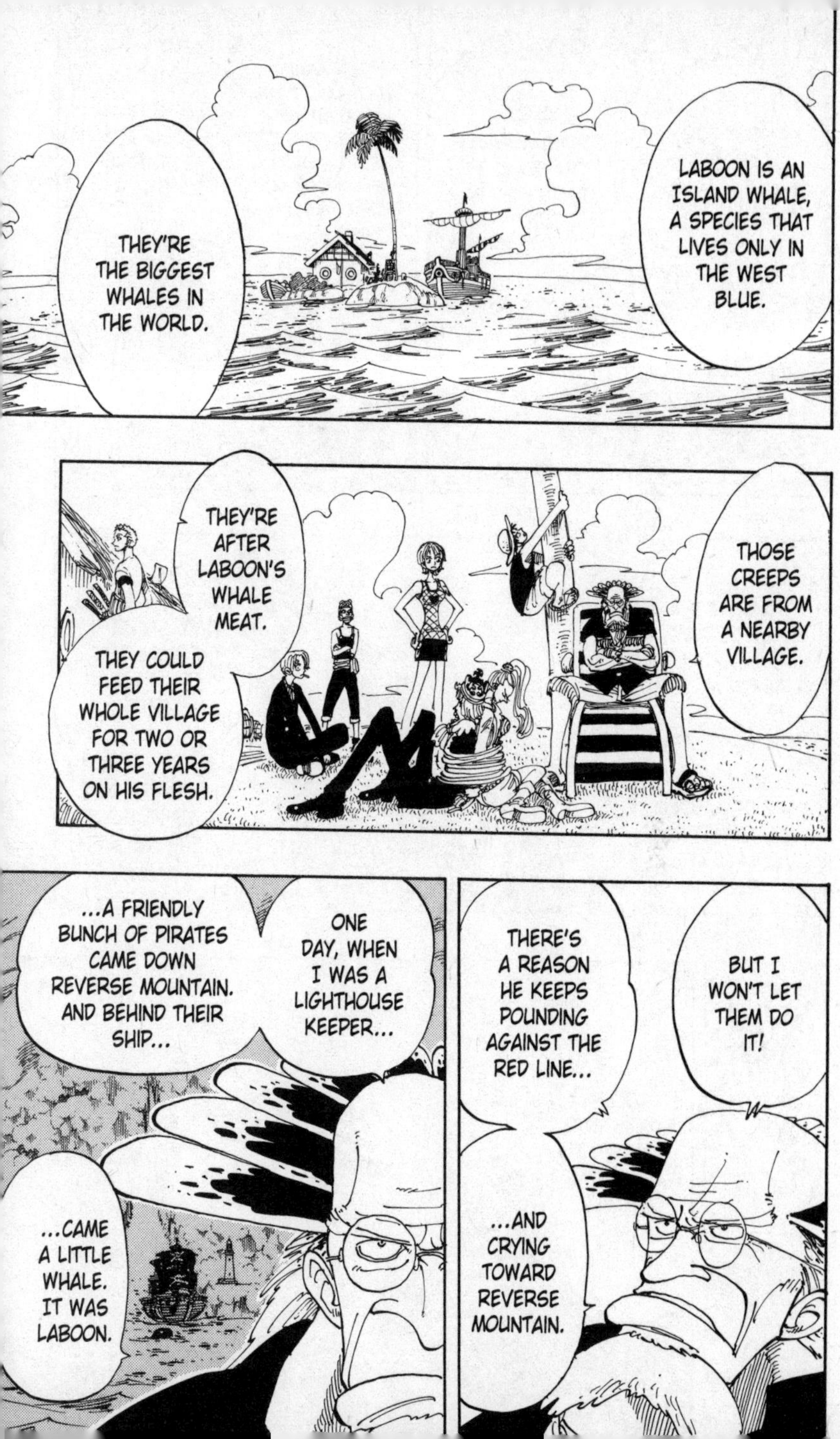
LABOON IS AN ISLAND WHALE, A SPECIES THAT LIVES ONLY IN THE WEST BLUE.
THEY'RE THE BIGGEST WHALES IN THE WORLD.
THOSE CREEPS ARE FROM A NEARBY VILLAGE.
THEY'RE AFTER LABOON'S WHALE MEAT.
THEY COULD FEED THEIR WHOLE VILLAGE FOR TWO OR THREE YEARS ON HIS FLESH.
BUT I WON'T LET THEM DO IT!
THERE'S A REASON HE KEEPS POUNDING AGAINST THE RED LINE...
...AND CRYING TOWARD REVERSE MOUNTAIN.
ONE DAY, WHEN I WAS A LIGHTHOUSE KEEPER...
...A FRIENDLY BUNCH OF PIRATES CAME DOWN REVERSE MOUNTAIN. AND BEHIND THEIR SHIP...
...CAME A LITTLE WHALE. IT WAS LABOON.

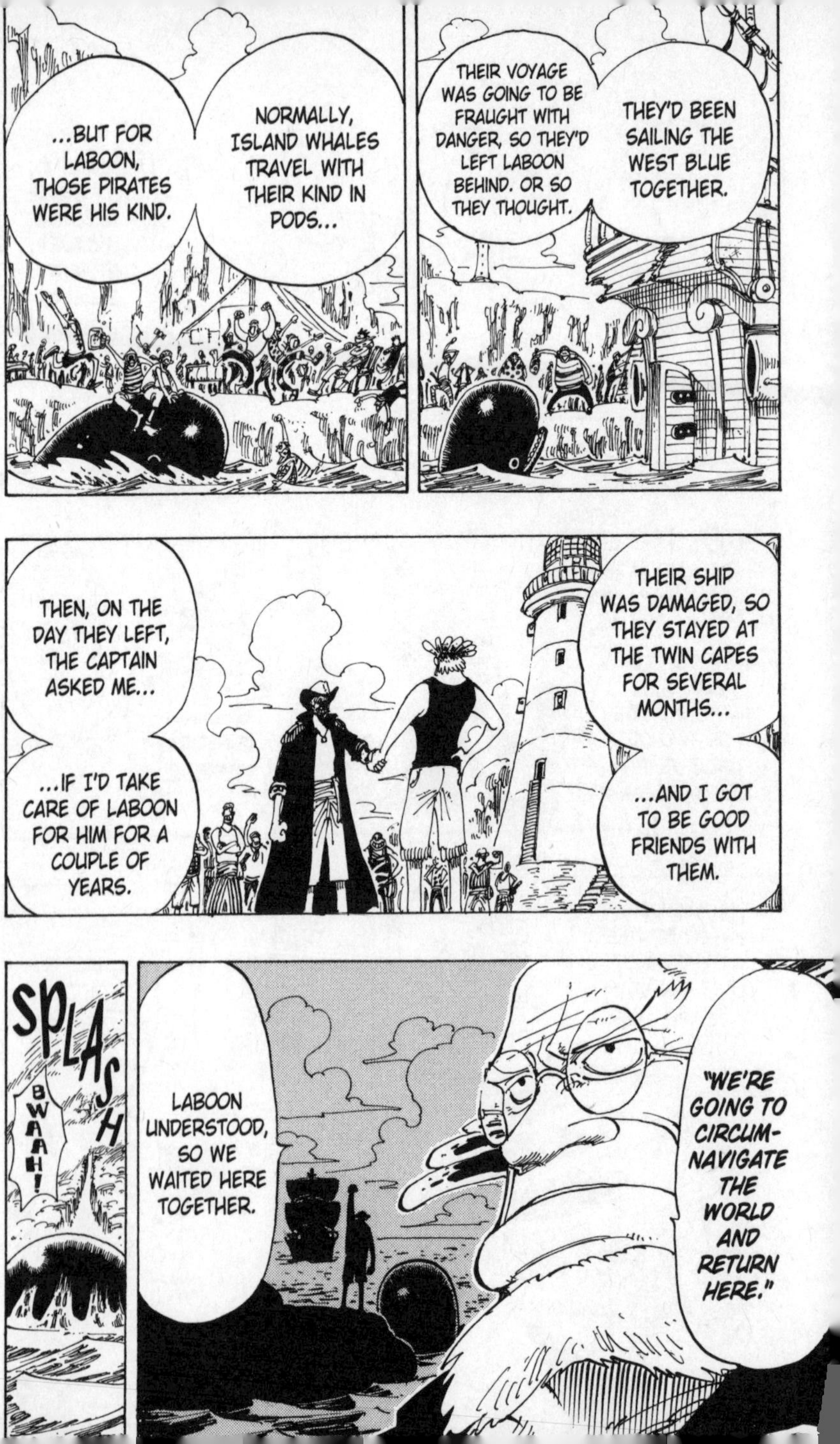
THEY'D BEEN SAILING THE WEST BLUE TOGETHER.
THEIR VOYAGE WAS GOING TO BE FRAUGHT WITH DANGER, SO THEY'D LEFT LABOON BEHIND. OR SO THEY THOUGHT.
NORMALLY, ISLAND WHALES TRAVEL WITH THEIR KIND IN PODS...
...BUT FOR LABOON, THOSE PIRATES WERE HIS KIND.
THEIR SHIP WAS DAMAGED, SO THEY STAYED AT THE TWIN CAPES FOR SEVERAL MONTHS...
...AND I GOT TO BE GOOD FRIENDS WITH THEM.
THEN, ON THE DAY THEY LEFT, THE CAPTAIN ASKED ME...
...IF I'D TAKE CARE OF LABOON FOR HIM FOR A COUPLE OF YEARS.
"WE'RE GOING TO CIRCUM-NAVIGATE THE WORLD AND RETURN HERE."
LABOON UNDERSTOOD, SO WE WAITED HERE TOGETHER.
SPLASH
BWAAH!

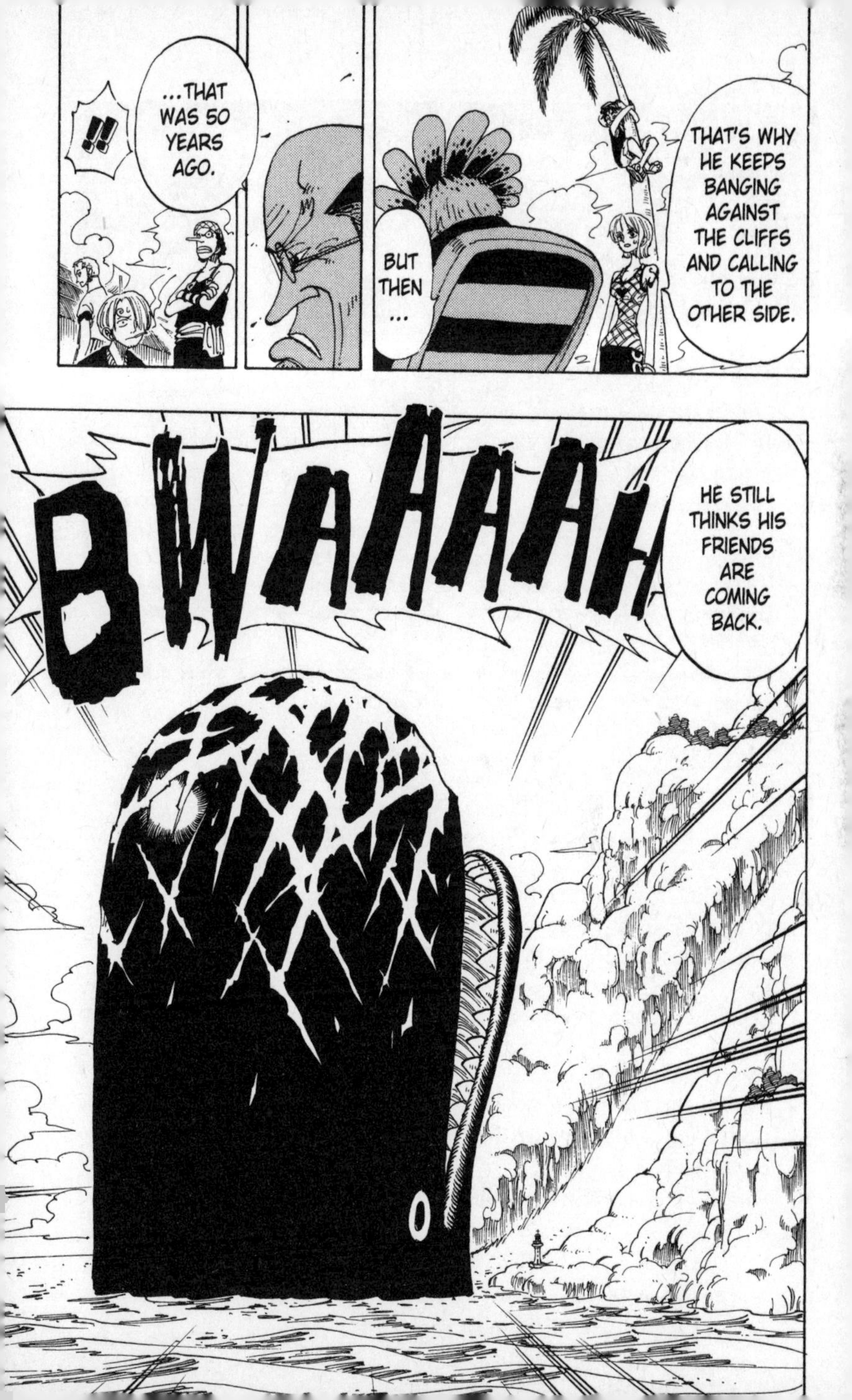
THAT'S WHY HE KEEPS BANGING AGAINST THE CLIFFS AND CALLING TO THE OTHER SIDE.
BUT THEN ...
...THAT WAS 50 YEARS AGO.
!!
HE STILL THINKS HIS FRIENDS ARE COMING BACK.
BWAAAAH

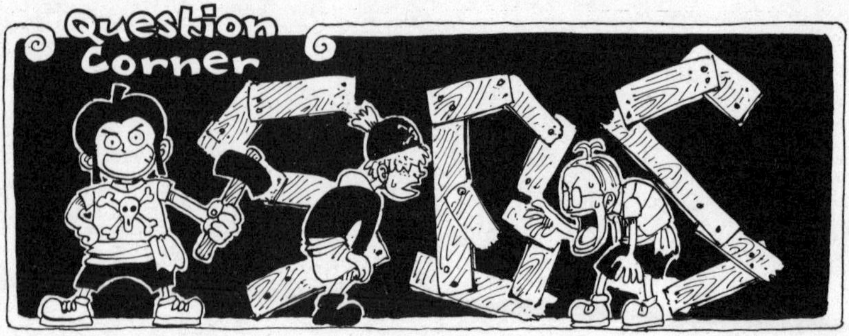
Question Corner

Q: How often do you get fan letters? Is it weekly?
If I mailed one on November 1, when would you receive it? Please let me know.

A: In Japan, fan letters go to Shueisha's *Weekly Shonen Jump* Editorial Department. Then, some part-timers sort the mail by author, and my editor brings me my letters each week. So if you're lucky, I might get your letter the day it arrives in the Editorial Department. Normally, I get them within a week or two.
(Outside Japan, the mail will take longer. Readers should send letters to the address below. --Ed.)

Eiichiro Oda/One Piece
c/o VIZ Media, LLC
P.O. Box 77010
San Francisco, CA 94107

Q: In volume 7, you wrote that you wear the same expression as your characters when you draw them, but is that true when you draw Nami's sexy expressions, too? Do you wear that "Mmm" expression?

A: Why of course. The sexiness of my expressions surpasses even those of the magazine queens--according to the town gossips.

Q: Hey, Ei-chan,* this is the first time I'm writing. (Giggle!) This is embarrassing. I have a question for you. Buggy the Clown comes apart, right? Does that go for all of his parts? Don't draw anything else until you've answered my question!!

A: Yes, that goes for all of his body parts.

(*"Ei" is short for Eiichiro. The reader is being playful here by adding the very informal "*-chan*" after it. --Ed.)

Chapter 104: CAPE PROMISE

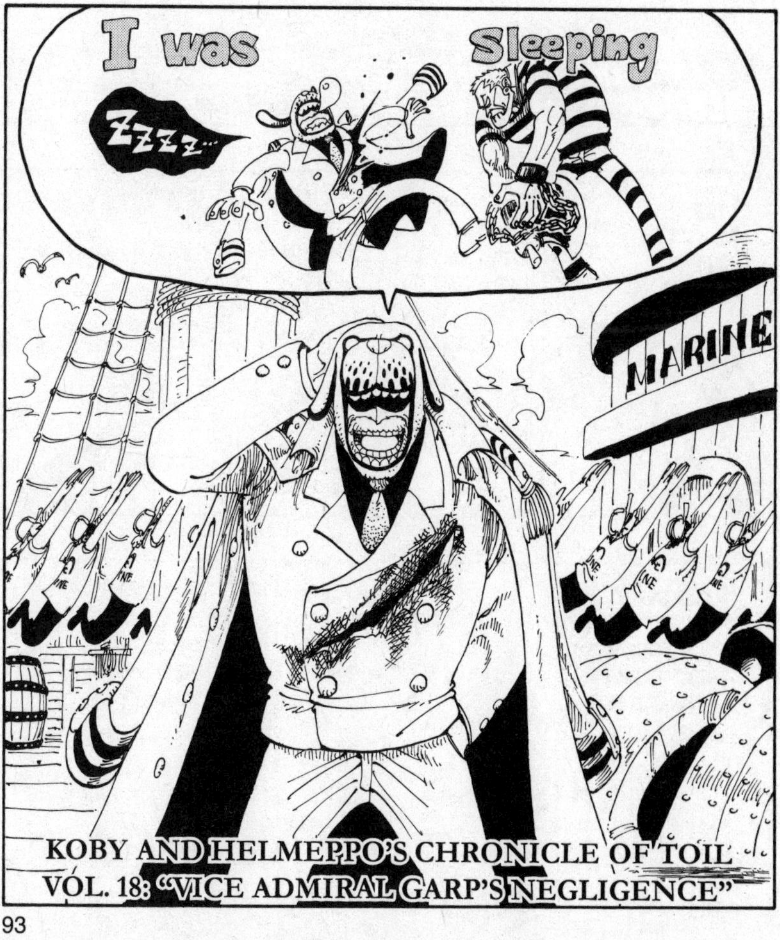
I was Sleeping
ZZZZ...
MARINE
KOBY AND HELMEPPO'S CHRONICLE OF TOIL
VOL. 18: "VICE ADMIRAL GARP'S NEGLIGENCE"

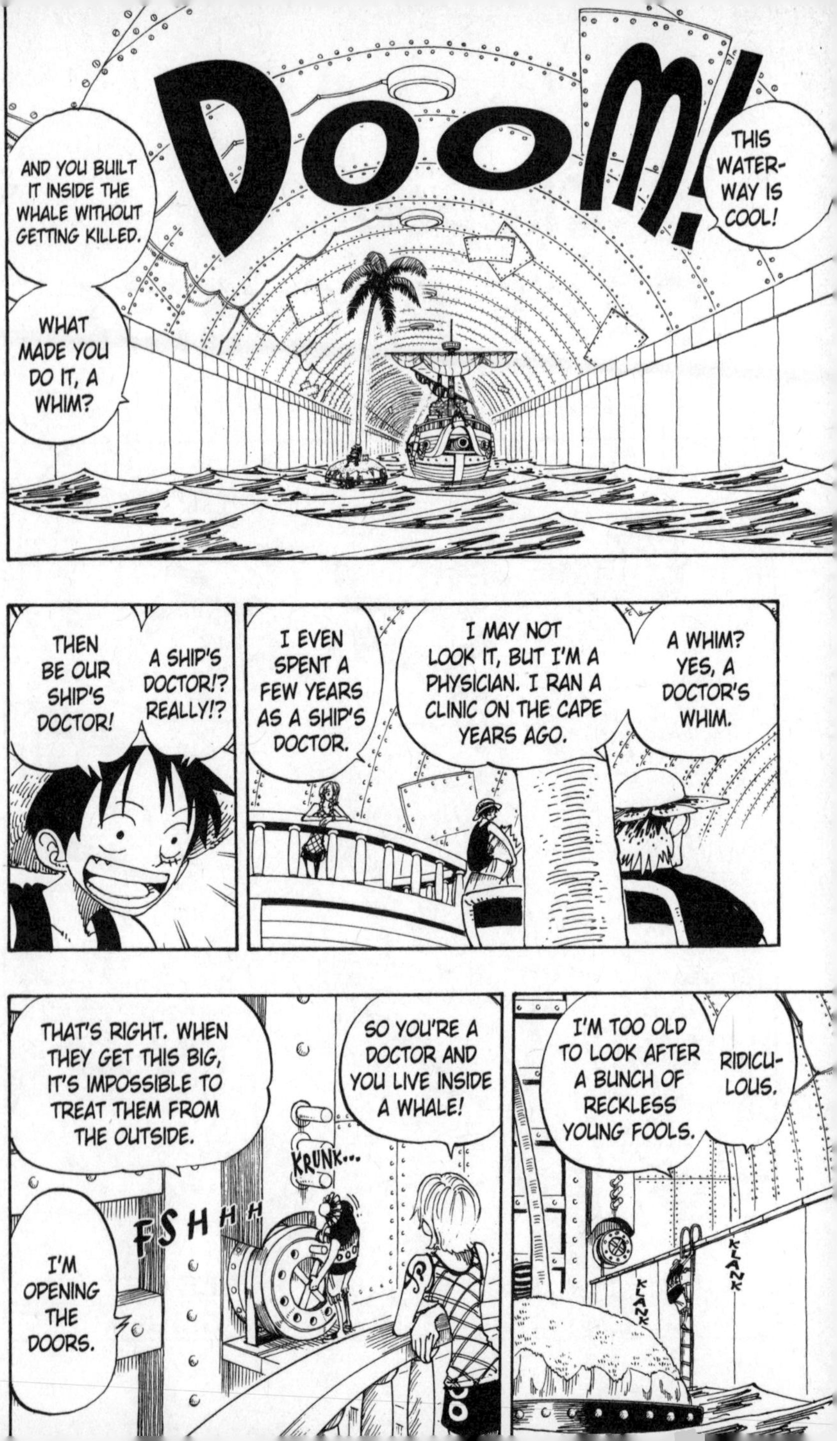
THIS WATER-WAY IS COOL!
DOOM!
AND YOU BUILT IT INSIDE THE WHALE WITHOUT GETTING KILLED.
WHAT MADE YOU DO IT, A WHIM?
A WHIM? YES, A DOCTOR'S WHIM.
I MAY NOT LOOK IT, BUT I'M A PHYSICIAN. I RAN A CLINIC ON THE CAPE YEARS AGO.
I EVEN SPENT A FEW YEARS AS A SHIP'S DOCTOR.
A SHIP'S DOCTOR!? REALLY!?
THEN BE OUR SHIP'S DOCTOR!
RIDICU-LOUS.
I'M TOO OLD TO LOOK AFTER A BUNCH OF RECKLESS YOUNG FOOLS.
KLANK
KLANK
SO YOU'RE A DOCTOR AND YOU LIVE INSIDE A WHALE!
THAT'S RIGHT. WHEN THEY GET THIS BIG, IT'S IMPOSSIBLE TO TREAT THEM FROM THE OUTSIDE.
KRUNK...
FSHHH
I'M OPENING THE DOORS.

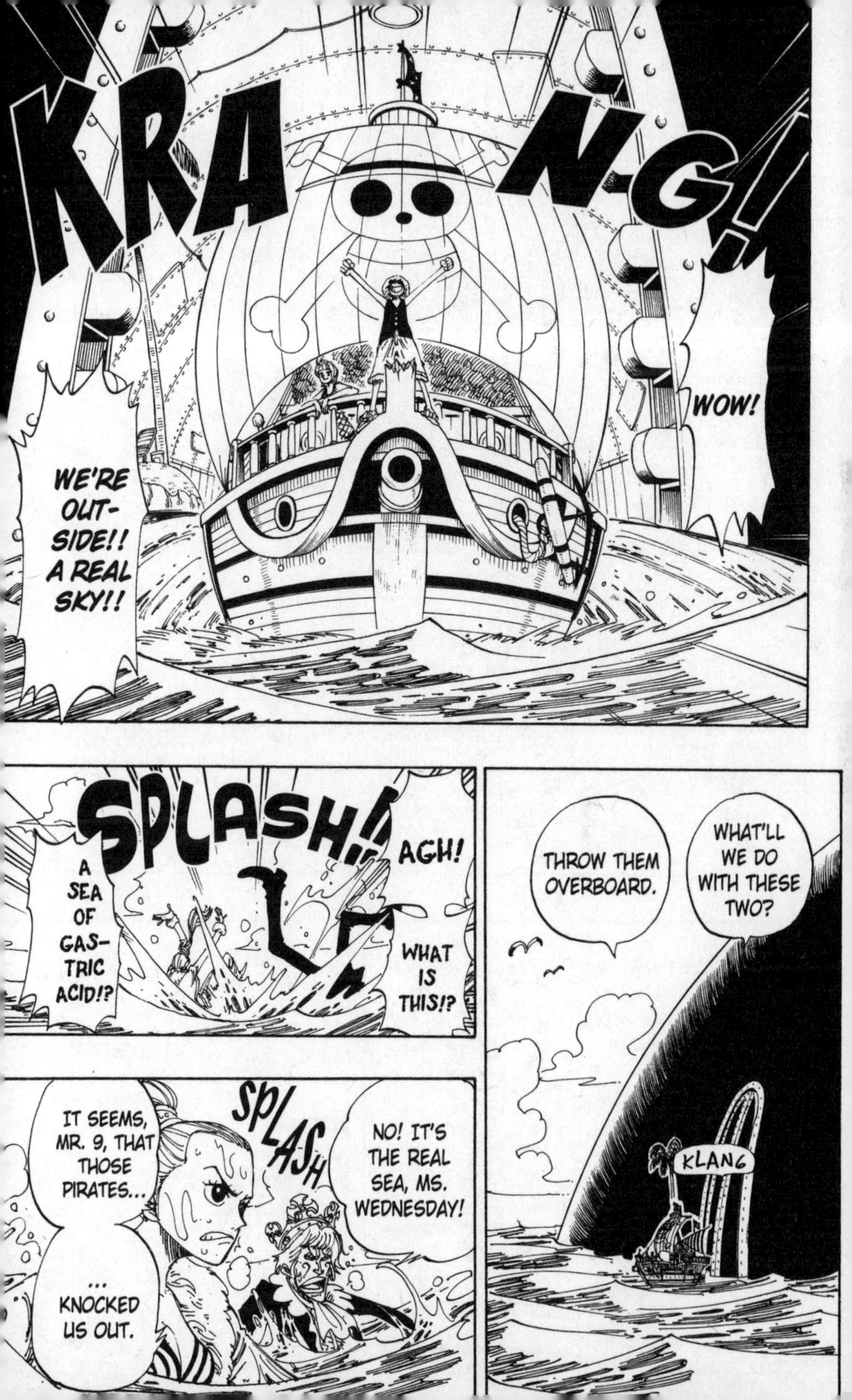
KRA-N-G!!
WOW!
WE'RE OUT-SIDE!! A REAL SKY!!
WHAT'LL WE DO WITH THESE TWO?
THROW THEM OVERBOARD.
KLANG
SPLASH!!
AGH!
WHAT IS THIS!?
A SEA OF GAS-TRIC ACID!?
SPLASH
NO! IT'S THE REAL SEA, MS. WEDNESDAY!
IT SEEMS, MR. 9, THAT THOSE PIRATES...
...KNOCKED US OUT.

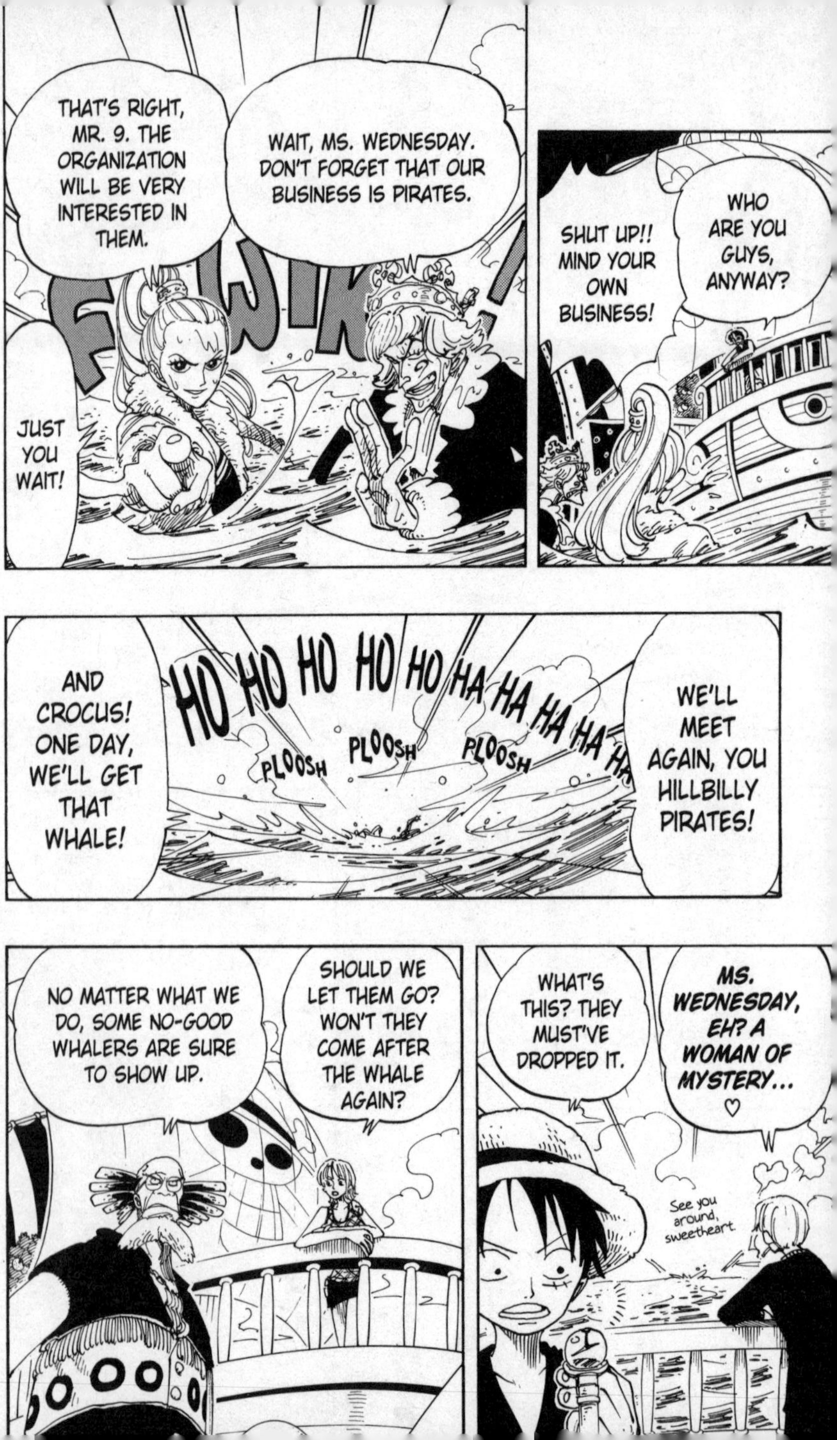
WHO ARE YOU GUYS, ANYWAY?
SHUT UP!! MIND YOUR OWN BUSINESS!
WAIT, MS. WEDNESDAY. DON'T FORGET THAT OUR BUSINESS IS PIRATES.
THAT'S RIGHT, MR. 9. THE ORGANIZATION WILL BE VERY INTERESTED IN THEM.
FWIK!
JUST YOU WAIT!
WE'LL MEET AGAIN, YOU HILLBILLY PIRATES!
HO HO HO HO HO HA HA HA HA HA
PLOOSH
PLOOSH
PLOOSH
AND CROCUS! ONE DAY, WE'LL GET THAT WHALE!
MS. WEDNESDAY, EH? A WOMAN OF MYSTERY... ♡
See you around, sweetheart.
WHAT'S THIS? THEY MUST'VE DROPPED IT.
SHOULD WE LET THEM GO? WON'T THEY COME AFTER THE WHALE AGAIN?
NO MATTER WHAT WE DO, SOME NO-GOOD WHALERS ARE SURE TO SHOW UP.

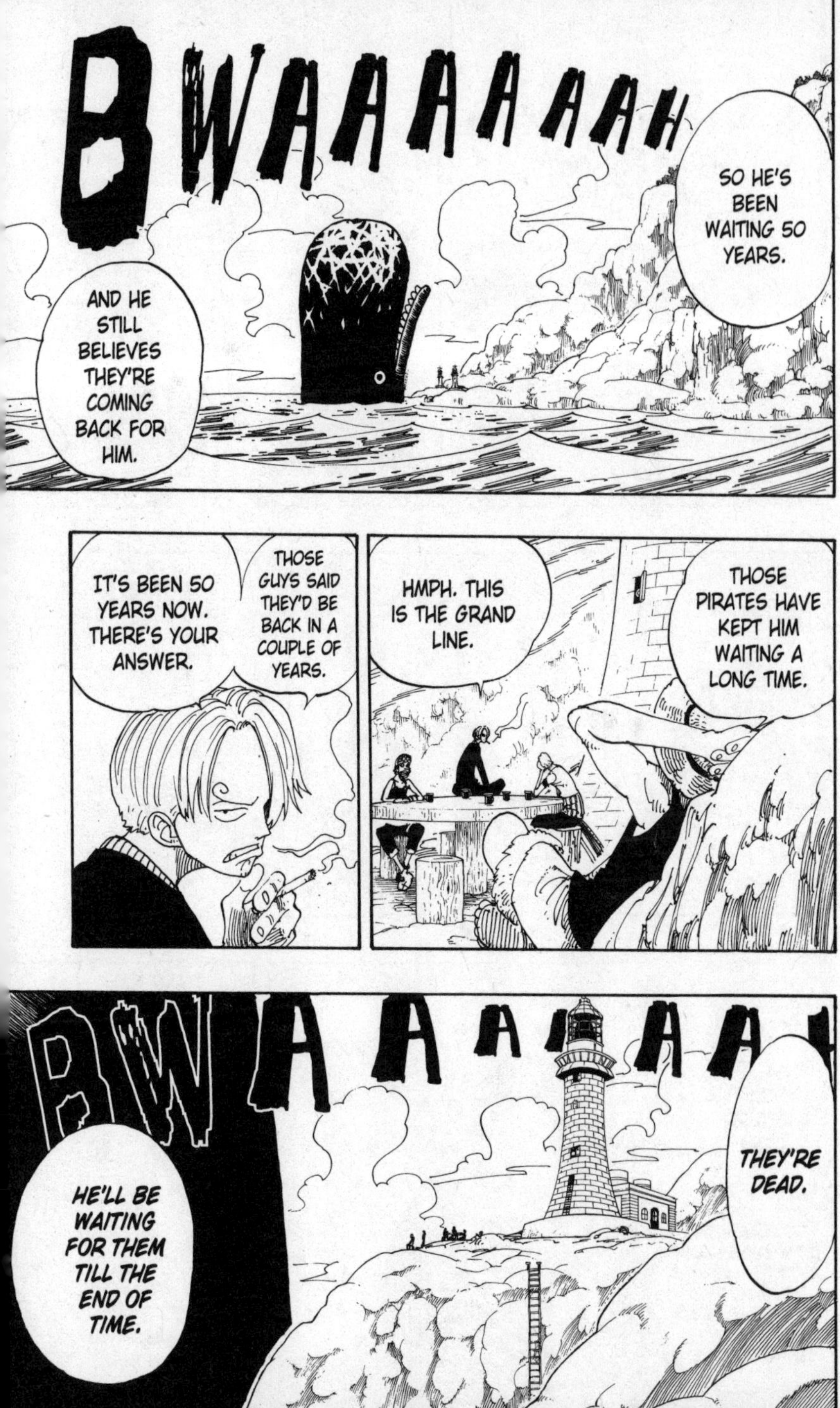
BWAAAAAAAH
SO HE'S BEEN WAITING 50 YEARS.
AND HE STILL BELIEVES THEY'RE COMING BACK FOR HIM.
THOSE PIRATES HAVE KEPT HIM WAITING A LONG TIME.
HMPH. THIS IS THE GRAND LINE.
THOSE GUYS SAID THEY'D BE BACK IN A COUPLE OF YEARS.
IT'S BEEN 50 YEARS NOW. THERE'S YOUR ANSWER.
BWAAAAA
THEY'RE DEAD.
HE'LL BE WAITING FOR THEM TILL THE END OF TIME.

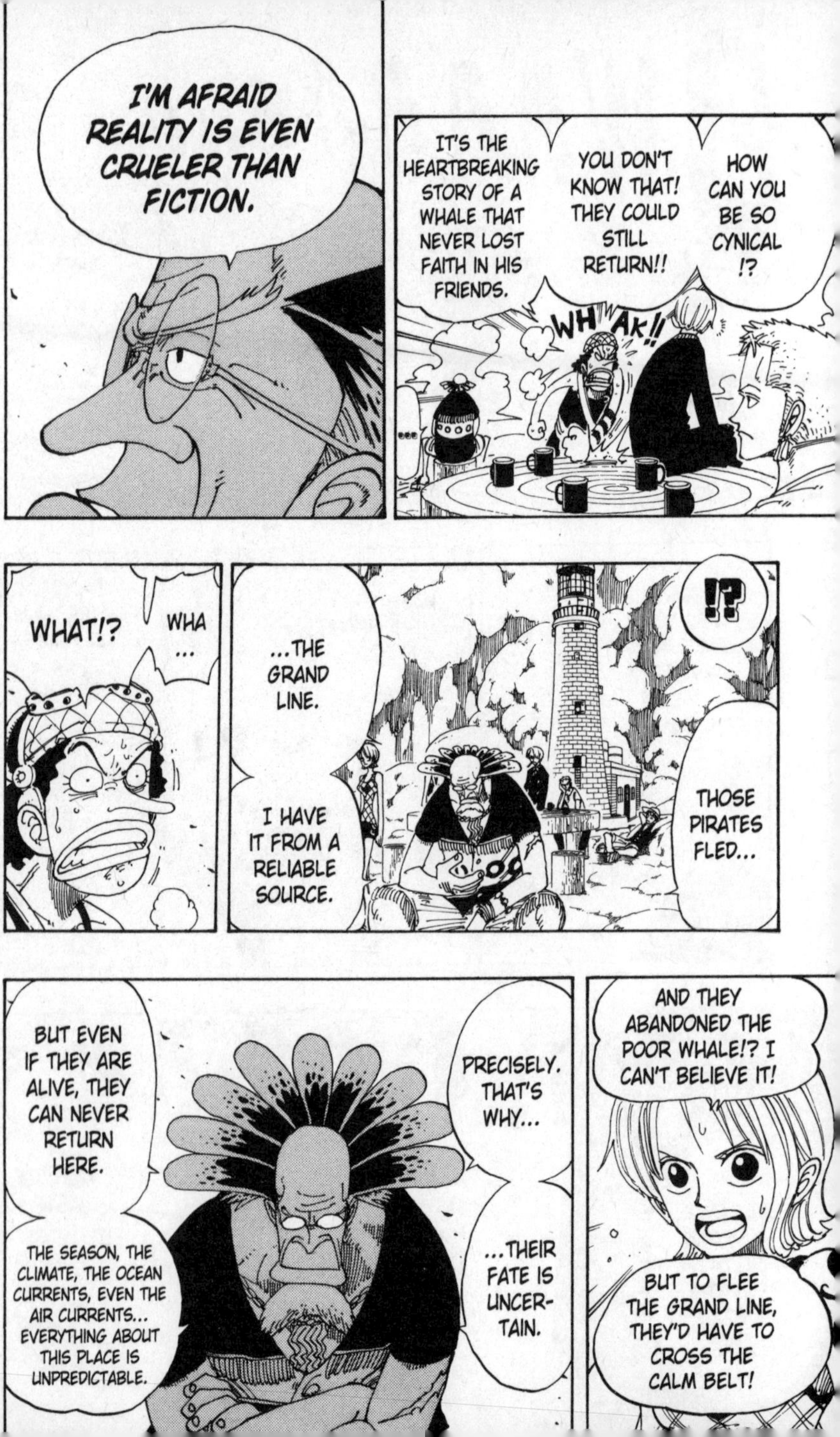
HOW CAN YOU BE SO CYNICAL !?
YOU DON'T KNOW THAT! THEY COULD STILL RETURN!!
IT'S THE HEARTBREAKING STORY OF A WHALE THAT NEVER LOST FAITH IN HIS FRIENDS.
WHAK!!
I'M AFRAID REALITY IS EVEN CRUELER THAN FICTION.
!?
THOSE PIRATES FLED...
...THE GRAND LINE.
I HAVE IT FROM A RELIABLE SOURCE.
WHA ...
WHAT!?
AND THEY ABANDONED THE POOR WHALE!? I CAN'T BELIEVE IT!
BUT TO FLEE THE GRAND LINE, THEY'D HAVE TO CROSS THE CALM BELT!
PRECISELY. THAT'S WHY...
...THEIR FATE IS UNCER-TAIN.
BUT EVEN IF THEY ARE ALIVE, THEY CAN NEVER RETURN HERE.
THE SEASON, THE CLIMATE, THE OCEAN CURRENTS, EVEN THE AIR CURRENTS... EVERYTHING ABOUT THIS PLACE IS UNPREDICTABLE.

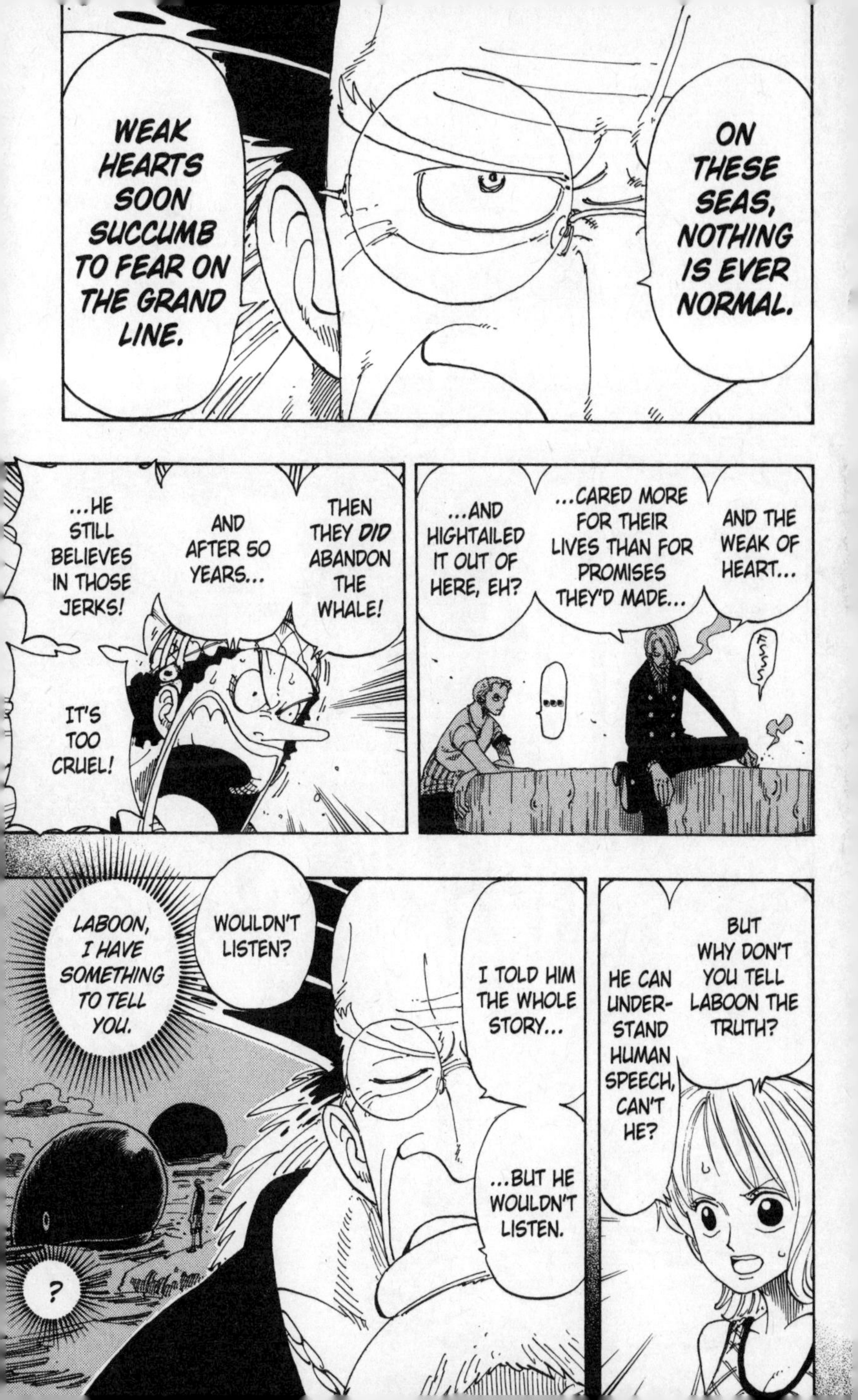
ON THESE SEAS, NOTHING IS EVER NORMAL.
WEAK HEARTS SOON SUCCUMB TO FEAR ON THE GRAND LINE.
AND THE WEAK OF HEART...
...CARED MORE FOR THEIR LIVES THAN FOR PROMISES THEY'D MADE...
...AND HIGHTAILED IT OUT OF HERE, EH?
FSSS
...
THEN THEY *DID* ABANDON THE WHALE!
AND AFTER 50 YEARS...
...HE STILL BELIEVES IN THOSE JERKS!
IT'S TOO CRUEL!
BUT WHY DON'T YOU TELL LABOON THE TRUTH?
HE CAN UNDER-STAND HUMAN SPEECH, CAN'T HE?
I TOLD HIM THE WHOLE STORY...
...BUT HE WOULDN'T LISTEN.
WOULDN'T LISTEN?
LABOON, I HAVE SOMETHING TO TELL YOU.
?

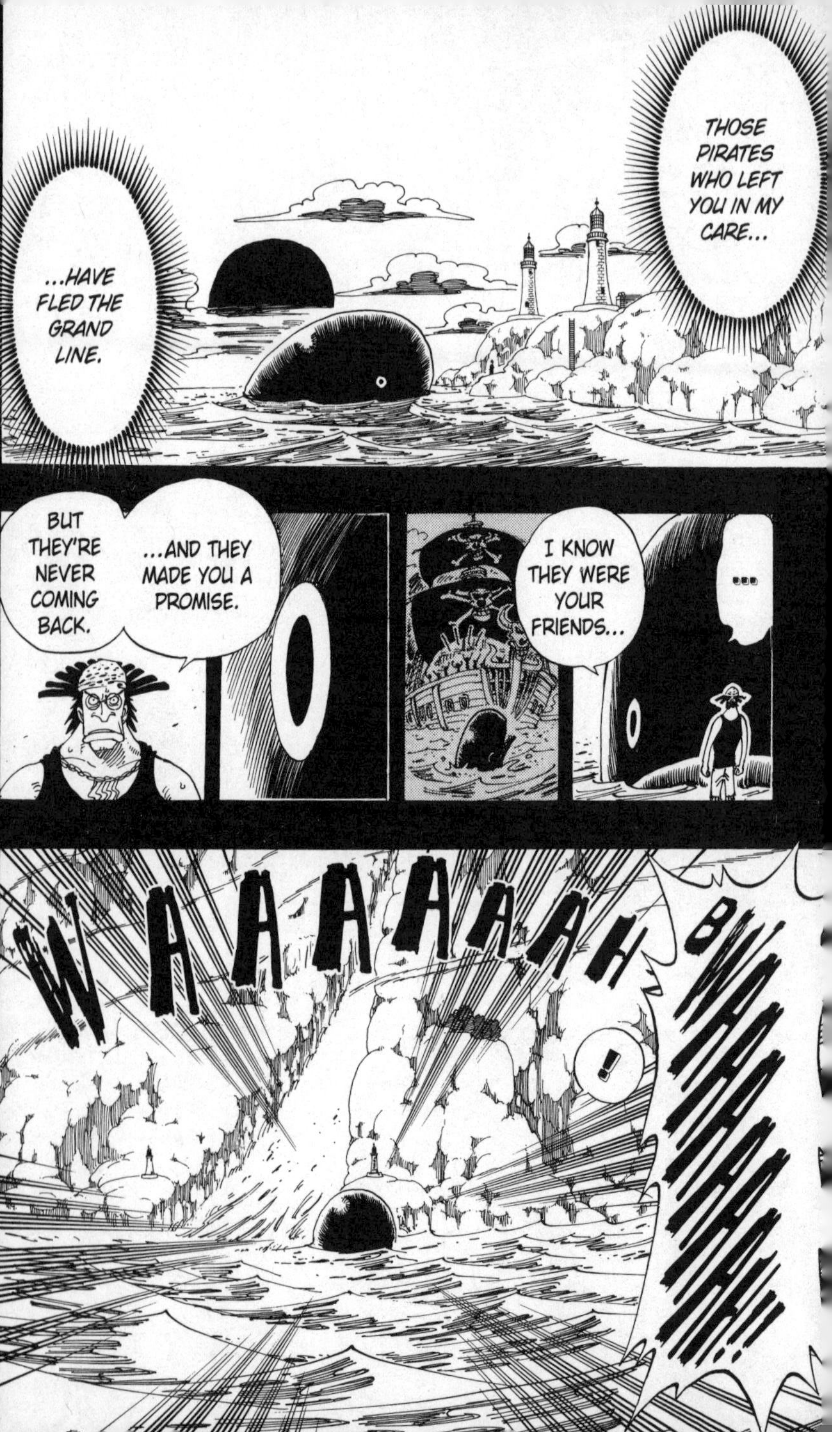
THOSE PIRATES WHO LEFT YOU IN MY CARE...
...HAVE FLED THE GRAND LINE.
...
I KNOW THEY WERE YOUR FRIENDS...
...AND THEY MADE YOU A PROMISE.
BUT THEY'RE NEVER COMING BACK.
BWAAAAAAAH!!
!
WAAAAAAH

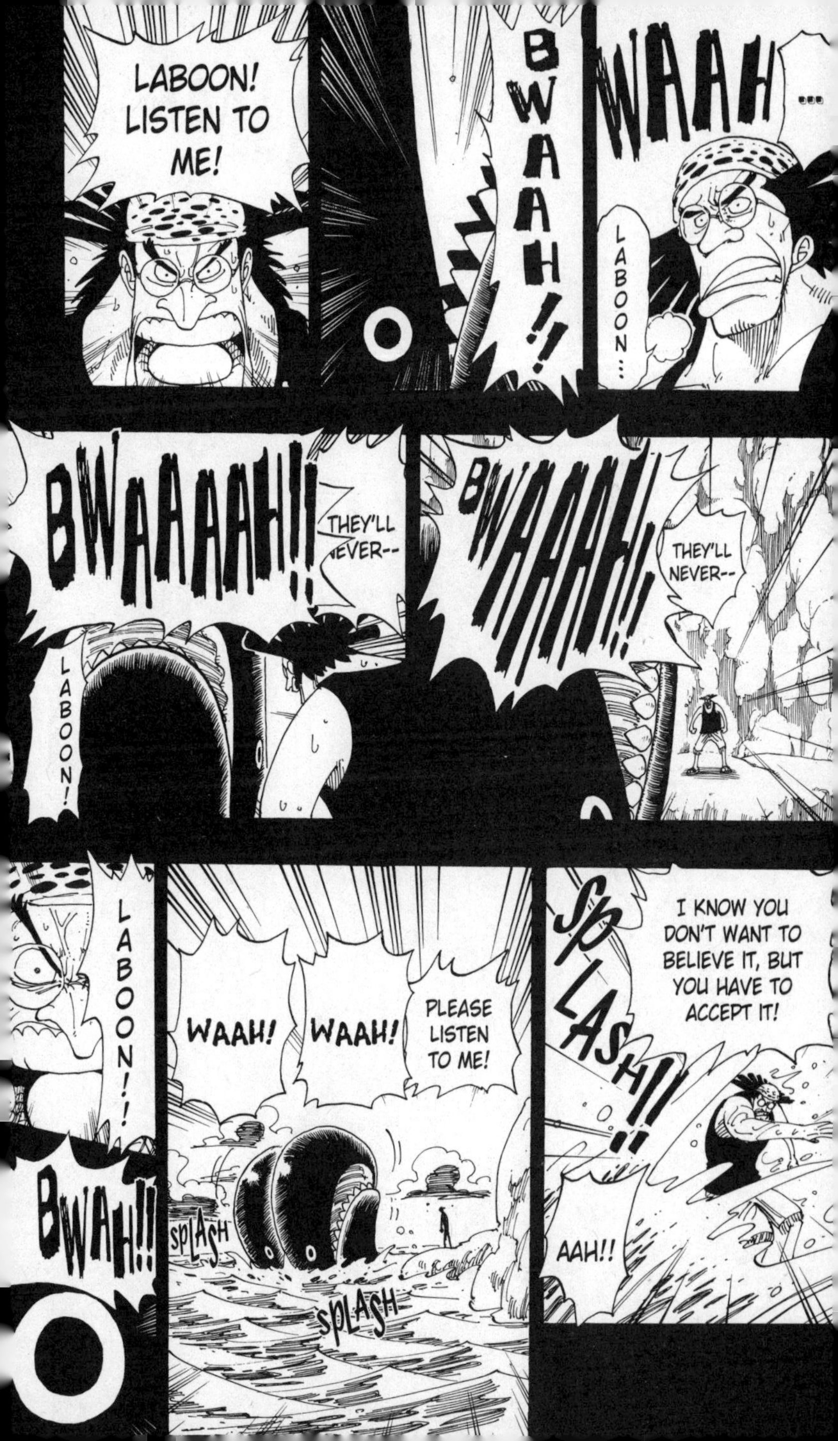
WAAH...
LABOON...
BWAAH!!
LABOON! LISTEN TO ME!
BWAAAH!!
THEY'LL NEVER--
BWAAAAH!!
THEY'LL NEVER--
LABOON!
SPLASH!!
I KNOW YOU DON'T WANT TO BELIEVE IT, BUT YOU HAVE TO ACCEPT IT!
AAH!!
PLEASE LISTEN TO ME!
WAAH!
WAAH!
SPLASH
SPLASH
LABOOON!!
BWAH!!

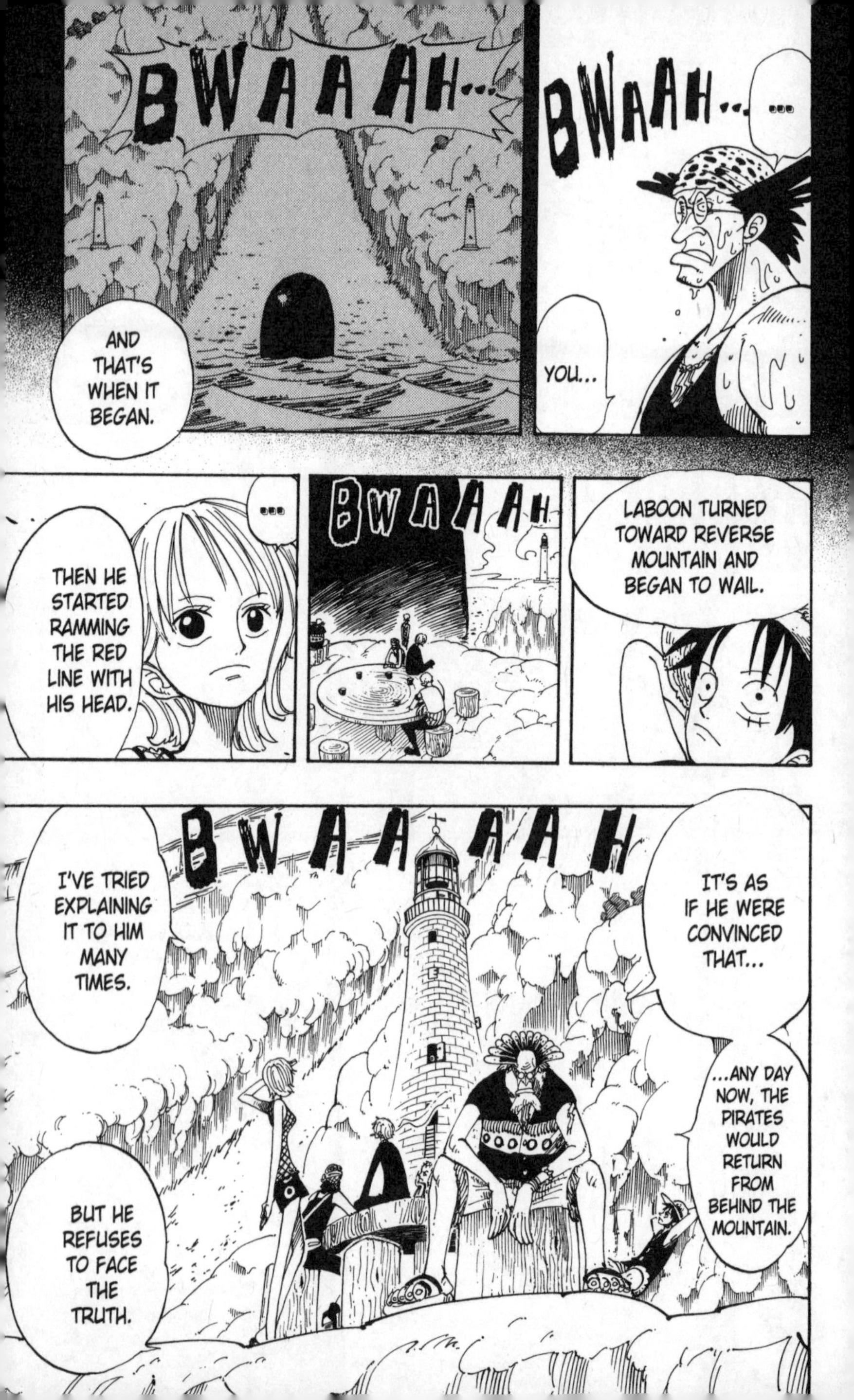
BWAAH... ...
...
YOU...
BWAAAAH...
AND THAT'S WHEN IT BEGAN.
LABOON TURNED TOWARD REVERSE MOUNTAIN AND BEGAN TO WAIL.
BWAAAAH
...
THEN HE STARTED RAMMING THE RED LINE WITH HIS HEAD.
IT'S AS IF HE WERE CONVINCED THAT...
...ANY DAY NOW, THE PIRATES WOULD RETURN FROM BEHIND THE MOUNTAIN.
BWAAAAAH
I'VE TRIED EXPLAINING IT TO HIM MANY TIMES.
BUT HE REFUSES TO FACE THE TRUTH.

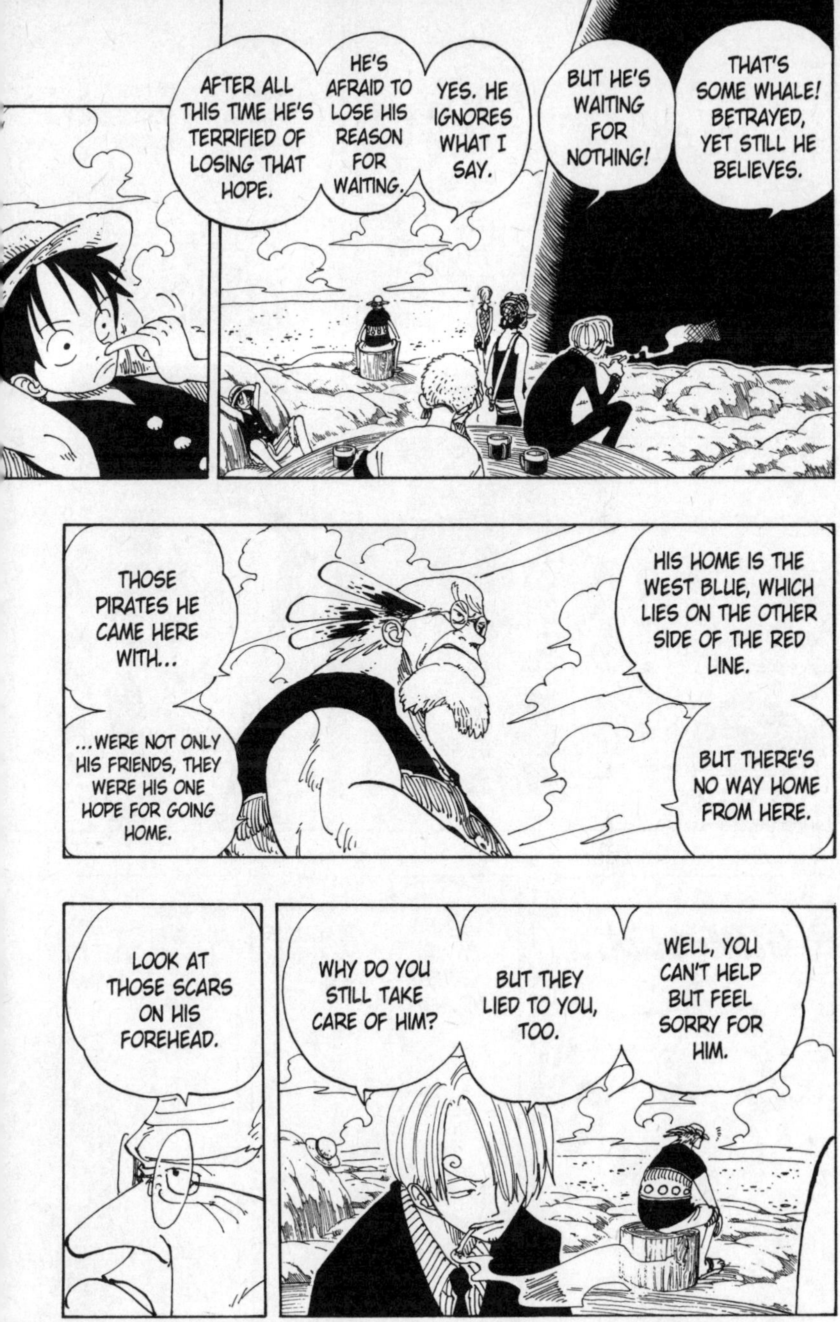
THAT'S SOME WHALE! BETRAYED, YET STILL HE BELIEVES.
BUT HE'S WAITING FOR NOTHING!
YES. HE IGNORES WHAT I SAY.
HE'S AFRAID TO LOSE HIS REASON FOR WAITING.
AFTER ALL THIS TIME HE'S TERRIFIED OF LOSING THAT HOPE.
HIS HOME IS THE WEST BLUE, WHICH LIES ON THE OTHER SIDE OF THE RED LINE.
BUT THERE'S NO WAY HOME FROM HERE.
THOSE PIRATES HE CAME HERE WITH...
...WERE NOT ONLY HIS FRIENDS, THEY WERE HIS ONE HOPE FOR GOING HOME.
WELL, YOU CAN'T HELP BUT FEEL SORRY FOR HIM.
BUT THEY LIED TO YOU, TOO.
WHY DO YOU STILL TAKE CARE OF HIM?
LOOK AT THOSE SCARS ON HIS FOREHEAD.

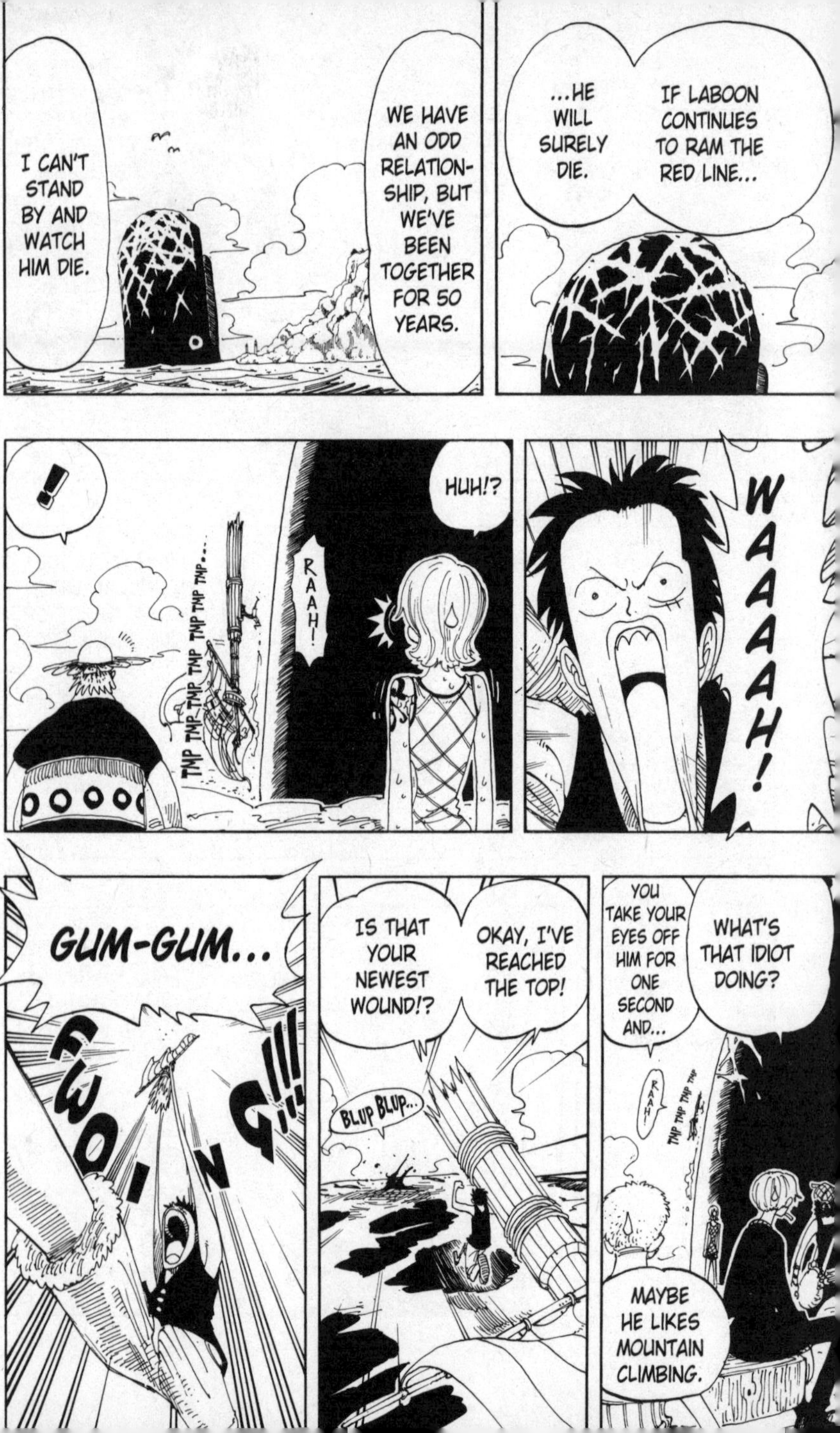
IF LABOON CONTINUES TO RAM THE RED LINE...
...HE WILL SURELY DIE.
WE HAVE AN ODD RELATION-SHIP, BUT WE'VE BEEN TOGETHER FOR 50 YEARS.
I CAN'T STAND BY AND WATCH HIM DIE.
WAAAAAH!
HUH!?
RAAAH!
!
TMP TMP TMP TMP TMP TMP TMP...
WHAT'S THAT IDIOT DOING?
YOU TAKE YOUR EYES OFF HIM FOR ONE SECOND AND...
RAAH!
TMP TMP TMP TMP
MAYBE HE LIKES MOUNTAIN CLIMBING.
OKAY, I'VE REACHED THE TOP!
IS THAT YOUR NEWEST WOUND!?
BLUP BLUP...
GUM-GUM...
FWOING!!!

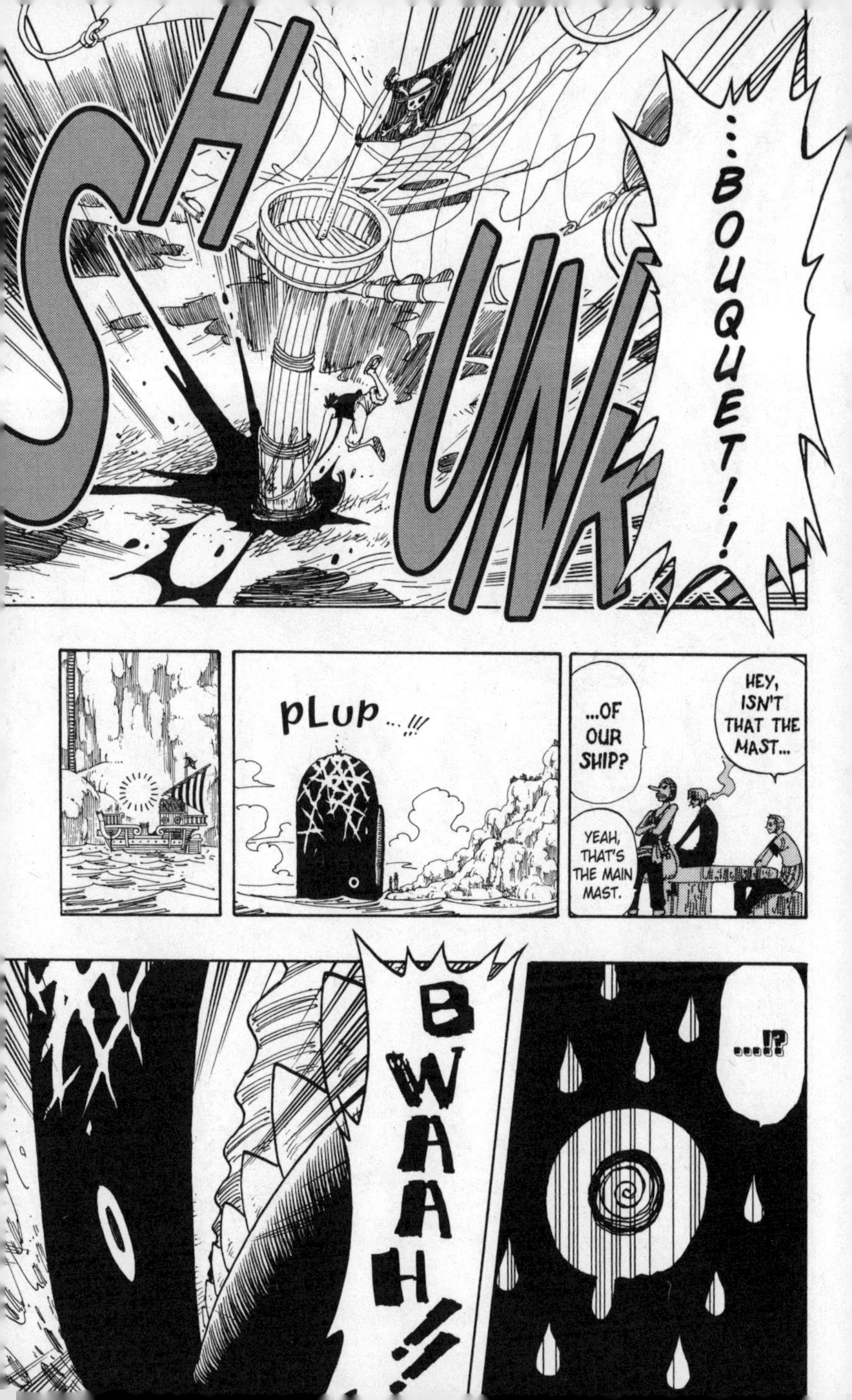
...BOUQUET!!
SHUNK
HEY, ISN'T THAT THE MAST...
...OF OUR SHIP?
YEAH, THAT'S THE MAIN MAST.
pLup...!!!
...!?
BWAAH!!

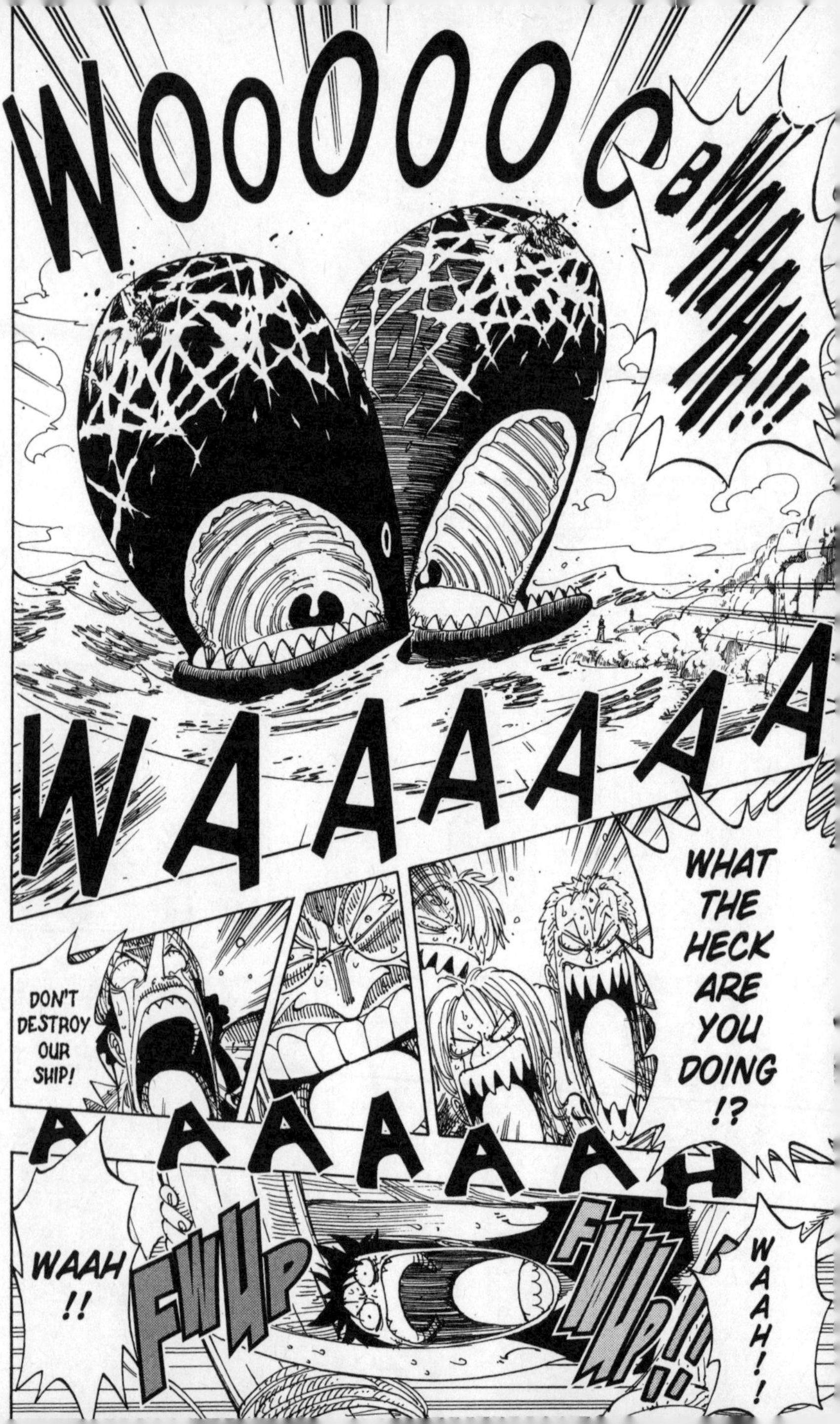
WOOOOOO
BWAAAH!!!
WAAAAAA
WHAT THE HECK ARE YOU DOING!?
DON'T DESTROY OUR SHIP!
AAAAAAH
WAAH!!
FWUP!!
FWUP
WAAH!!

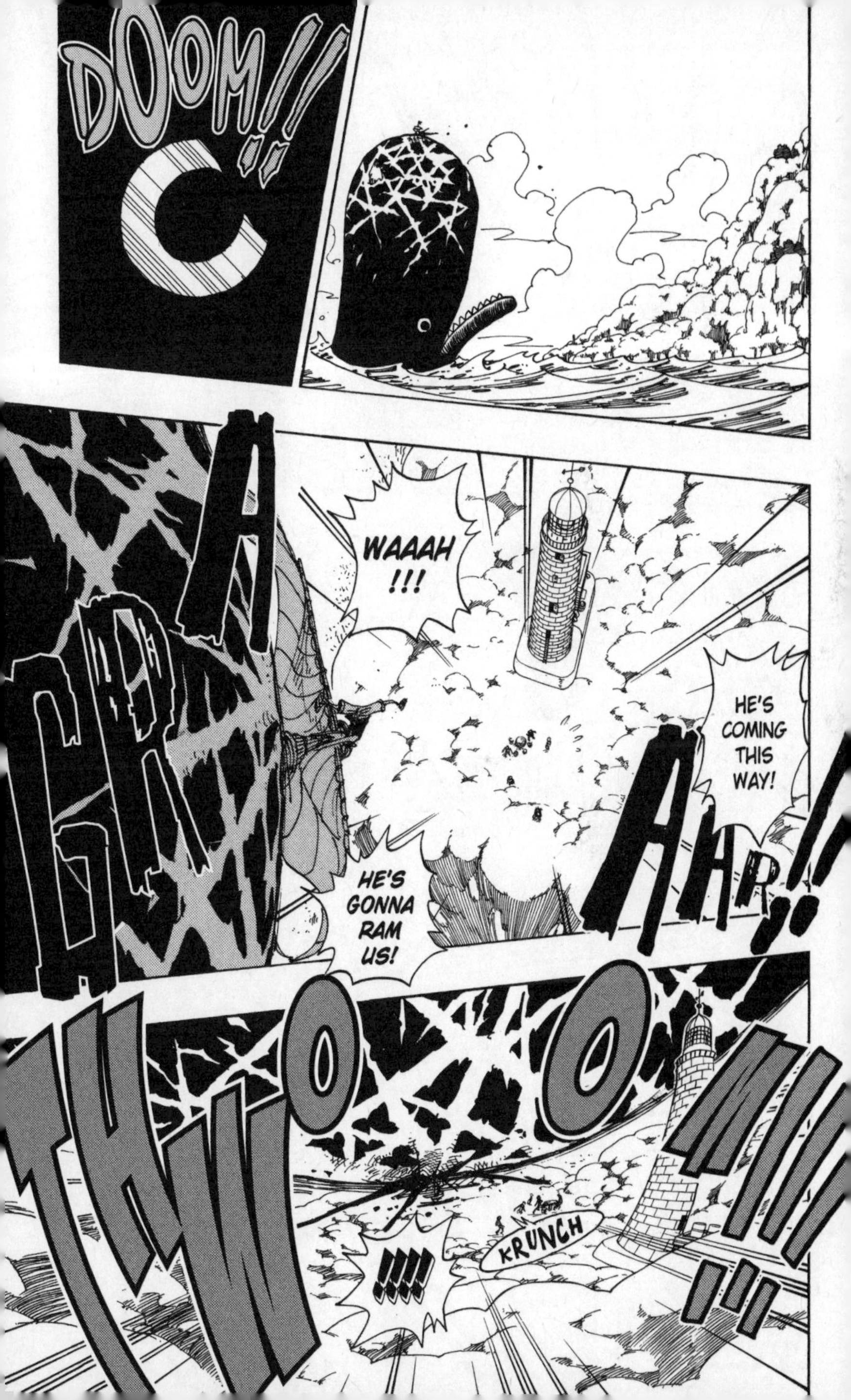
DOOM!!
HE'S COMING THIS WAY!
AHR!!
WAAAH!!!
HE'S GONNA RAM US!
GRAA
THWOOOM!!!
KRUNCH
!!!!!

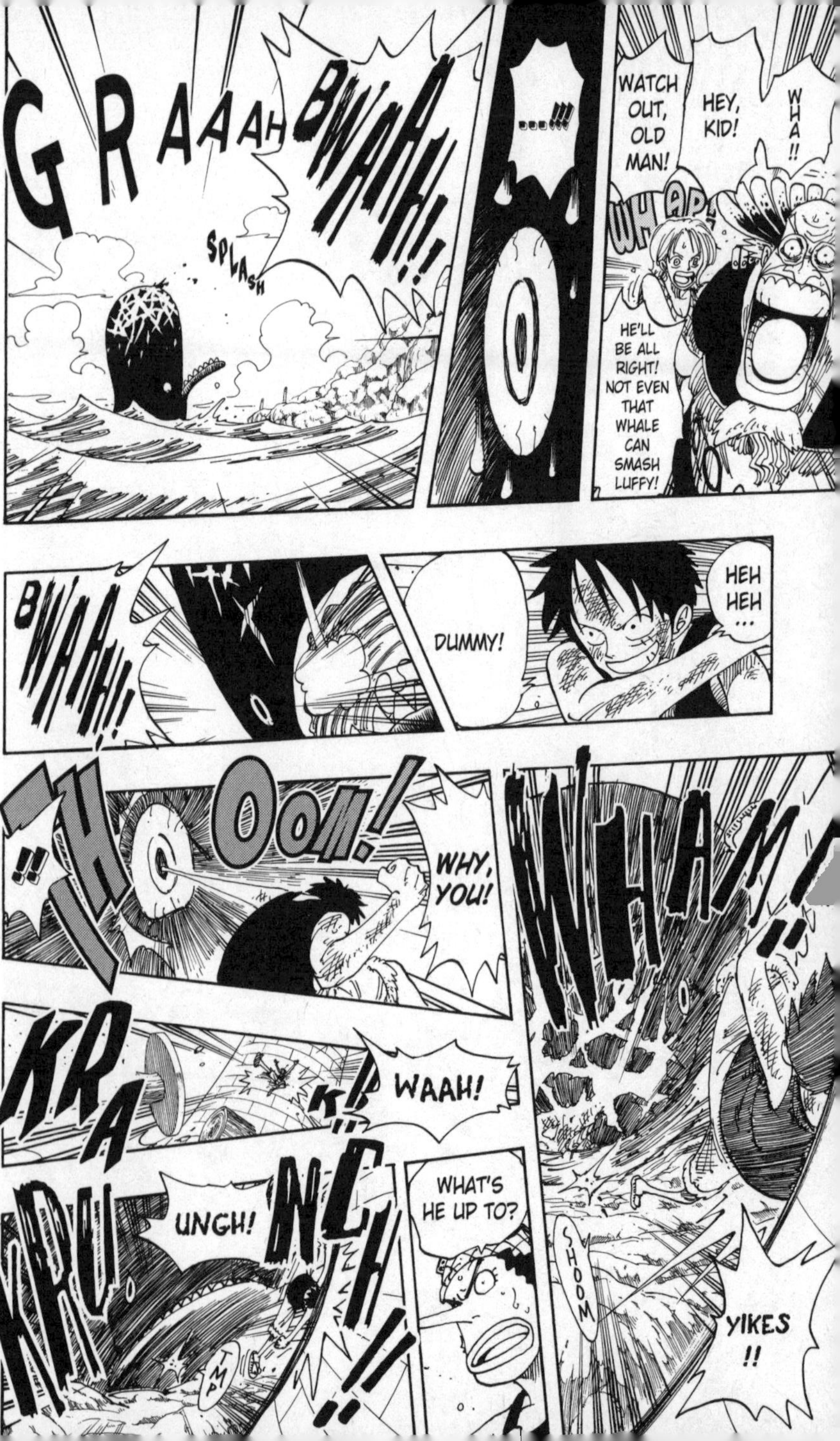
WATCH OUT, OLD MAN!
HEY, KID!
WHA!!
WHAP
HE'LL BE ALL RIGHT! NOT EVEN THAT WHALE CAN SMASH LUFFY!
...!!!
GRAAAAH
BWAAAH!!
SPLASH
HEH HEH...
DUMMY!
BWAAAH!!
WHAM!!
SHOOM
YIKES!!
ZHOOOM!
!!
WHY, YOU!
KRAK!!
WAAH!
WHAT'S HE UP TO?
KRUNCH!!
UNGH!
TMP

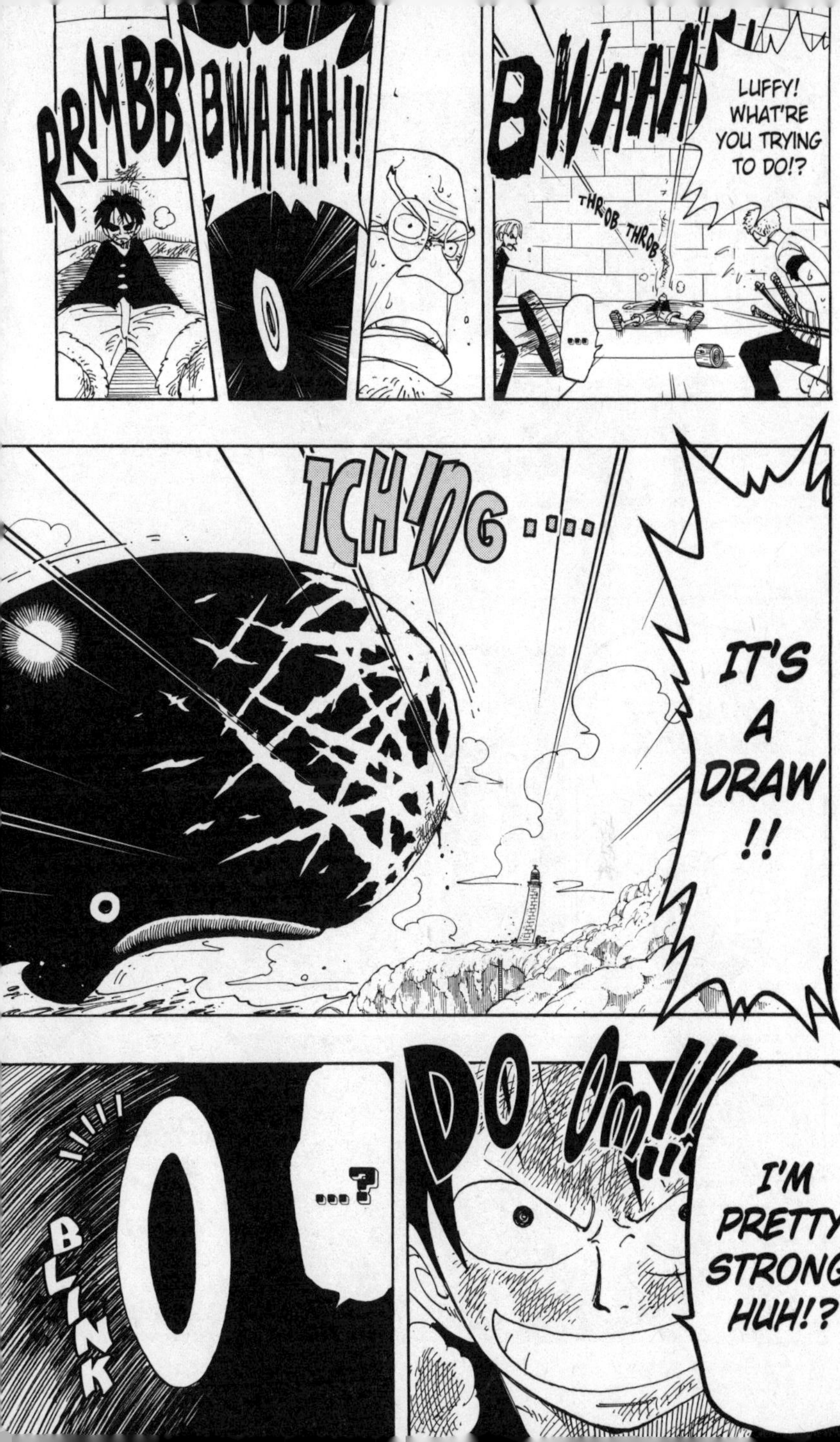
BWAAA
LUFFY! WHAT'RE YOU TRYING TO DO!?
THROB THROB
...
BWAAAH!!
RRMBB
TCHING....
IT'S A DRAW!!
DOOM!!
I'M PRETTY STRONG, HUH!?
...?
BLINK

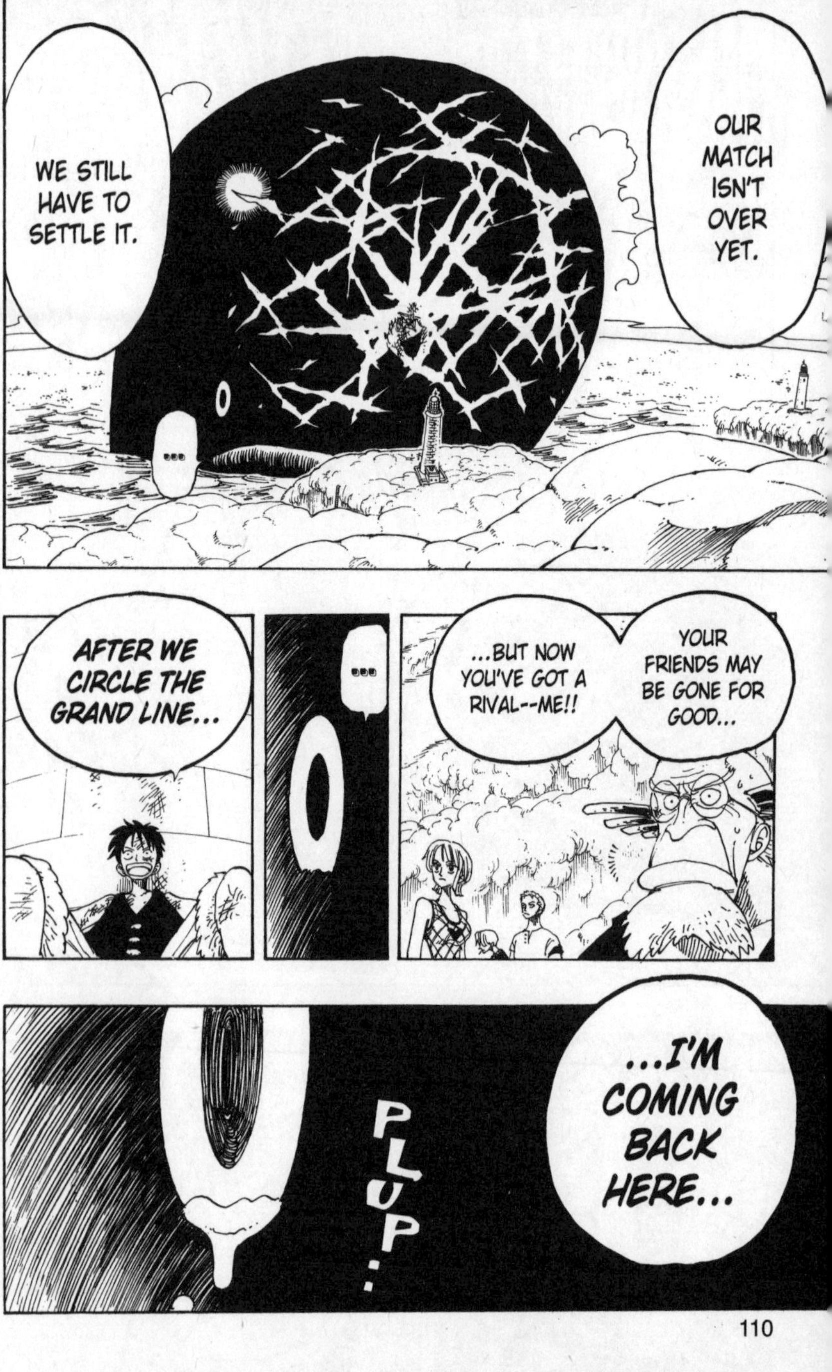
OUR MATCH ISN'T OVER YET.
WE STILL HAVE TO SETTLE IT.
...
YOUR FRIENDS MAY BE GONE FOR GOOD...
...BUT NOW YOU'VE GOT A RIVAL--ME!!
...
AFTER WE CIRCLE THE GRAND LINE...
...I'M COMING BACK HERE...
PLUP..

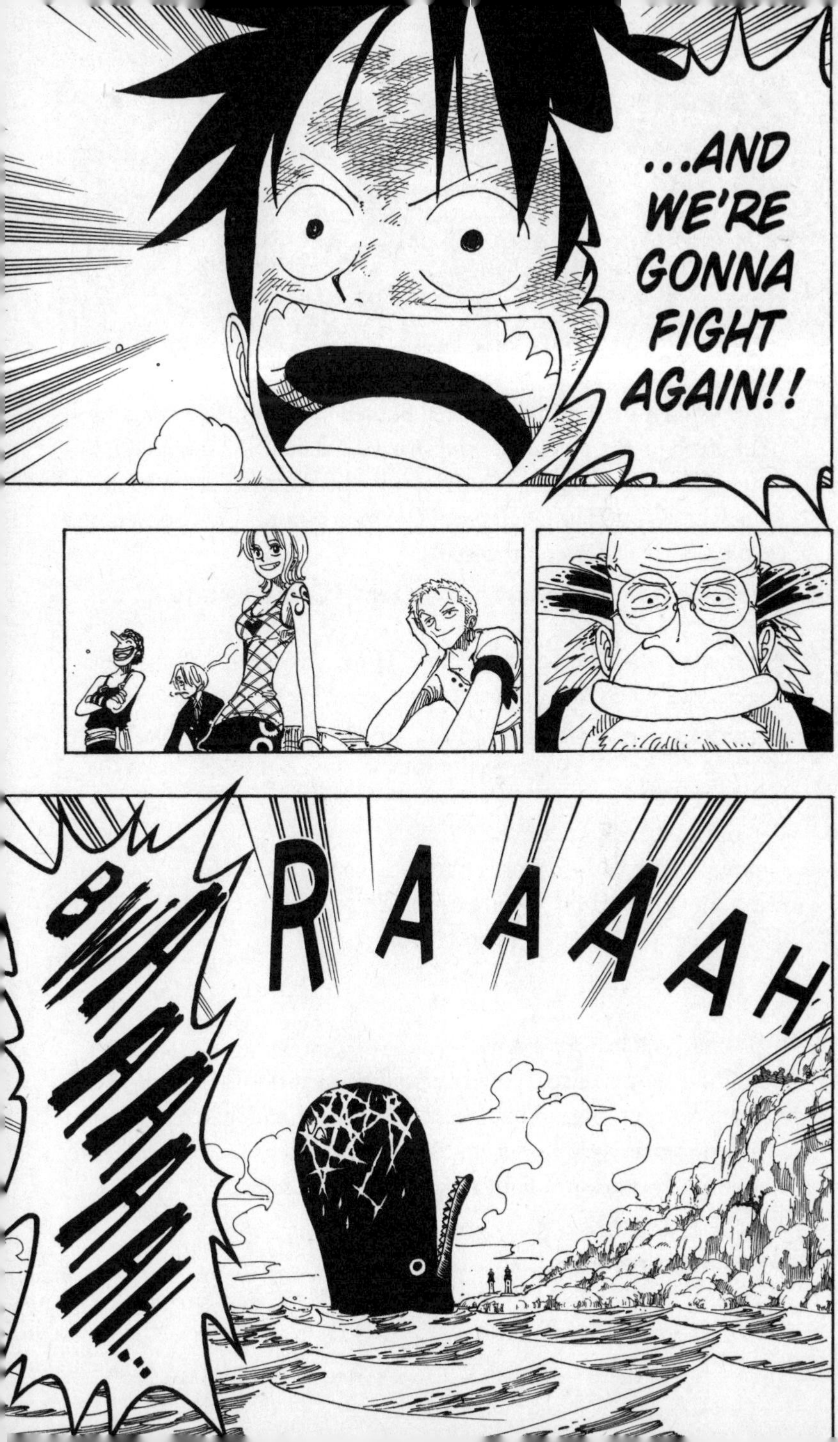
...AND WE'RE GONNA FIGHT AGAIN!!
RAAAAH
BWAAAAAAH...

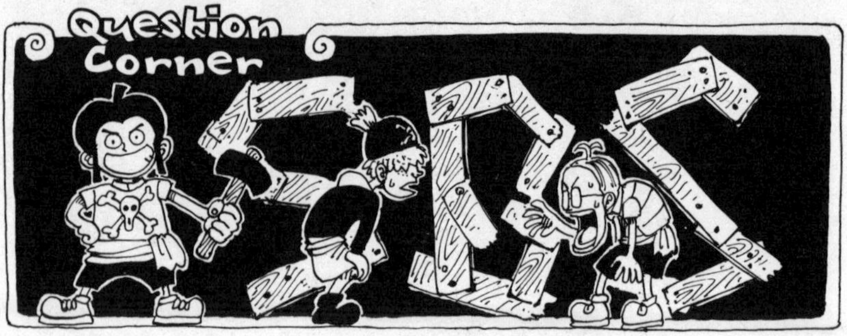
Question Corner
SBS

Q: I'm president of the International Somewhat Cool Hair Federation. Chef Zeff of the restaurant ship has cool hair color, length, and luster--all really cool!! So Chef Zeff has been chosen as the 41st Somewhat Cool Hair Champion! Congratulations! Oda Sensei, may we please have your comments!?

A: Well, I'm curious about the other 40 champions.

Q: I've mulled this over for some time. How…how can Arlong wear finger rings when he's got webbed fingers? Please tell me.

A: He sticks them right into his fingers. They're more like pierced rings than normal rings.

Q: Brrrring… Brrring… Click…
Umm…hello? Is this Mino@nta*? Listen to this… Huh? You're not Mino@nta? Huh? Oda Sensei? Oh, sorry. Wrong number… Click… Beep… Beep… Beep… Beep…

A: It's okay...

Q: (Episode I) Help, Oda Baby!
I think this guy named Yamada who lives next door is a Fish-Man! I mean, he's got gills on his face. Huh? I feel a sudden chill. Maybe I turned the air conditioner up too high. I–I sense something there... *Vwmm* (the sound of a light saber being activated).
To be continued…

A: I'm not saving you.

(*Mino@nta is a thinly disguised reference to a popular TV host in Japan who takes calls from viewers during his show. --Ed.)

Chapter 105:
LOG POSE

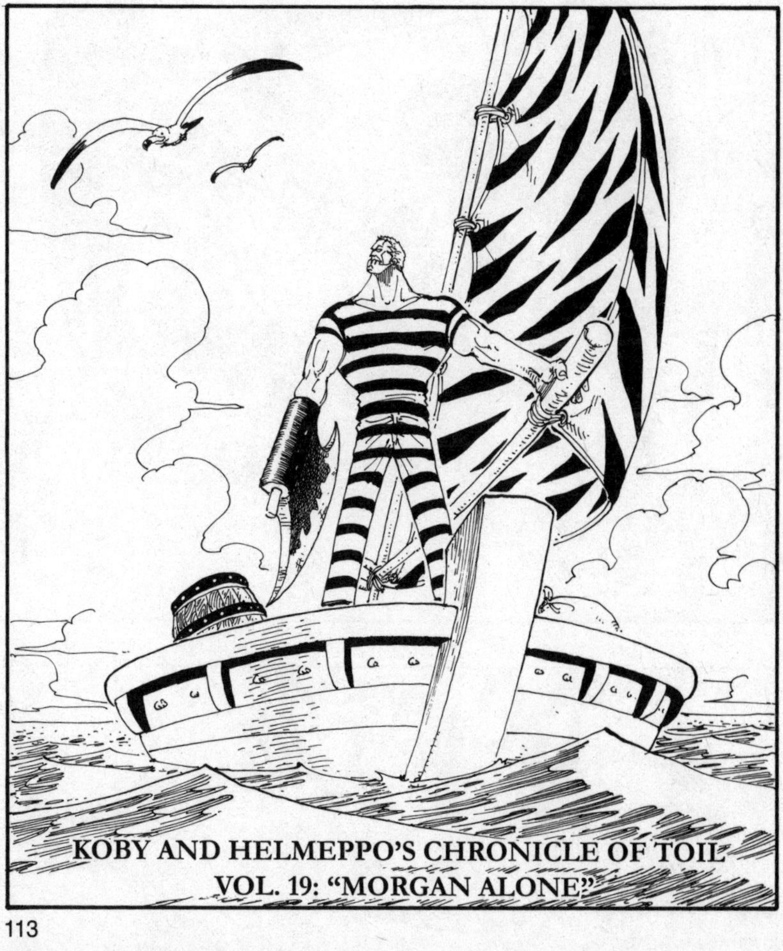
KOBY AND HELMEPPO'S CHRONICLE OF TOIL
VOL. 19: "MORGAN ALONE"

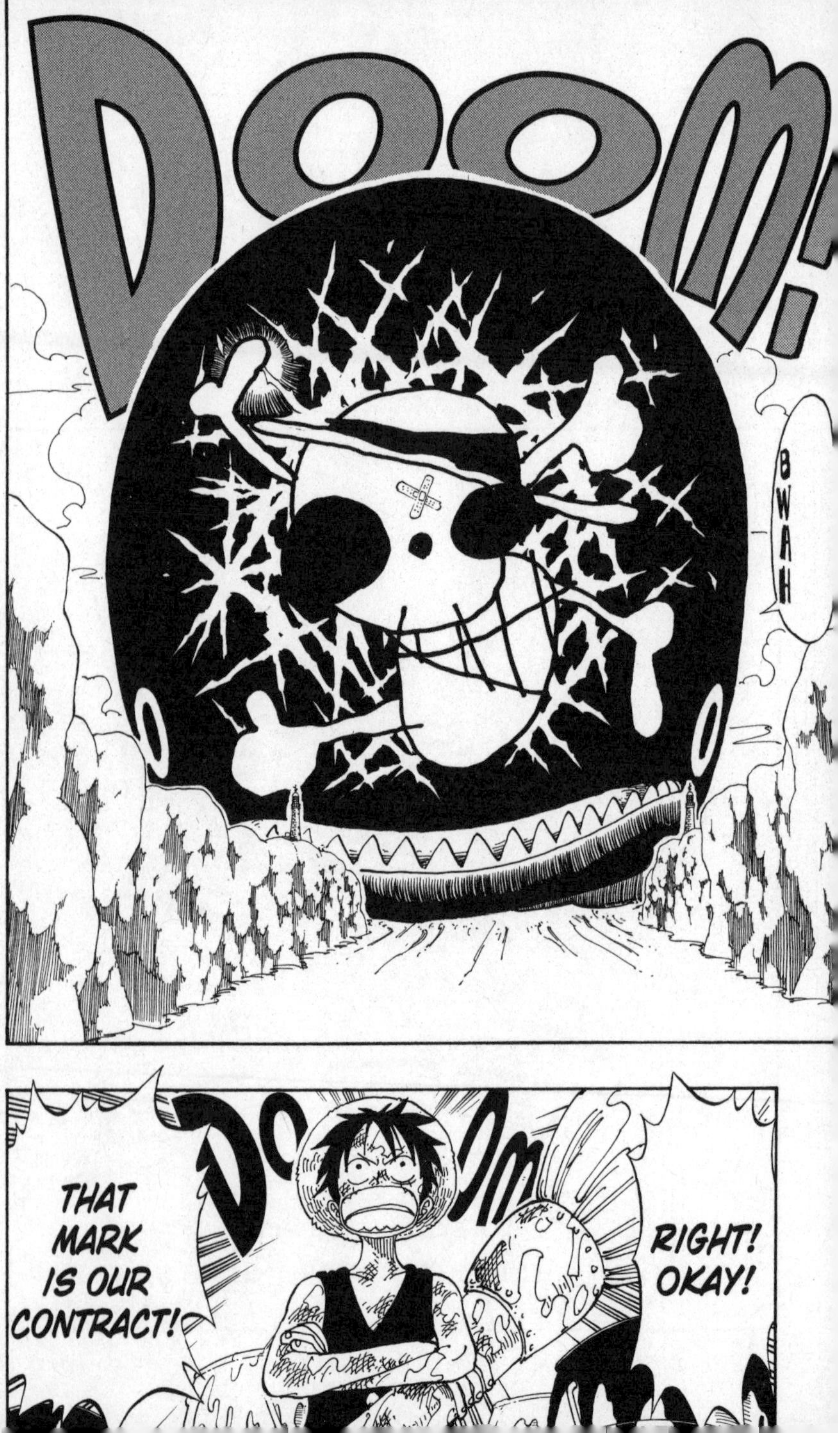
DOOM!
BWAH
DOOM
THAT MARK IS OUR CONTRACT!
RIGHT! OKAY!

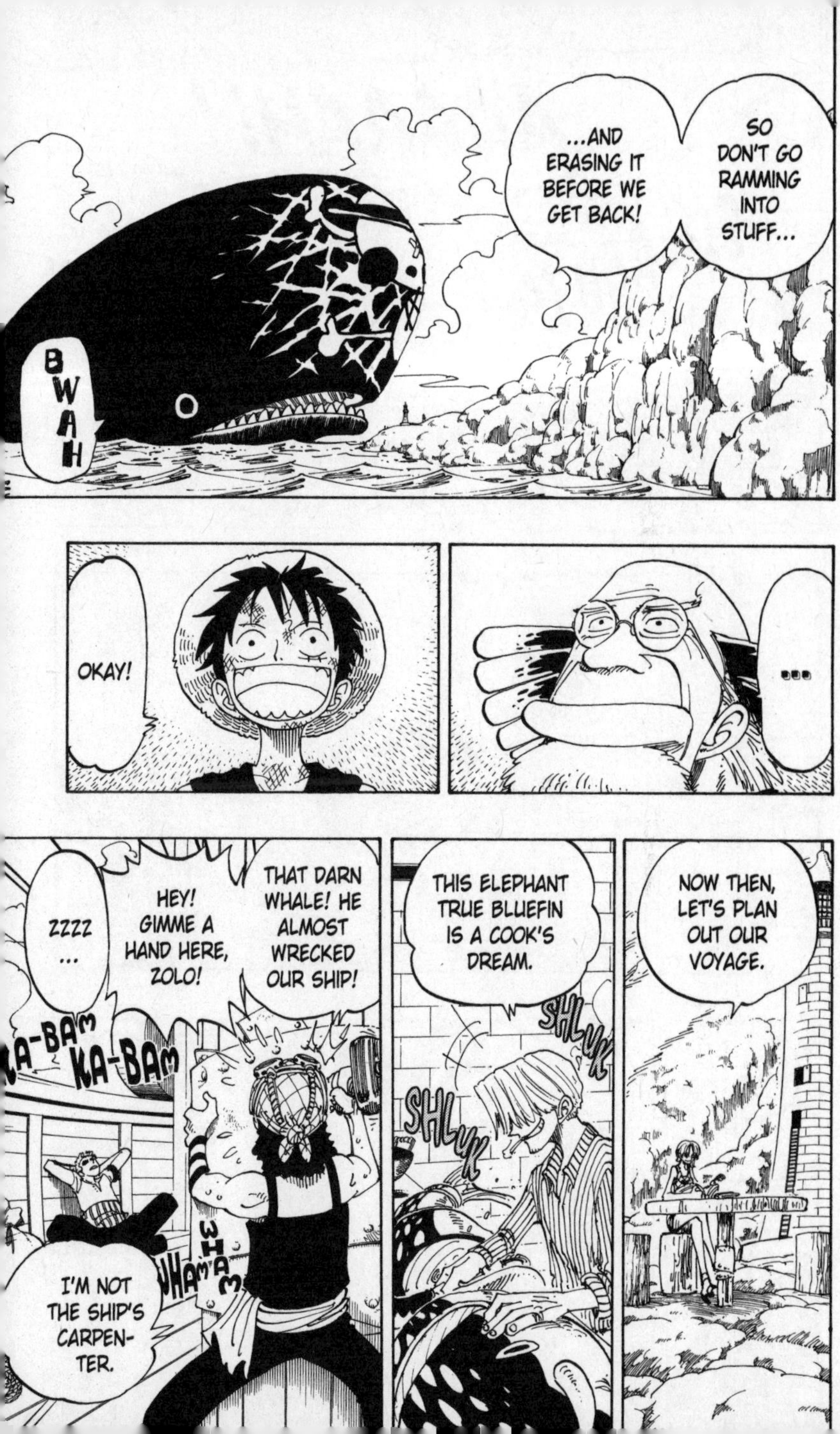
SO DON'T GO RAMMING INTO STUFF...
...AND ERASING IT BEFORE WE GET BACK!
BWAH
...
OKAY!
NOW THEN, LET'S PLAN OUT OUR VOYAGE.
THIS ELEPHANT TRUE BLUEFIN IS A COOK'S DREAM.
SHLUK
SHLUK
THAT DARN WHALE! HE ALMOST WRECKED OUR SHIP!
HEY! GIMME A HAND HERE, ZOLO!
ZZZZ ...
KA-BAM
KA-BAM
WHAM
WHAM
I'M NOT THE SHIP'S CARPENTER.

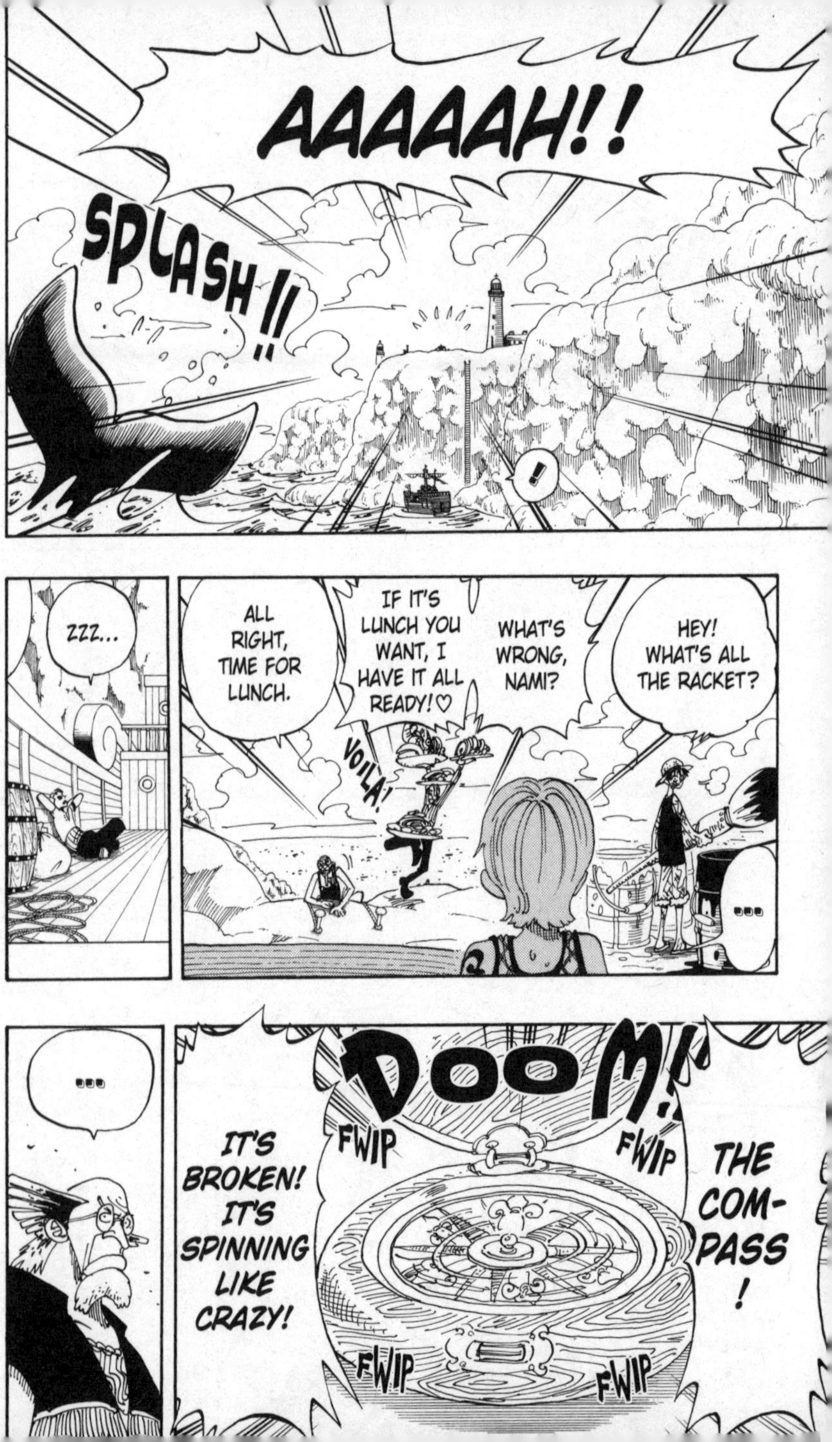
AAAAAH!!
SPLASH!!
!
HEY! WHAT'S ALL THE RACKET?
...
WHAT'S WRONG, NAMI?
IF IT'S LUNCH YOU WANT, I HAVE IT ALL READY!♡
VOILA!
ALL RIGHT, TIME FOR LUNCH.
ZZZ...
DOOM!!
THE COM-PASS!
FWIP
FWIP
IT'S BROKEN! IT'S SPINNING LIKE CRAZY!
FWIP
FWIP
...

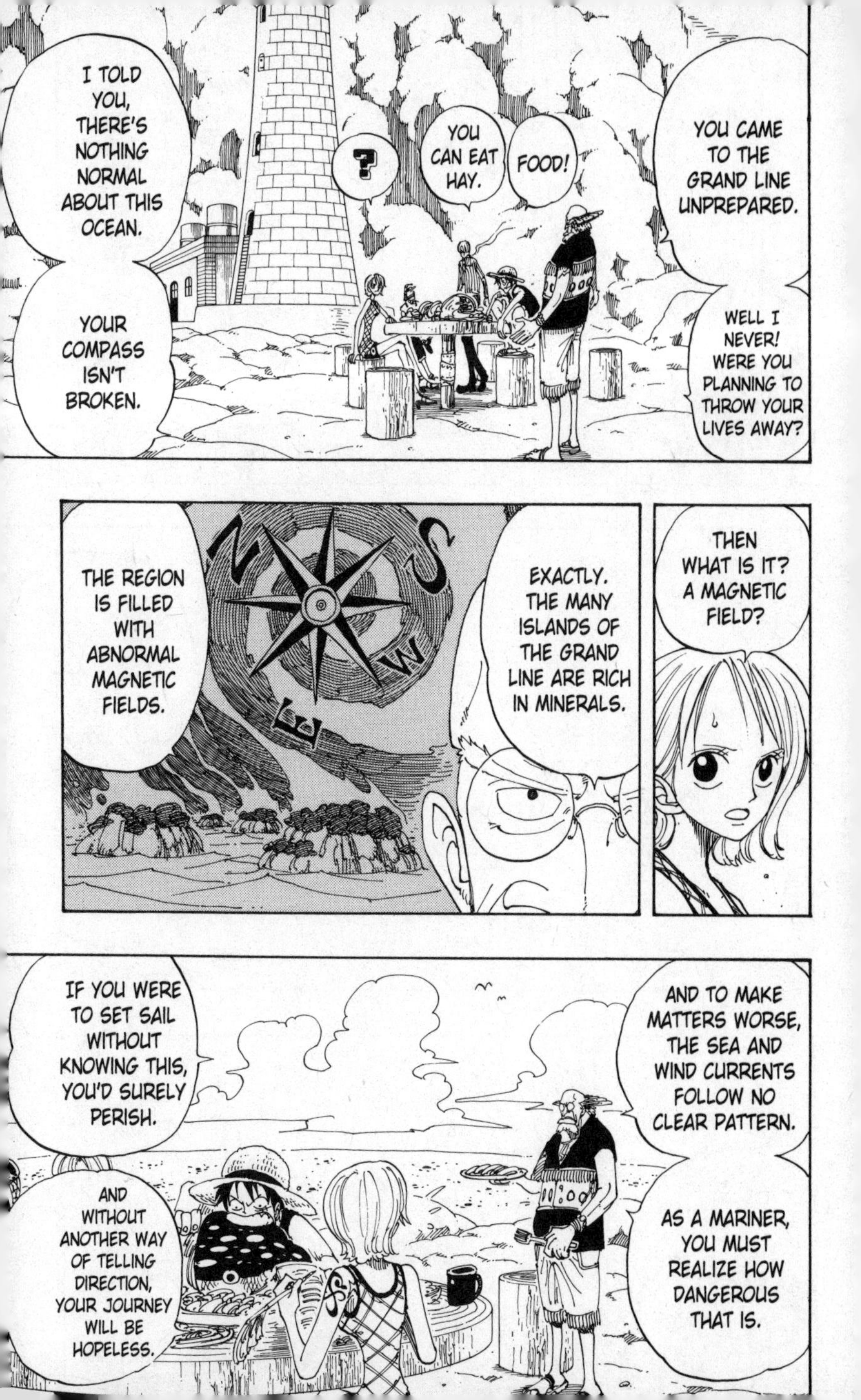
YOU CAME TO THE GRAND LINE UNPREPARED.
WELL I NEVER! WERE YOU PLANNING TO THROW YOUR LIVES AWAY?
FOOD!
YOU CAN EAT HAY.
?
I TOLD YOU, THERE'S NOTHING NORMAL ABOUT THIS OCEAN.
YOUR COMPASS ISN'T BROKEN.
THEN WHAT IS IT? A MAGNETIC FIELD?
EXACTLY. THE MANY ISLANDS OF THE GRAND LINE ARE RICH IN MINERALS.
THE REGION IS FILLED WITH ABNORMAL MAGNETIC FIELDS.
AND TO MAKE MATTERS WORSE, THE SEA AND WIND CURRENTS FOLLOW NO CLEAR PATTERN.
AS A MARINER, YOU MUST REALIZE HOW DANGEROUS THAT IS.
IF YOU WERE TO SET SAIL WITHOUT KNOWING THIS, YOU'D SURELY PERISH.
AND WITHOUT ANOTHER WAY OF TELLING DIRECTION, YOUR JOURNEY WILL BE HOPELESS.

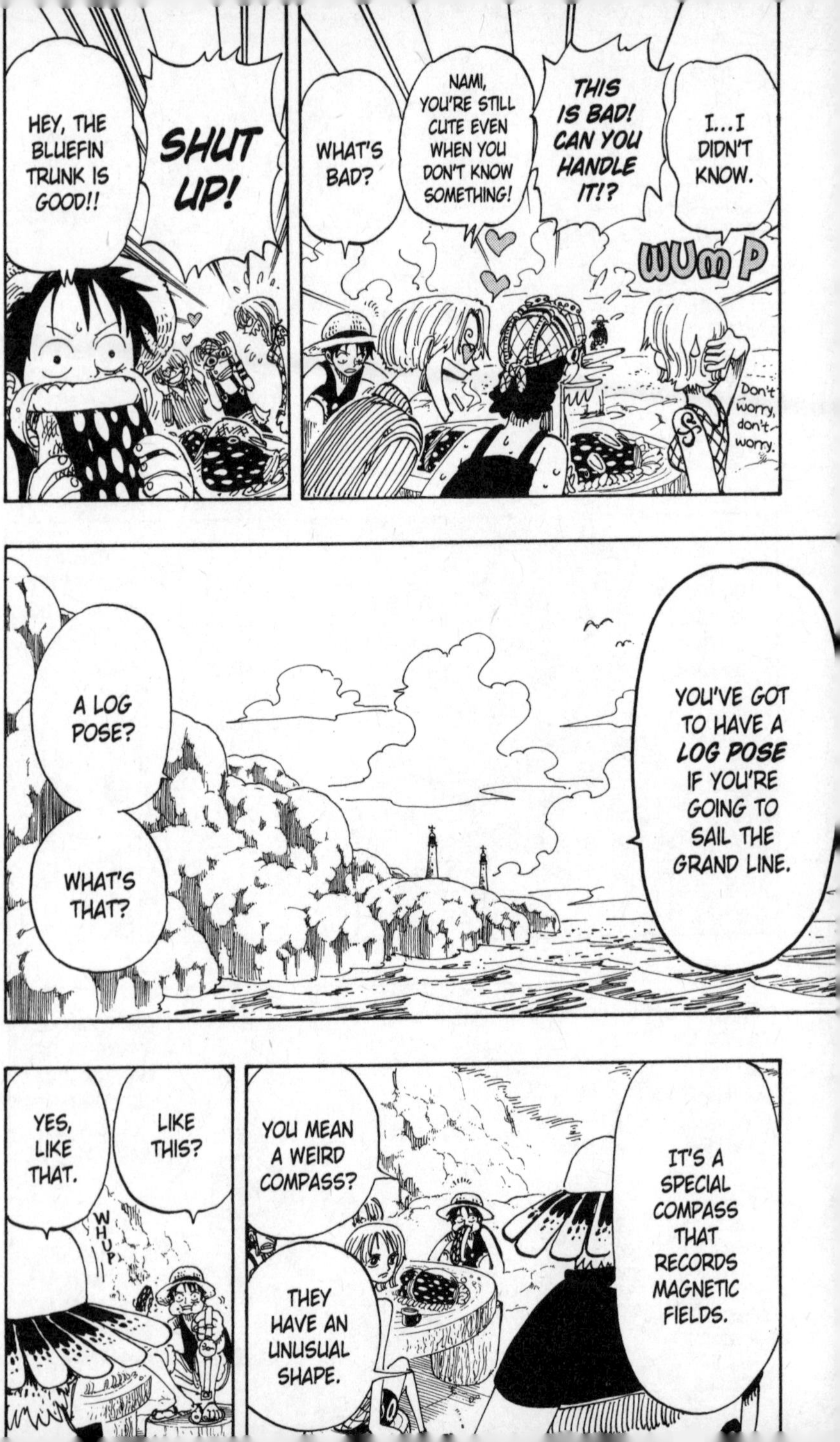
I...I DIDN'T KNOW.
THIS IS BAD! CAN YOU HANDLE IT!?
NAMI, YOU'RE STILL CUTE EVEN WHEN YOU DON'T KNOW SOMETHING!
WHAT'S BAD?
WUMP
Don't worry, don't worry.
HEY, THE BLUEFIN TRUNK IS GOOD!!
SHUT UP!
YOU'VE GOT TO HAVE A LOG POSE IF YOU'RE GOING TO SAIL THE GRAND LINE.
A LOG POSE?
WHAT'S THAT?
IT'S A SPECIAL COMPASS THAT RECORDS MAGNETIC FIELDS.
YOU MEAN A WEIRD COMPASS?
THEY HAVE AN UNUSUAL SHAPE.
LIKE THIS?
YES, LIKE THAT.
WHUP

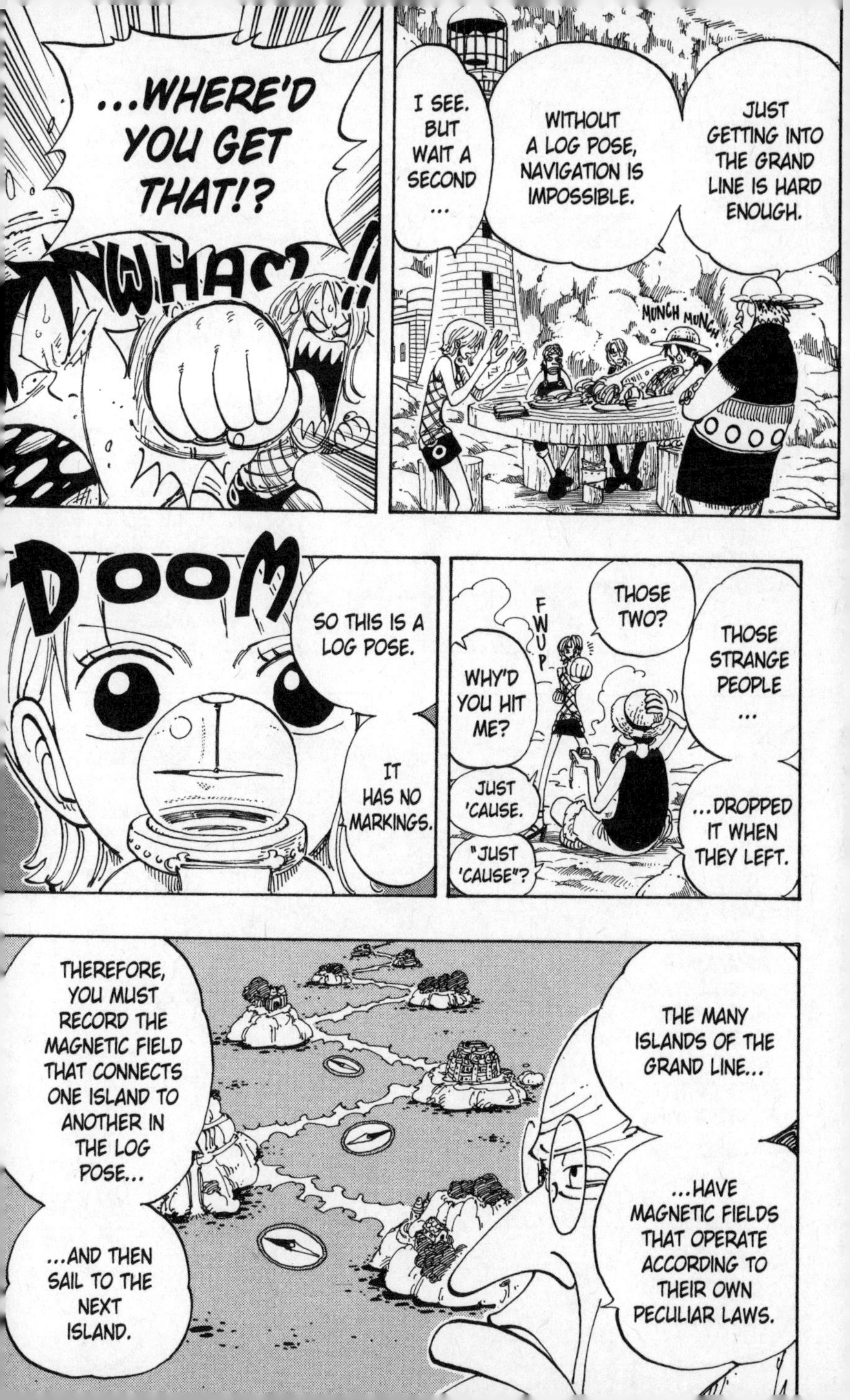
JUST GETTING INTO THE GRAND LINE IS HARD ENOUGH.
WITHOUT A LOG POSE, NAVIGATION IS IMPOSSIBLE.
I SEE. BUT WAIT A SECOND ...
MUNCH MUNCH
...WHERE'D YOU GET THAT!?
WHAM!!
THOSE STRANGE PEOPLE ...
...DROPPED IT WHEN THEY LEFT.
THOSE TWO?
FWUP
WHY'D YOU HIT ME?
JUST 'CAUSE.
"JUST 'CAUSE"?
DOOM
SO THIS IS A LOG POSE.
IT HAS NO MARKINGS.
THE MANY ISLANDS OF THE GRAND LINE...
...HAVE MAGNETIC FIELDS THAT OPERATE ACCORDING TO THEIR OWN PECULIAR LAWS.
THEREFORE, YOU MUST RECORD THE MAGNETIC FIELD THAT CONNECTS ONE ISLAND TO ANOTHER IN THE LOG POSE...
...AND THEN SAIL TO THE NEXT ISLAND.

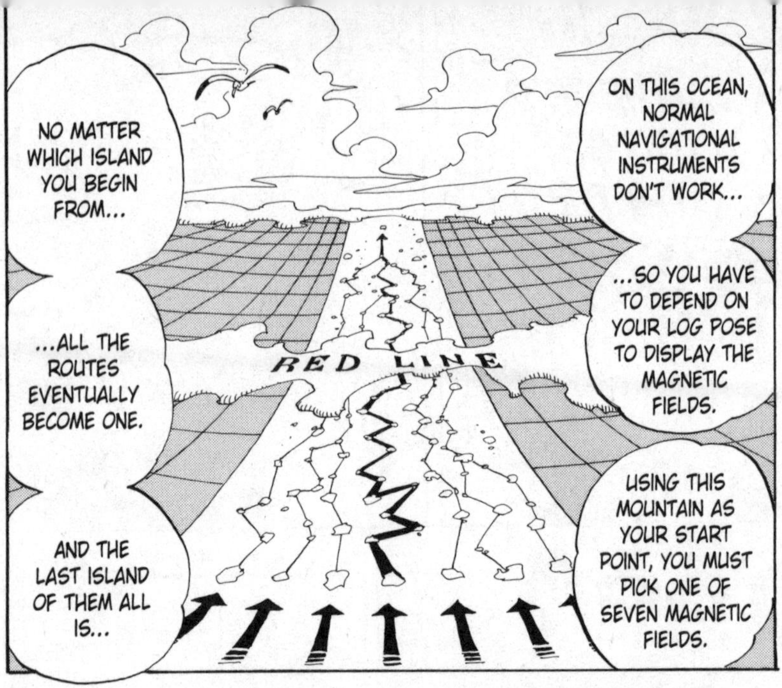
ON THIS OCEAN, NORMAL NAVIGATIONAL INSTRUMENTS DON'T WORK...
...SO YOU HAVE TO DEPEND ON YOUR LOG POSE TO DISPLAY THE MAGNETIC FIELDS.
USING THIS MOUNTAIN AS YOUR START POINT, YOU MUST PICK ONE OF SEVEN MAGNETIC FIELDS.
RED LINE
NO MATTER WHICH ISLAND YOU BEGIN FROM...
...ALL THE ROUTES EVENTUALLY BECOME ONE.
AND THE LAST ISLAND OF THEM ALL IS...

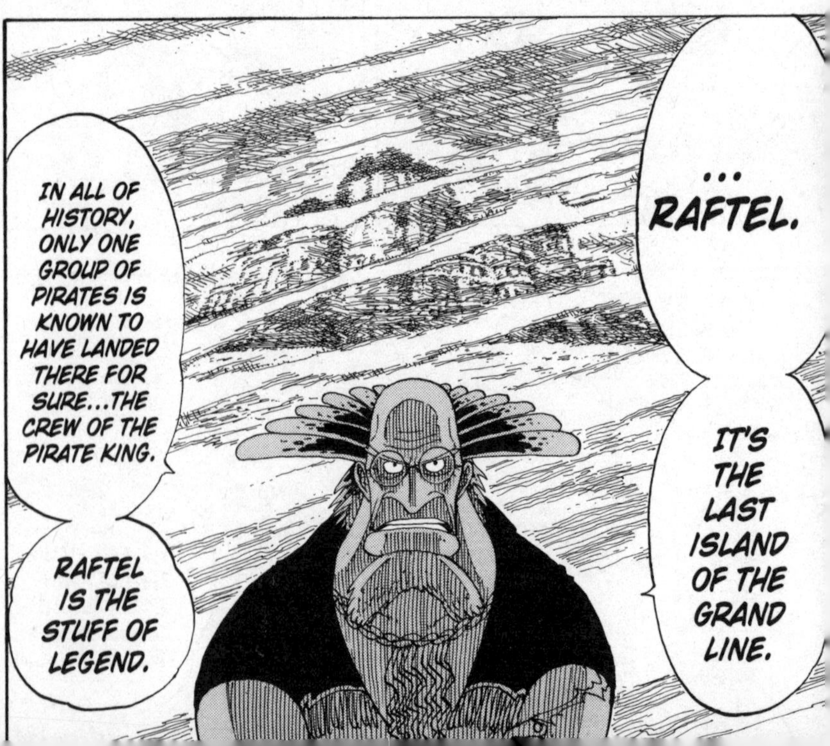
... RAFTEL.
IT'S THE LAST ISLAND OF THE GRAND LINE.
IN ALL OF HISTORY, ONLY ONE GROUP OF PIRATES IS KNOWN TO HAVE LANDED THERE FOR SURE...THE CREW OF THE PIRATE KING.
RAFTEL IS THE STUFF OF LEGEND.

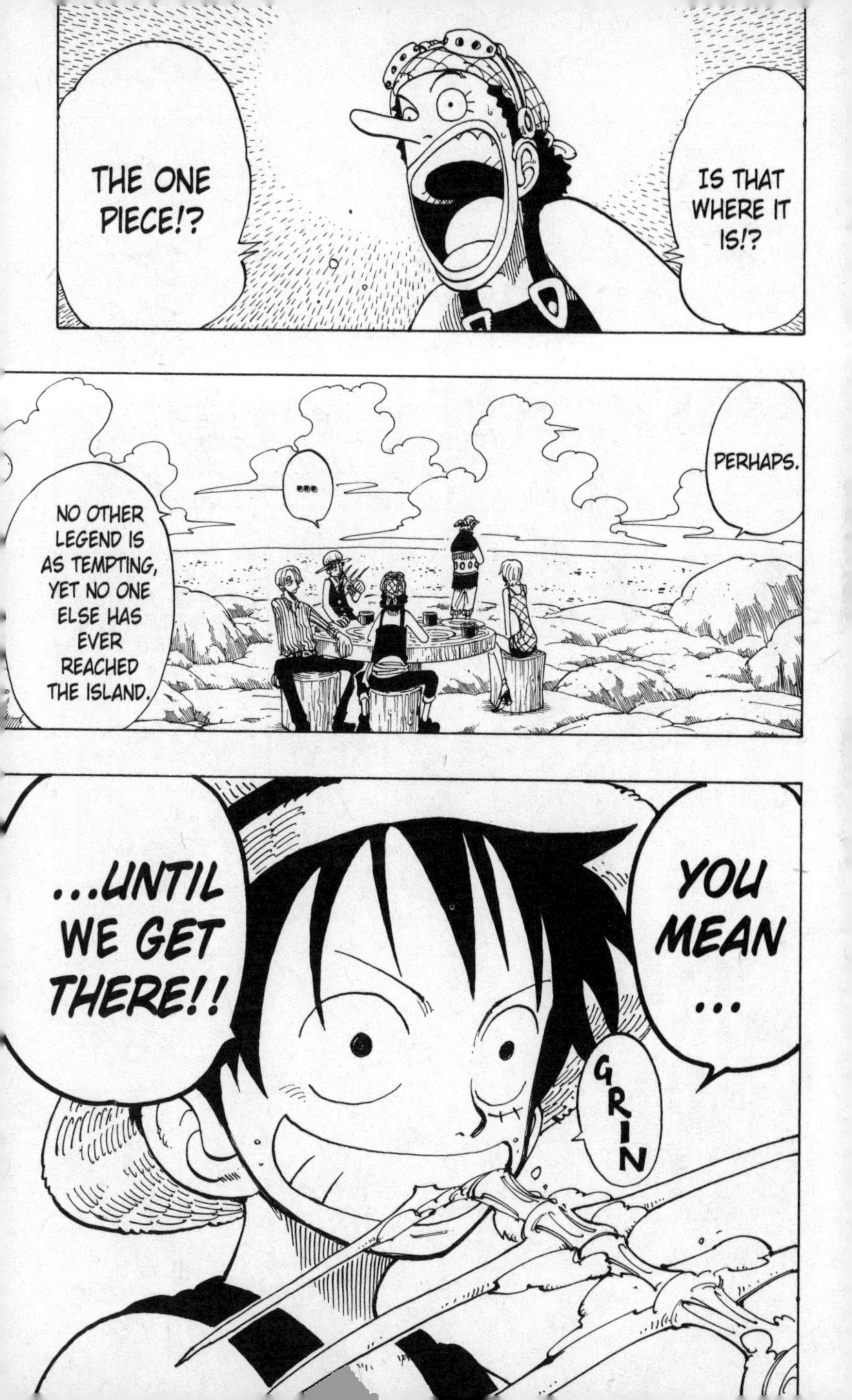
IS THAT WHERE IT IS!?
THE ONE PIECE!?
PERHAPS.
...
NO OTHER LEGEND IS AS TEMPTING, YET NO ONE ELSE HAS EVER REACHED THE ISLAND.
YOU MEAN...
GRIN
...UNTIL WE GET THERE!!

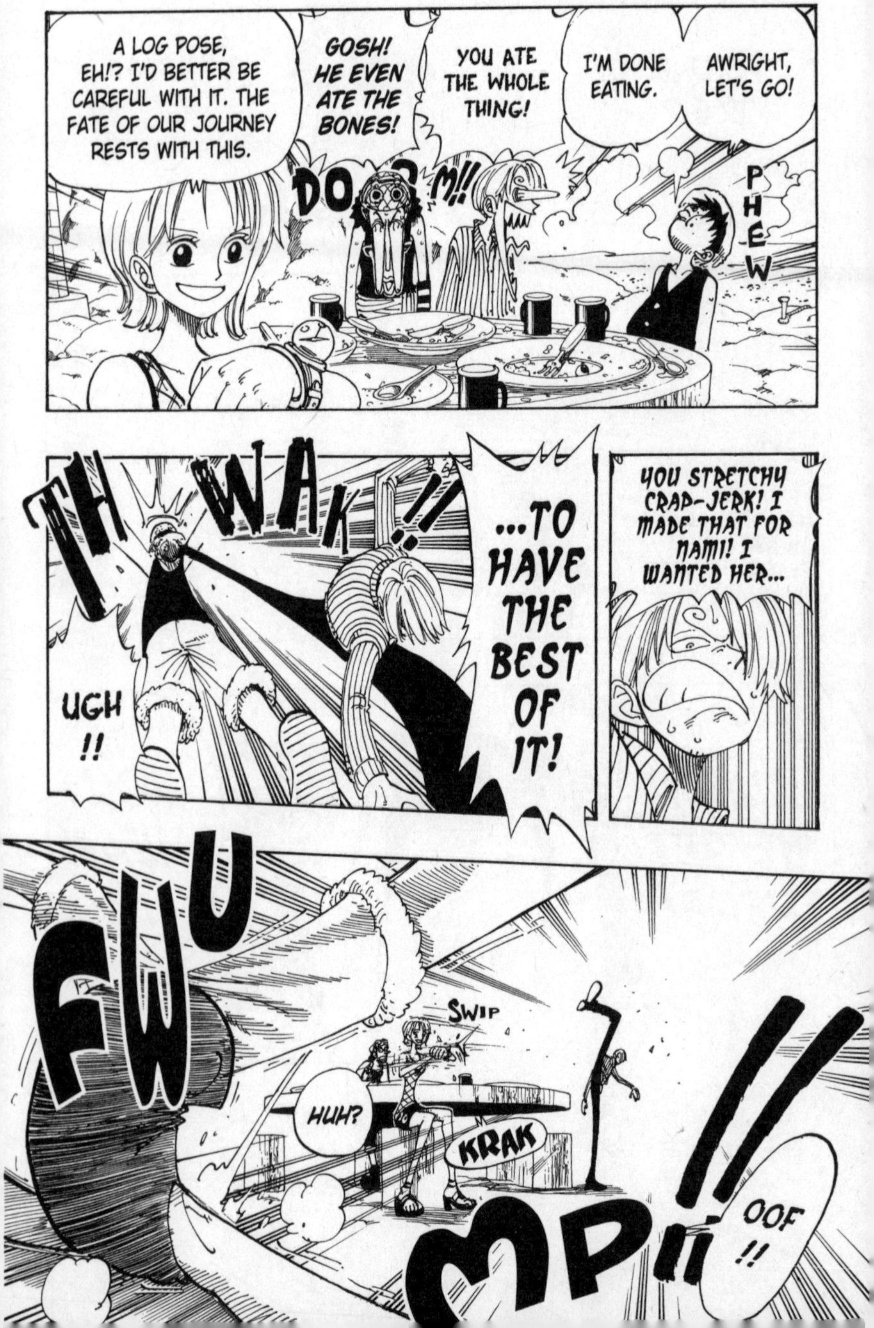
AWRIGHT, LET'S GO!
I'M DONE EATING.
PHEW
YOU ATE THE WHOLE THING!
GOSH! HE EVEN ATE THE BONES!
DO M!!
A LOG POSE, EH!? I'D BETTER BE CAREFUL WITH IT. THE FATE OF OUR JOURNEY RESTS WITH THIS.
YOU STRETCHY CRAP-JERK! I MADE THAT FOR NAMI! I WANTED HER...
...TO HAVE THE BEST OF IT!
THWAK!!
UGH!!
OOF!!
SWIP
KRAK
HUH?
FWU
MP!!

READ THIS WAY

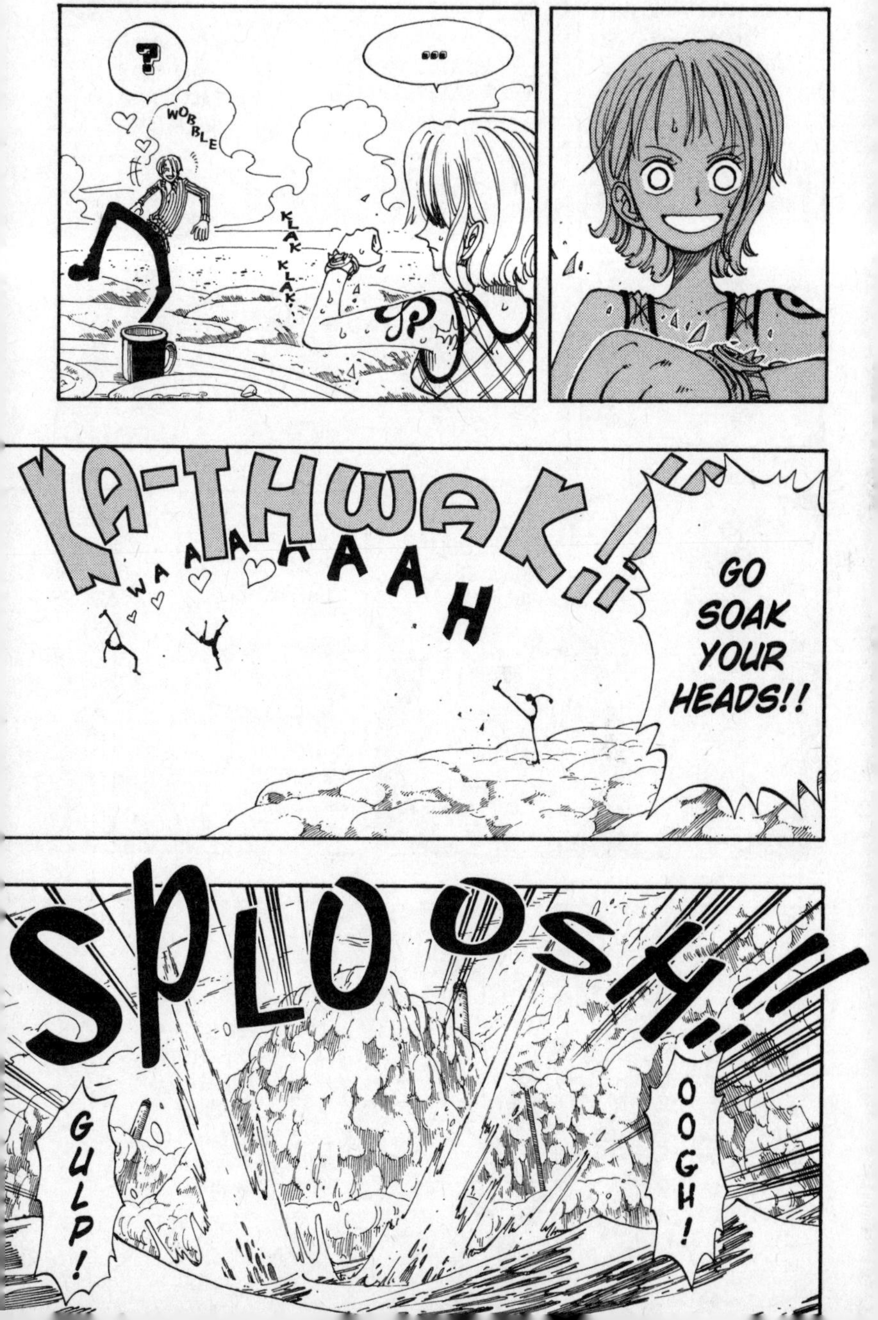
...
?
WOBBLE
KLAK KLAK...
KA-THWAK!!
GO SOAK YOUR HEADS!!
WAAAAAAH
SPLOOSH!!
OOGH!
GULP!

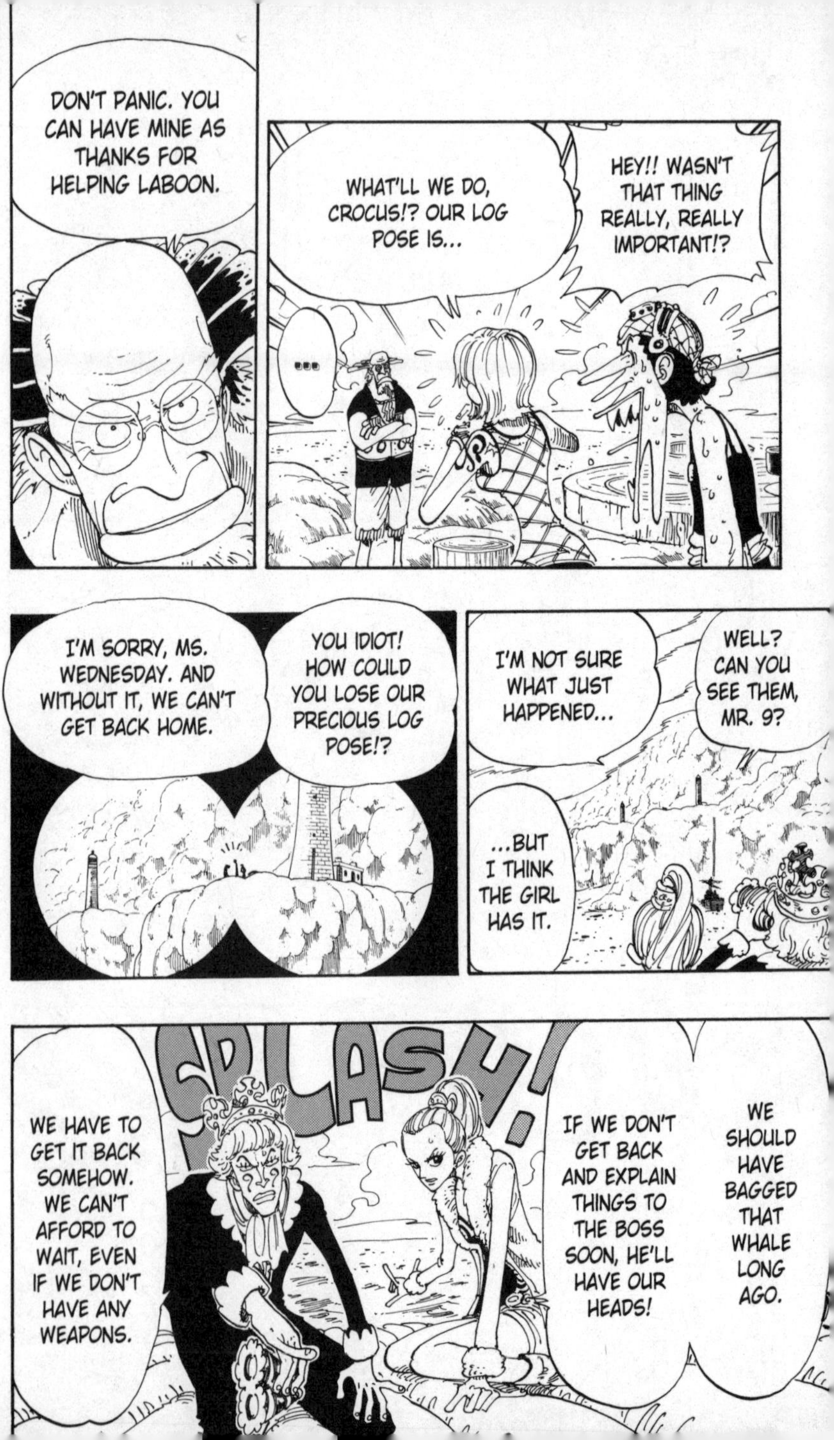
HEY!! WASN'T THAT THING REALLY, REALLY IMPORTANT!?
WHAT'LL WE DO, CROCUS!? OUR LOG POSE IS...
...
DON'T PANIC. YOU CAN HAVE MINE AS THANKS FOR HELPING LABOON.
WELL? CAN YOU SEE THEM, MR. 9?
I'M NOT SURE WHAT JUST HAPPENED...
...BUT I THINK THE GIRL HAS IT.
YOU IDIOT! HOW COULD YOU LOSE OUR PRECIOUS LOG POSE!?
I'M SORRY, MS. WEDNESDAY. AND WITHOUT IT, WE CAN'T GET BACK HOME.
SPLASH!
WE SHOULD HAVE BAGGED THAT WHALE LONG AGO.
IF WE DON'T GET BACK AND EXPLAIN THINGS TO THE BOSS SOON, HE'LL HAVE OUR HEADS!
WE HAVE TO GET IT BACK SOMEHOW. WE CAN'T AFFORD TO WAIT, EVEN IF WE DON'T HAVE ANY WEAPONS.

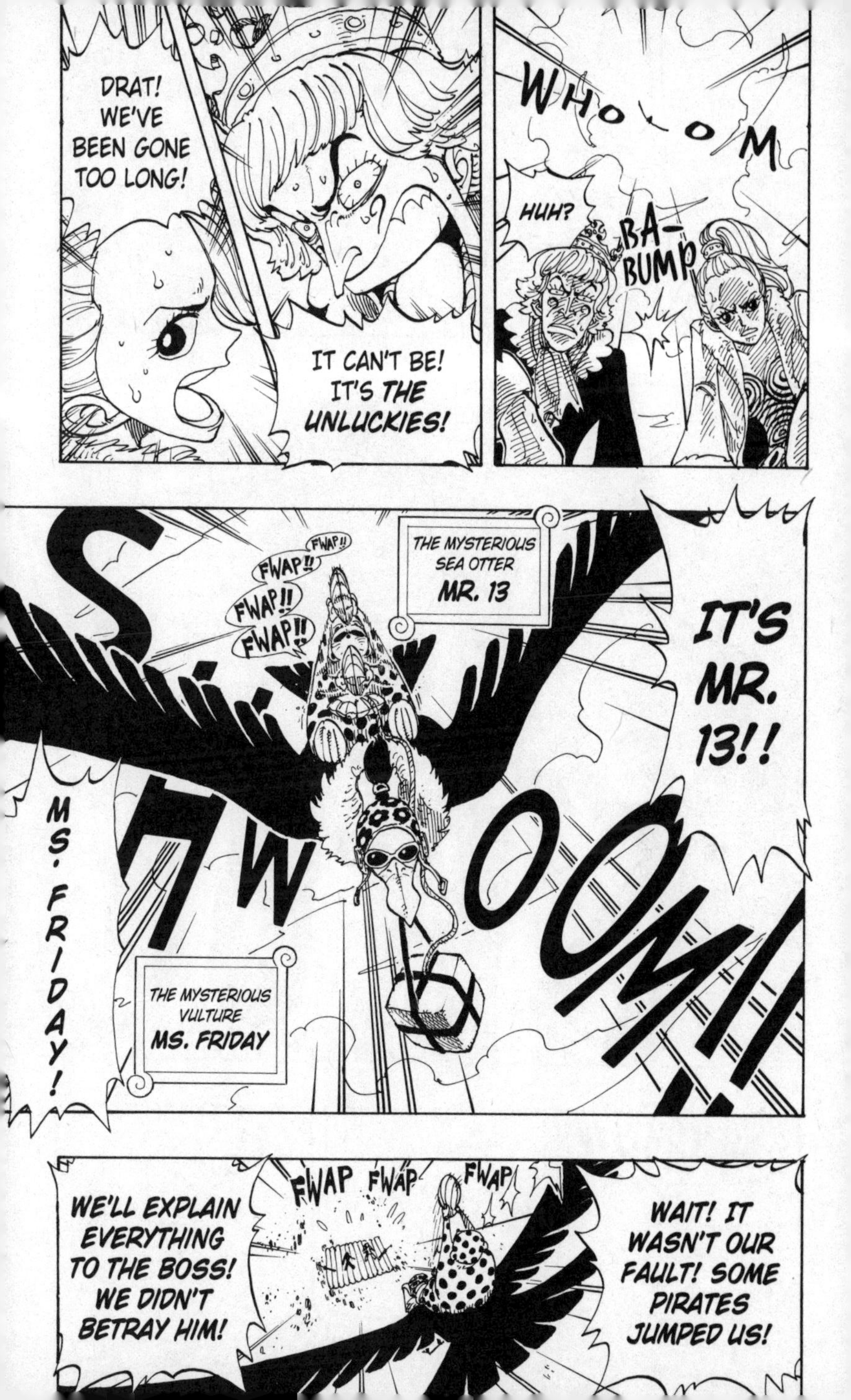
WHOOOM
HUH?
BA-BUMP
DRAT! WE'VE BEEN GONE TOO LONG!
IT CAN'T BE! IT'S THE UNLUCKIES!
SHWOOM
IT'S MR. 13!!
THE MYSTERIOUS SEA OTTER MR. 13
FWAP!!
FWAP!!
FWAP!!
FWAP!!
MS. FRIDAY!
THE MYSTERIOUS VULTURE MS. FRIDAY
WAIT! IT WASN'T OUR FAULT! SOME PIRATES JUMPED US!
FWAP FWAP FWAP
WE'LL EXPLAIN EVERYTHING TO THE BOSS! WE DIDN'T BETRAY HIM!

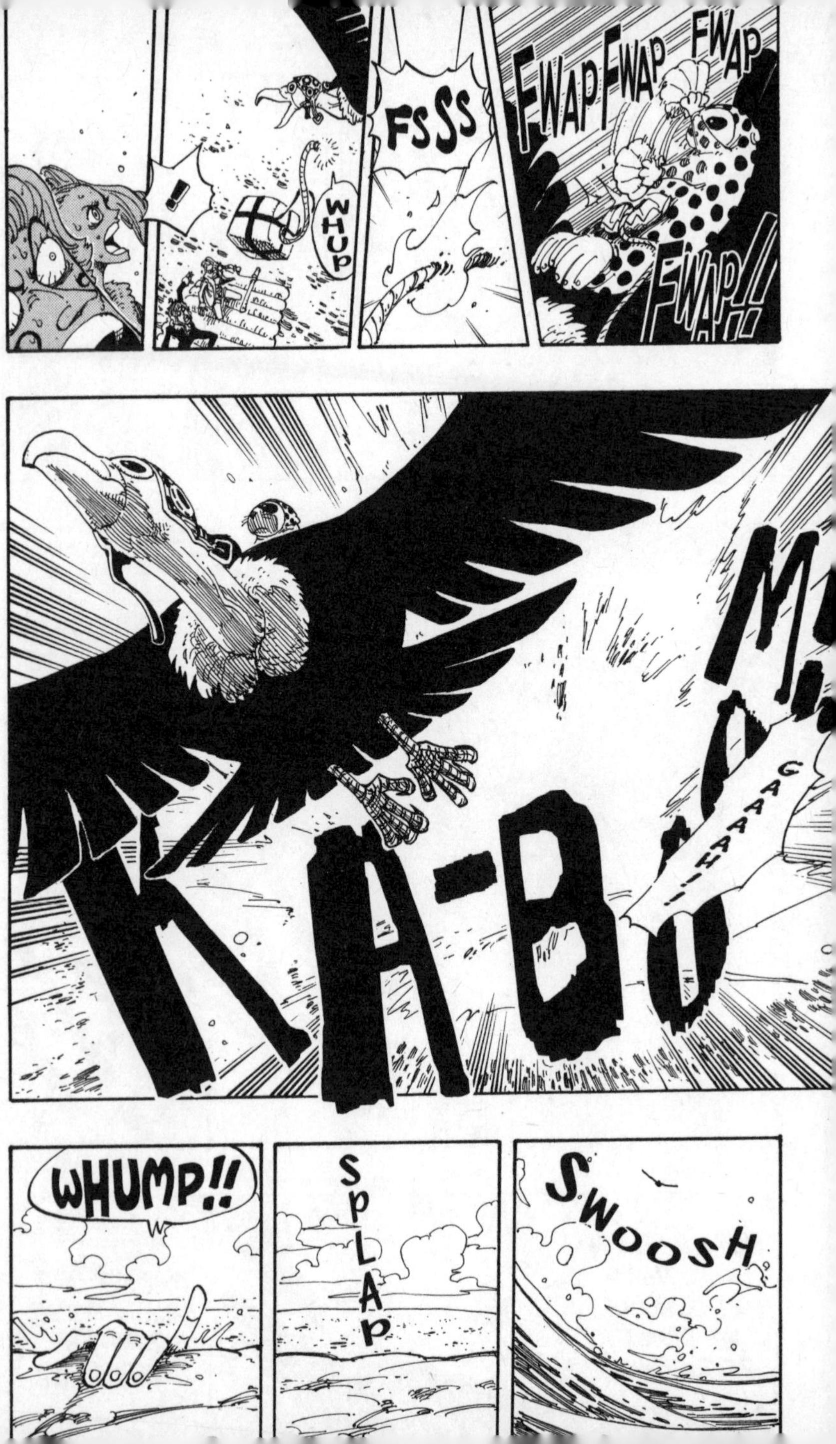
FWAP FWAP FWAP
FWAP!!
FSSS
WHUP
!
KA-BOOM
GAAAAH!!
SWOOSH
SPLAP
WHUMP!!

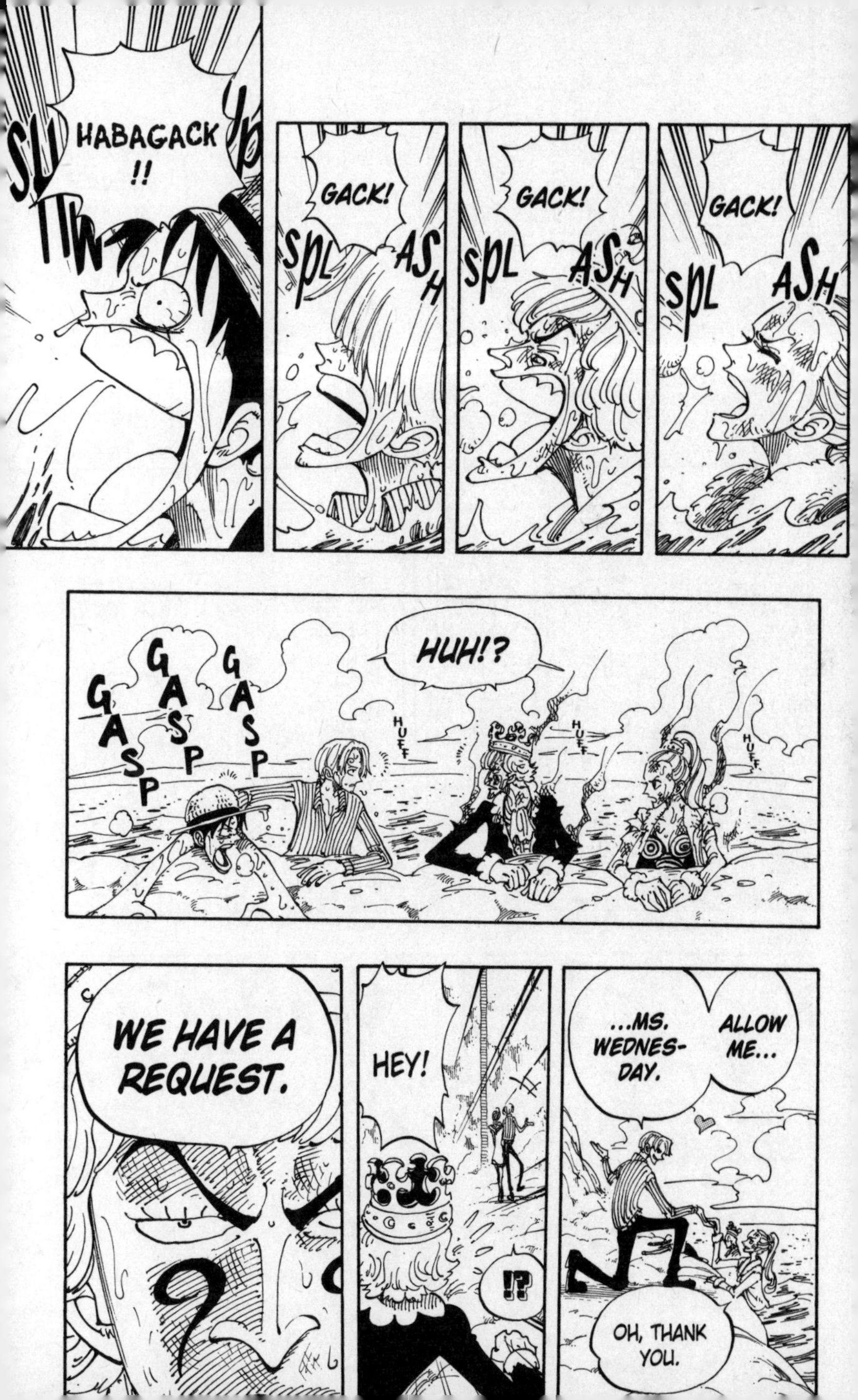
GACK!
SPLASH
GACK!
SPLASH
GACK!
SPLASH
HABAGACK !!
HUFF
HUFF
HUH!?
HUFF
GASP
GASP
GASP
ALLOW ME...
...MS. WEDNES-DAY.
OH, THANK YOU.
HEY!
!?
WE HAVE A REQUEST.

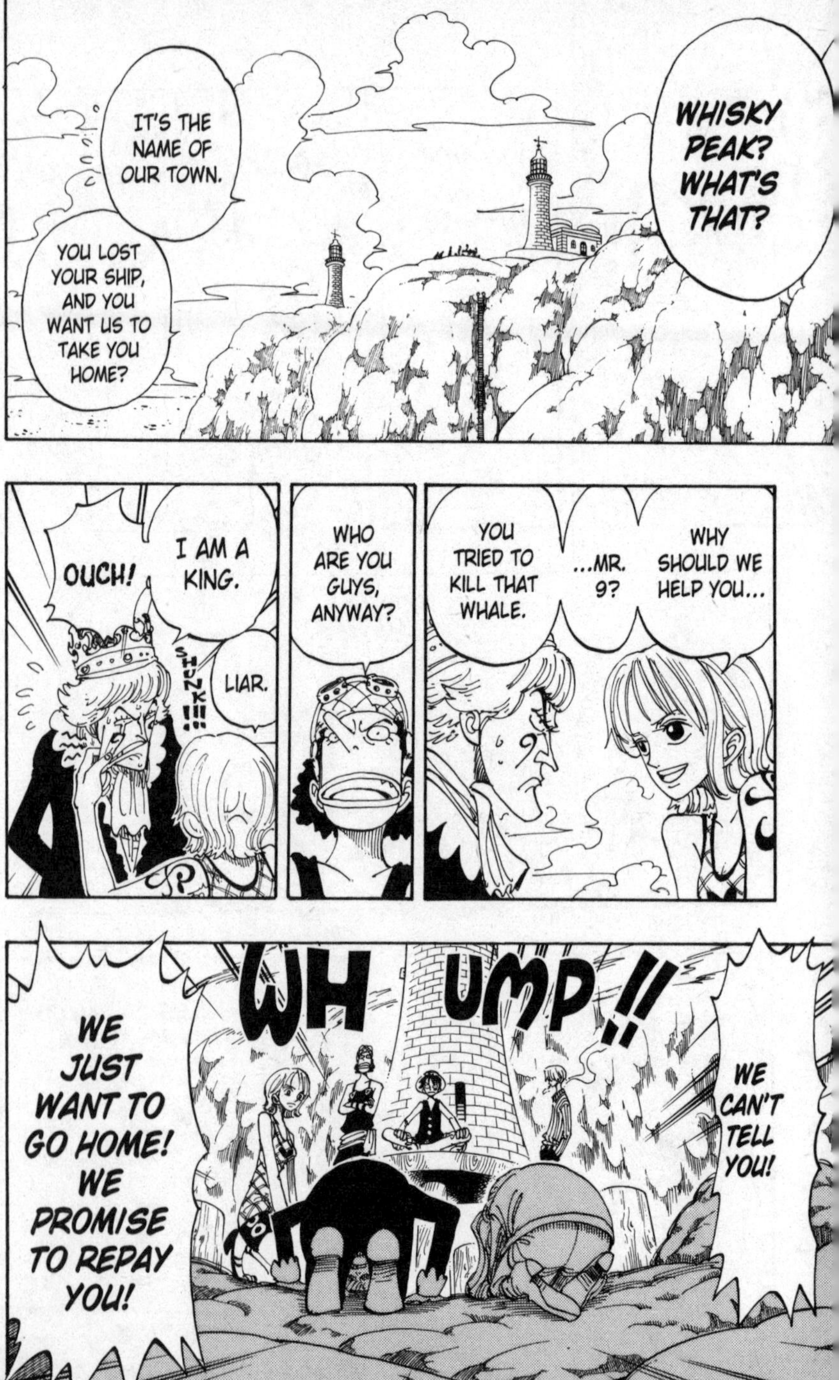

WHISKY PEAK? WHAT'S THAT?
IT'S THE NAME OF OUR TOWN.
YOU LOST YOUR SHIP, AND YOU WANT US TO TAKE YOU HOME?
WHY SHOULD WE HELP YOU...
...MR. 9?
YOU TRIED TO KILL THAT WHALE.
WHO ARE YOU GUYS, ANYWAY?
I AM A KING.
OUCH!
SHUNK!!!
LIAR.
WHUMP!!
WE CAN'T TELL YOU!
WE JUST WANT TO GO HOME! WE PROMISE TO REPAY YOU!

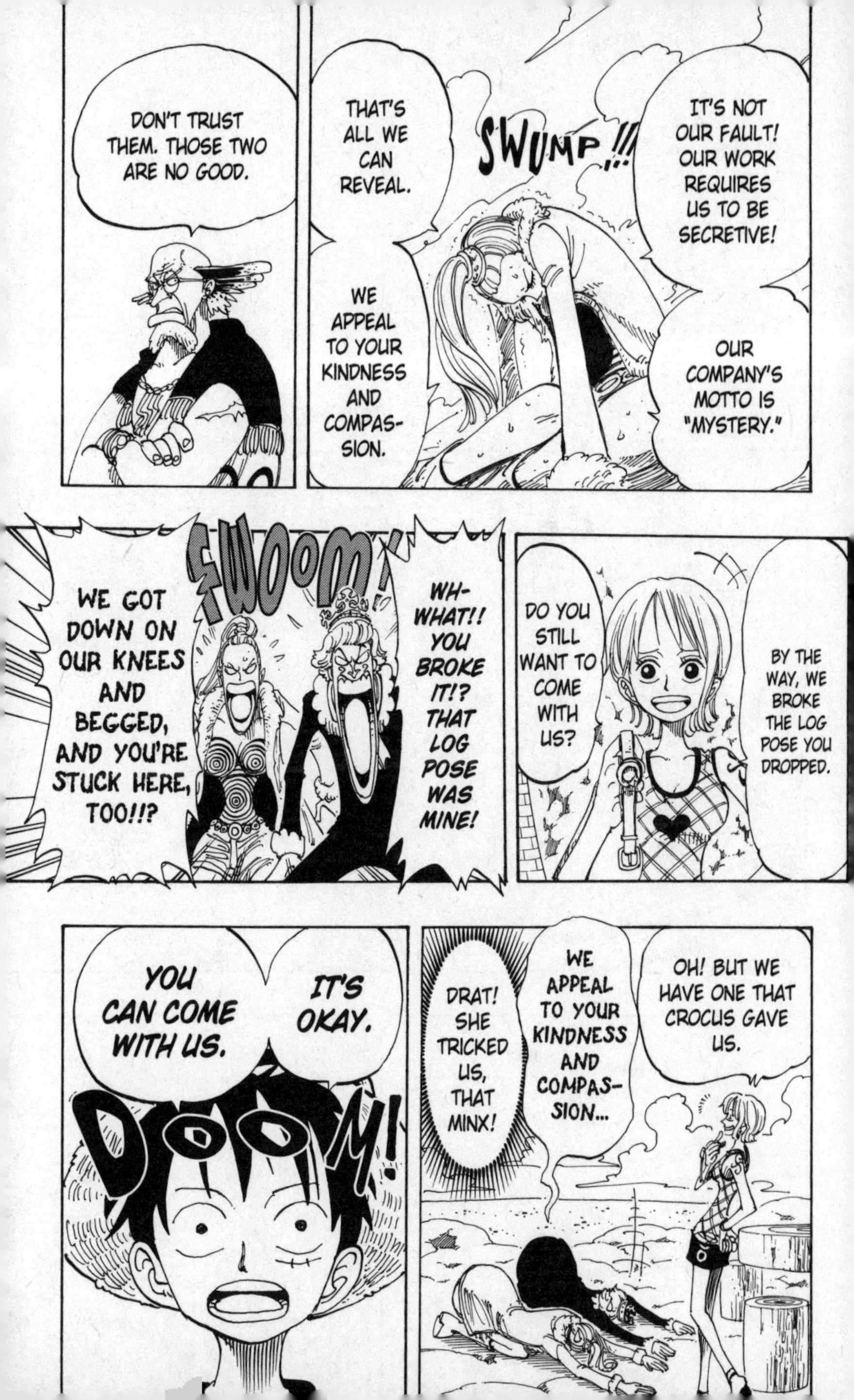
IT'S NOT OUR FAULT! OUR WORK REQUIRES US TO BE SECRETIVE!
SWUMP!!!
OUR COMPANY'S MOTTO IS "MYSTERY."
THAT'S ALL WE CAN REVEAL.
WE APPEAL TO YOUR KINDNESS AND COMPAS-SION.
DON'T TRUST THEM. THOSE TWO ARE NO GOOD.
BY THE WAY, WE BROKE THE LOG POSE YOU DROPPED.
DO YOU STILL WANT TO COME WITH US?
WH-WHAT!! YOU BROKE IT!? THAT LOG POSE WAS MINE!
FWOOM!
WE GOT DOWN ON OUR KNEES AND BEGGED, AND YOU'RE STUCK HERE, TOO!!?
OH! BUT WE HAVE ONE THAT CROCUS GAVE US.
WE APPEAL TO YOUR KINDNESS AND COMPAS-SION...
DRAT! SHE TRICKED US, THAT MINX!
IT'S OKAY.
YOU CAN COME WITH US.
DOOM!

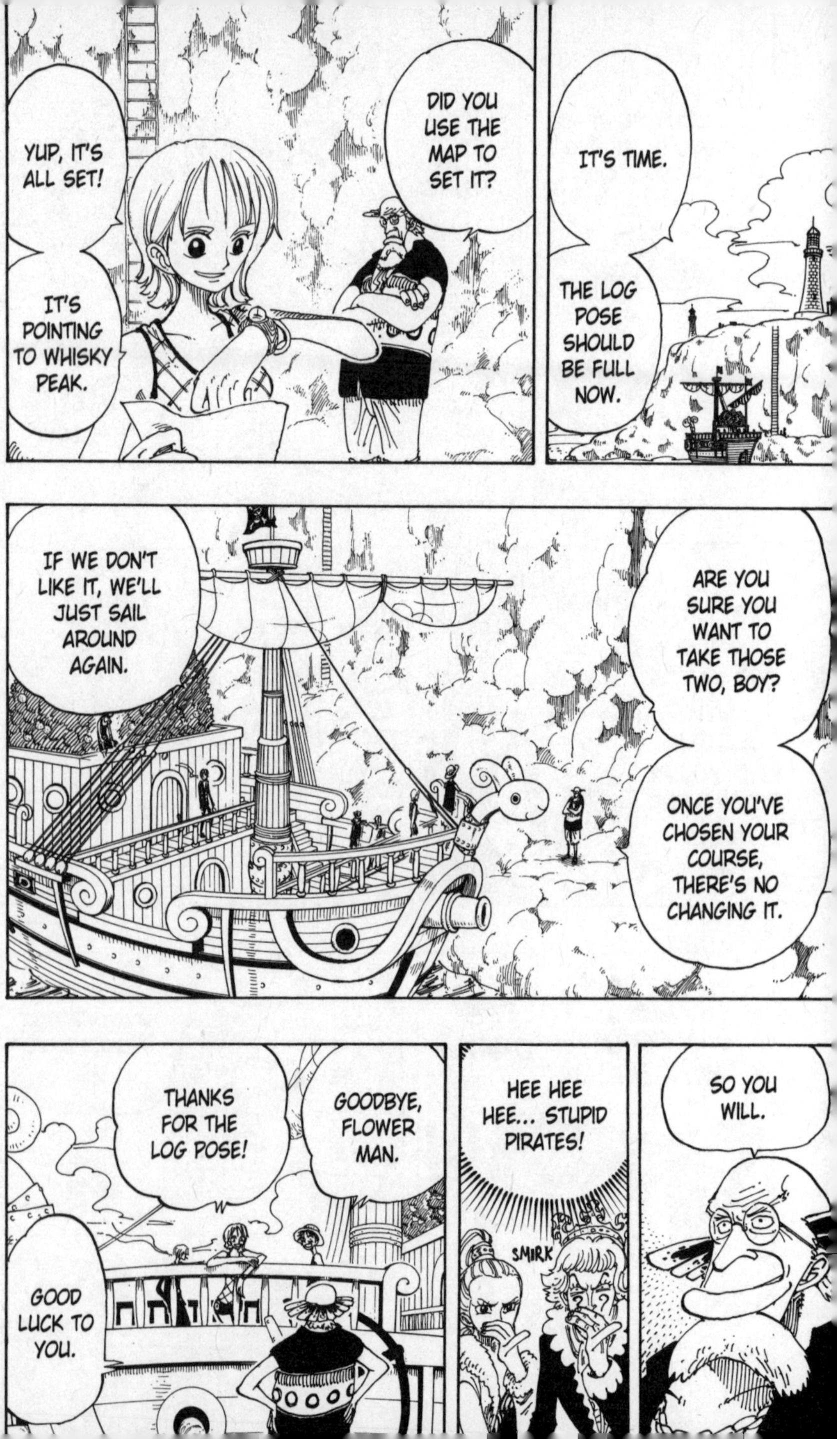
IT'S TIME.
THE LOG POSE SHOULD BE FULL NOW.
DID YOU USE THE MAP TO SET IT?
YUP, IT'S ALL SET!
IT'S POINTING TO WHISKY PEAK.
ARE YOU SURE YOU WANT TO TAKE THOSE TWO, BOY?
ONCE YOU'VE CHOSEN YOUR COURSE, THERE'S NO CHANGING IT.
IF WE DON'T LIKE IT, WE'LL JUST SAIL AROUND AGAIN.
SO YOU WILL.
HEE HEE HEE... STUPID PIRATES!
SMIRK
GOODBYE, FLOWER MAN.
THANKS FOR THE LOG POSE!
GOOD LUCK TO YOU.

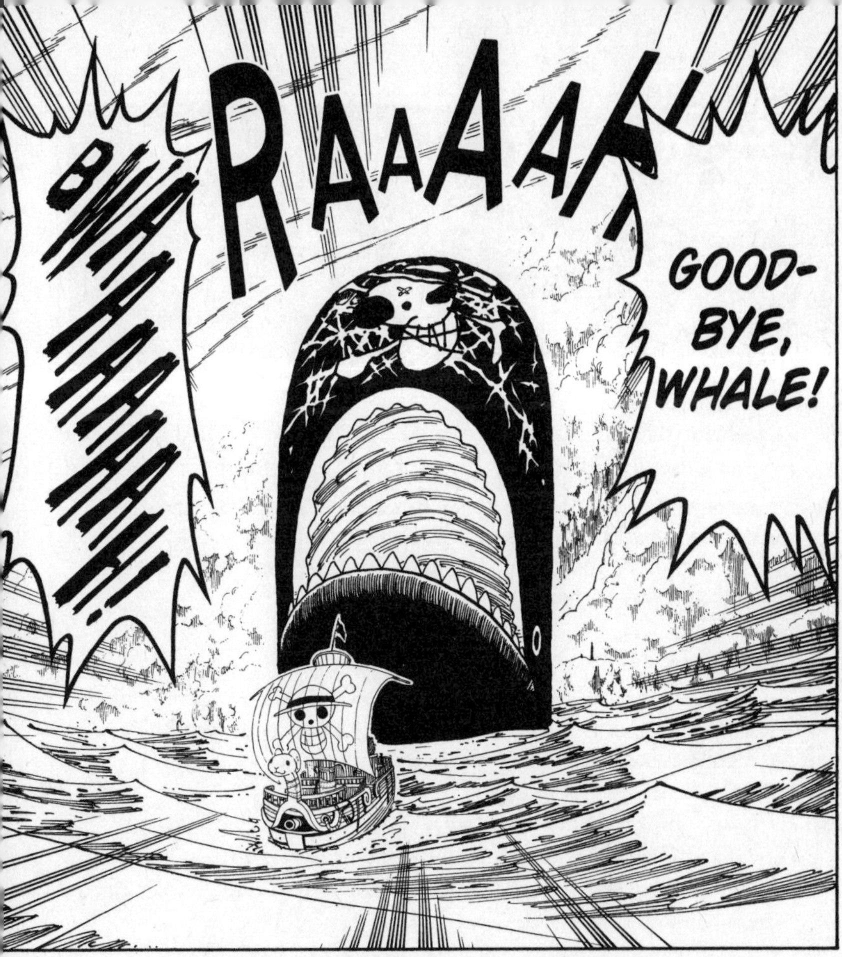
RAAAAA
GOOD-BYE, WHALE!
BWAAAAAAH!!

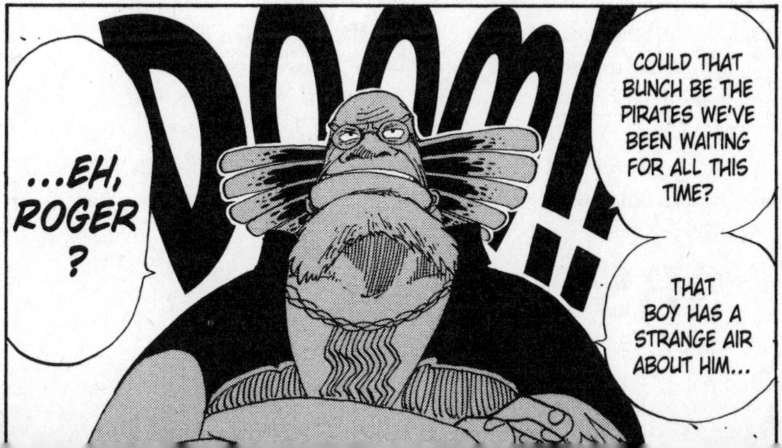
COULD THAT BUNCH BE THE PIRATES WE'VE BEEN WAITING FOR ALL THIS TIME?
THAT BOY HAS A STRANGE AIR ABOUT HIM...
DOOM!!
...EH, ROGER?

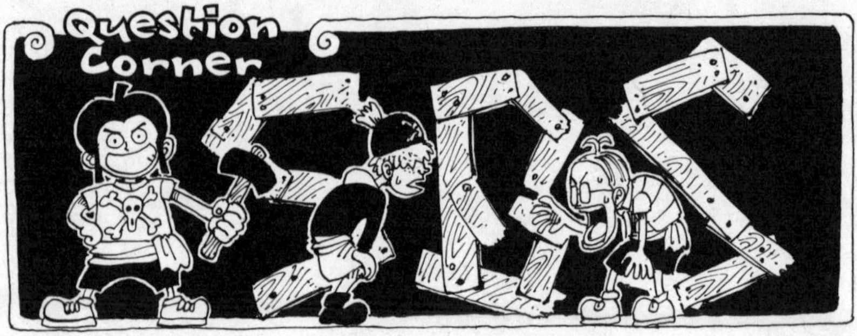
Question Corner
SBS

Q: To what extent can Buggy split himself up? I've been thinking about it so much that I've let my hair grow for three days straight.

A: Buggy, eh? Well, I'll just say, into big chunks. Too small and he'd lose control of himself. But that aside, since you've been growing your hair, why don't you enter the Cool Hair Contest that came up earlier?

Q: All right! Let's start the SBS Corner!

A: Bwah ha ha ha! Yay! I brought that up right out of the blue! Surprised? There have been a lot of postcards like that lately. And postcards like this:

Q: On page 78 of volume 9, the panel shows the kanji characters *koi* (love) and *sake* (rice wine), but you didn't mean *koi* (carp) and *sake* (salmon), did you? I mean, you wouldn't do that, would you? By the way, what kind of Fish-Men are they?

A: That's such old material, I can't remember. Umm... Anyway...

Q: Hello! This postcard is to Oda Sensei, who else? Oh, I forgot to introduce myself. I'm Timmy Maiko! Does the name "Timmy" ring a bell? That's right, it's just like Timmy Ueda! I'm Ueda's younger sister. My brother owes you for volume 10. This time, I'm writing the thank you postcard. I'm the *hee-hee* ♡ loving sister, and that's where I'll stop before Oda Sensei puts an end to this. After all, I am a member of the SBS hijacking gang.

SBS is over!

A: Aaargh! Not again! Why, you--Timmy!

Chapter 106:
THE TOWN OF WELCOME

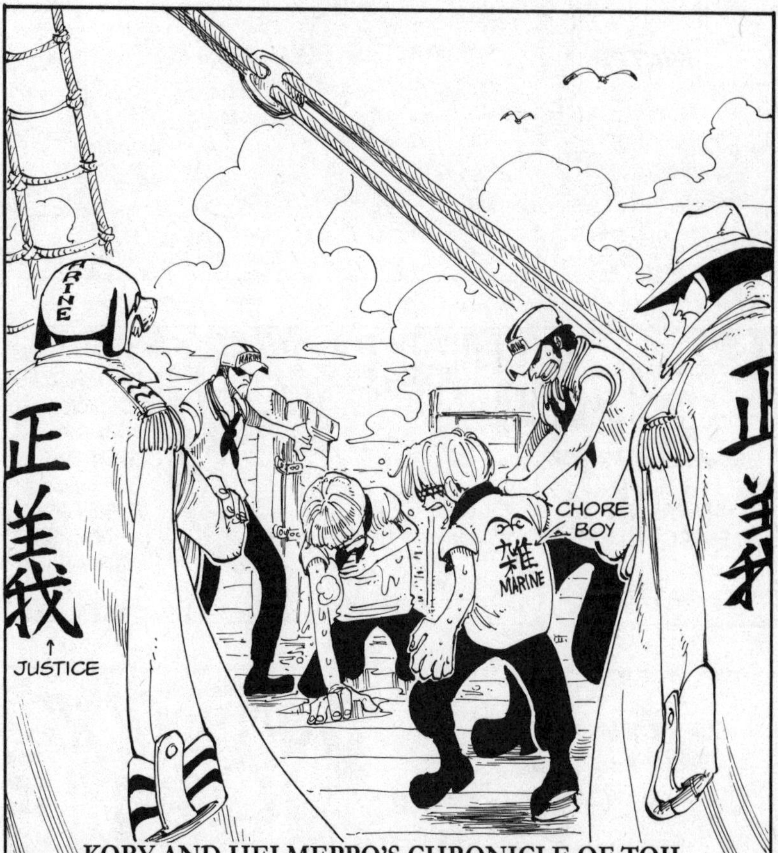
MARINE
正義
↑
JUSTICE
MARINE
MARINE
雑
MARINE
CHORE BOY
正義
KOBY AND HELMEPPO'S CHRONICLE OF TOIL
VOL. 20: "HELMEPPO'S RETURN"

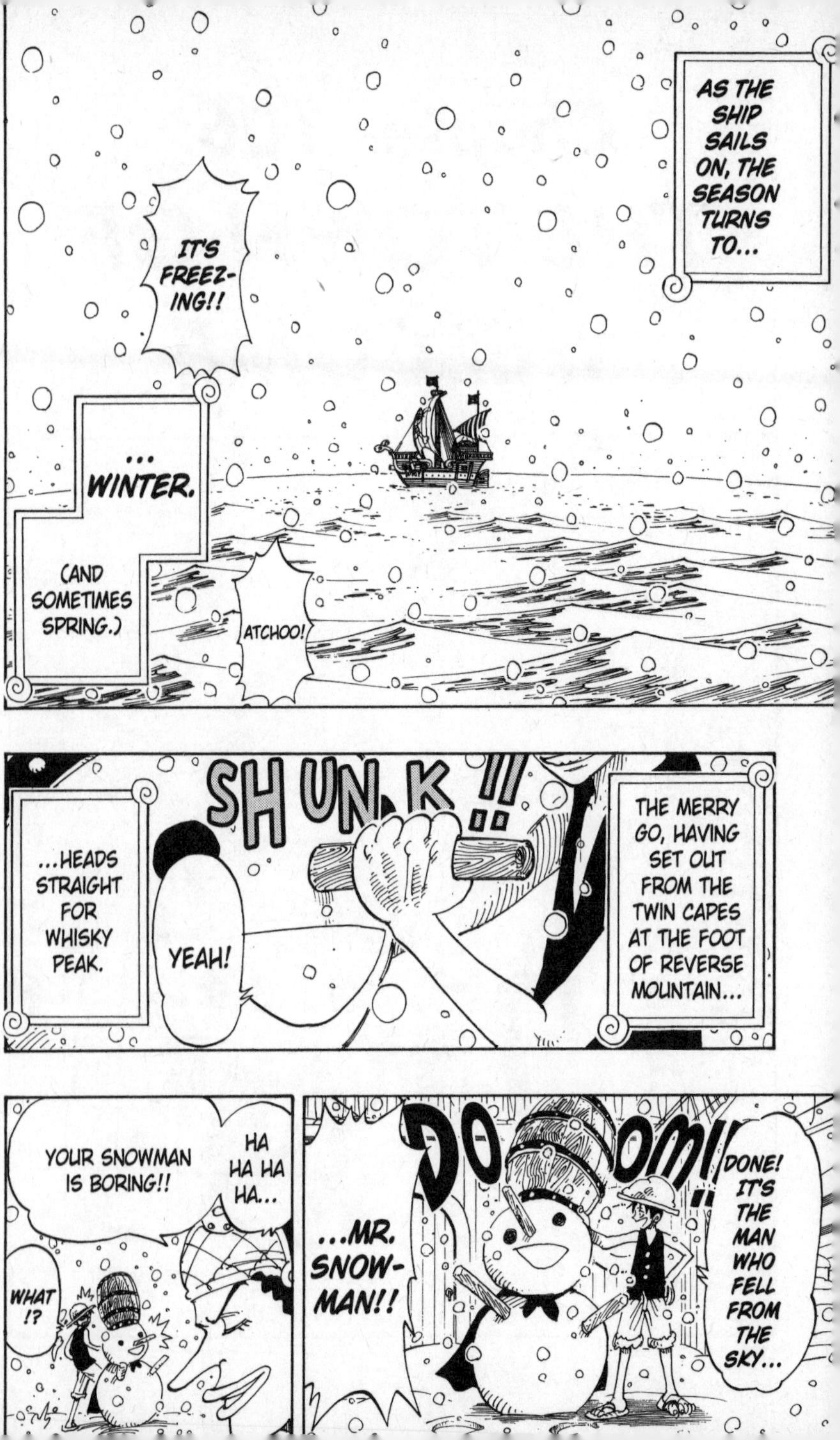
AS THE SHIP SAILS ON, THE SEASON TURNS TO...
IT'S FREEZING!!
...WINTER.
ATCHOO!
(AND SOMETIMES SPRING.)
THE MERRY GO, HAVING SET OUT FROM THE TWIN CAPES AT THE FOOT OF REVERSE MOUNTAIN...
SHUNK!!
...HEADS STRAIGHT FOR WHISKY PEAK.
YEAH!
DONE! IT'S THE MAN WHO FELL FROM THE SKY...
DO OM!!
...MR. SNOWMAN!!
HA HA HA HA...
YOUR SNOWMAN IS BORING!!
WHAT!?

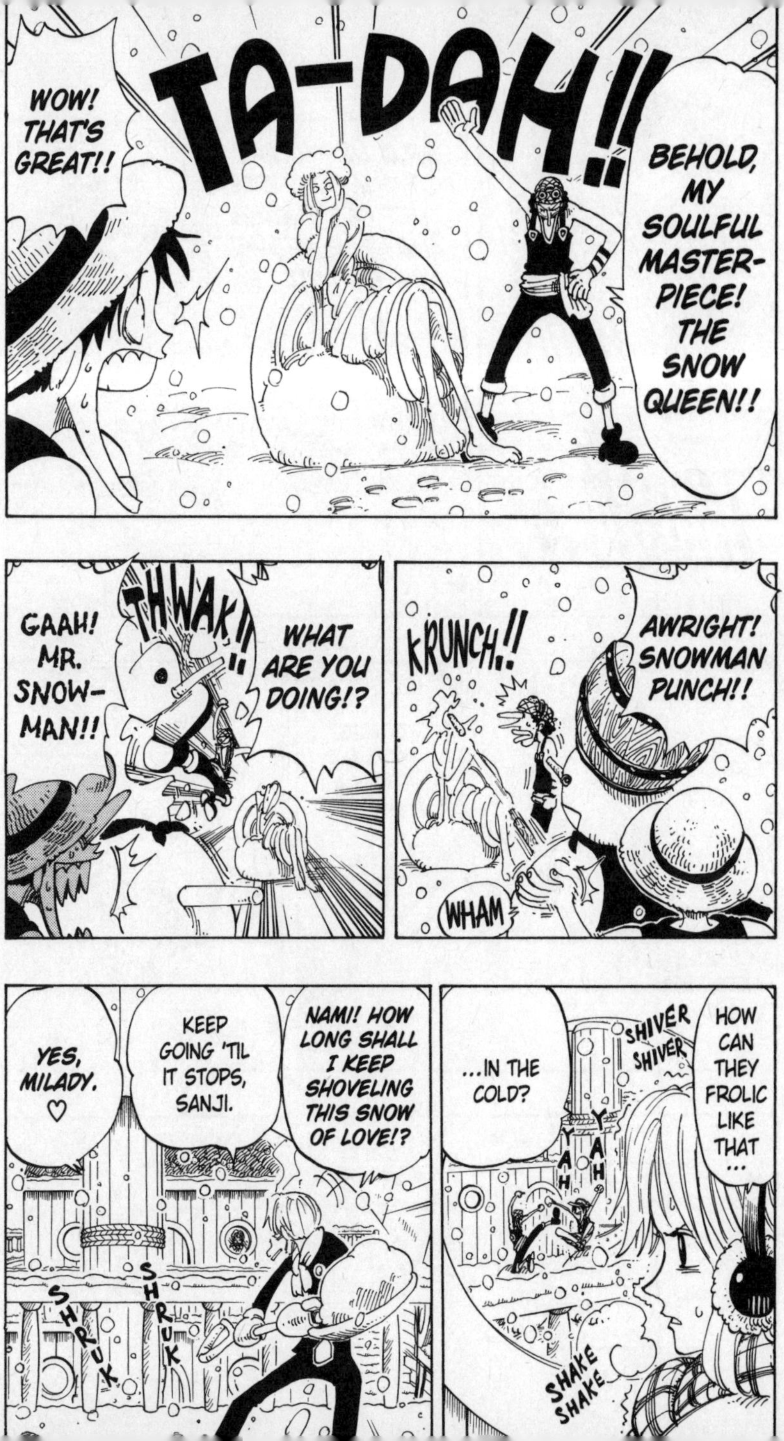
TA-DAH!!
BEHOLD, MY SOULFUL MASTER-PIECE! THE SNOW QUEEN!!
WOW! THAT'S GREAT!!
AWRIGHT! SNOWMAN PUNCH!!
KRUNCH!!
WHAM
WHAT ARE YOU DOING!?
THWAK!!
GAAH! MR. SNOW-MAN!!
HOW CAN THEY FROLIC LIKE THAT ...
SHIVER SHIVER
...IN THE COLD?
YAH YAH
SHAKE SHAKE
NAMI! HOW LONG SHALL I KEEP SHOVELING THIS SNOW OF LOVE!?
KEEP GOING 'TIL IT STOPS, SANJI.
YES, MILADY. ♡
SHRUK SHRUK

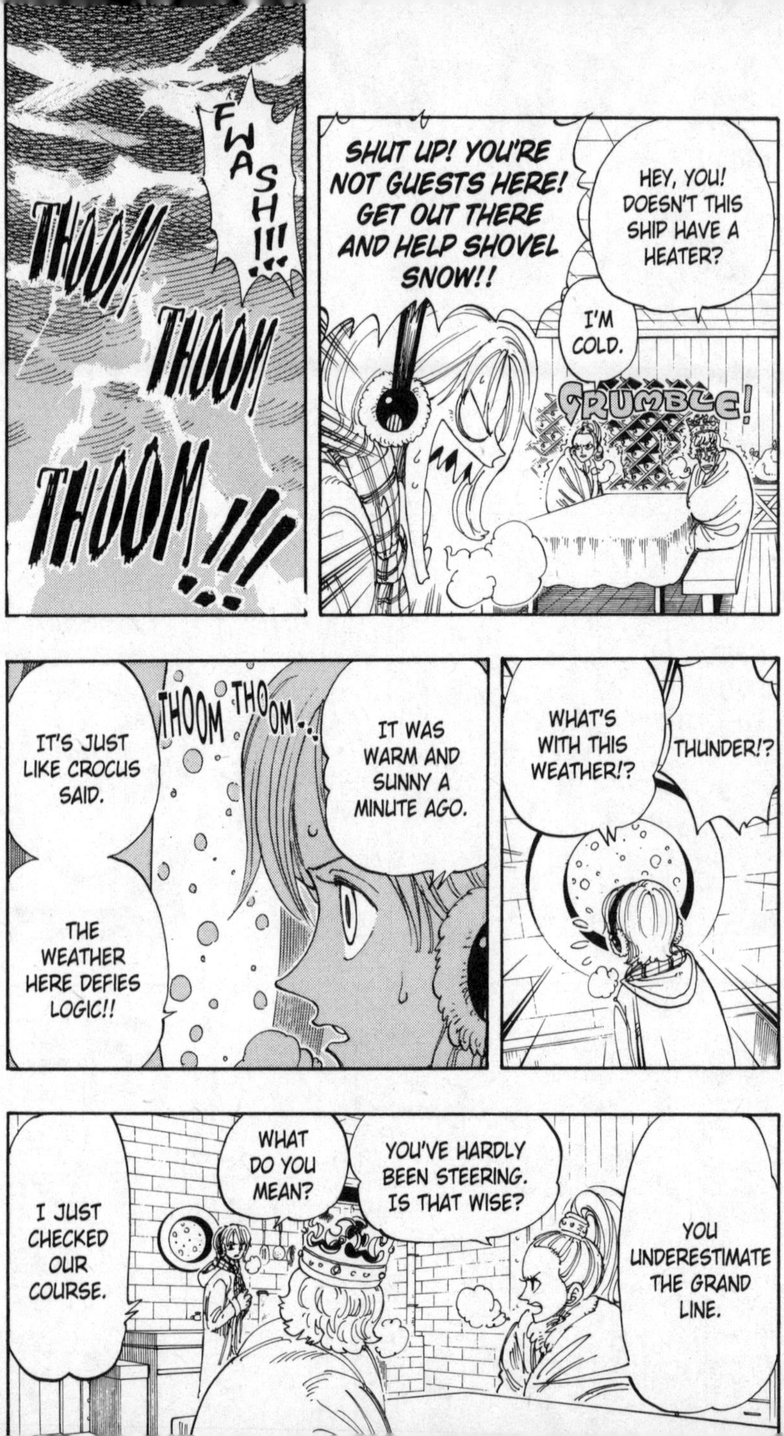
HEY, YOU! DOESN'T THIS SHIP HAVE A HEATER?
I'M COLD.
SHUT UP! YOU'RE NOT GUESTS HERE! GET OUT THERE AND HELP SHOVEL SNOW!!
GRUMBLE!
FWASH!!!
THOOM
THOOM
THOOM!!
WHAT'S WITH THIS WEATHER!?
THUNDER!?
IT WAS WARM AND SUNNY A MINUTE AGO.
THOOM THOOM..
IT'S JUST LIKE CROCUS SAID.
THE WEATHER HERE DEFIES LOGIC!!
YOU UNDERESTIMATE THE GRAND LINE.
YOU'VE HARDLY BEEN STEERING. IS THAT WISE?
WHAT DO YOU MEAN?
I JUST CHECKED OUR COURSE.

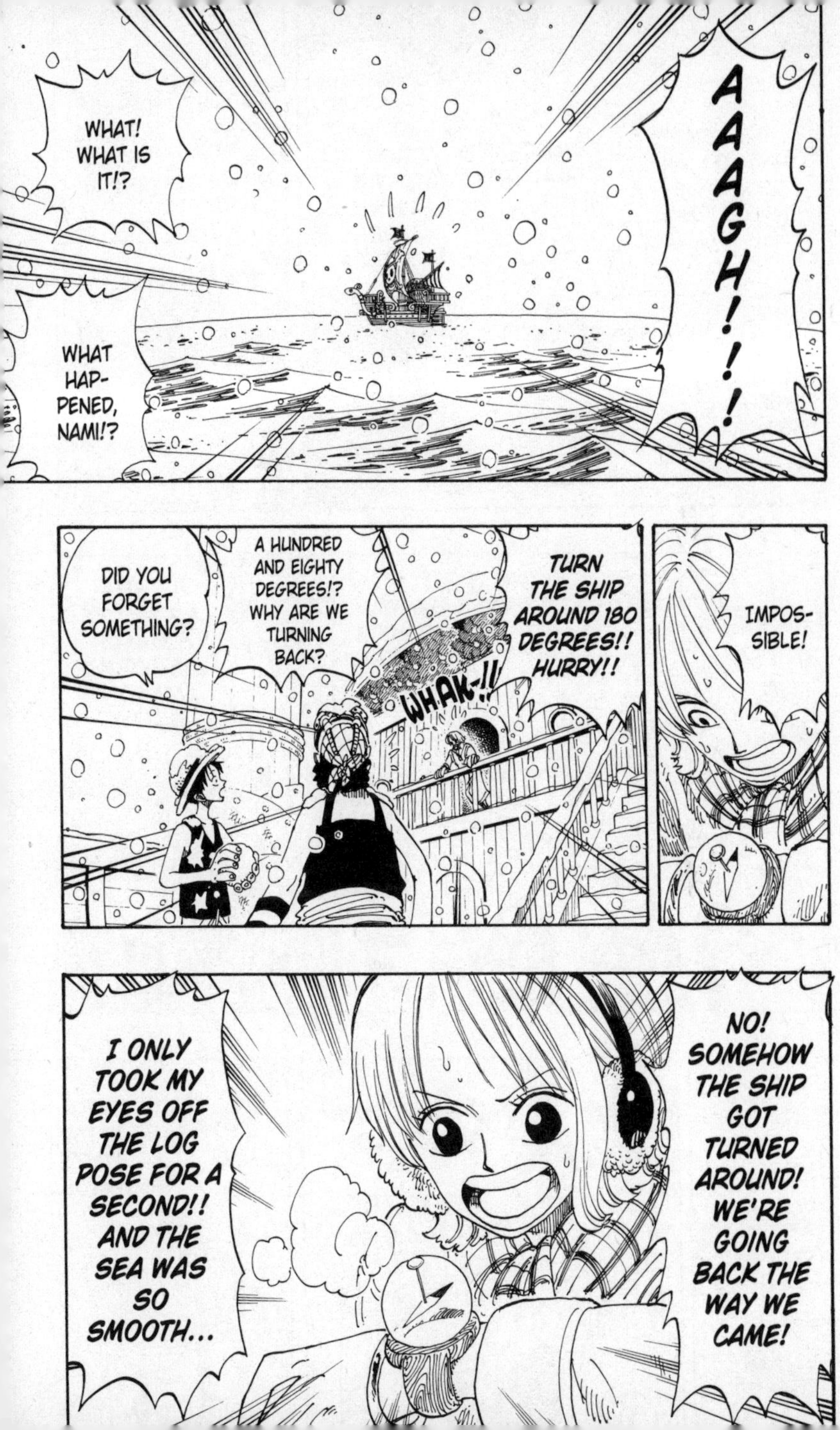
AAAGH!!!
WHAT! WHAT IS IT!?
WHAT HAP-PENED, NAMI!?
IMPOS-SIBLE!
TURN THE SHIP AROUND 180 DEGREES!! HURRY!!
WHAK-!!
A HUNDRED AND EIGHTY DEGREES!? WHY ARE WE TURNING BACK?
DID YOU FORGET SOMETHING?
NO! SOMEHOW THE SHIP GOT TURNED AROUND! WE'RE GOING BACK THE WAY WE CAME!
I ONLY TOOK MY EYES OFF THE LOG POSE FOR A SECOND!! AND THE SEA WAS SO SMOOTH...

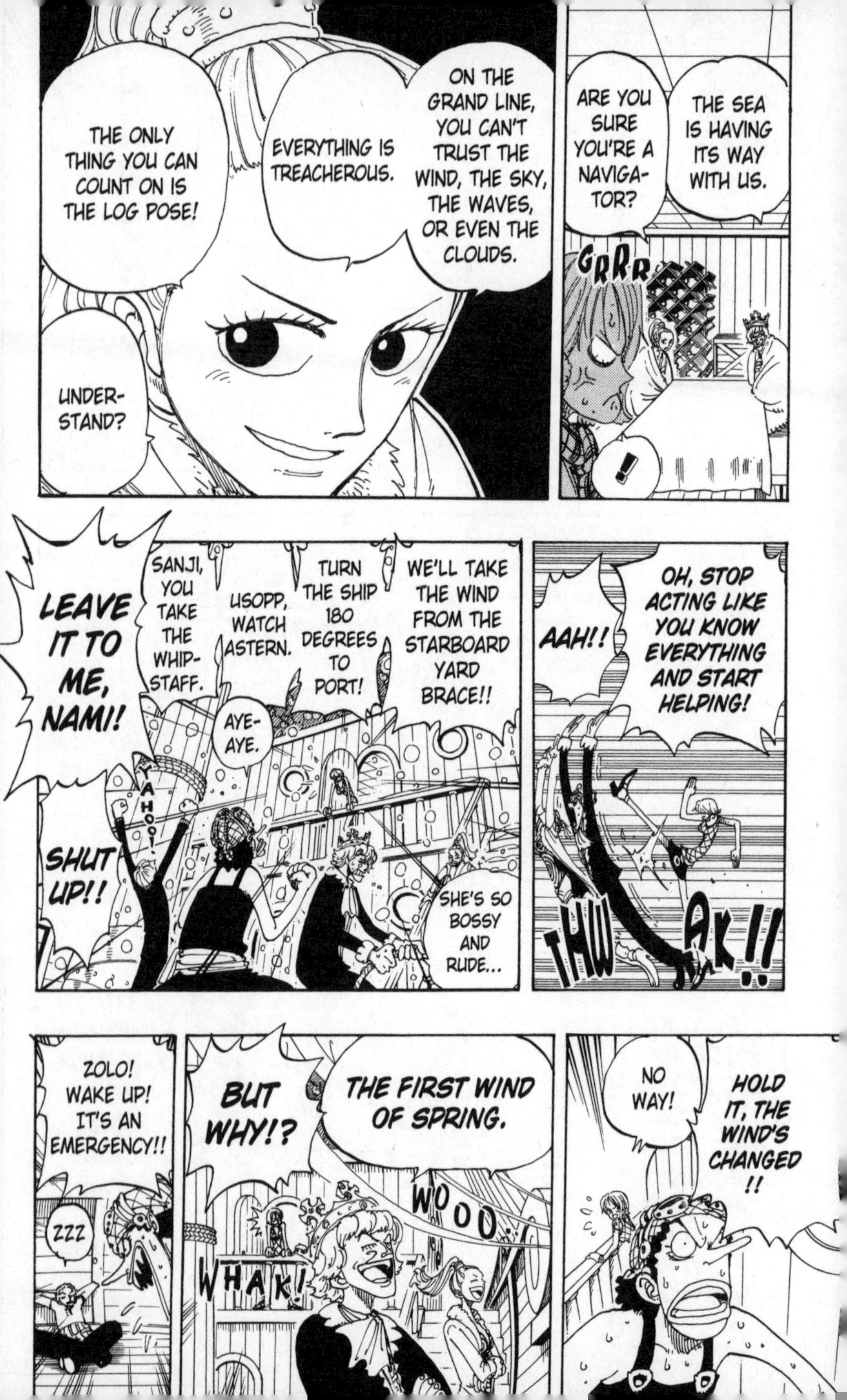
THE SEA IS HAVING ITS WAY WITH US.
ARE YOU SURE YOU'RE A NAVIGA-TOR?
GRRR
!
ON THE GRAND LINE, YOU CAN'T TRUST THE WIND, THE SKY, THE WAVES, OR EVEN THE CLOUDS.
EVERYTHING IS TREACHEROUS.
THE ONLY THING YOU CAN COUNT ON IS THE LOG POSE!
UNDER-STAND?
OH, STOP ACTING LIKE YOU KNOW EVERYTHING AND START HELPING!
AAH!!
THWAK!!
WE'LL TAKE THE WIND FROM THE STARBOARD YARD BRACE!!
TURN THE SHIP 180 DEGREES TO PORT!
USOPP, WATCH ASTERN.
SANJI, YOU TAKE THE WHIP-STAFF.
AYE-AYE.
LEAVE IT TO ME, NAMI!
YAHOO!
SHE'S SO BOSSY AND RUDE...
SHUT UP!!
HOLD IT, THE WIND'S CHANGED!!
NO WAY!
THE FIRST WIND OF SPRING.
BUT WHY!?
WOOO
WHAK!
ZOLO! WAKE UP! IT'S AN EMERGENCY!!
ZZZ

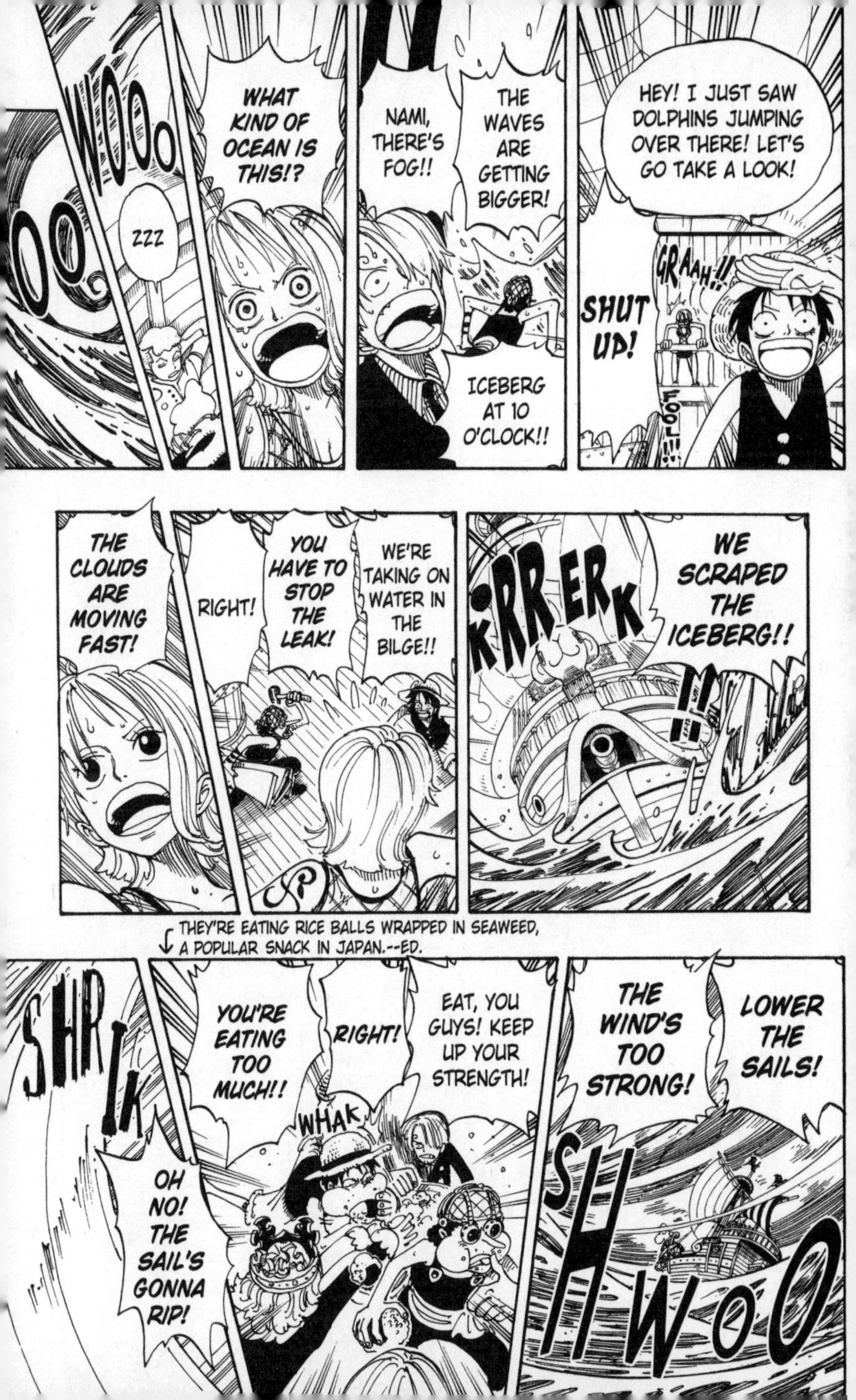
HEY! I JUST SAW DOLPHINS JUMPING OVER THERE! LET'S GO TAKE A LOOK!
GRAAH!!
SHUT UP!
FOOL!!!
THE WAVES ARE GETTING BIGGER!
NAMI, THERE'S FOG!!
ICEBERG AT 10 O'CLOCK!!
WHAT KIND OF OCEAN IS THIS!?
WOOOO
ZZZ
OOO
WE SCRAPED THE ICEBERG!!
KRRERK
!!
WE'RE TAKING ON WATER IN THE BILGE!!
YOU HAVE TO STOP THE LEAK!
RIGHT!
THE CLOUDS ARE MOVING FAST!
LOWER THE SAILS!
THE WIND'S TOO STRONG!
SHWOOO
EAT, YOU GUYS! KEEP UP YOUR STRENGTH!
RIGHT!
YOU'RE EATING TOO MUCH!!
WHAK
SHRIK
OH NO! THE SAIL'S GONNA RIP!

THEY'RE EATING RICE BALLS WRAPPED IN SEAWEED, A POPULAR SNACK IN JAPAN.--ED.

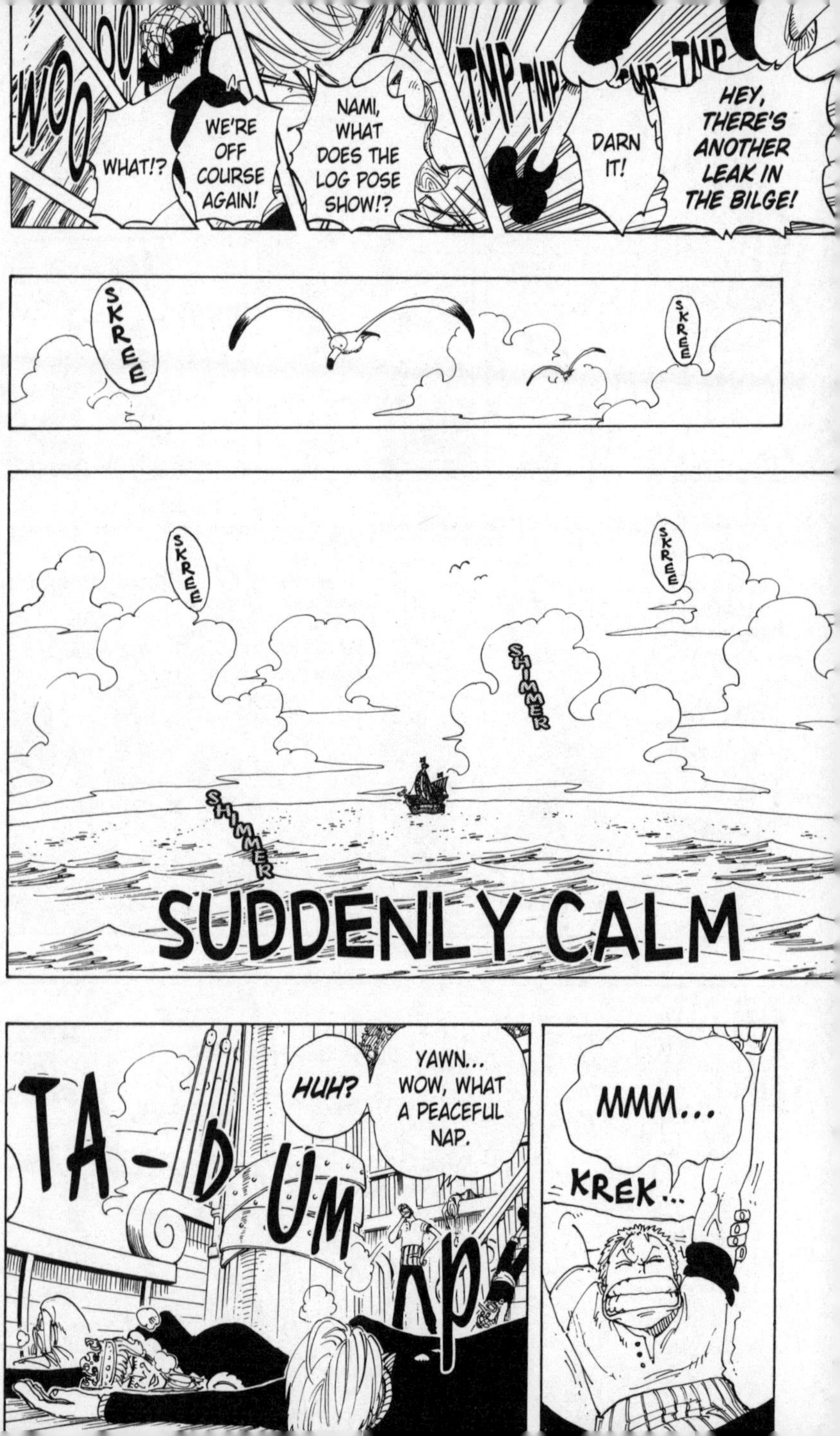
HEY, THERE'S ANOTHER LEAK IN THE BILGE!
TMP TMP
DARN IT!
TMP TMP
NAMI, WHAT DOES THE LOG POSE SHOW!?
WE'RE OFF COURSE AGAIN!
WHAT!?
WOOOO
SKREE
SKREE
SKREE
SKREE
SHIMMER
SHIMMER
SUDDENLY CALM
MMM...
KREK...
YAWN... WOW, WHAT A PEACEFUL NAP.
HUH?
TA-DUMP

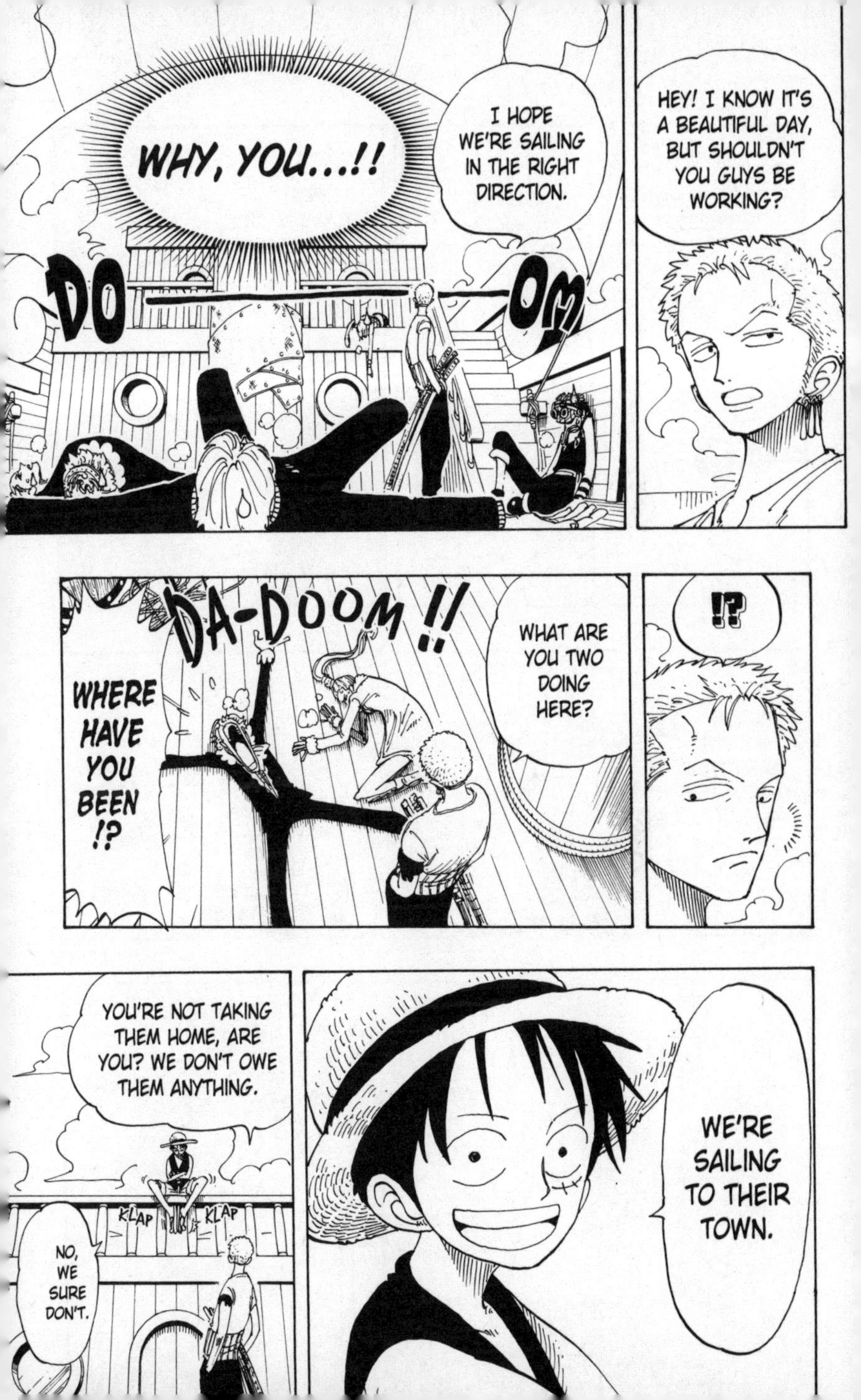

HEY! I KNOW IT'S A BEAUTIFUL DAY, BUT SHOULDN'T YOU GUYS BE WORKING?
I HOPE WE'RE SAILING IN THE RIGHT DIRECTION.
WHY, YOU...!!
DO-OM
!?
WHAT ARE YOU TWO DOING HERE?
DA-DOOM!!
WHERE HAVE YOU BEEN!?
WE'RE SAILING TO THEIR TOWN.
YOU'RE NOT TAKING THEM HOME, ARE YOU? WE DON'T OWE THEM ANYTHING.
KLAP KLAP
NO, WE SURE DON'T.

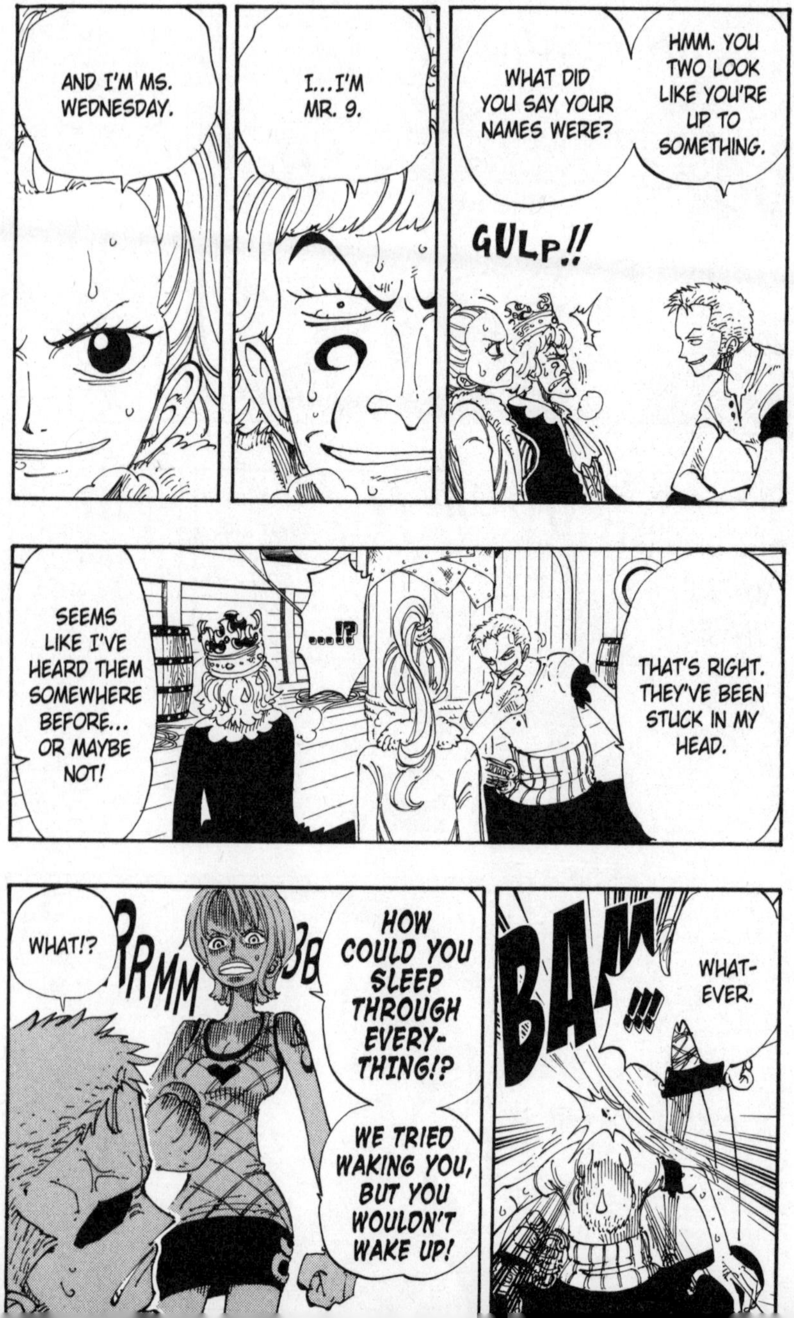
HMM. YOU TWO LOOK LIKE YOU'RE UP TO SOMETHING.
WHAT DID YOU SAY YOUR NAMES WERE?
GULP!!
I...I'M MR. 9.
AND I'M MS. WEDNESDAY.
THAT'S RIGHT. THEY'VE BEEN STUCK IN MY HEAD.
...!?
SEEMS LIKE I'VE HEARD THEM SOMEWHERE BEFORE... OR MAYBE NOT!
WHAT-EVER.
BAM!!!
HOW COULD YOU SLEEP THROUGH EVERY-THING!?
WE TRIED WAKING YOU, BUT YOU WOULDN'T WAKE UP!
RRMM
WHAT!?

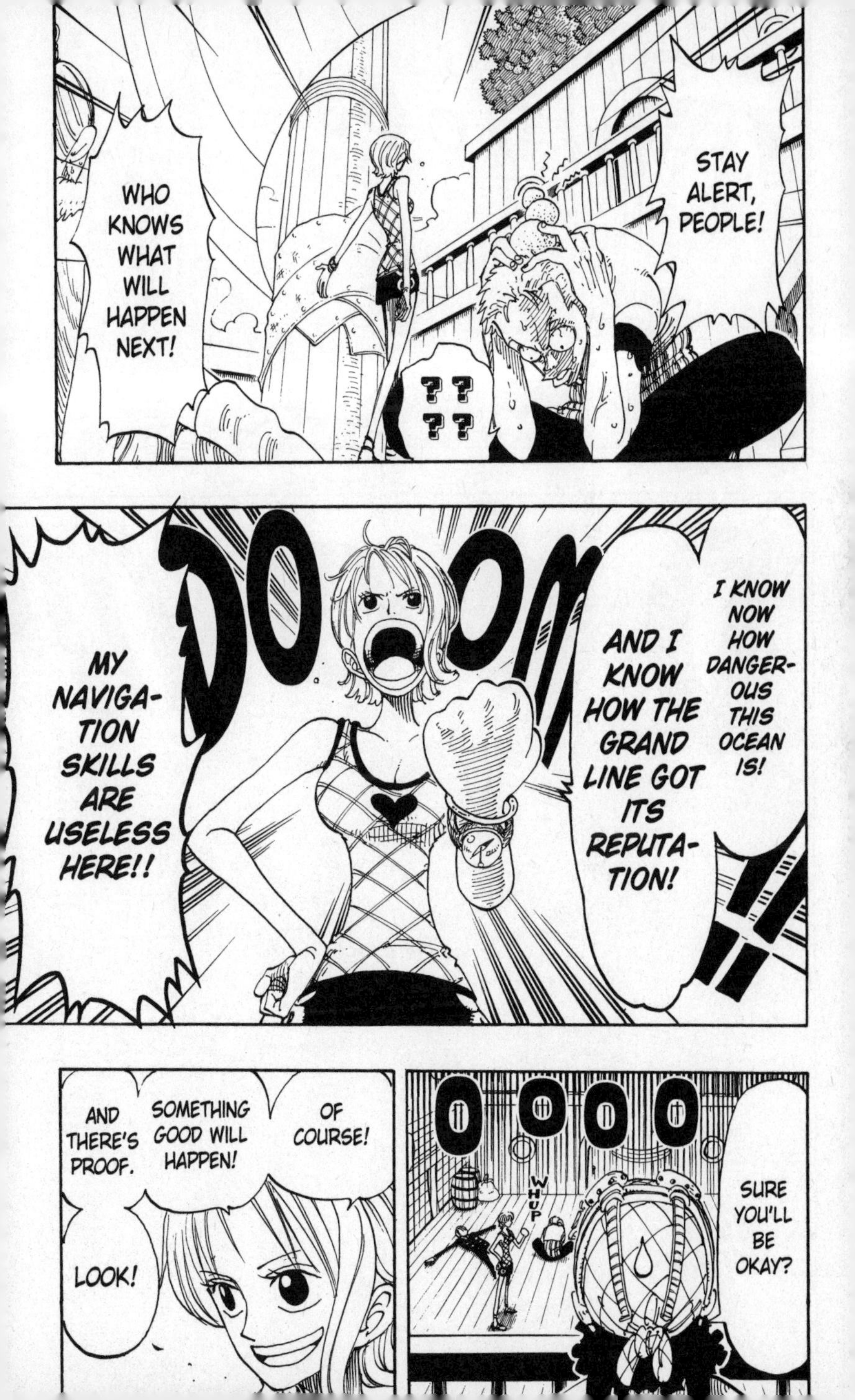
STAY ALERT, PEOPLE!
WHO KNOWS WHAT WILL HAPPEN NEXT!
??
??
I KNOW NOW HOW DANGER-OUS THIS OCEAN IS!
AND I KNOW HOW THE GRAND LINE GOT ITS REPUTA-TION!
DOOM
MY NAVIGA-TION SKILLS ARE USELESS HERE!!
SURE YOU'LL BE OKAY?
WHUP
OF COURSE!
SOMETHING GOOD WILL HAPPEN!
AND THERE'S PROOF.
LOOK!

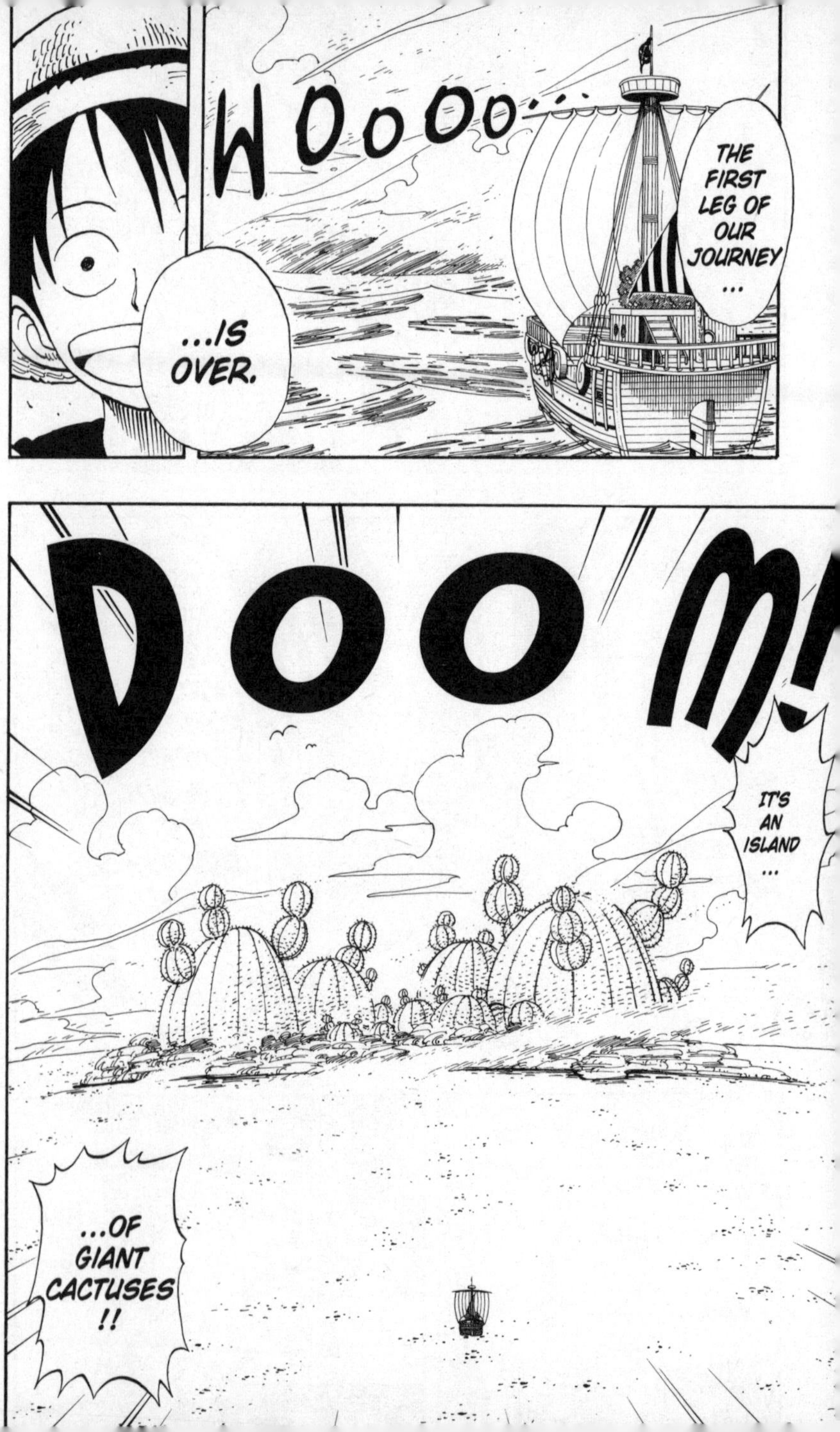
THE FIRST LEG OF OUR JOURNEY ...
WOOOO...
...IS OVER.
DOOM!
IT'S AN ISLAND ...
...OF GIANT CACTUSES !!

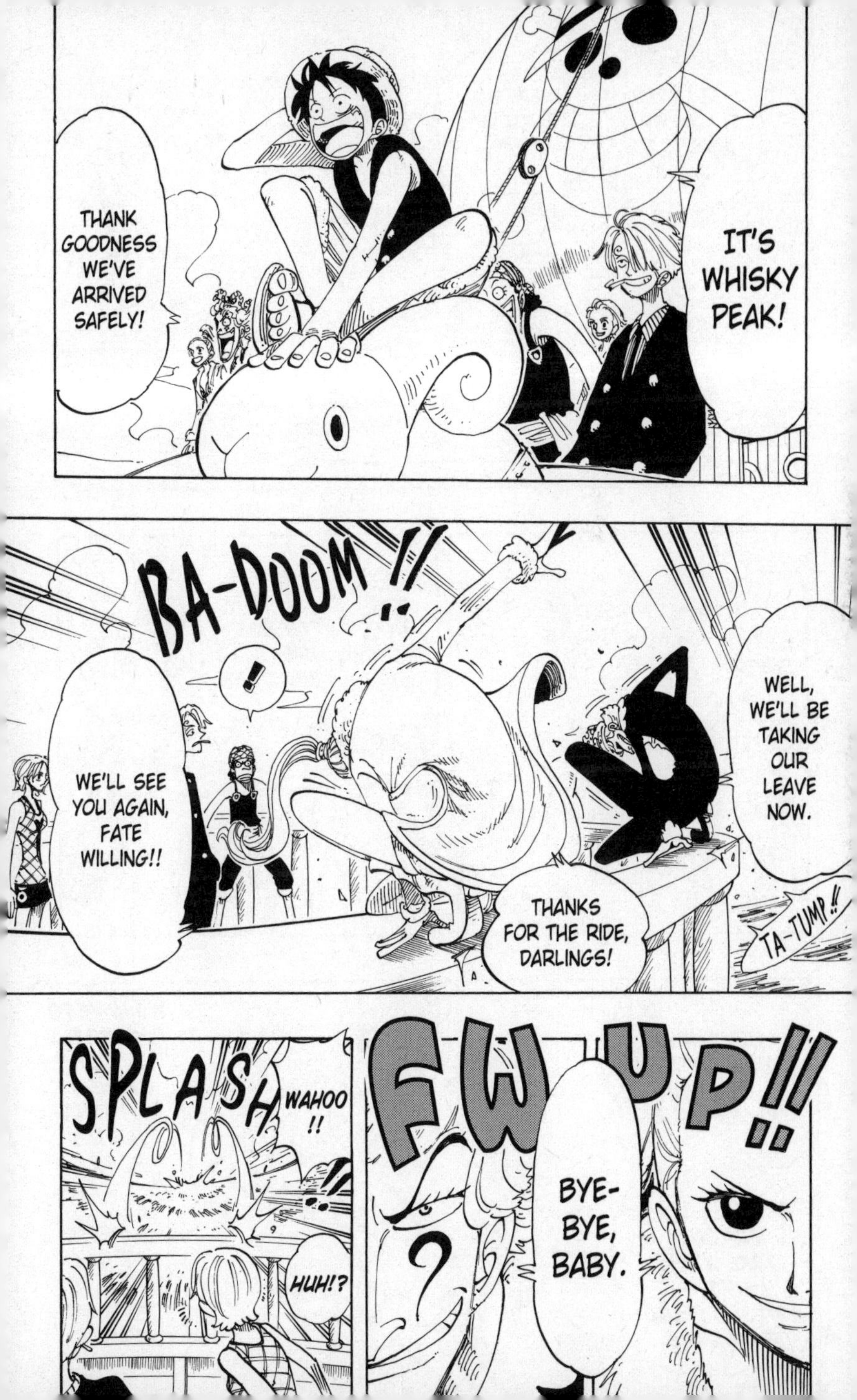
IT'S WHISKY PEAK!
THANK GOODNESS WE'VE ARRIVED SAFELY!
WELL, WE'LL BE TAKING OUR LEAVE NOW.
BA-DOOM!!
!
TA-TUMP!!
THANKS FOR THE RIDE, DARLINGS!
WE'LL SEE YOU AGAIN, FATE WILLING!!
FWUP!!
BYE-BYE, BABY.
?
SPLASH
WAHOO!!
HUH!?

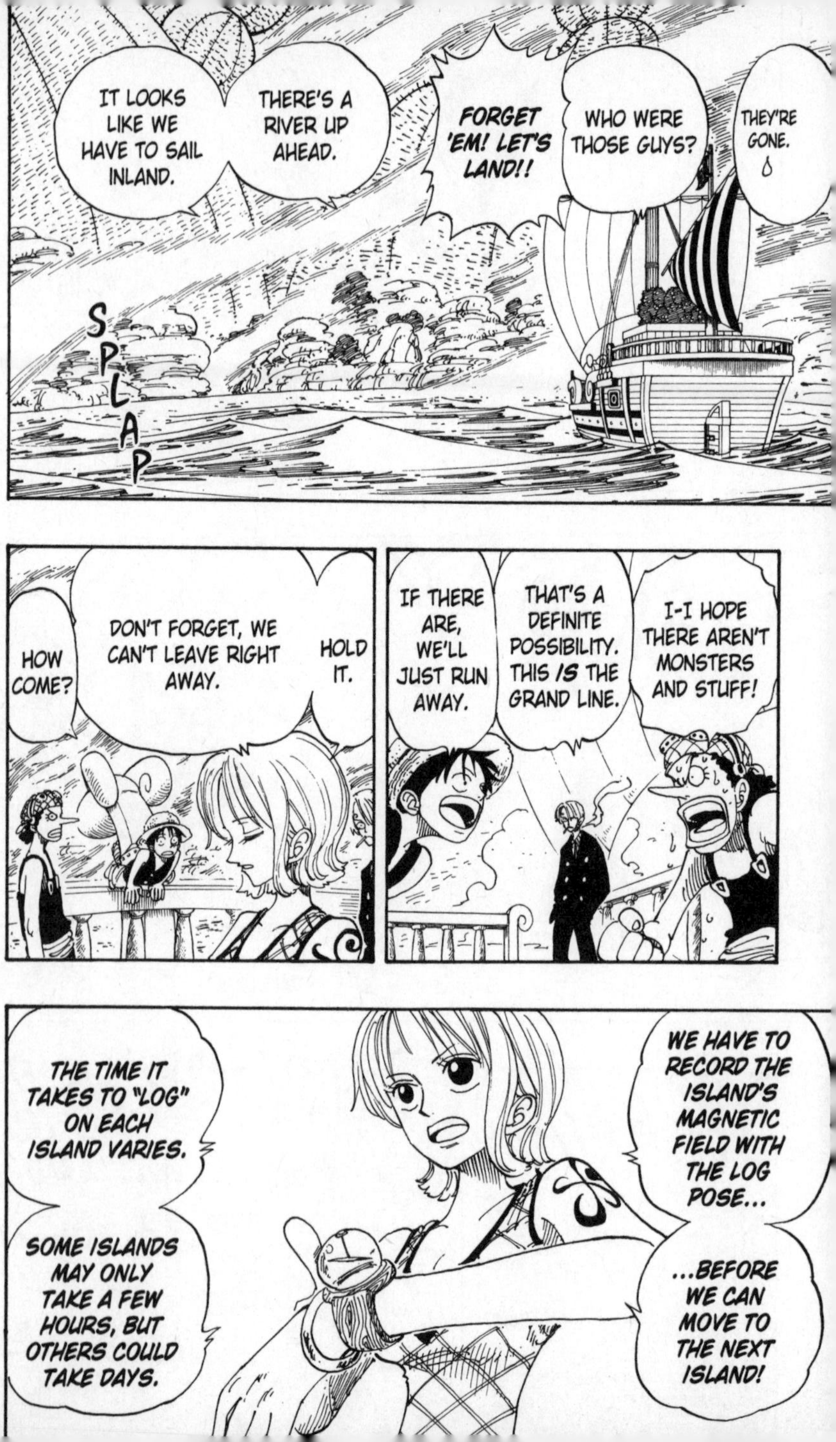
THEY'RE GONE.
WHO WERE THOSE GUYS?
FORGET 'EM! LET'S LAND!!
THERE'S A RIVER UP AHEAD.
IT LOOKS LIKE WE HAVE TO SAIL INLAND.
SPLAP
I-I HOPE THERE AREN'T MONSTERS AND STUFF!
THAT'S A DEFINITE POSSIBILITY. THIS *IS* THE GRAND LINE.
IF THERE ARE, WE'LL JUST RUN AWAY.
HOLD IT.
DON'T FORGET, WE CAN'T LEAVE RIGHT AWAY.
HOW COME?
WE HAVE TO RECORD THE ISLAND'S MAGNETIC FIELD WITH THE LOG POSE...
...BEFORE WE CAN MOVE TO THE NEXT ISLAND!
THE TIME IT TAKES TO "LOG" ON EACH ISLAND VARIES.
SOME ISLANDS MAY ONLY TAKE A FEW HOURS, BUT OTHERS COULD TAKE DAYS.

READ THIS WAY

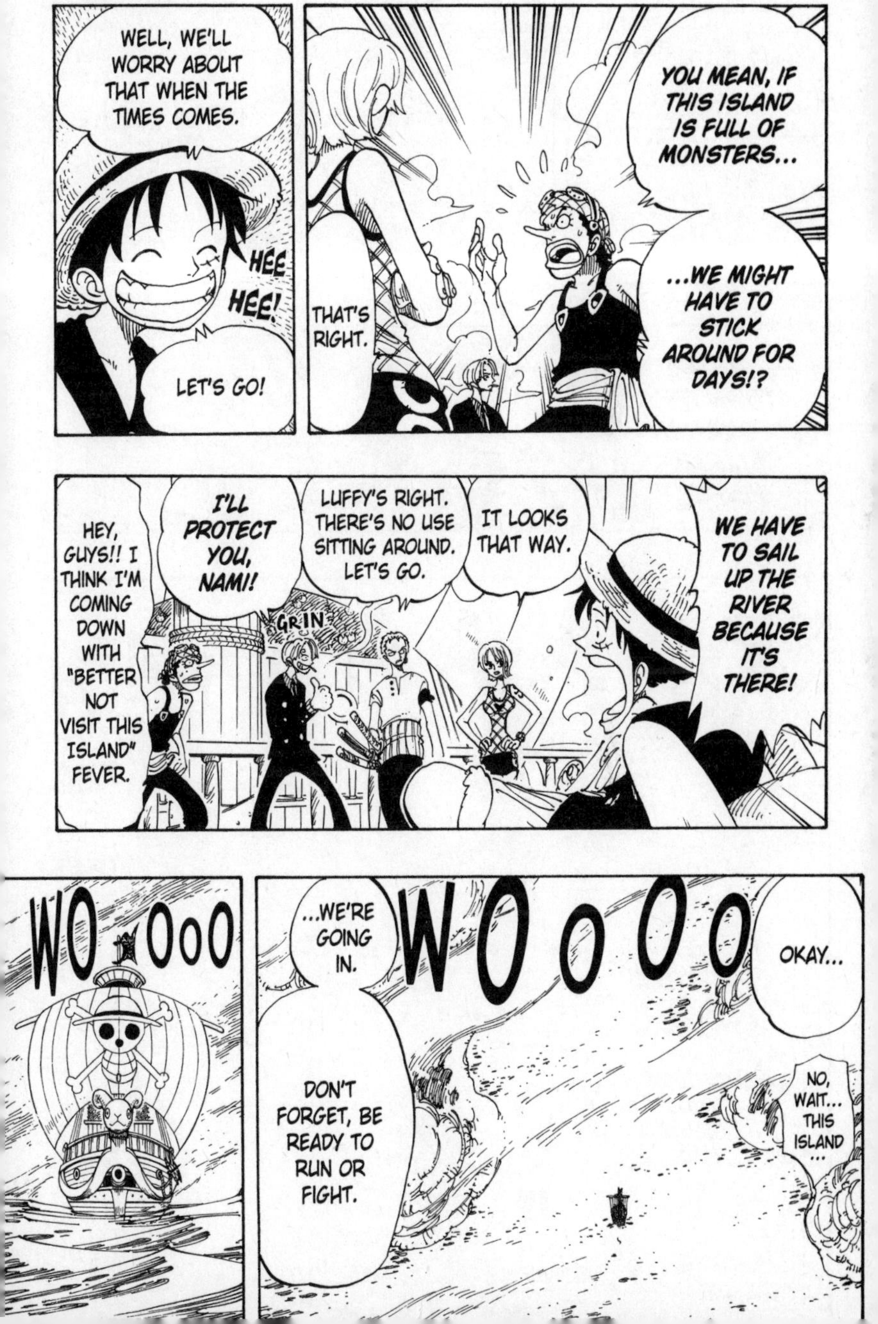
YOU MEAN, IF THIS ISLAND IS FULL OF MONSTERS...
...WE MIGHT HAVE TO STICK AROUND FOR DAYS!?
THAT'S RIGHT.
WELL, WE'LL WORRY ABOUT THAT WHEN THE TIMES COMES.
HEE HEE!
LET'S GO!
WE HAVE TO SAIL UP THE RIVER BECAUSE IT'S THERE!
IT LOOKS THAT WAY.
LUFFY'S RIGHT. THERE'S NO USE SITTING AROUND. LET'S GO.
I'LL PROTECT YOU, NAMI!
GRIN
HEY, GUYS!! I THINK I'M COMING DOWN WITH "BETTER NOT VISIT THIS ISLAND" FEVER.
OKAY...
NO, WAIT... THIS ISLAND ...
WOoOO
...WE'RE GOING IN.
DON'T FORGET, BE READY TO RUN OR FIGHT.
WO OOO

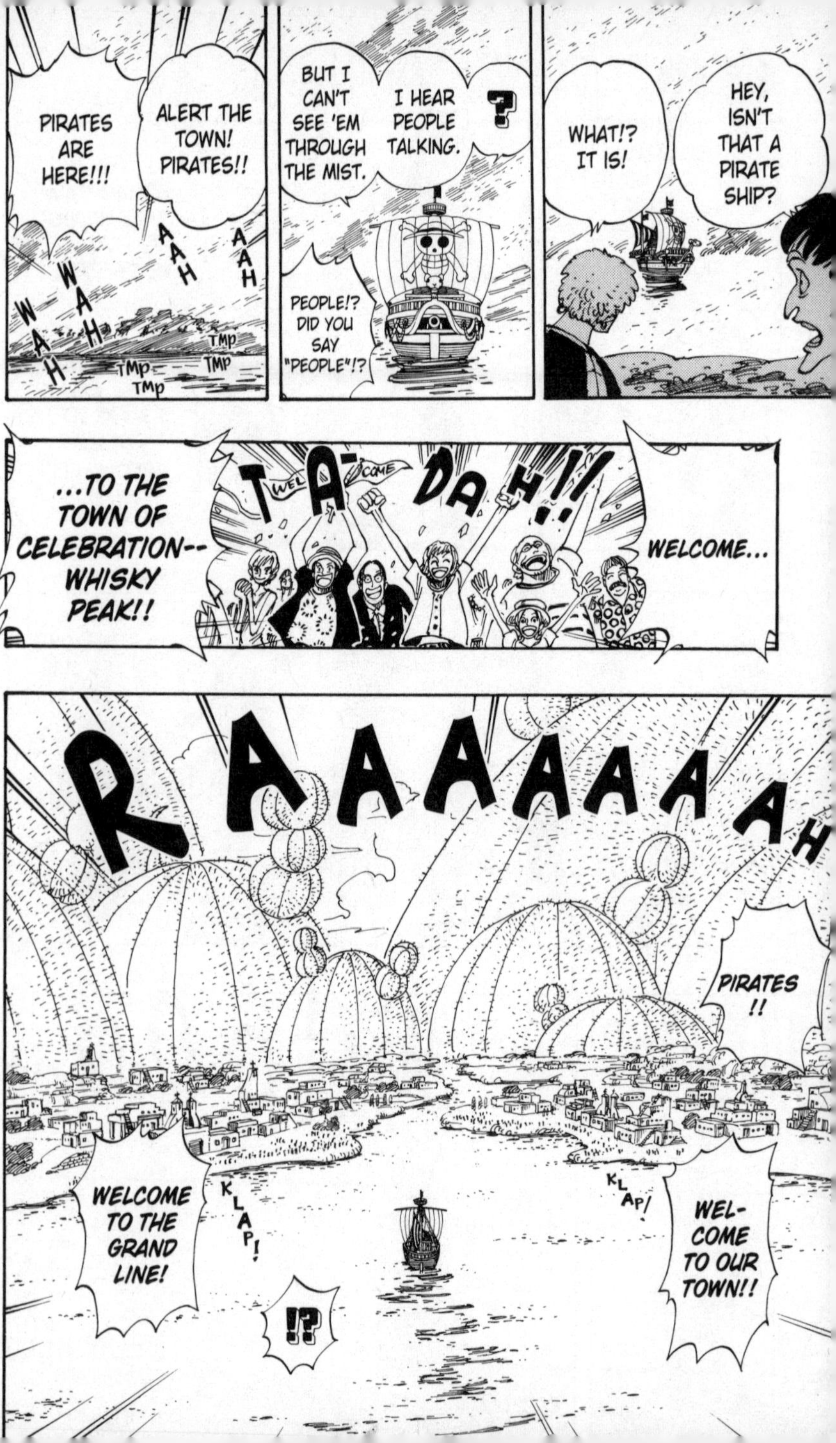
HEY, ISN'T THAT A PIRATE SHIP?
WHAT!? IT IS!
?
I HEAR PEOPLE TALKING.
BUT I CAN'T SEE 'EM THROUGH THE MIST.
PEOPLE!? DID YOU SAY "PEOPLE"!?
ALERT THE TOWN! PIRATES!!
PIRATES ARE HERE!!!
AAH
AAH
WAH
WAH
TMP TMP
TMP TMP
WELCOME...
TA-DA!!
WELCOME
...TO THE TOWN OF CELEBRATION--WHISKY PEAK!!
RAAAAAAAH
PIRATES!!
WEL-COME TO OUR TOWN!!
KLAP!
!?
KLAP!
WELCOME TO THE GRAND LINE!

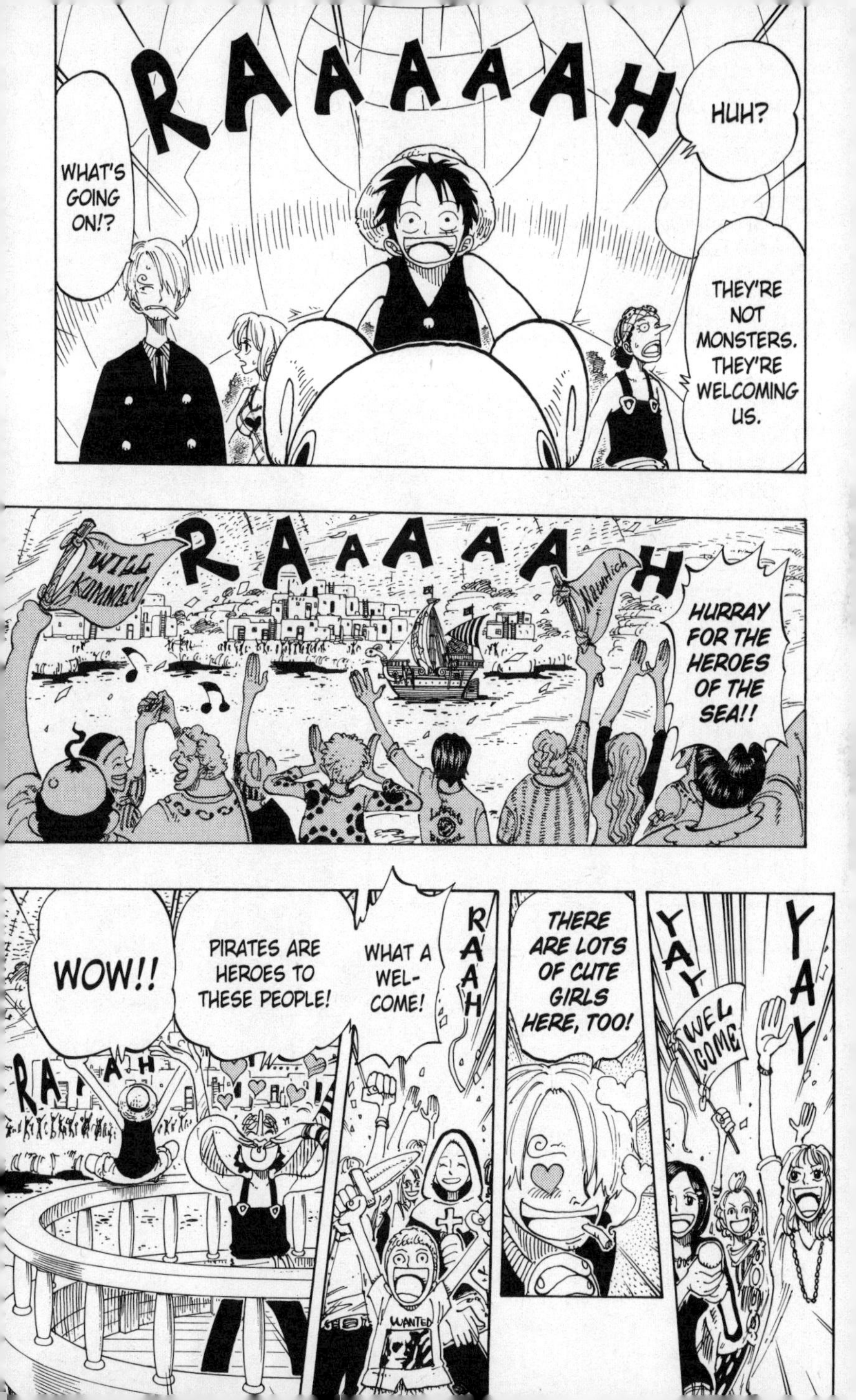
HUH?
RAAAAAH
WHAT'S GOING ON!?
THEY'RE NOT MONSTERS. THEY'RE WELCOMING US.
HURRAY FOR THE HEROES OF THE SEA!!
RAAAAAH
WILL KOMMEN
YAY
WEL COME
YAY
THERE ARE LOTS OF CUTE GIRLS HERE, TOO!
RAAH
WHAT A WEL-COME!
PIRATES ARE HEROES TO THESE PEOPLE!
WOW!!
WANTED

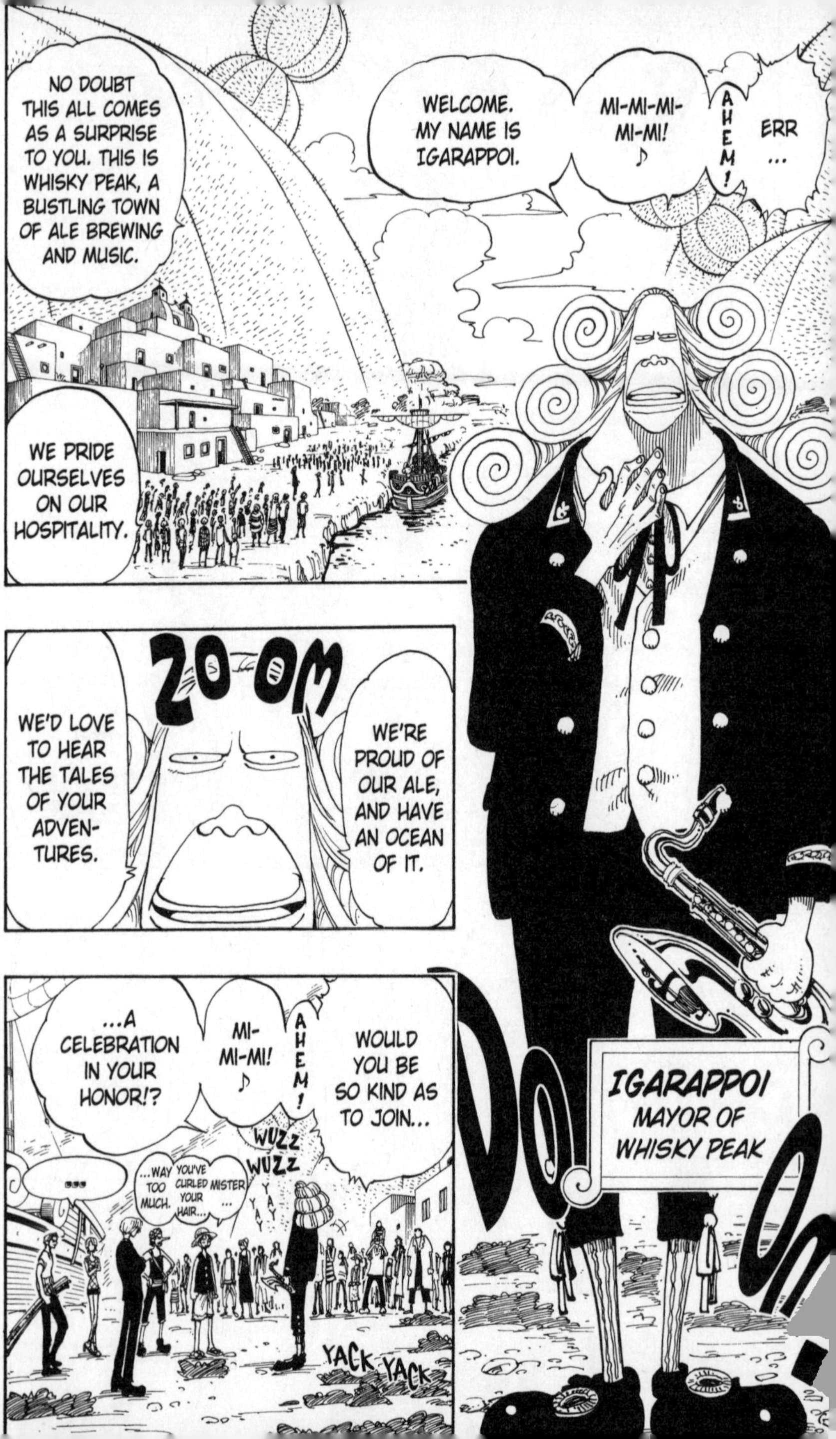

ERR ...
AHEM!
MI-MI-MI-MI-MI! ♪
WELCOME. MY NAME IS IGARAPPOI.
IGARAPPOI
MAYOR OF WHISKY PEAK
NO DOUBT THIS ALL COMES AS A SURPRISE TO YOU. THIS IS WHISKY PEAK, A BUSTLING TOWN OF ALE BREWING AND MUSIC.
WE PRIDE OURSELVES ON OUR HOSPITALITY.
ZO-OM
WE'RE PROUD OF OUR ALE, AND HAVE AN OCEAN OF IT.
WE'D LOVE TO HEAR THE TALES OF YOUR ADVEN-TURES.
WOULD YOU BE SO KIND AS TO JOIN...
AHEM!
MI-MI-MI! ♪
...A CELEBRATION IN YOUR HONOR!?
WUZZ WUZZ
YAY YAY
MISTER ...
YOU'VE CURLED YOUR HAIR...
...WAY TOO MUCH.
...
YACK YACK

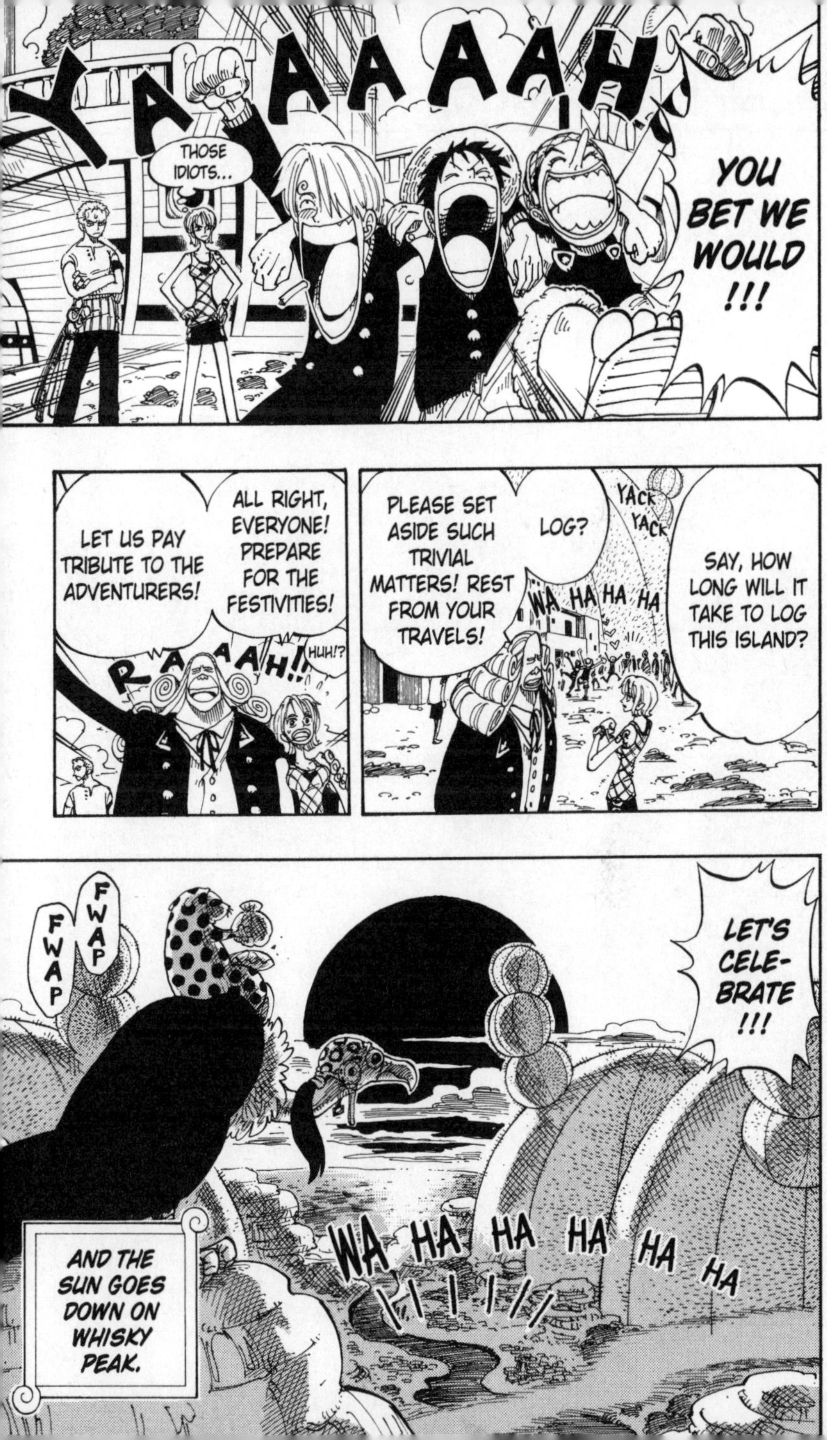
YAAAAH!
YOU BET WE WOULD!!!
THOSE IDIOTS...
SAY, HOW LONG WILL IT TAKE TO LOG THIS ISLAND?
YACK YACK
LOG?
PLEASE SET ASIDE SUCH TRIVIAL MATTERS! REST FROM YOUR TRAVELS!
WA HA HA HA
ALL RIGHT, EVERYONE! PREPARE FOR THE FESTIVITIES!
LET US PAY TRIBUTE TO THE ADVENTURERS!
HUH!?
RAAAH!!
LET'S CELEBRATE!!!
FWAP
FWAP
WA HA HA HA HA HA
AND THE SUN GOES DOWN ON WHISKY PEAK.

Chapter 107: MOONLIGHT AND TOMBSTONES

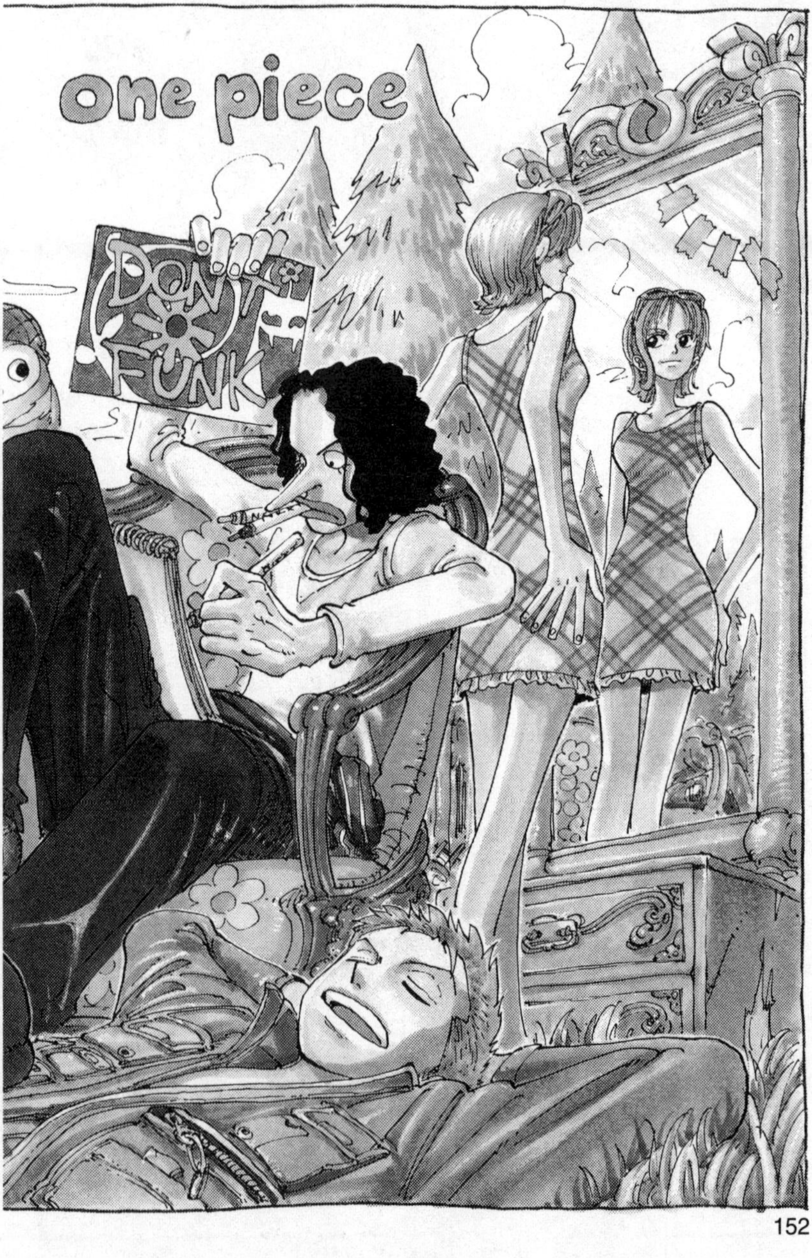
one piece
DON'T FUNK

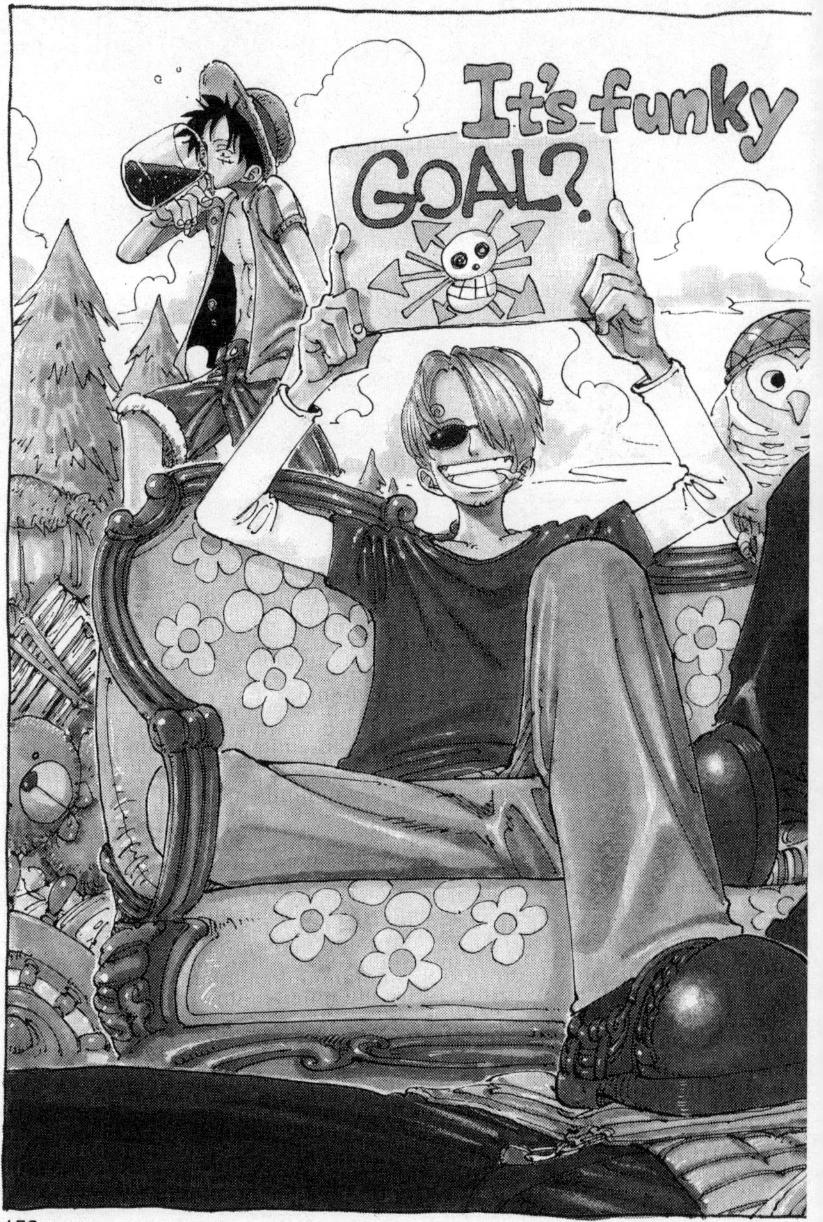
It's funky
GOAL?

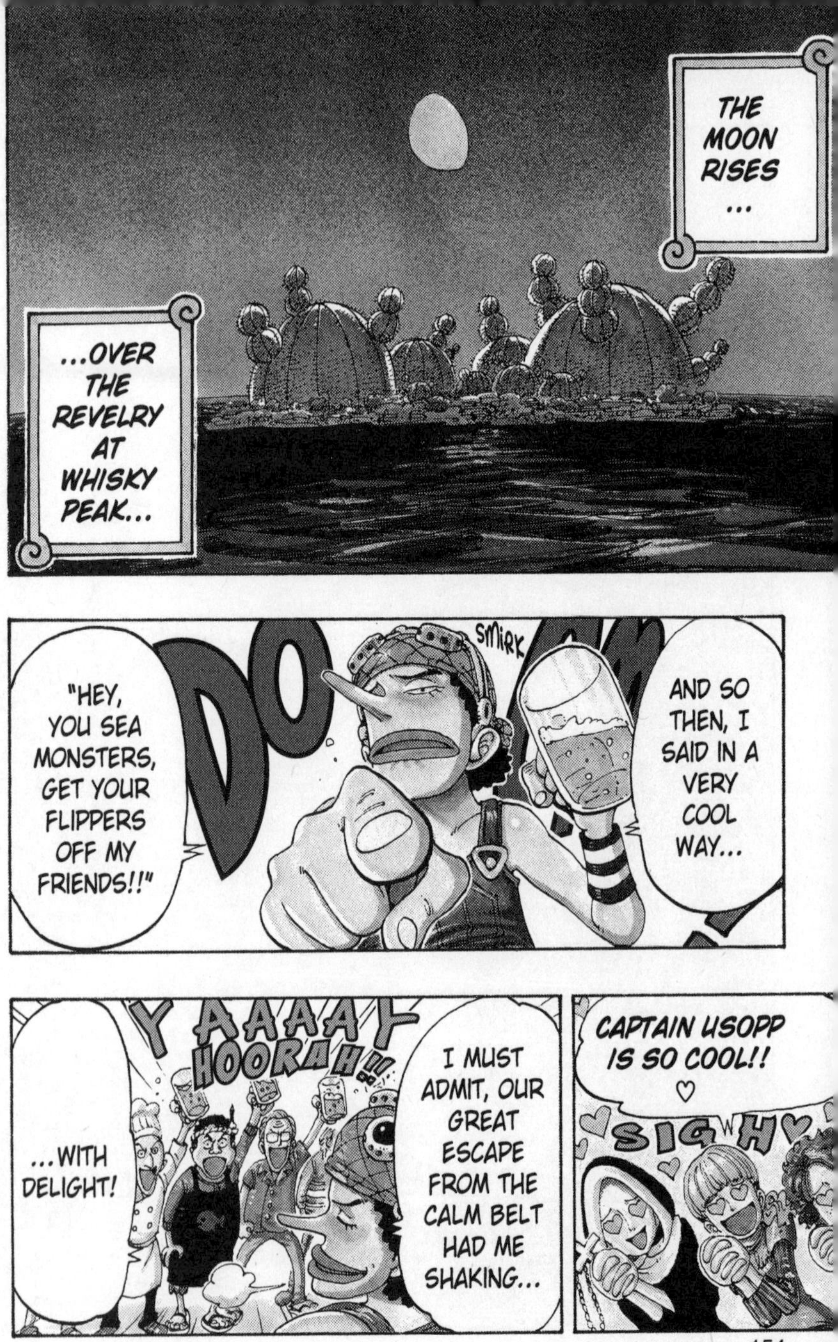
THE MOON RISES...
...OVER THE REVELRY AT WHISKY PEAK...
AND SO THEN, I SAID IN A VERY COOL WAY...
SMIRK
DO
"HEY, YOU SEA MONSTERS, GET YOUR FLIPPERS OFF MY FRIENDS!!"
CAPTAIN USOPP IS SO COOL!! ♡
SIGH
I MUST ADMIT, OUR GREAT ESCAPE FROM THE CALM BELT HAD ME SHAKING...
YAAAY
HOORAH!!
...WITH DELIGHT!

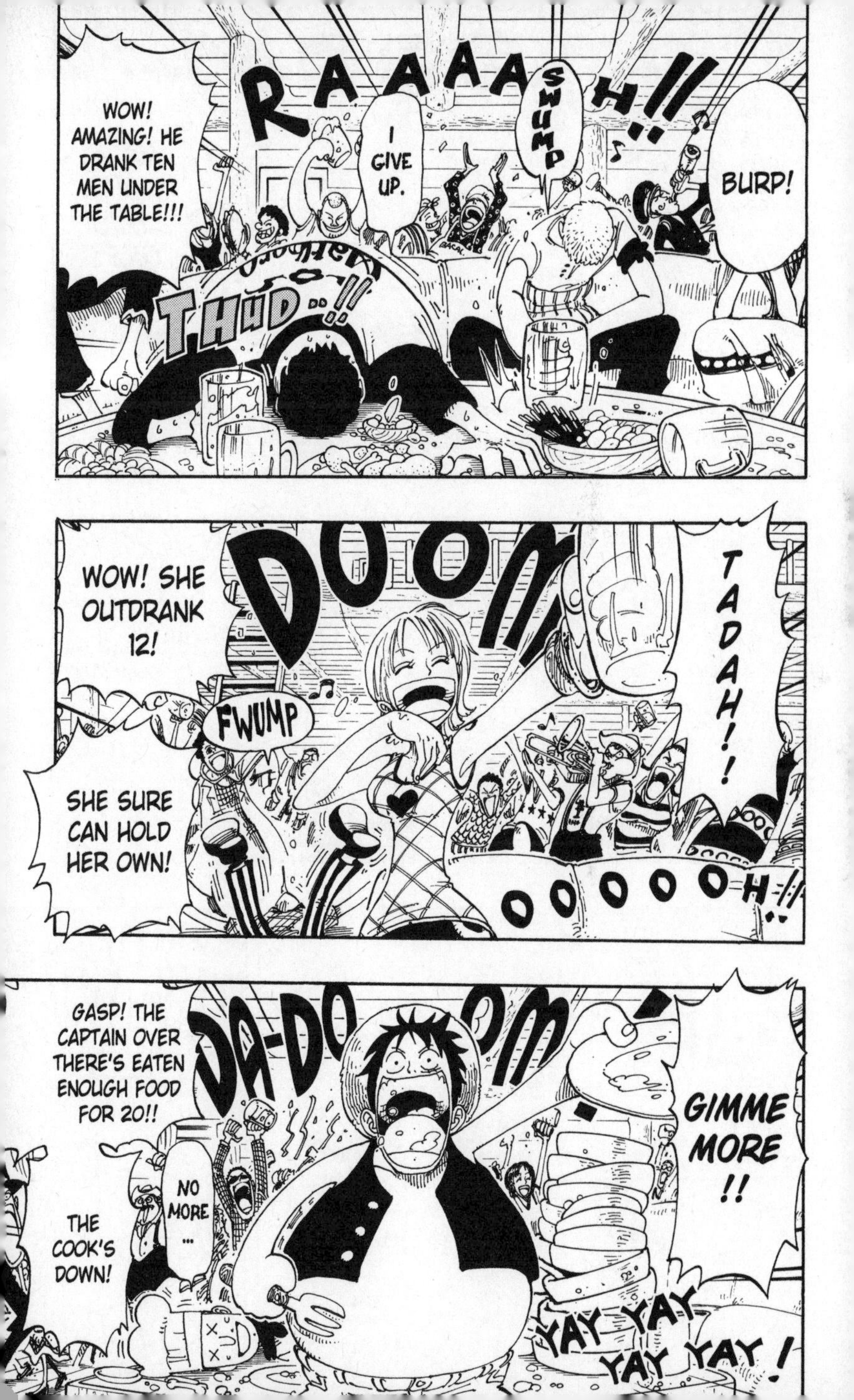
BURP!
SWUMP
RAAAAH!!
I GIVE UP.
WOW! AMAZING! HE DRANK TEN MEN UNDER THE TABLE!!!
THUD..!!
TADAH!!
DOOOOOOOOH!!
WOW! SHE OUTDRANK 12!
FWUMP
SHE SURE CAN HOLD HER OWN!
GIMME MORE!!
DA-DOOM!
GASP! THE CAPTAIN OVER THERE'S EATEN ENOUGH FOOD FOR 20!!
YAY YAY YAY YAY!
NO MORE...
THE COOK'S DOWN!

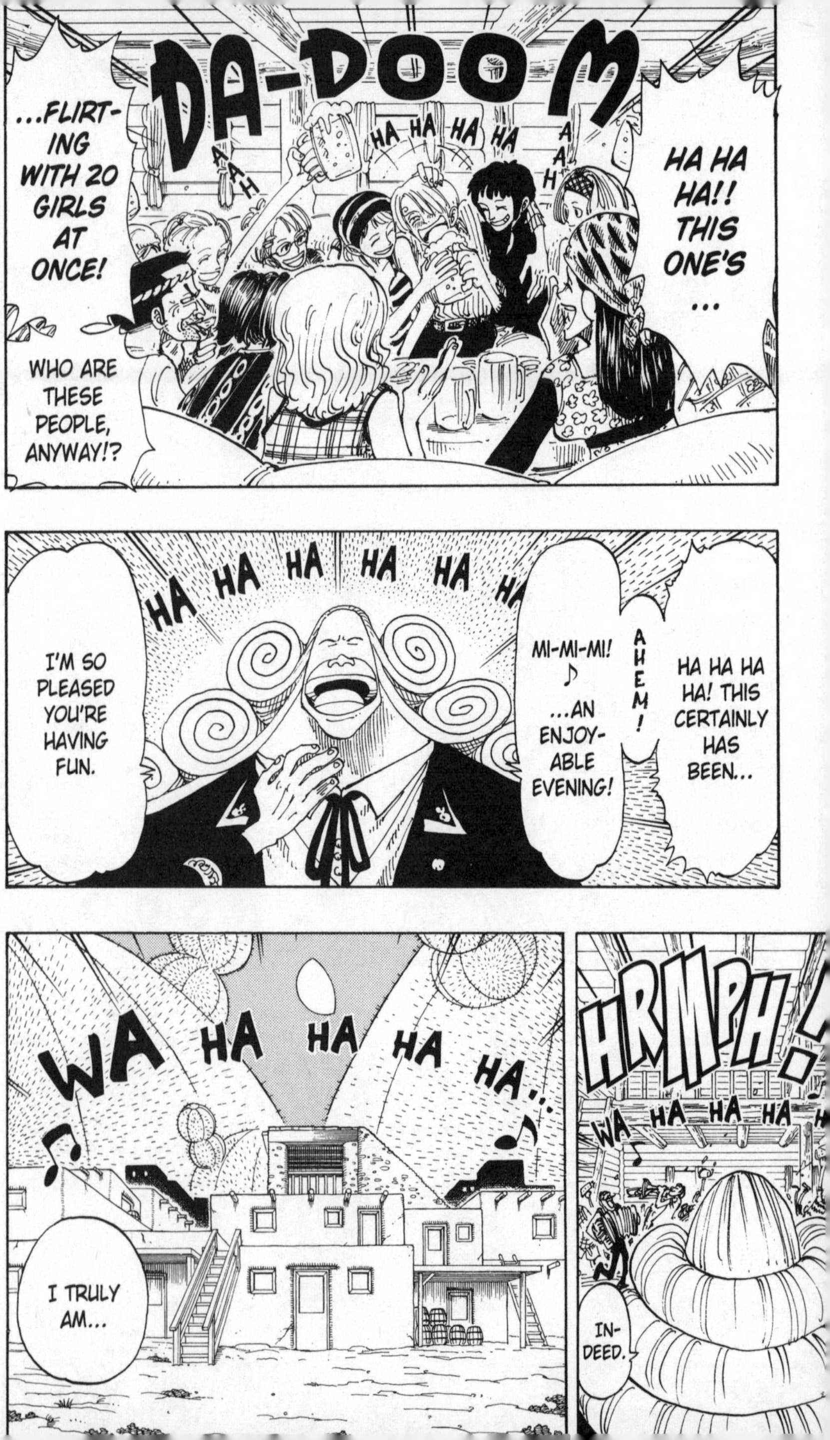
HA HA HA!! THIS ONE'S ...
DA-DOOM
HA HA HA HA
AAAH
AAAH
...FLIRTING WITH 20 GIRLS AT ONCE!
WHO ARE THESE PEOPLE, ANYWAY!?
HA HA HA HA! THIS CERTAINLY HAS BEEN...
AHEM!
MI-MI-MI! ♪ ...AN ENJOYABLE EVENING!
HA HA HA HA HA HA
I'M SO PLEASED YOU'RE HAVING FUN.
HRMPH!
WA HA HA HA HA
INDEED.
WA HA HA HA HA..
I TRULY AM...

READ THIS WAY

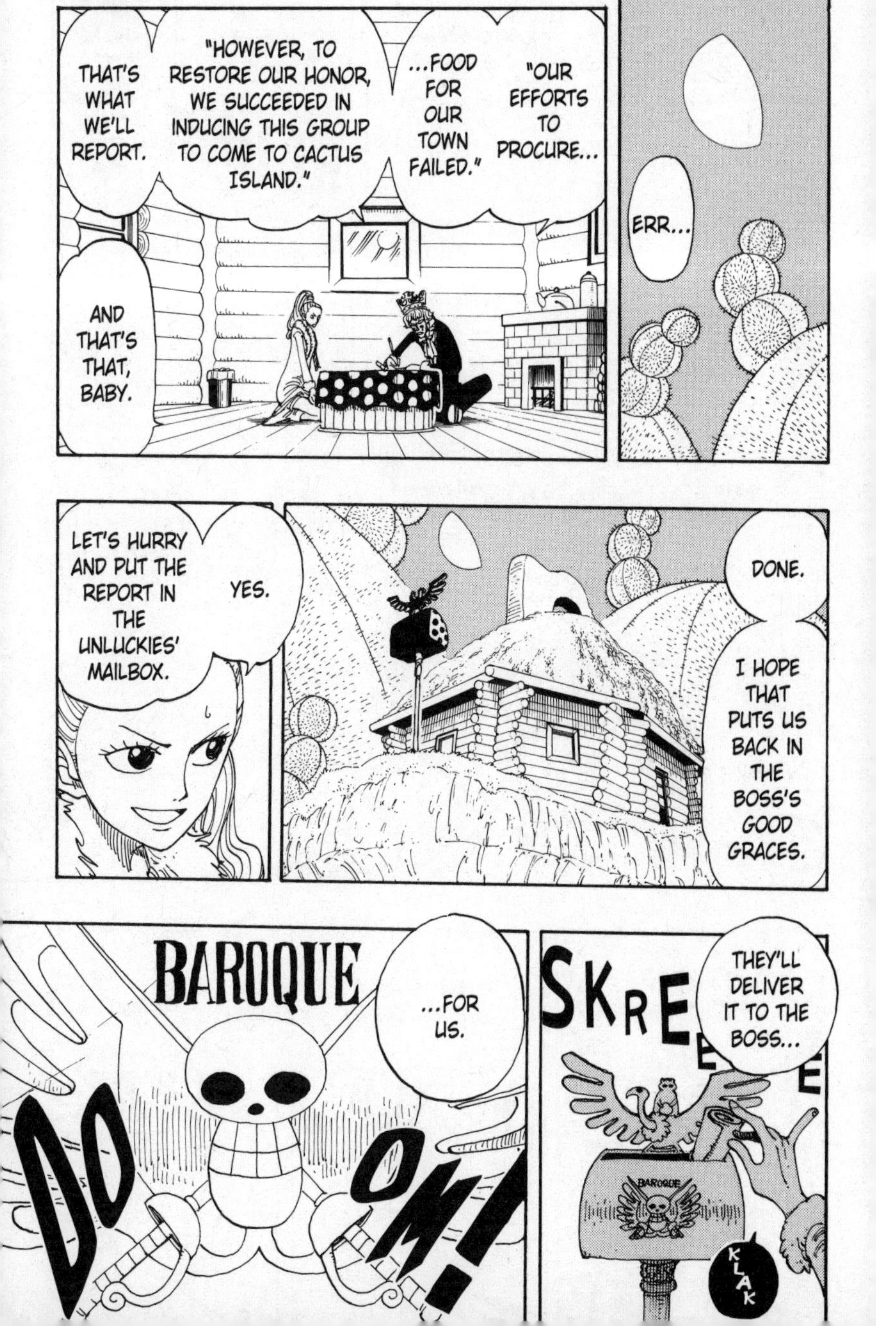
ERR...
"OUR EFFORTS TO PROCURE...
...FOOD FOR OUR TOWN FAILED."
"HOWEVER, TO RESTORE OUR HONOR, WE SUCCEEDED IN INDUCING THIS GROUP TO COME TO CACTUS ISLAND."
THAT'S WHAT WE'LL REPORT.
AND THAT'S THAT, BABY.
DONE.
I HOPE THAT PUTS US BACK IN THE BOSS'S GOOD GRACES.
LET'S HURRY AND PUT THE REPORT IN THE UNLUCKIES' MAILBOX.
YES.
SKREEEE
THEY'LL DELIVER IT TO THE BOSS...
BAROQUE
KLAK
BAROQUE
...FOR US.
DOOM!

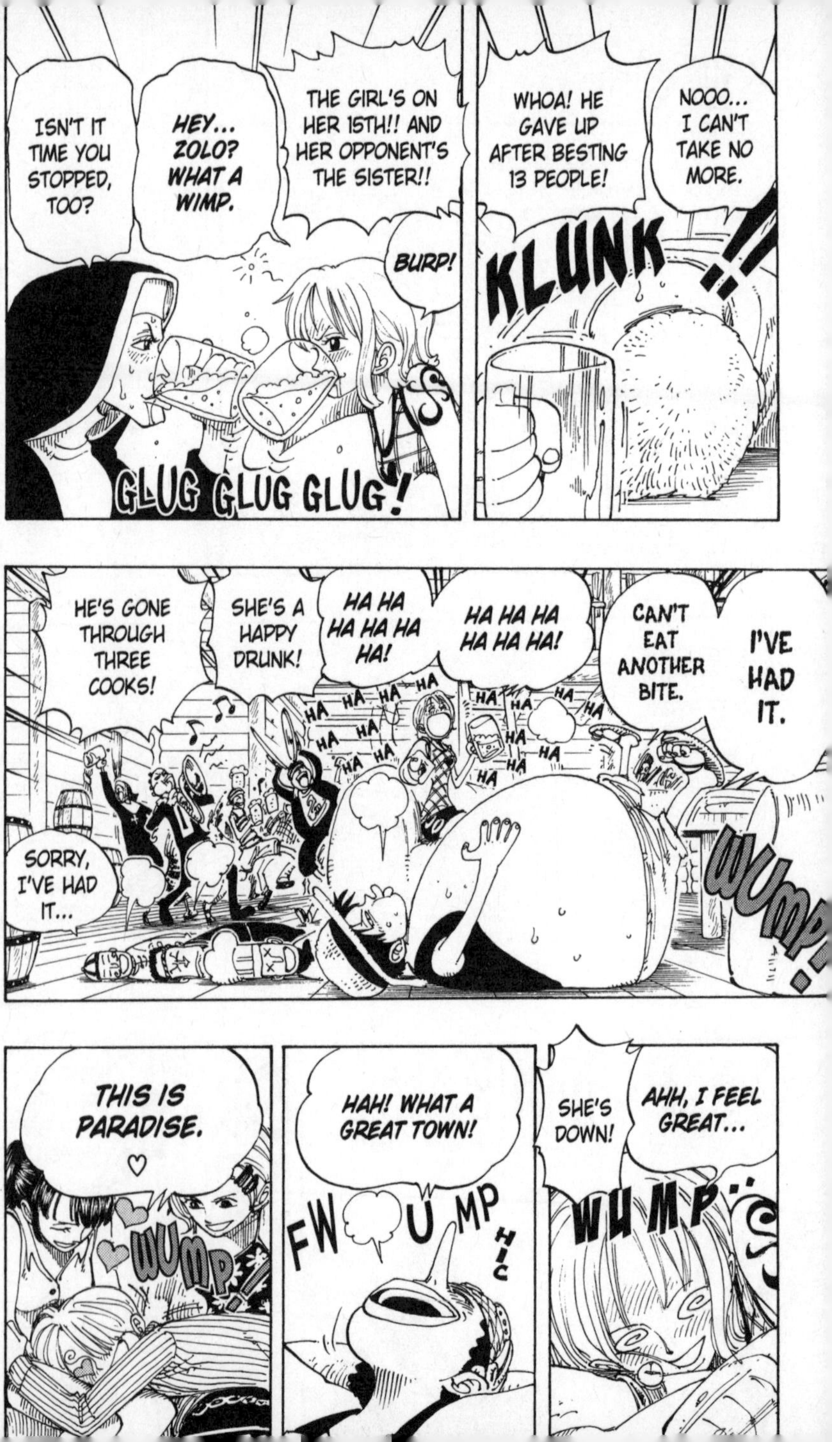
NOOO... I CAN'T TAKE NO MORE.
WHOA! HE GAVE UP AFTER BESTING 13 PEOPLE!
KLUNK!!
THE GIRL'S ON HER 15TH!! AND HER OPPONENT'S THE SISTER!!
HEY... ZOLO? WHAT A WIMP.
ISN'T IT TIME YOU STOPPED, TOO?
BURP!
GLUG GLUG GLUG!
I'VE HAD IT.
CAN'T EAT ANOTHER BITE.
WUMP!!
HA HA HA HA HA HA!
HA HA HA HA HA HA!
SHE'S A HAPPY DRUNK!
HE'S GONE THROUGH THREE COOKS!
SORRY, I'VE HAD IT...
AHH, I FEEL GREAT...
SHE'S DOWN!
WUMP..
HAH! WHAT A GREAT TOWN!
FWUMP
HIC
THIS IS PARADISE.
WUMP!!

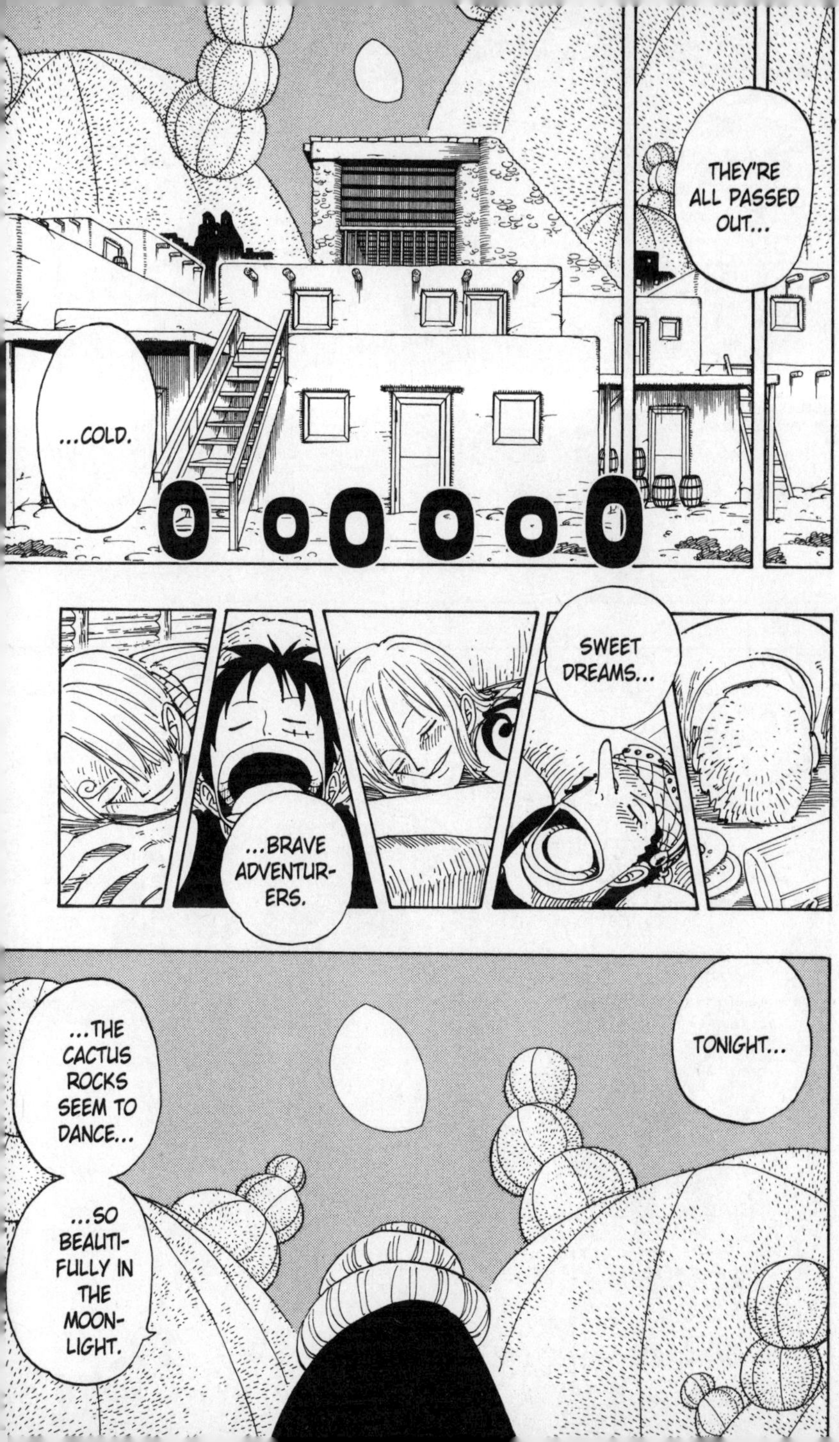
THEY'RE ALL PASSED OUT...
...COLD.
OOOOOO
SWEET DREAMS...
...BRAVE ADVENTURERS.
TONIGHT...
...THE CACTUS ROCKS SEEM TO DANCE...
...SO BEAUTIFULLY IN THE MOONLIGHT.

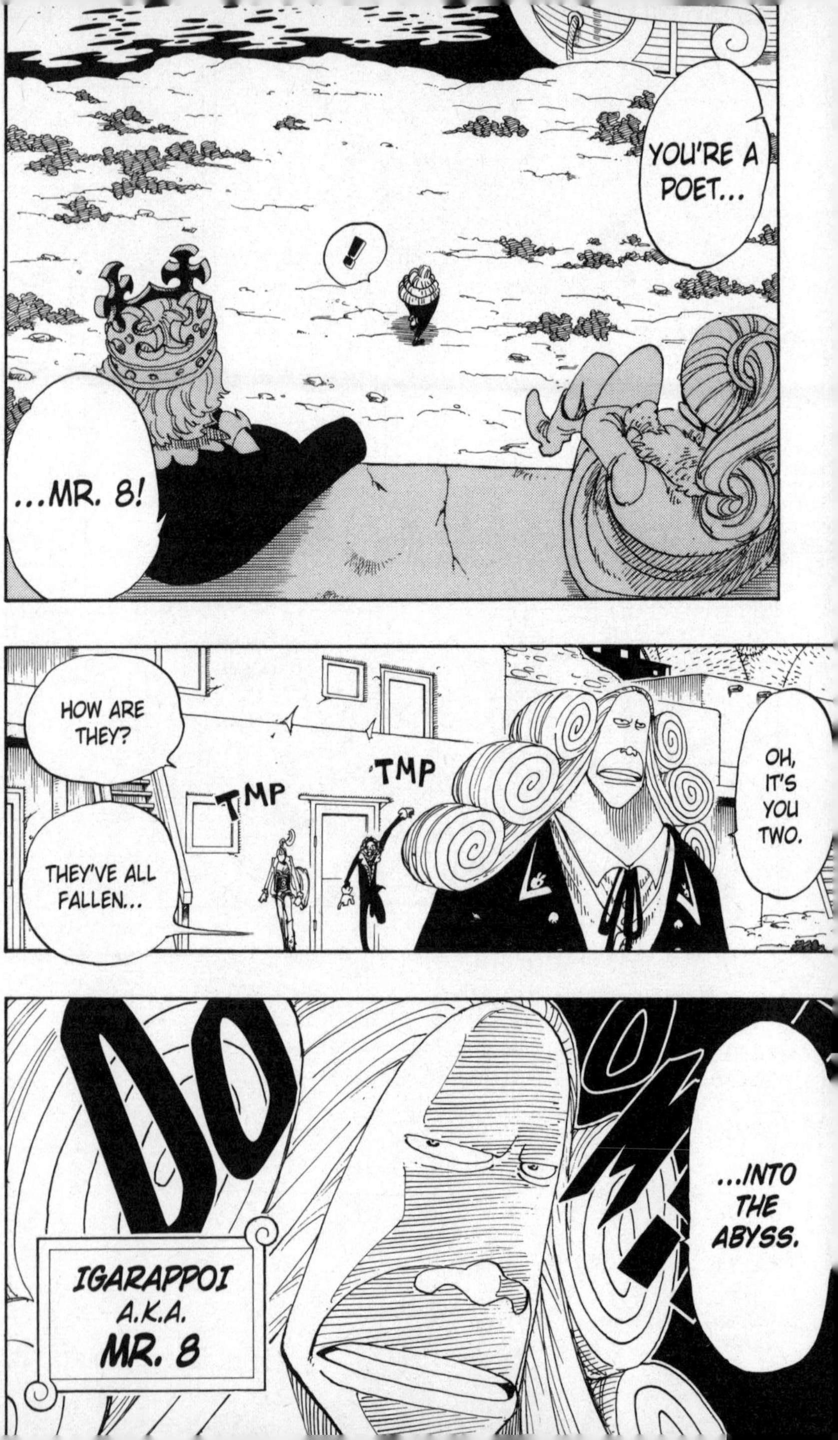
YOU'RE A POET...
!
...MR. 8!
OH, IT'S YOU TWO.
TMP
TMP
HOW ARE THEY?
THEY'VE ALL FALLEN...
DOOM
...INTO THE ABYSS.
IGARAPPOI A.K.A. MR. 8

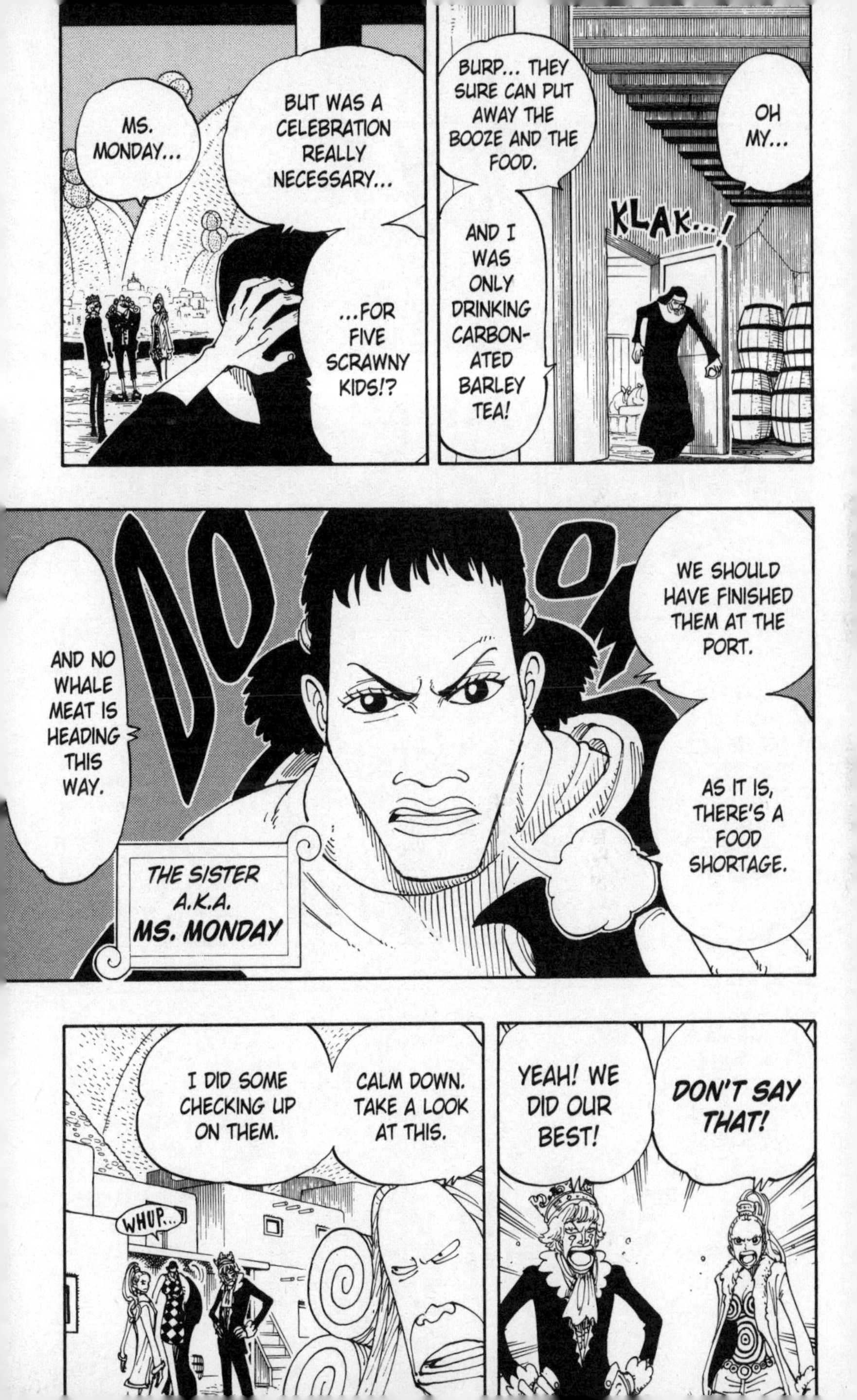
KLAK...!
OH MY...
BURP... THEY SURE CAN PUT AWAY THE BOOZE AND THE FOOD.
AND I WAS ONLY DRINKING CARBON-ATED BARLEY TEA!
BUT WAS A CELEBRATION REALLY NECESSARY...
MS. MONDAY...
...FOR FIVE SCRAWNY KIDS!?
WE SHOULD HAVE FINISHED THEM AT THE PORT.
AS IT IS, THERE'S A FOOD SHORTAGE.
AND NO WHALE MEAT IS HEADING THIS WAY.
THE SISTER A.K.A. MS. MONDAY
DON'T SAY THAT!
YEAH! WE DID OUR BEST!
CALM DOWN. TAKE A LOOK AT THIS.
I DID SOME CHECKING UP ON THEM.
WHUP...

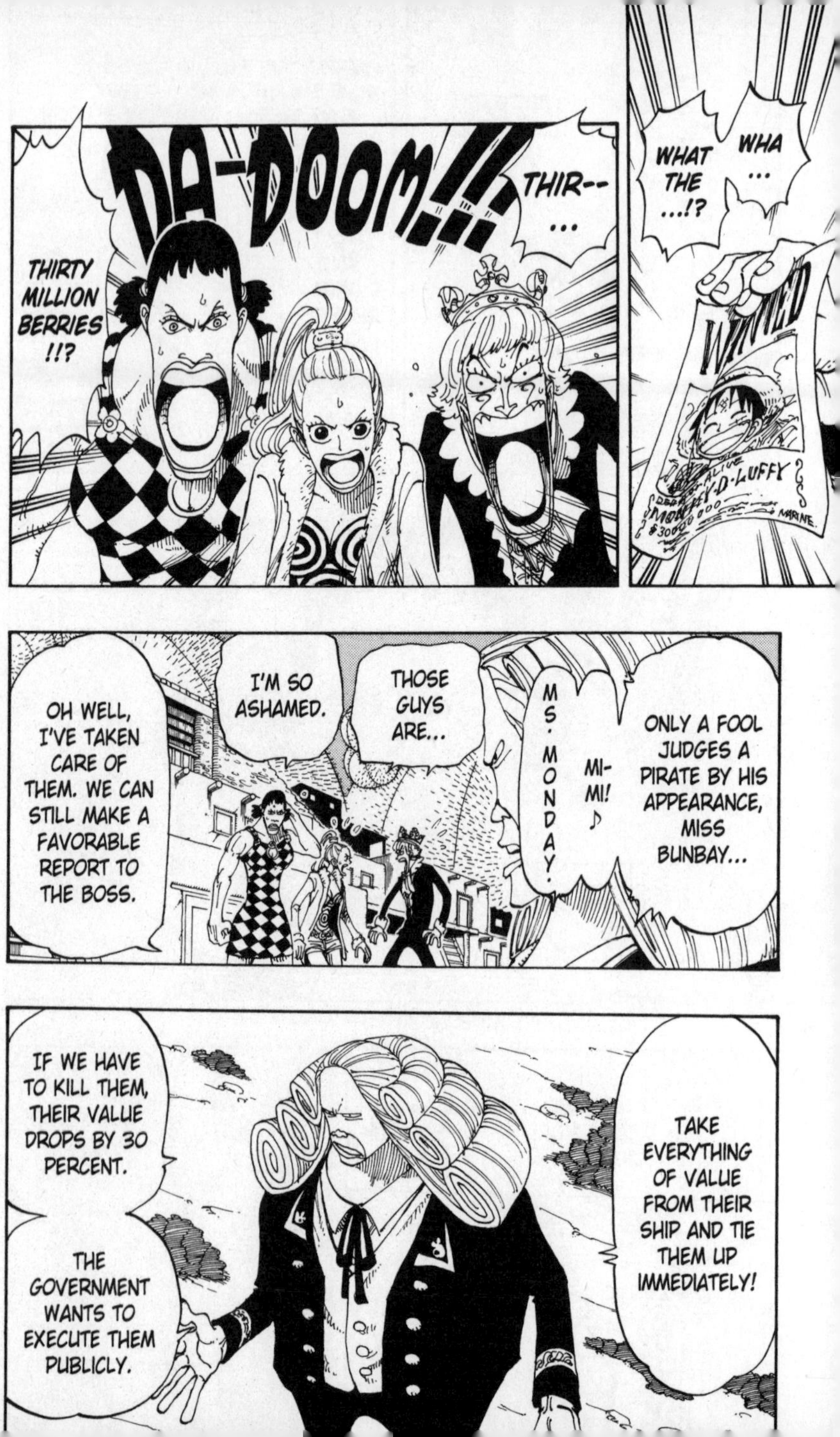
WHA ...
WHAT THE ...!?
THIR-- ...
DA-DOOM!!!
THIRTY MILLION BERRIES !!?
ONLY A FOOL JUDGES A PIRATE BY HIS APPEARANCE, MISS BUNBAY...
MI-MI! ♪
MS. MONDAY.
THOSE GUYS ARE...
I'M SO ASHAMED.
OH WELL, I'VE TAKEN CARE OF THEM. WE CAN STILL MAKE A FAVORABLE REPORT TO THE BOSS.
TAKE EVERYTHING OF VALUE FROM THEIR SHIP AND TIE THEM UP IMMEDIATELY!
IF WE HAVE TO KILL THEM, THEIR VALUE DROPS BY 30 PERCENT.
THE GOVERNMENT WANTS TO EXECUTE THEM PUBLICLY.

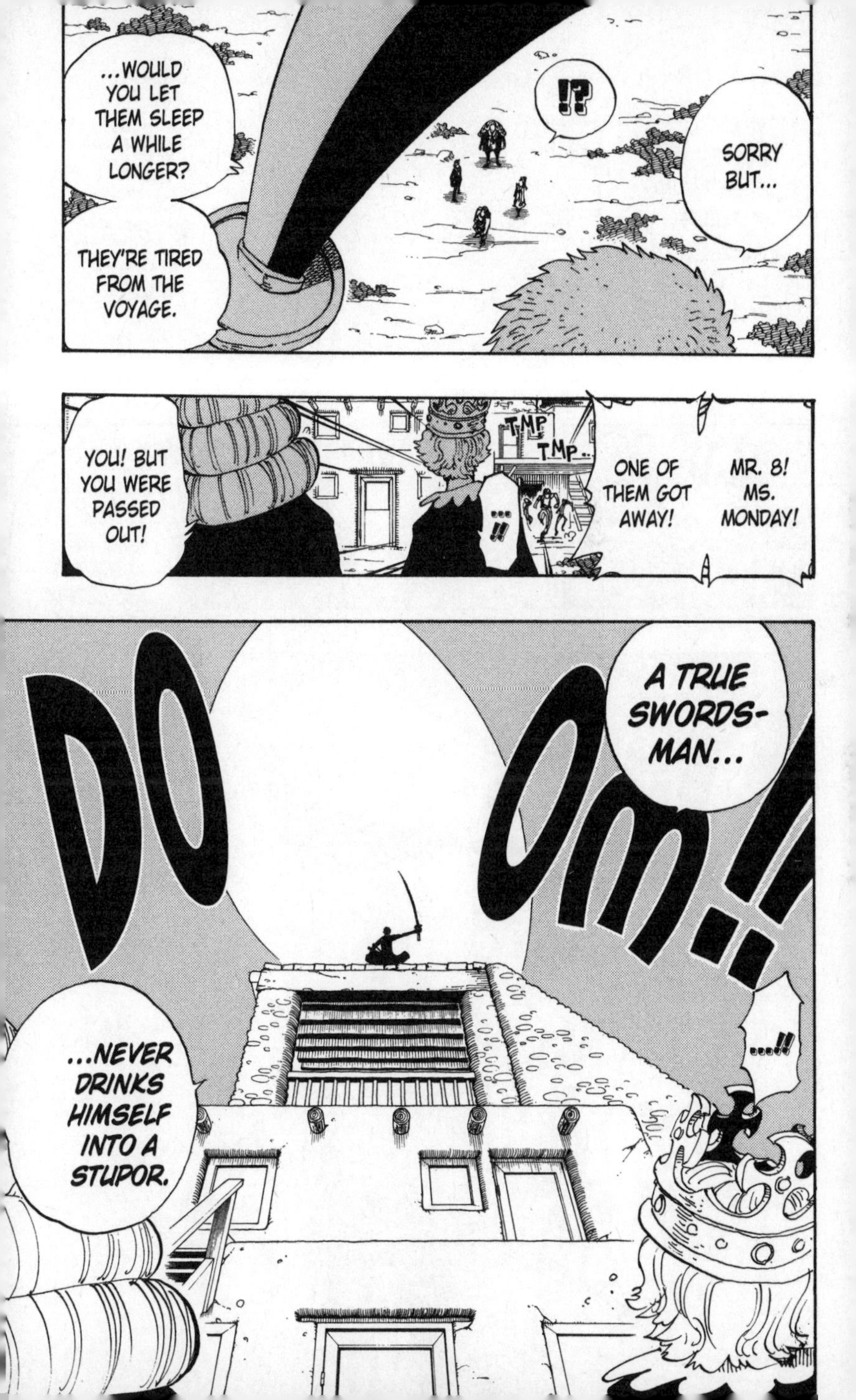

SORRY BUT...
!?
...WOULD YOU LET THEM SLEEP A WHILE LONGER?
THEY'RE TIRED FROM THE VOYAGE.
MR. 8! MS. MONDAY!
ONE OF THEM GOT AWAY!
TMP TMP...
...!!
YOU! BUT YOU WERE PASSED OUT!
A TRUE SWORDS-MAN...
DOOM!!
...!!
...NEVER DRINKS HIMSELF INTO A STUPOR.

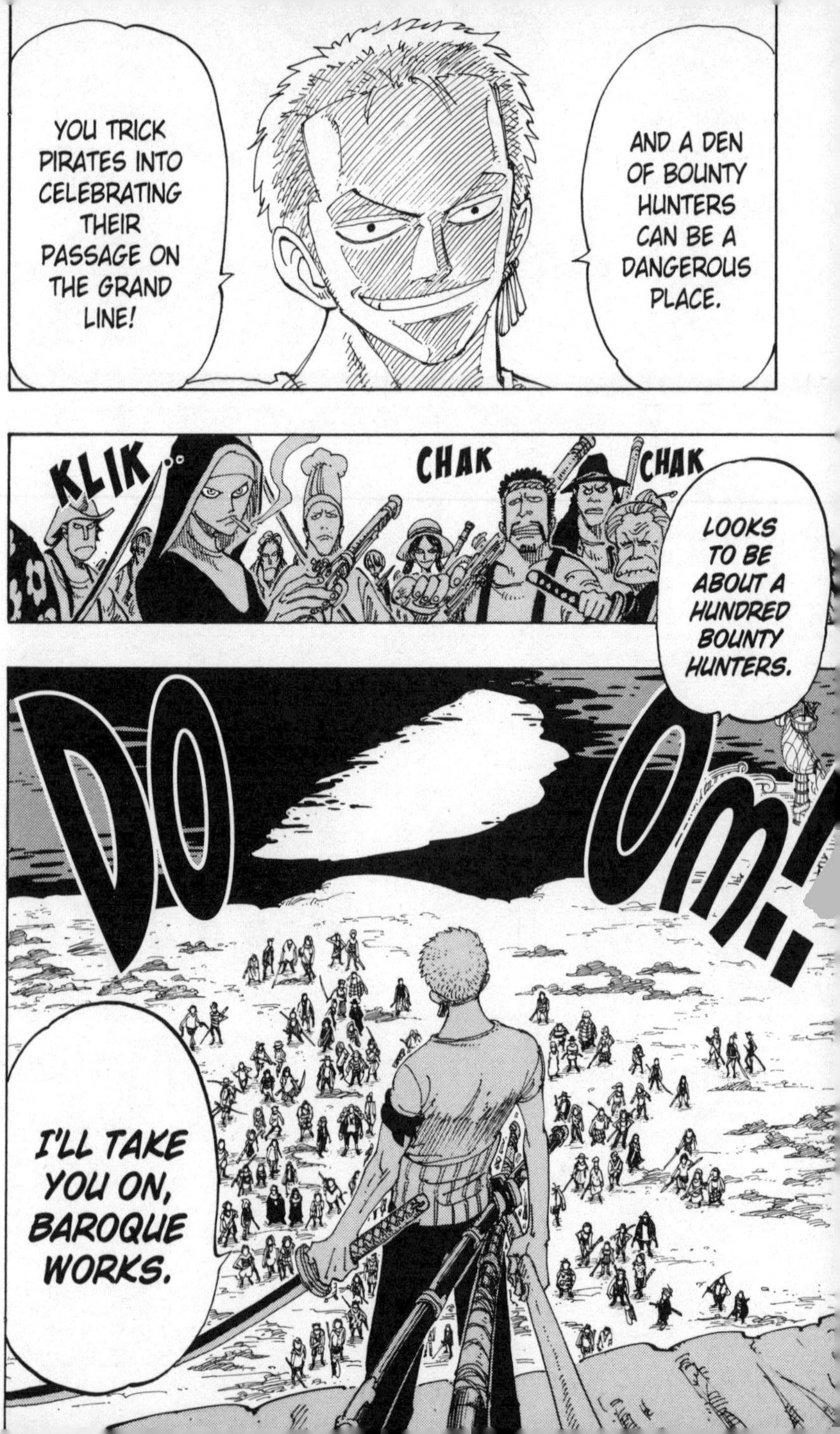
AND A DEN OF BOUNTY HUNTERS CAN BE A DANGEROUS PLACE.
YOU TRICK PIRATES INTO CELEBRATING THEIR PASSAGE ON THE GRAND LINE!
LOOKS TO BE ABOUT A HUNDRED BOUNTY HUNTERS.
CHAK
CHAK
KLIK
DOOM!!
I'LL TAKE YOU ON, BAROQUE WORKS.

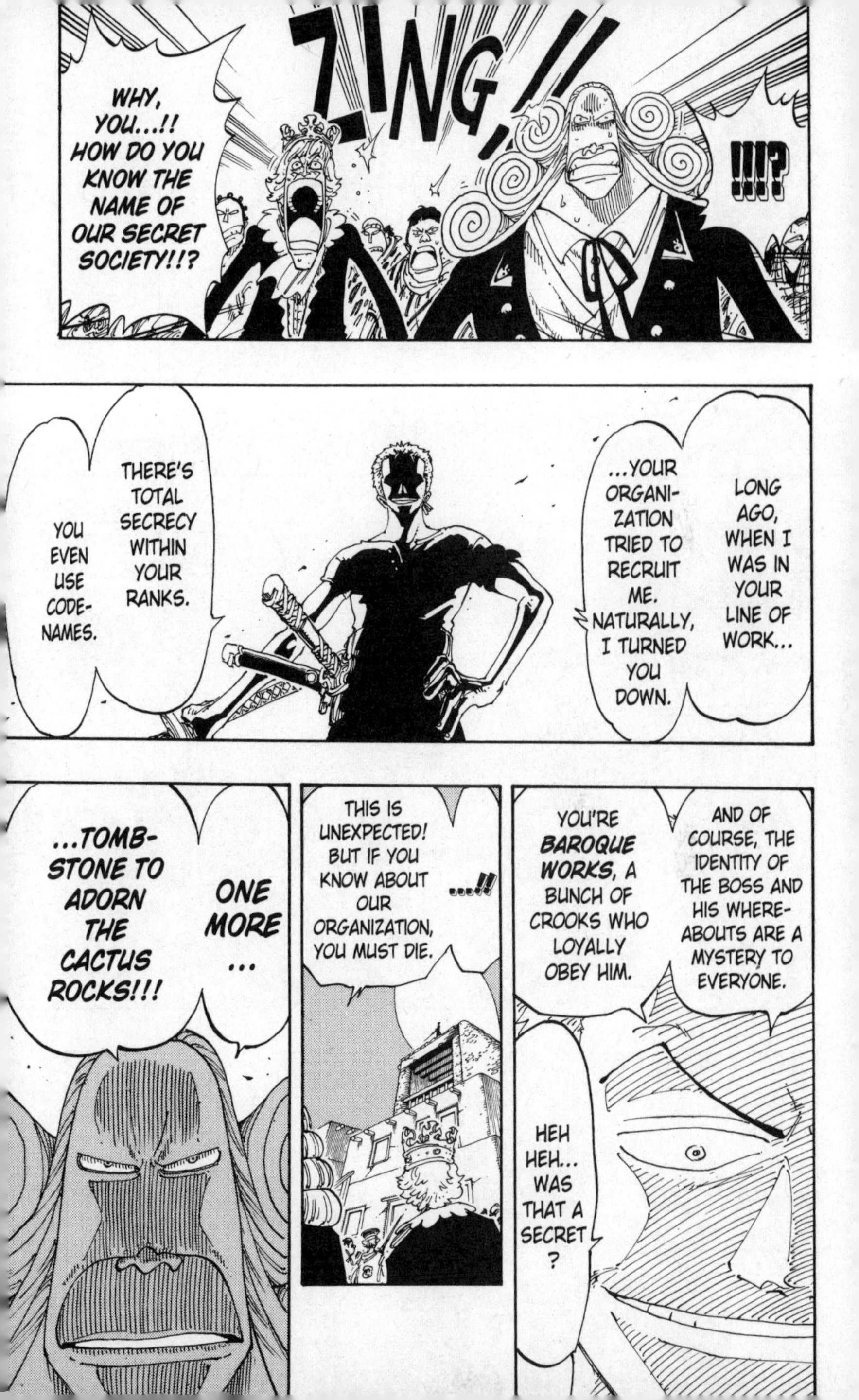
ZING!!
!!!?
WHY, YOU...!! HOW DO YOU KNOW THE NAME OF OUR SECRET SOCIETY!!?
LONG AGO, WHEN I WAS IN YOUR LINE OF WORK...
...YOUR ORGANI-ZATION TRIED TO RECRUIT ME. NATURALLY, I TURNED YOU DOWN.
THERE'S TOTAL SECRECY WITHIN YOUR RANKS.
YOU EVEN USE CODE-NAMES.
AND OF COURSE, THE IDENTITY OF THE BOSS AND HIS WHERE-ABOUTS ARE A MYSTERY TO EVERYONE.
YOU'RE BAROQUE WORKS, A BUNCH OF CROOKS WHO LOYALLY OBEY HIM.
HEH HEH... WAS THAT A SECRET?
...!!
THIS IS UNEXPECTED! BUT IF YOU KNOW ABOUT OUR ORGANIZATION, YOU MUST DIE.
ONE MORE...
...TOMB-STONE TO ADORN THE CACTUS ROCKS!!!

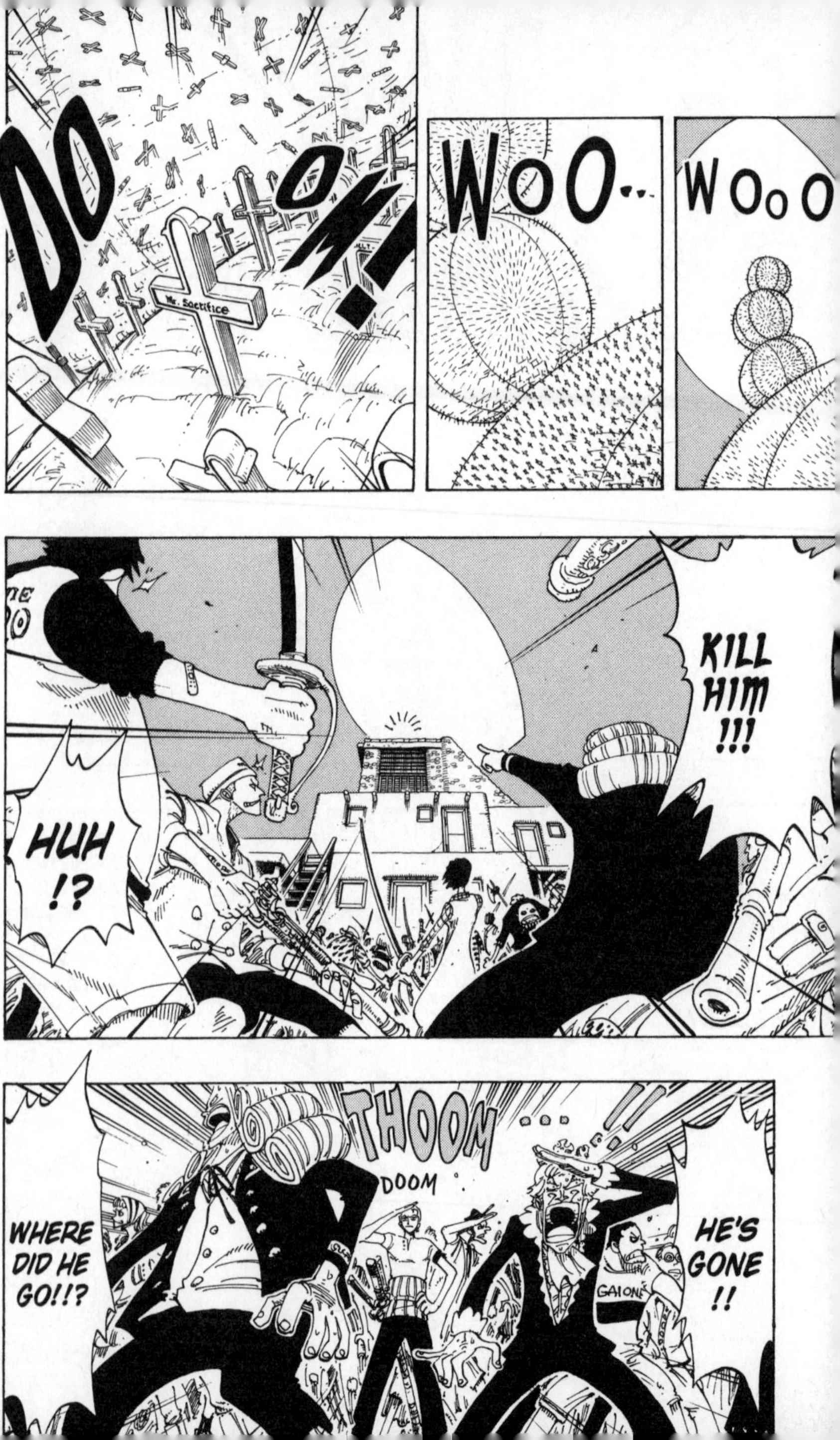
WOOO
WOO...
DOOM!
Mr. Sacrifice
KILL HIM!!!
HUH!?
THOOM...!!
HE'S GONE!!
GAIONE
DOOM
WHERE DID HE GO!!?

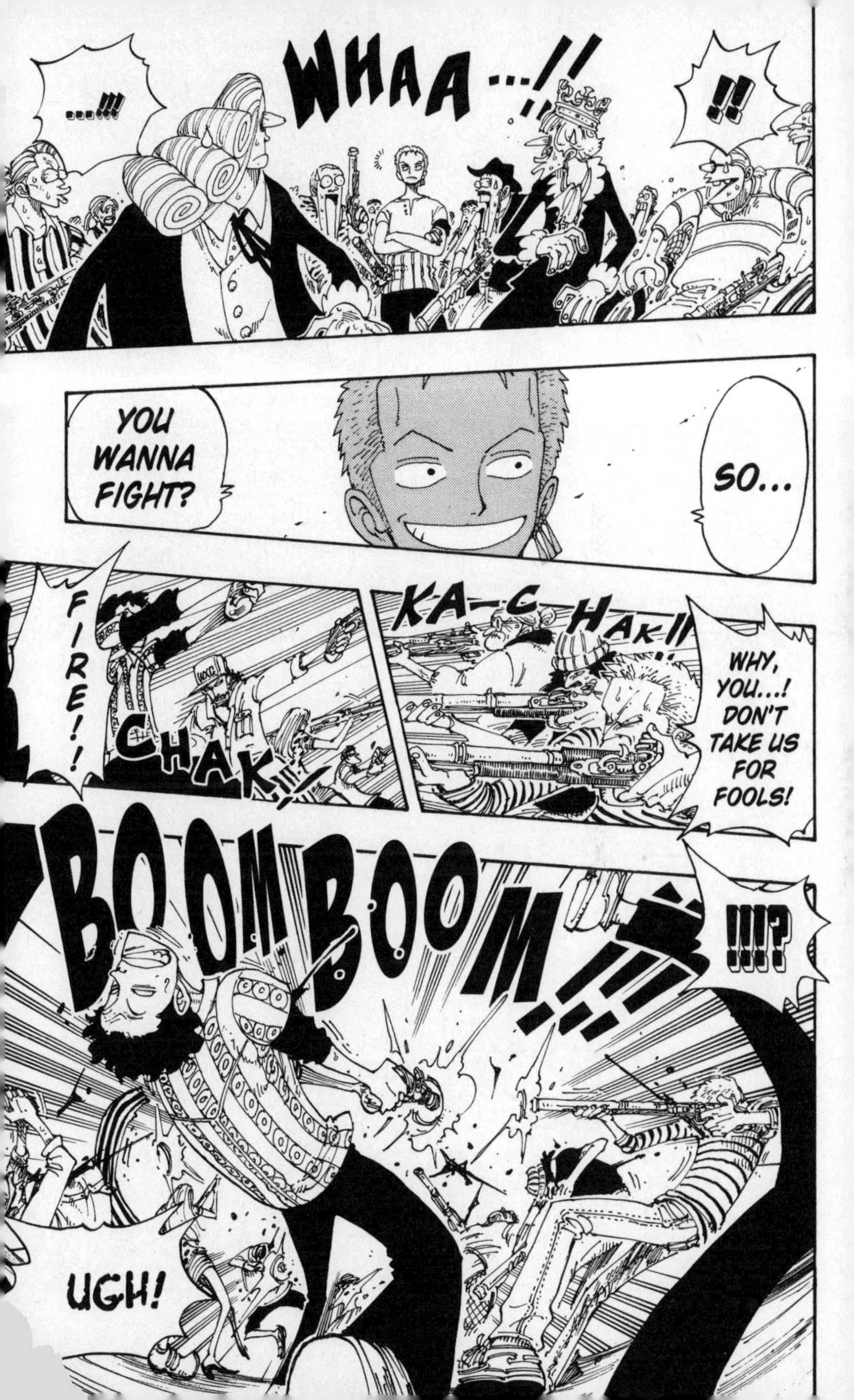
!!
WHAA...!!
...!!!
SO...
YOU WANNA FIGHT?
KA-CHAK!!
WHY, YOU...! DON'T TAKE US FOR FOOLS!
FIRE!!
CHAK!!
!!!?
BOOM BOOM!!!
UGH!

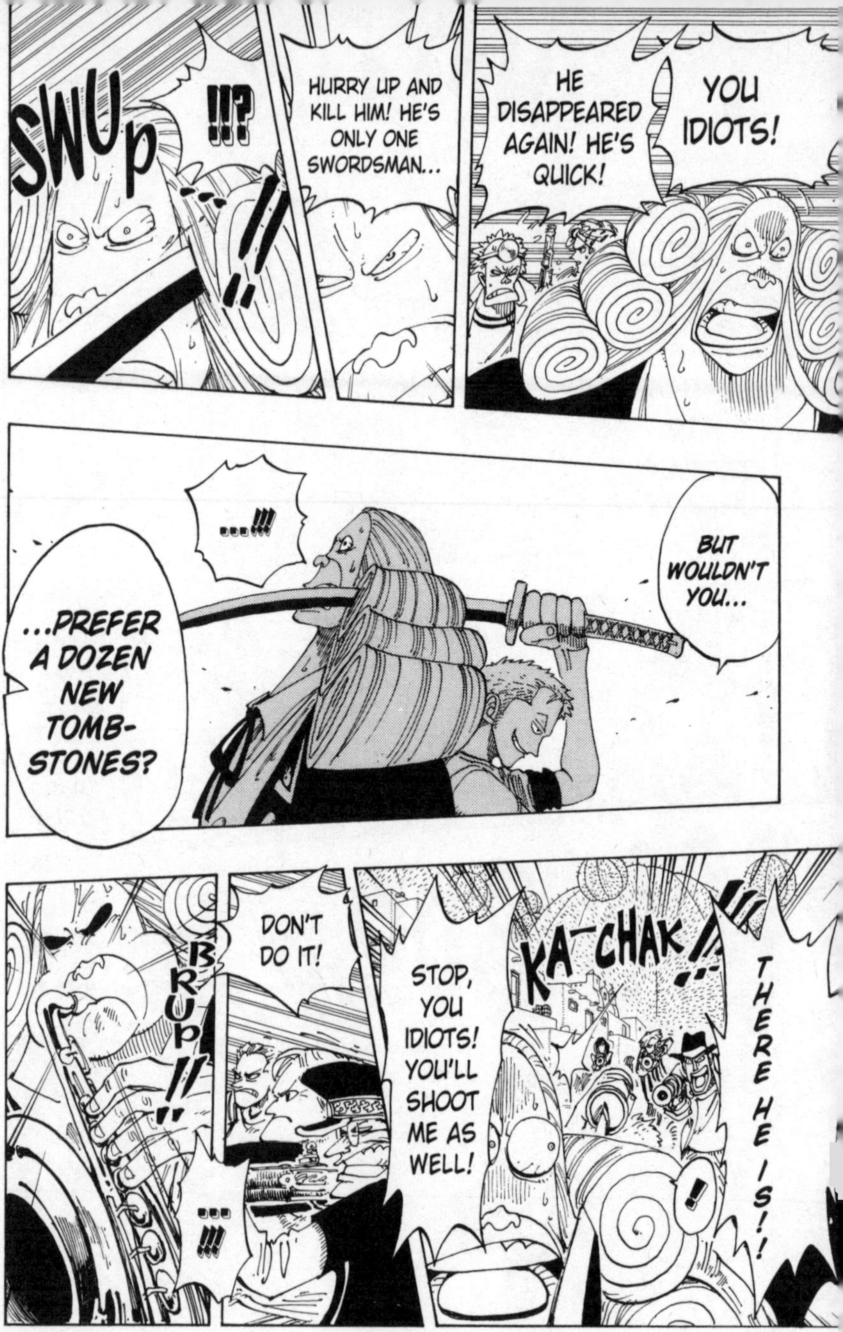
YOU IDIOTS!
HE DISAPPEARED AGAIN! HE'S QUICK!
HURRY UP AND KILL HIM! HE'S ONLY ONE SWORDSMAN...
SWUp
!!?
...!!
BUT WOULDN'T YOU...
...!!!
...PREFER A DOZEN NEW TOMB-STONES?
THERE HE IS!!
KA-CHAK !!
!
STOP, YOU IDIOTS! YOU'LL SHOOT ME AS WELL!
DON'T DO IT!
BRUP!!
...!!!

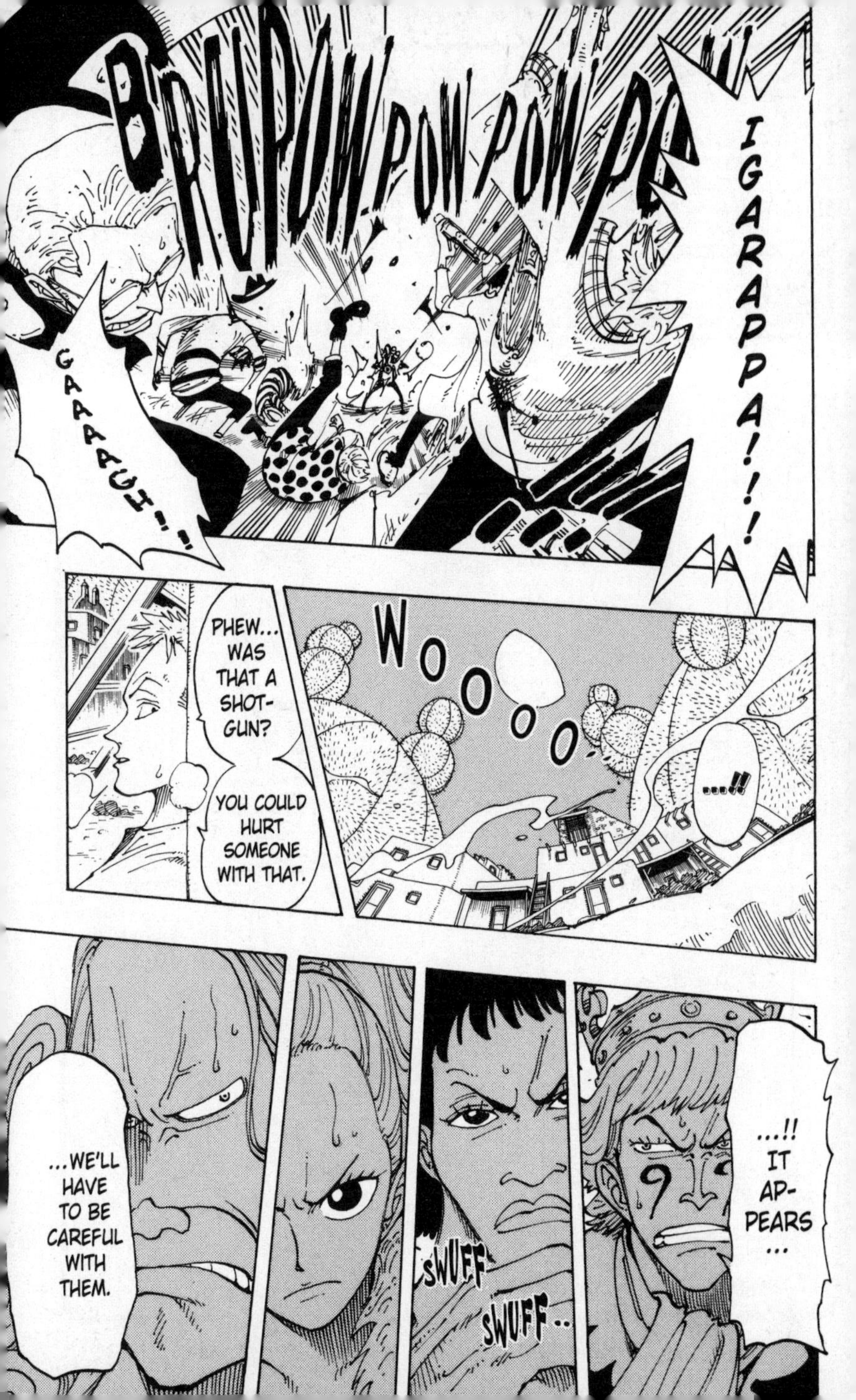
IGARAPPA!!!
BRRUPOW POW POW POW PE
GAAAAAGH!!!
WOOOOO
...!!
PHEW... WAS THAT A SHOT-GUN?
YOU COULD HURT SOMEONE WITH THAT.
...!! IT AP-PEARS...
SWUFF
SWUFF...
...WE'LL HAVE TO BE CAREFUL WITH THEM.

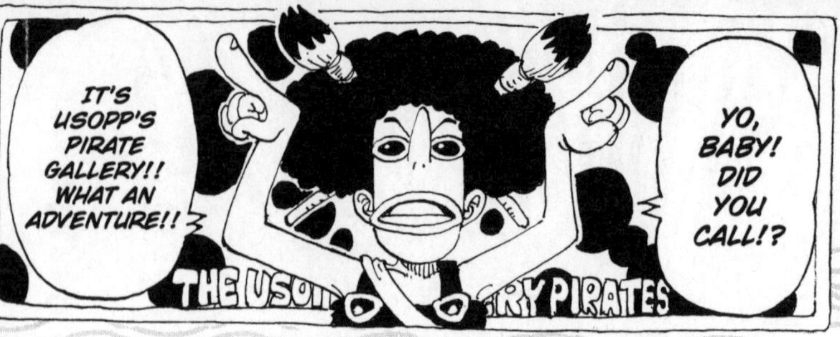
IT'S USOPP'S PIRATE GALLERY!! WHAT AN ADVENTURE!!
YO, BABY! DID YOU CALL!?

A PIRATE REUNION (HOLD THE ONION)

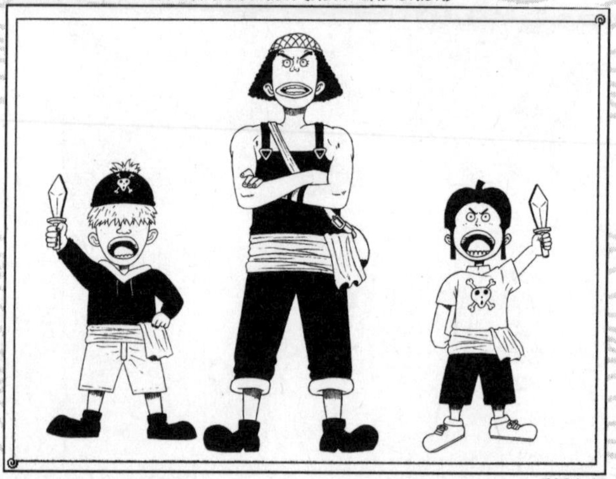

JACK, 15

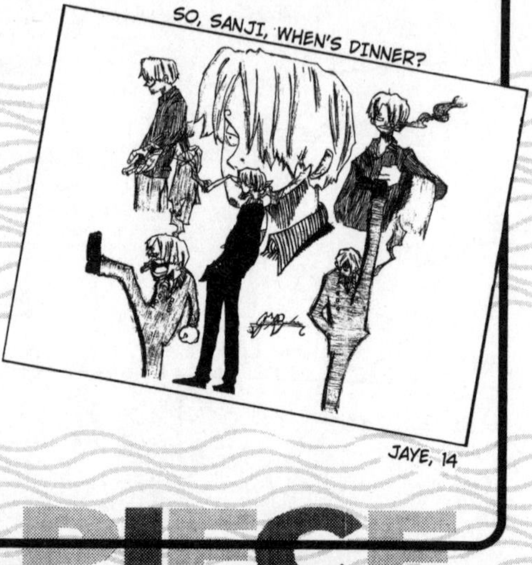

SO, SANJI, WHEN'S DINNER?

JAYE, 14

DON'T BE LATE FOR CLASS!

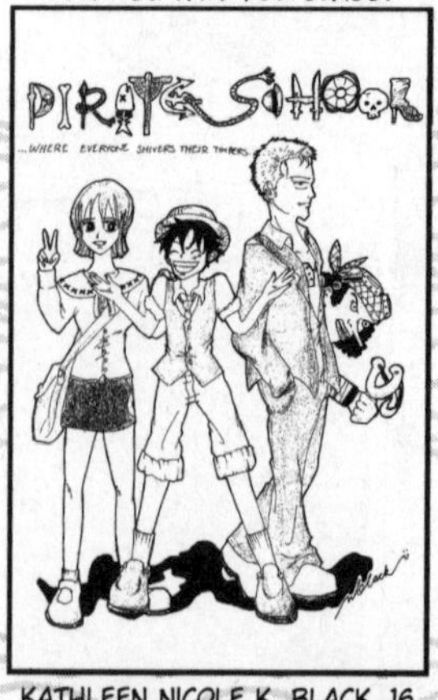
PIRATE SCHOOL
...WHERE EVERYONE SHIVERS THEIR TIMBERS

KATHLEEN NICOLE K. BLACK, 16

ONE PIECE

Chapter 108:
100 BOUNTY HUNTERS

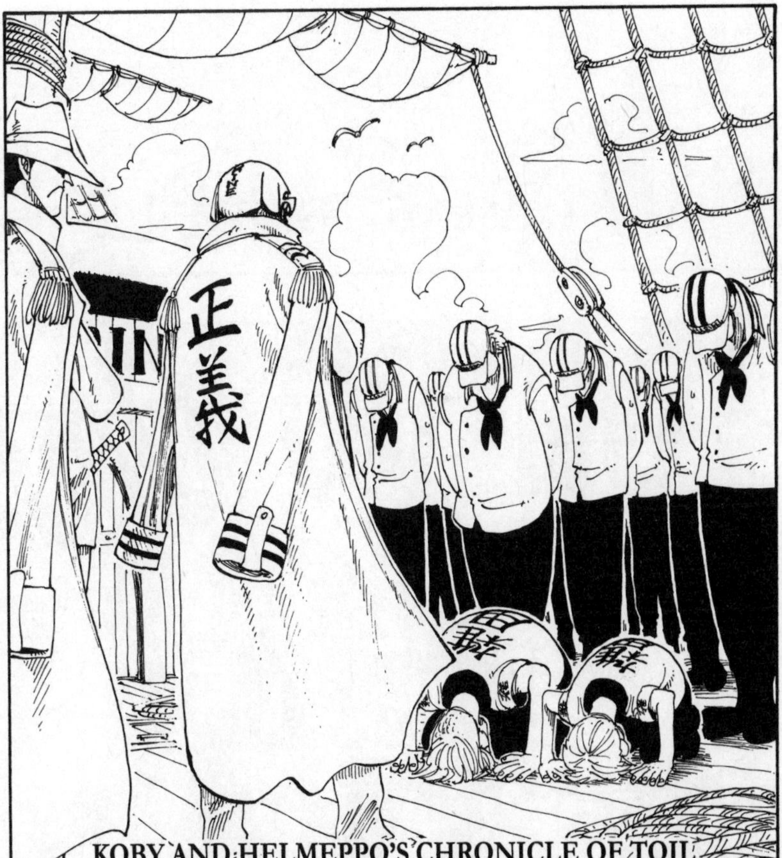
正義
KOBY AND HELMEPPO'S CHRONICLE OF TOIL
VOL. 21: "BEGGING FORGIVENESS"

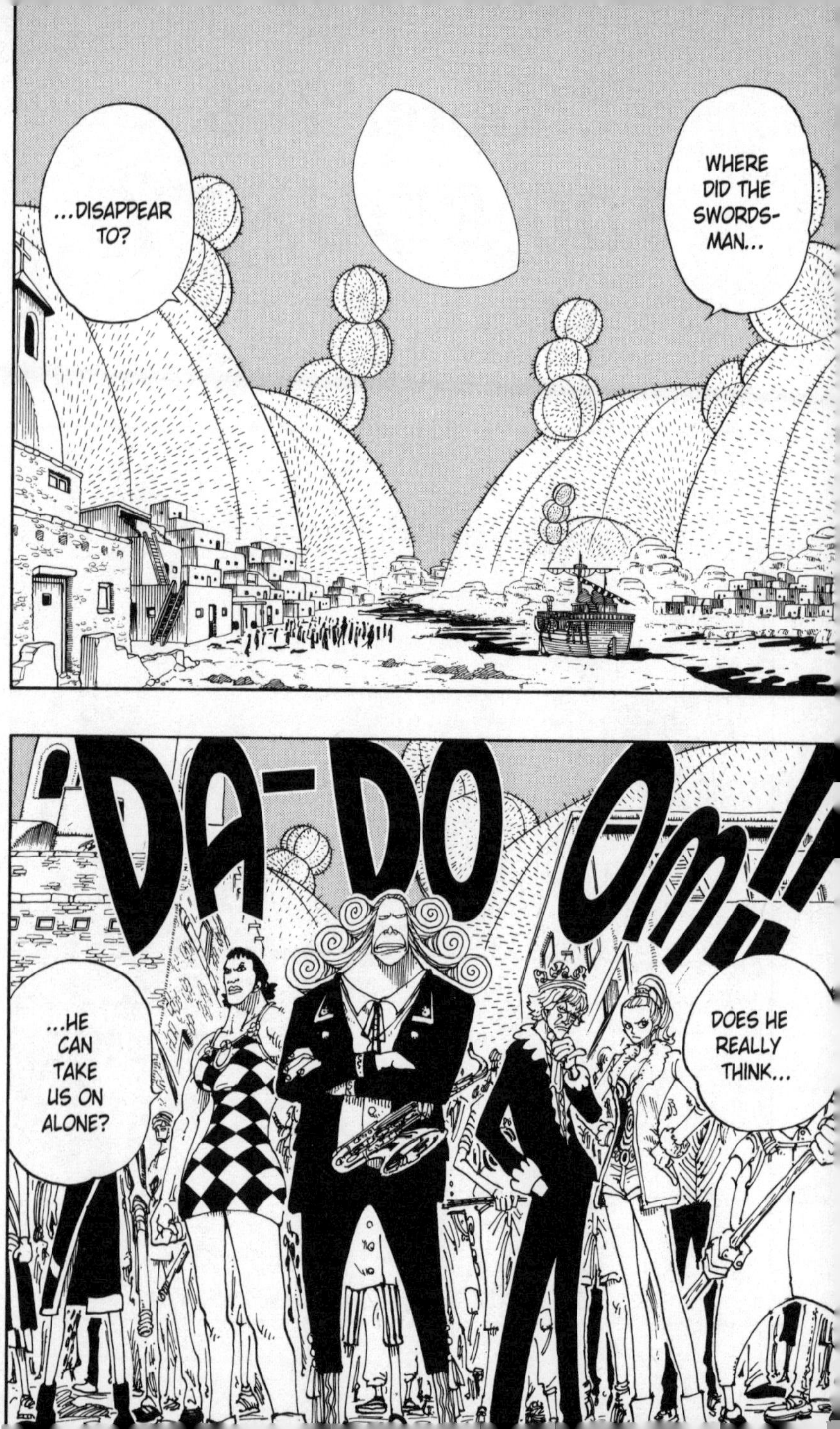
WHERE DID THE SWORDS-MAN...
...DISAPPEAR TO?
DA-DOOM!!
DOES HE REALLY THINK...
...HE CAN TAKE US ON ALONE?

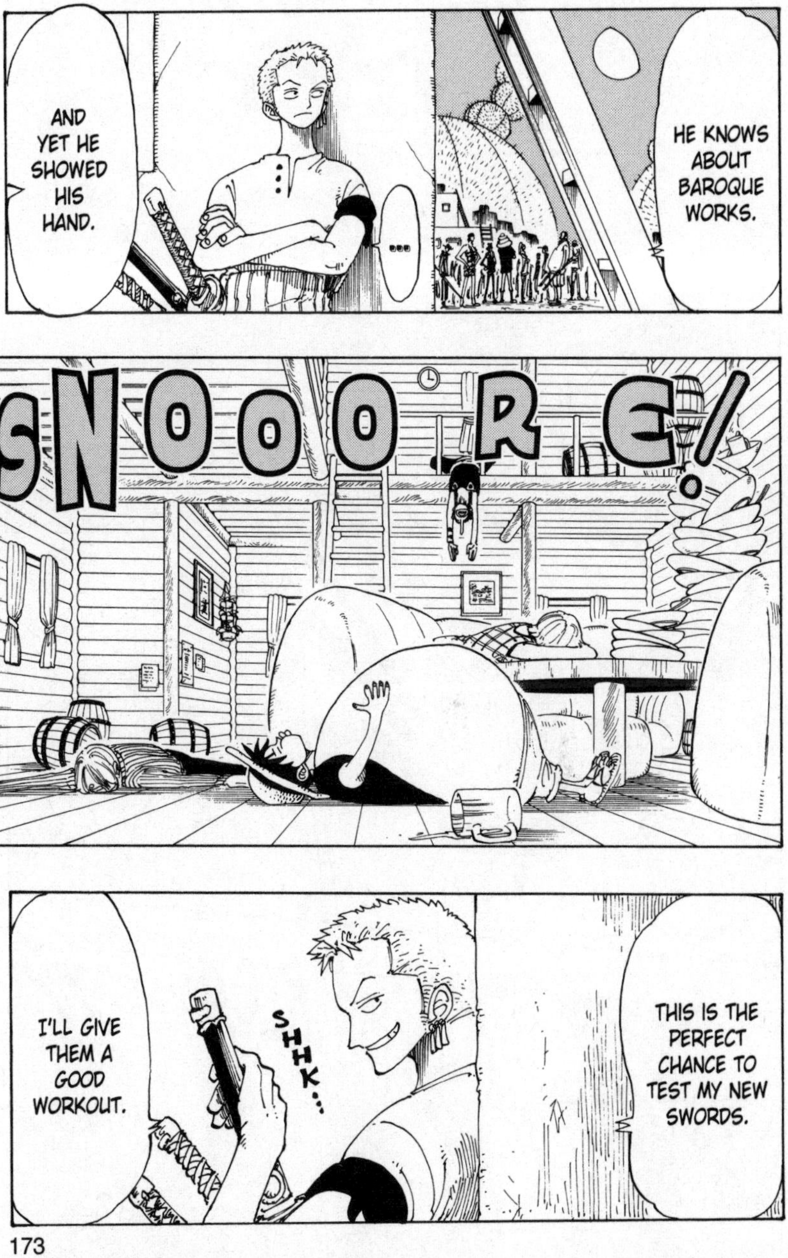
HE KNOWS ABOUT BAROQUE WORKS.
AND YET HE SHOWED HIS HAND.
...
SNOOORE!
THIS IS THE PERFECT CHANCE TO TEST MY NEW SWORDS.
SHHK...
I'LL GIVE THEM A GOOD WORKOUT.

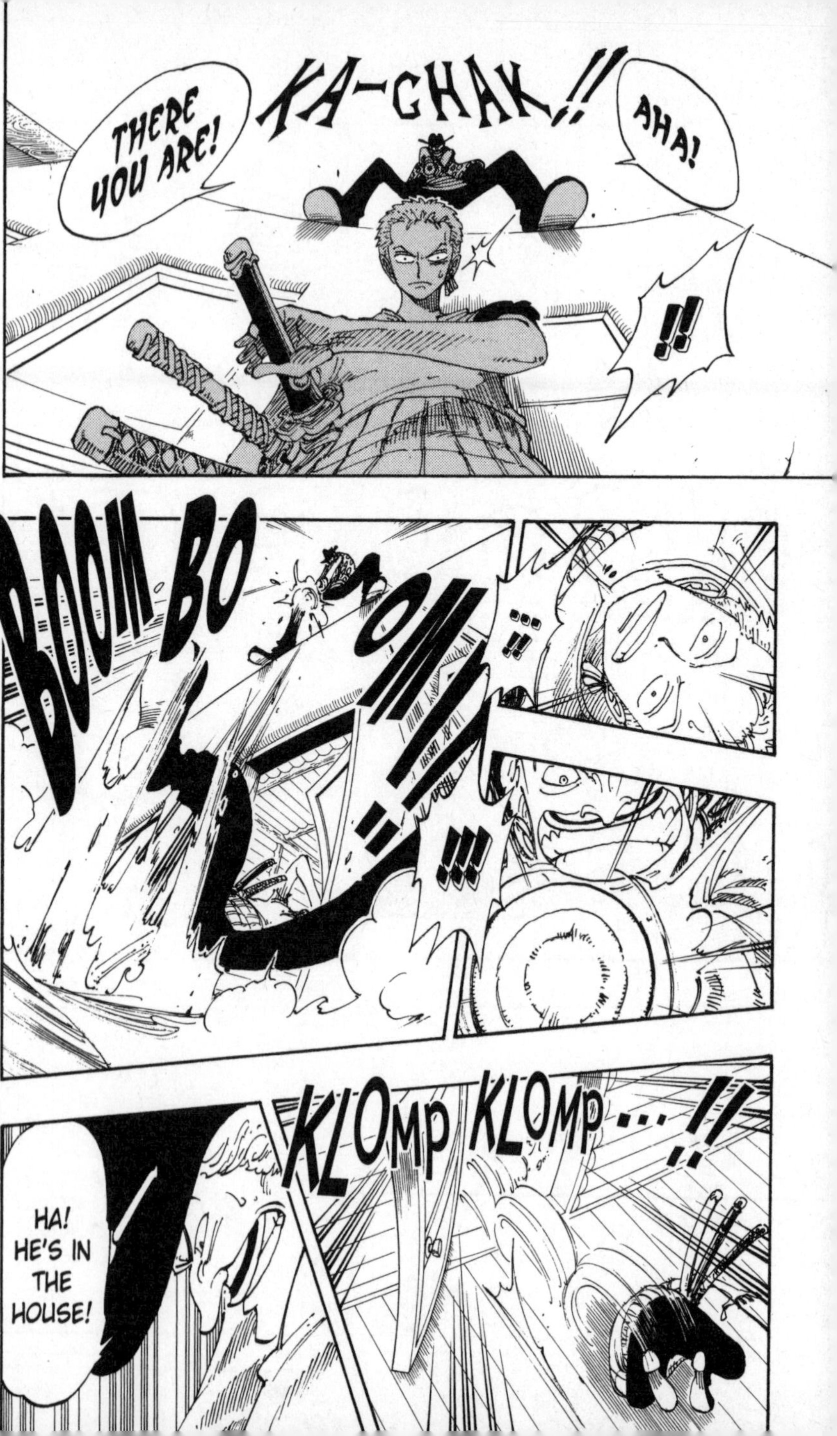
AHA!
KA-CHAK!!
THERE YOU ARE!
!!
BOOM BOOM!!
...!!
!!!
KLOMP KLOMP...!!
HA! HE'S IN THE HOUSE!

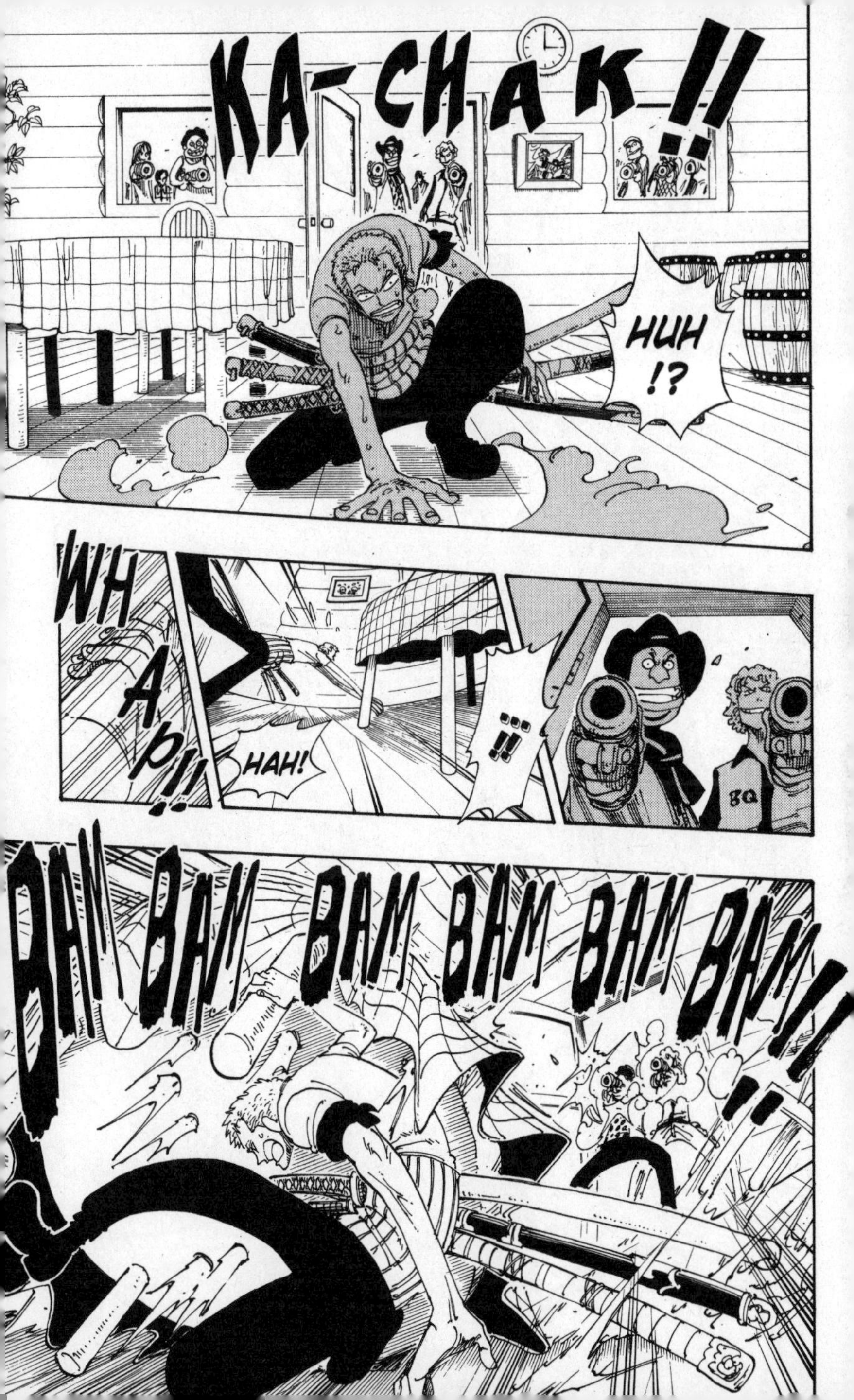
KA-CHAK!!
HUH !?
!!
BQ
HAH!
WHAP!!
BAM BAM BAM BAM BAM BAM!!

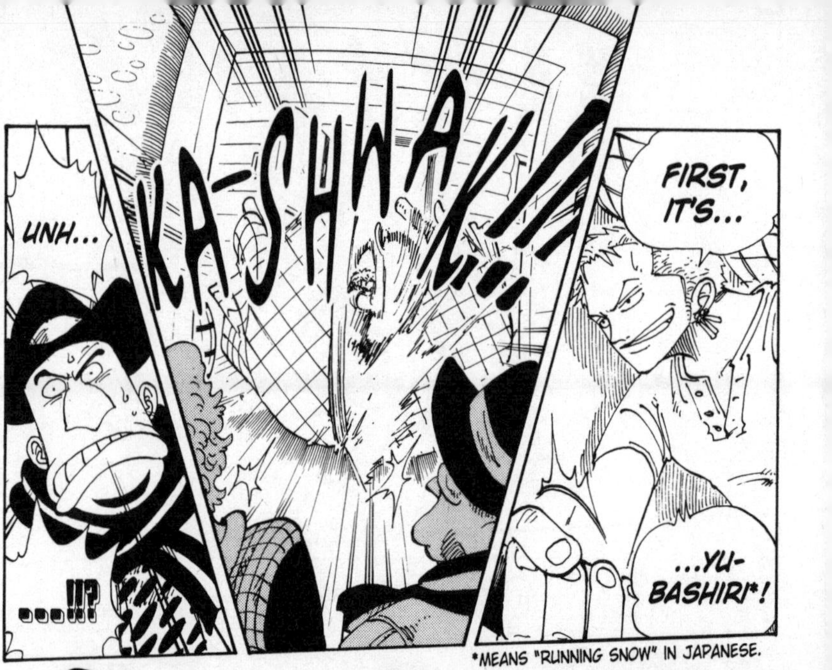
FIRST, IT'S...
...YU-BASHIRI*!
KA-SHWAKK!!
UNH...
...!!?

*MEANS "RUNNING SNOW" IN JAPANESE.

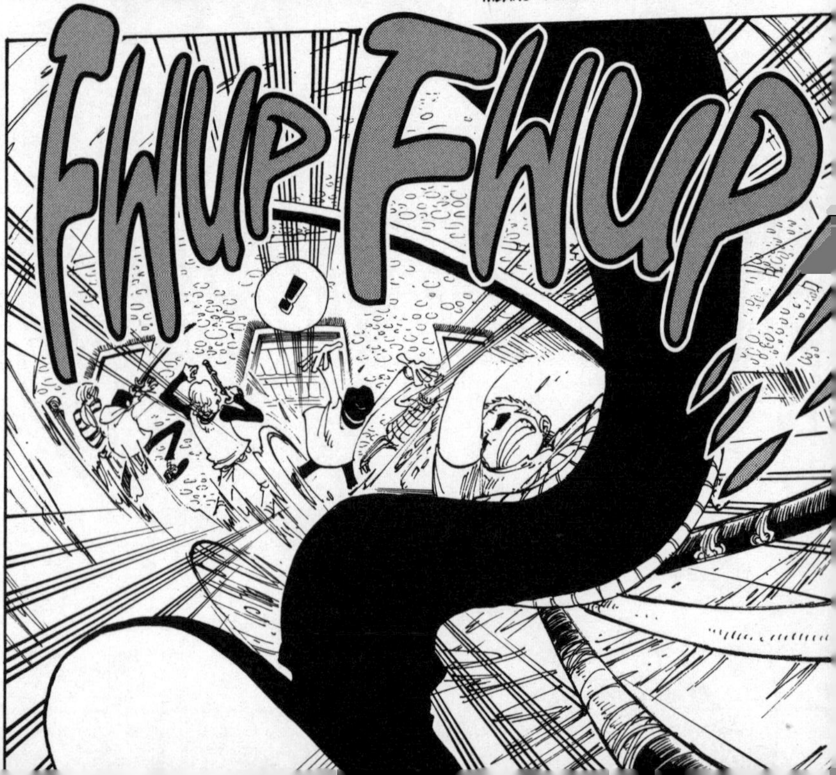
FWUP FWUP
!

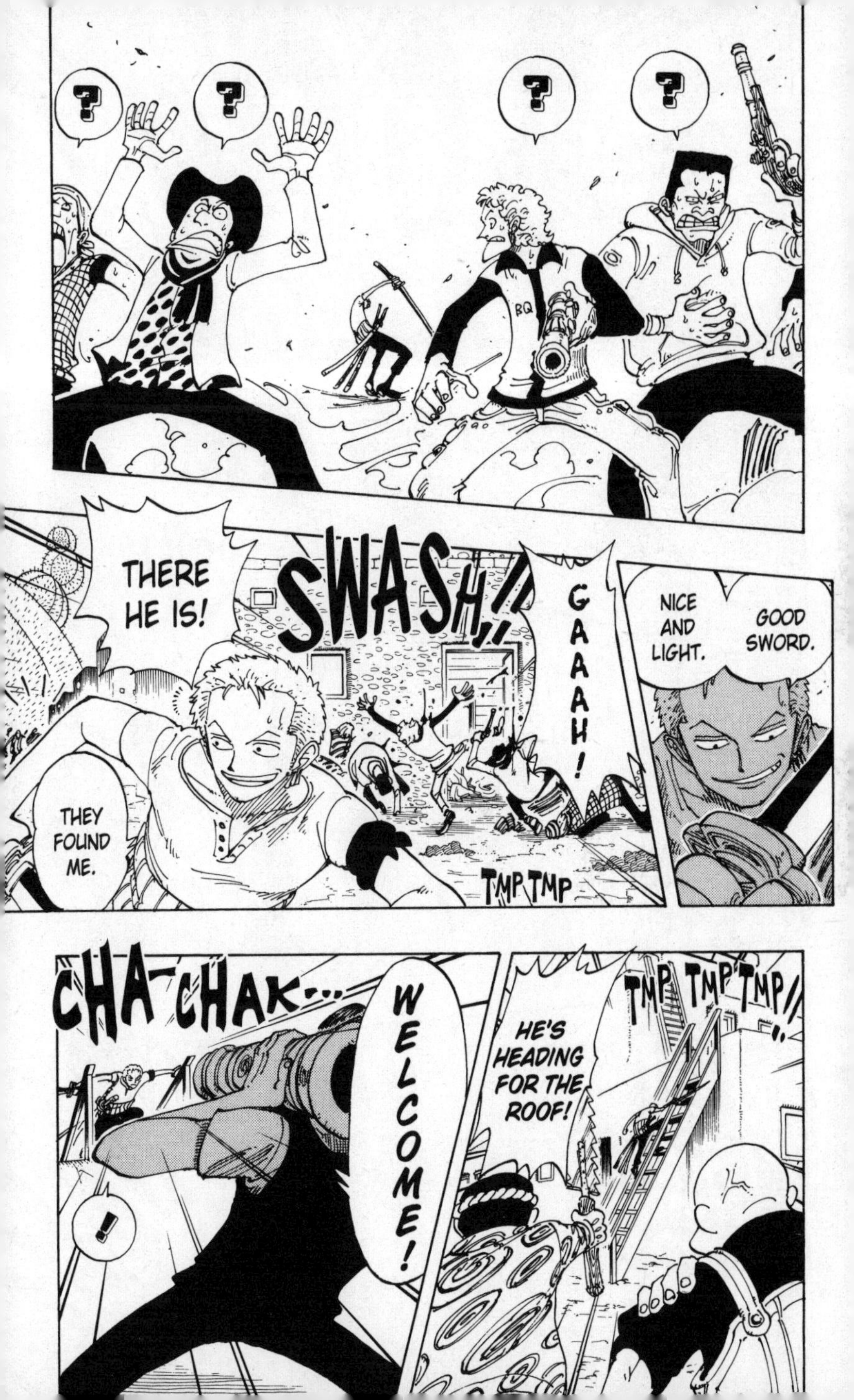
?
?
?
?
GOOD SWORD.
NICE AND LIGHT.
GAAAH!
SWASH!!
THERE HE IS!
TMP TMP
THEY FOUND ME.
TMP TMP TMP!!
HE'S HEADING FOR THE ROOF!
WELCOME!
CHA-CHAK...
!

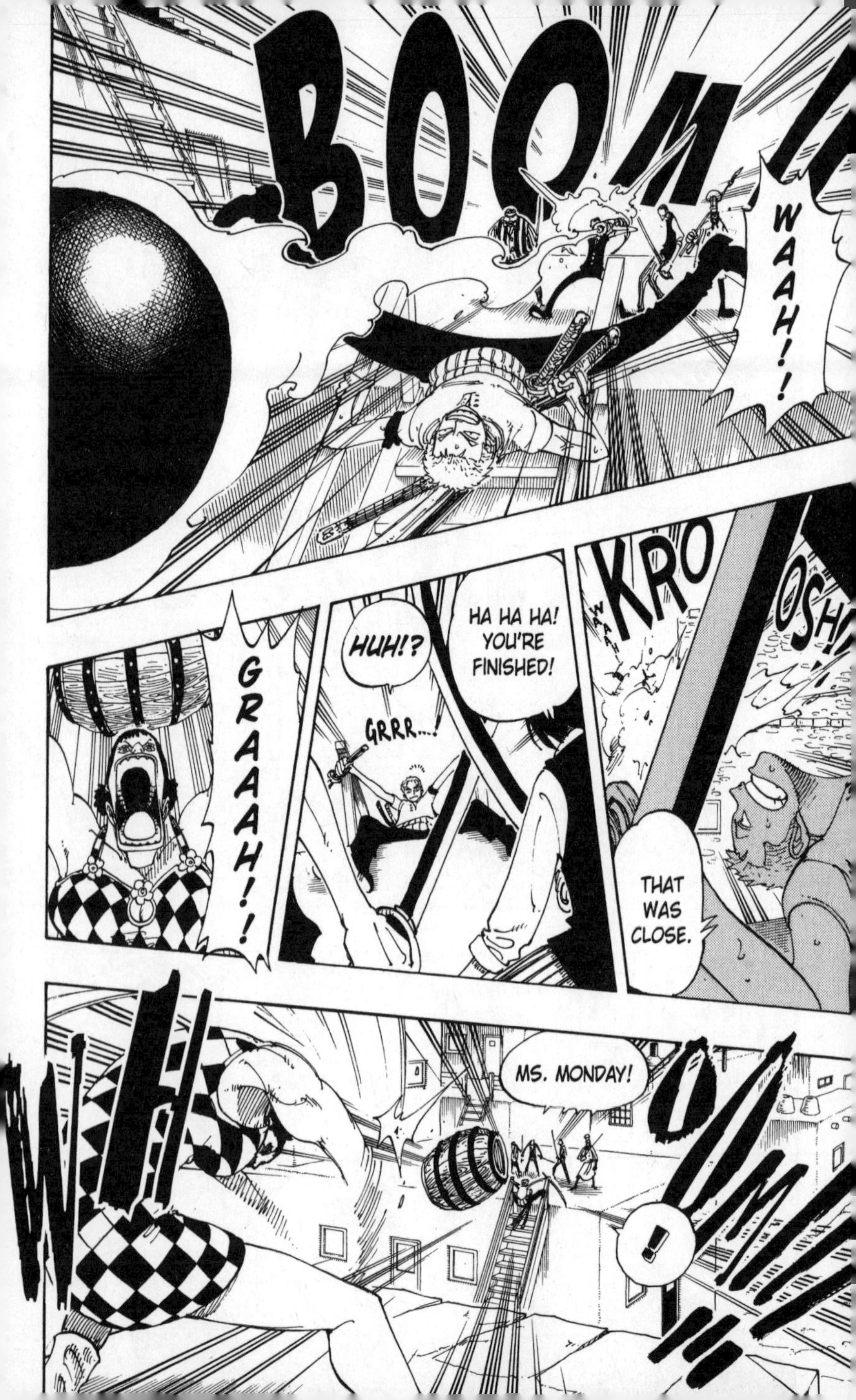
BOOM
WAAH!!
KROSH!!
WAAAH
THAT WAS CLOSE.
HA HA HA! YOU'RE FINISHED!
HUH!?
GRRR...!
GRAAAAH!!
MS. MONDAY!
!

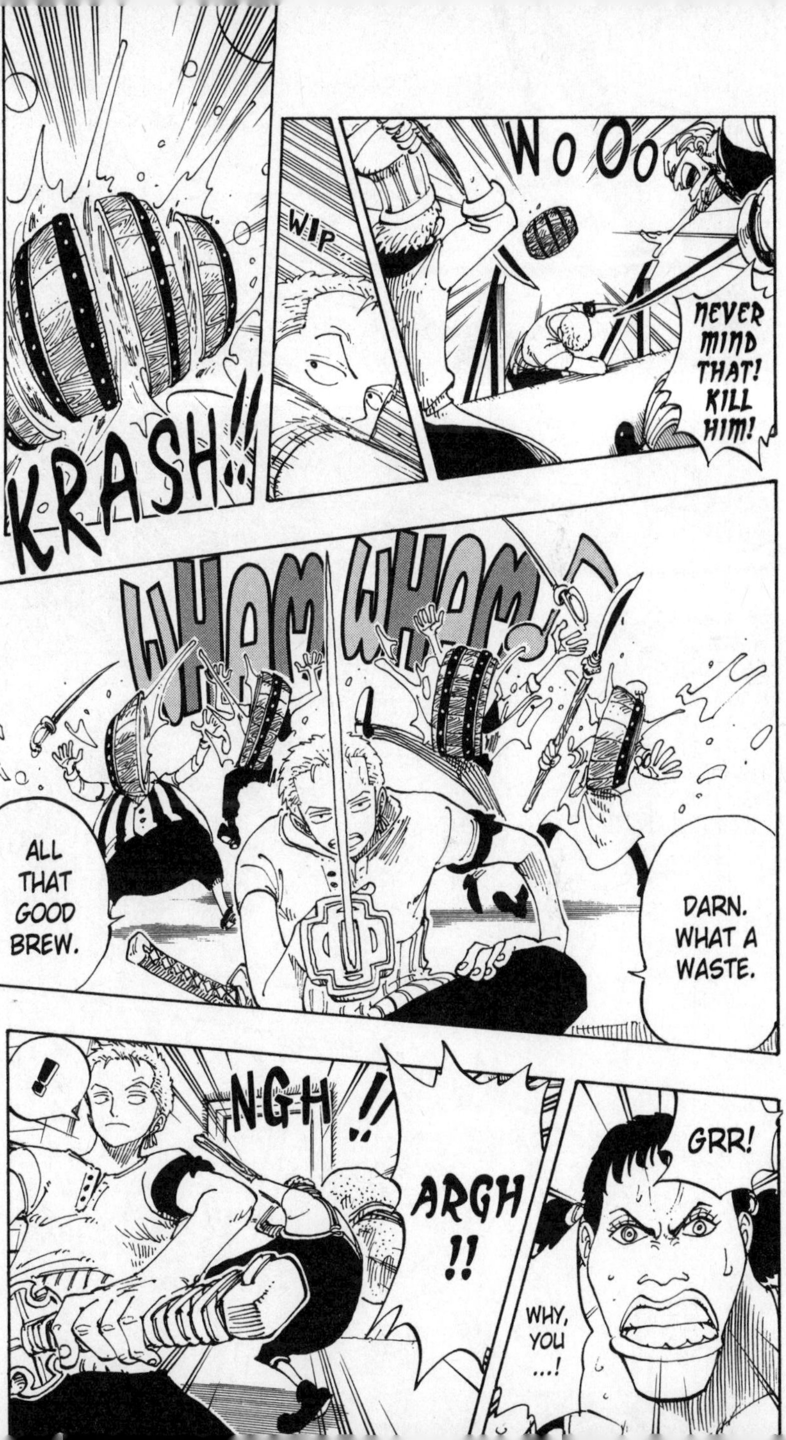
WO OO
NEVER MIND THAT! KILL HIM!
WIP
KRASH!!
WHAM WHAM
DARN. WHAT A WASTE.
ALL THAT GOOD BREW.
GRR!
WHY, YOU ...!
ARGH !!
NGH !!
!

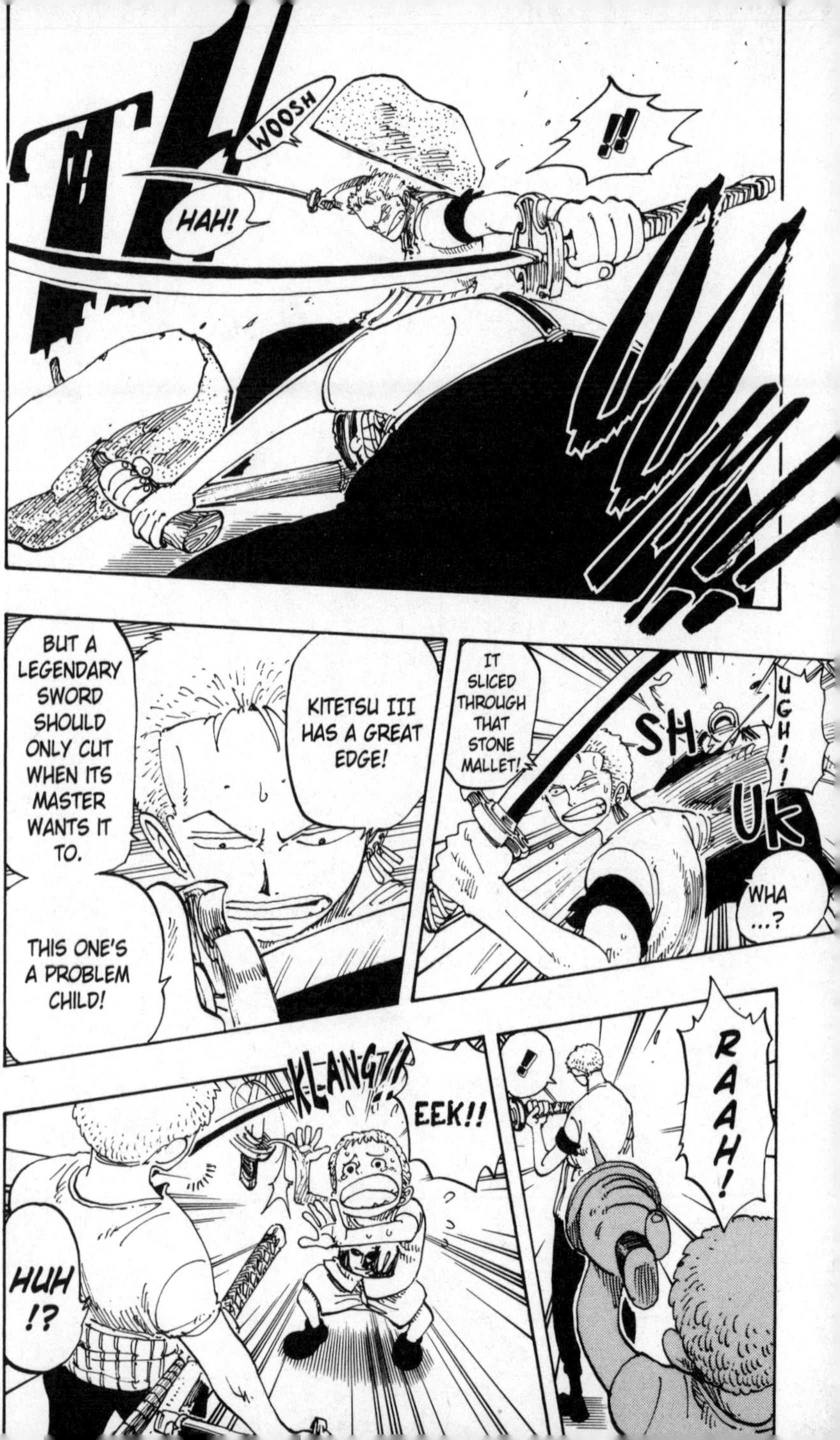
!!
WOOSH
HAH!
UGH!!
SH
UK
IT SLICED THROUGH THAT STONE MALLET!
WHA ...?
KITETSU III HAS A GREAT EDGE!
BUT A LEGENDARY SWORD SHOULD ONLY CUT WHEN ITS MASTER WANTS IT TO.
THIS ONE'S A PROBLEM CHILD!
RAAH!
!
KLANG!!
EEK!!
HUH!?

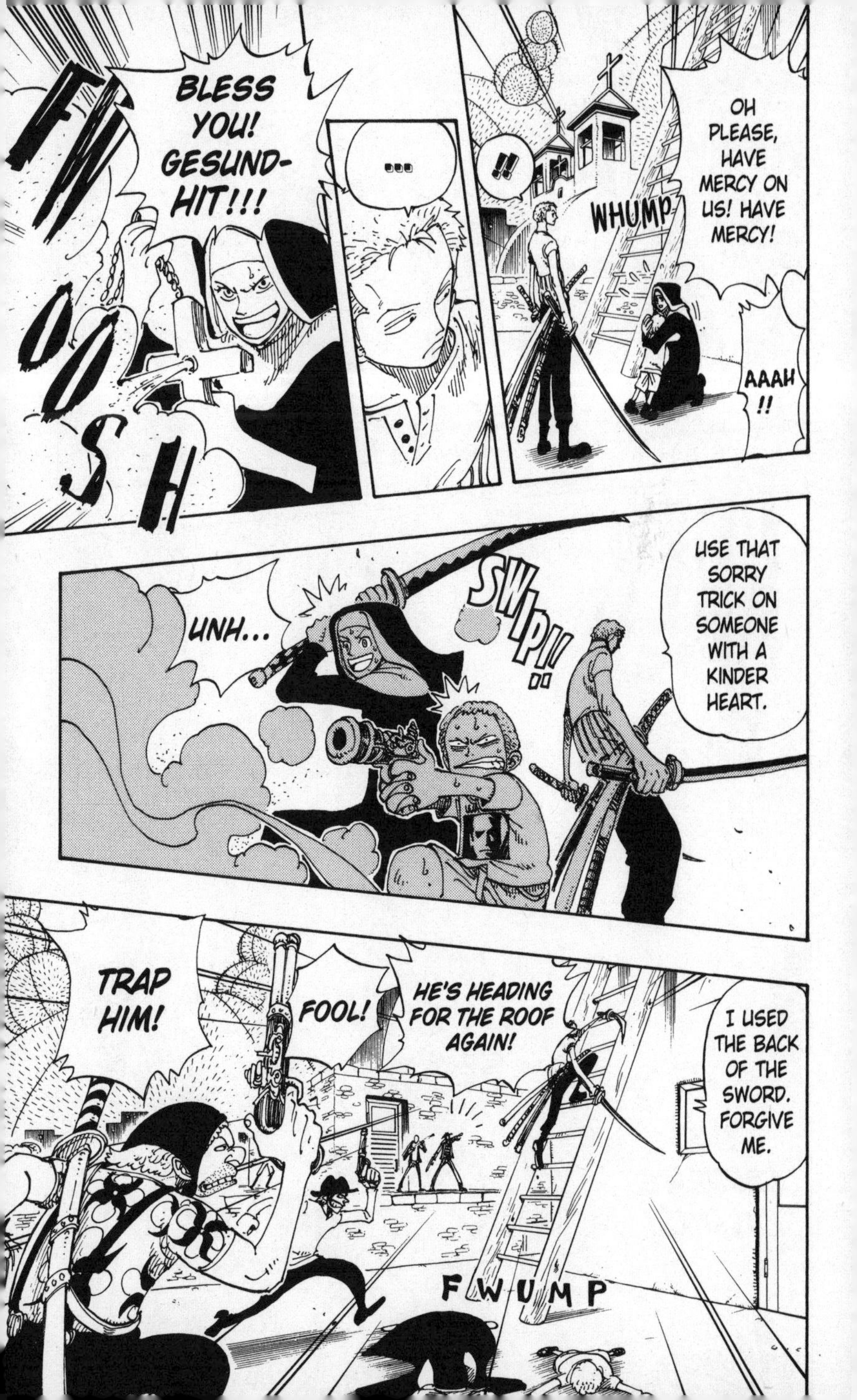
OH PLEASE, HAVE MERCY ON US! HAVE MERCY!
AAAH !!
WHUMP
!!
...
BLESS YOU! GESUNDHIT!!!
FWOOSH
USE THAT SORRY TRICK ON SOMEONE WITH A KINDER HEART.
SWIP!!
UNH...
I USED THE BACK OF THE SWORD. FORGIVE ME.
HE'S HEADING FOR THE ROOF AGAIN!
FOOL!
TRAP HIM!
FWUMP

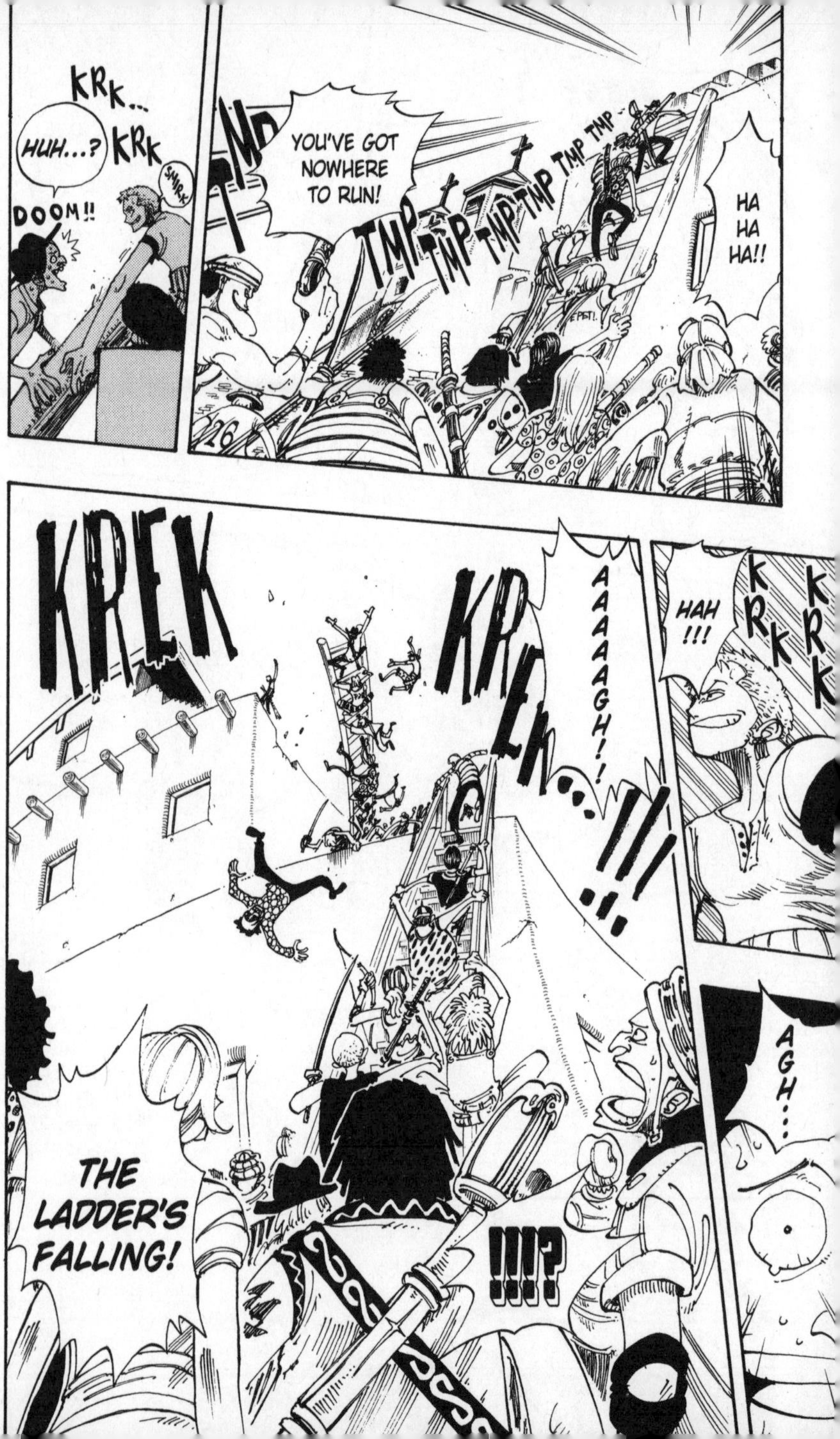

HA HA HA!!
YOU'VE GOT NOWHERE TO RUN!
TMP TMP TMP TMP TMP TMP TMP
KRK... KRK
HUH...?
SMIRK
DOOM!!
KRK KRK
HAH!!!
AGH...
KREK
KREK...!!!
AAAAAAGH!!
THE LADDER'S FALLING!
!!!?

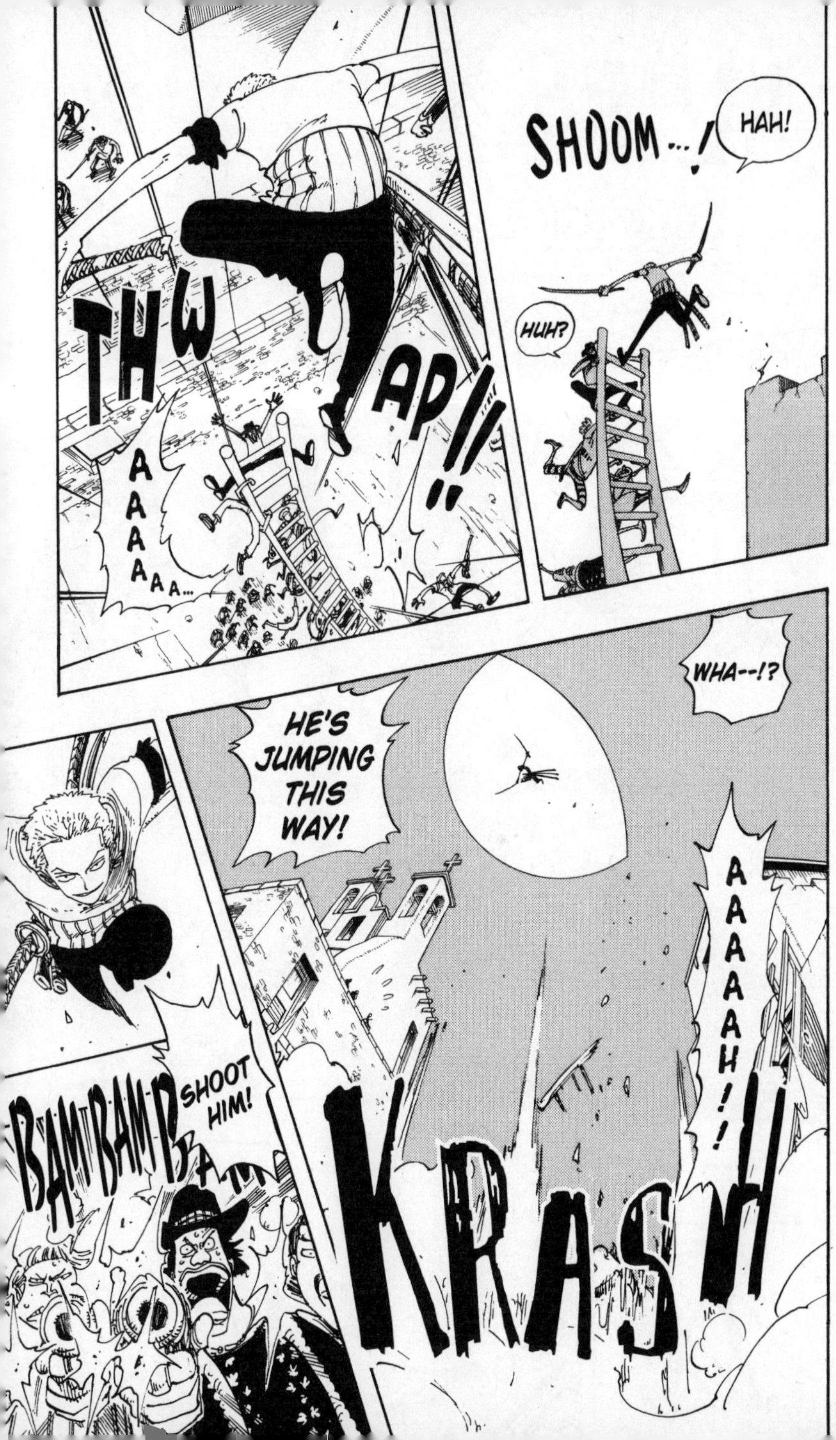
HAH!
SHOOM...!
HUH?
THWAP!!
AAAAAAA...
WHA--!?
HE'S JUMPING THIS WAY!
AAAAAAH!!!
KRASH
SHOOT HIM!
BAM BAM BAM

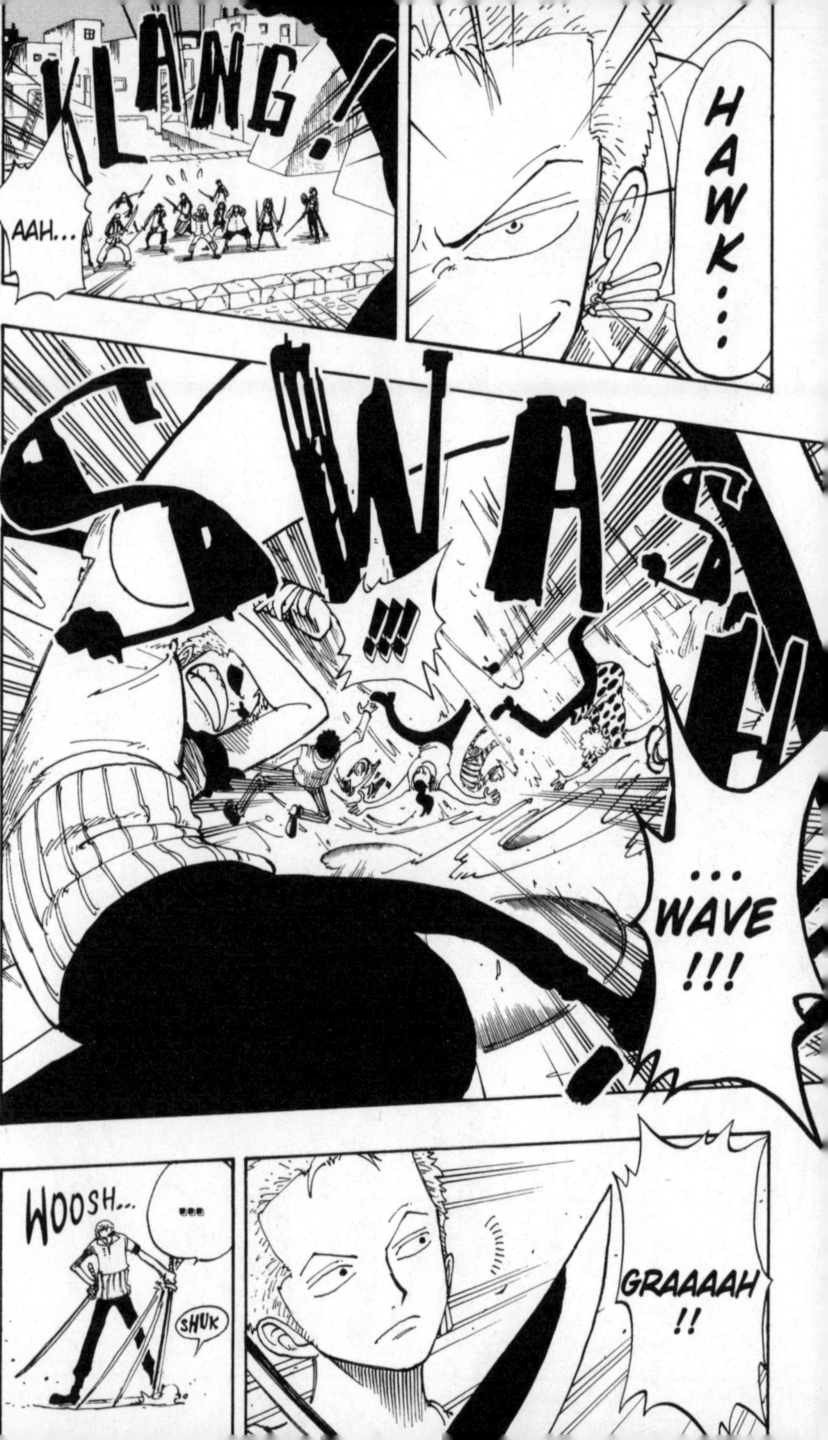
HAWK...
KLANG!
AAH...
SWASH!!!
...WAVE!!!
GRAAAAH!!
WOOSH...
...
SHUK

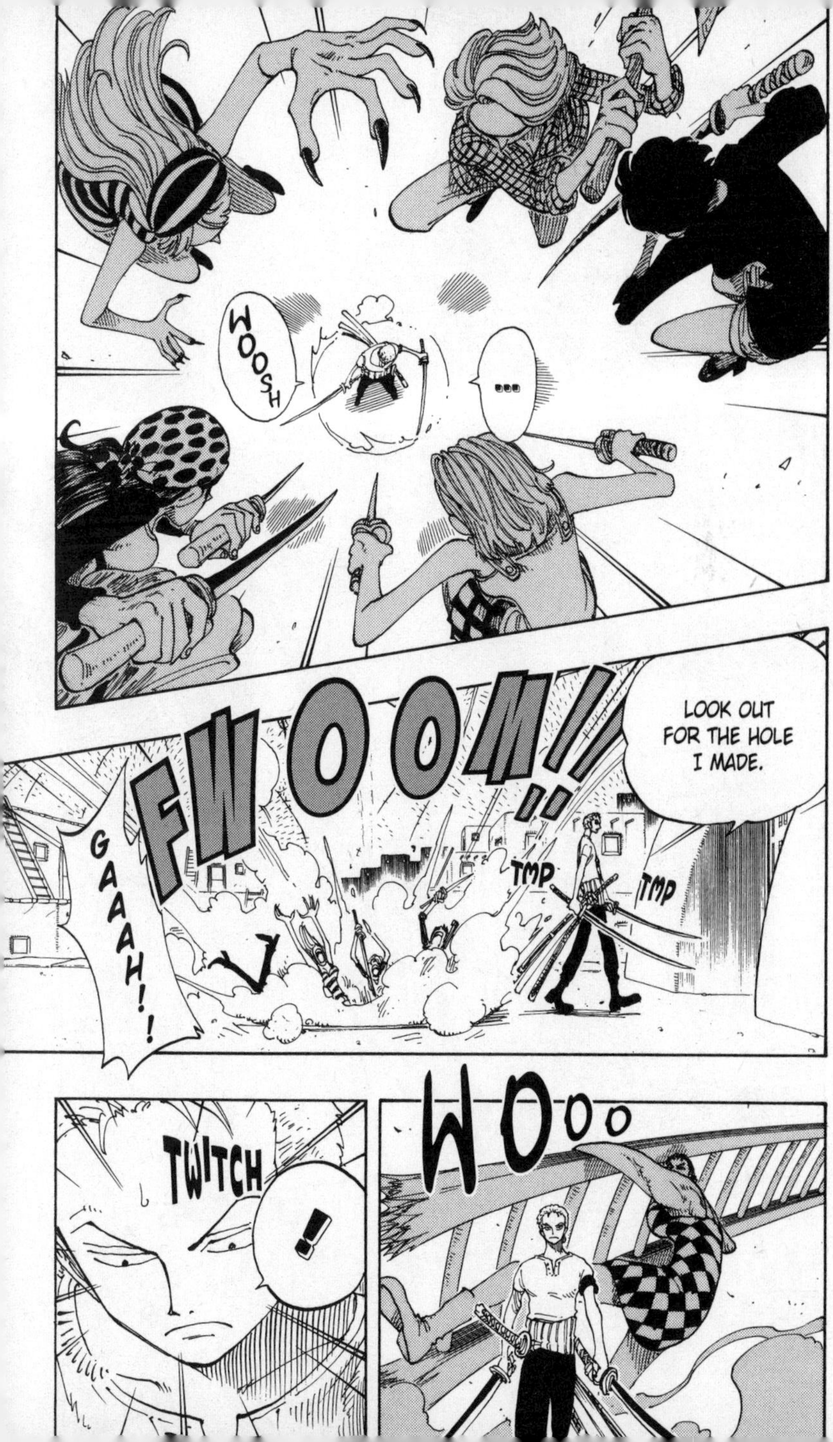
...
WOOSH
LOOK OUT FOR THE HOLE I MADE.
TMP
TMP
FWOOM!!
GAAAH!!
WOOO
!
TWITCH

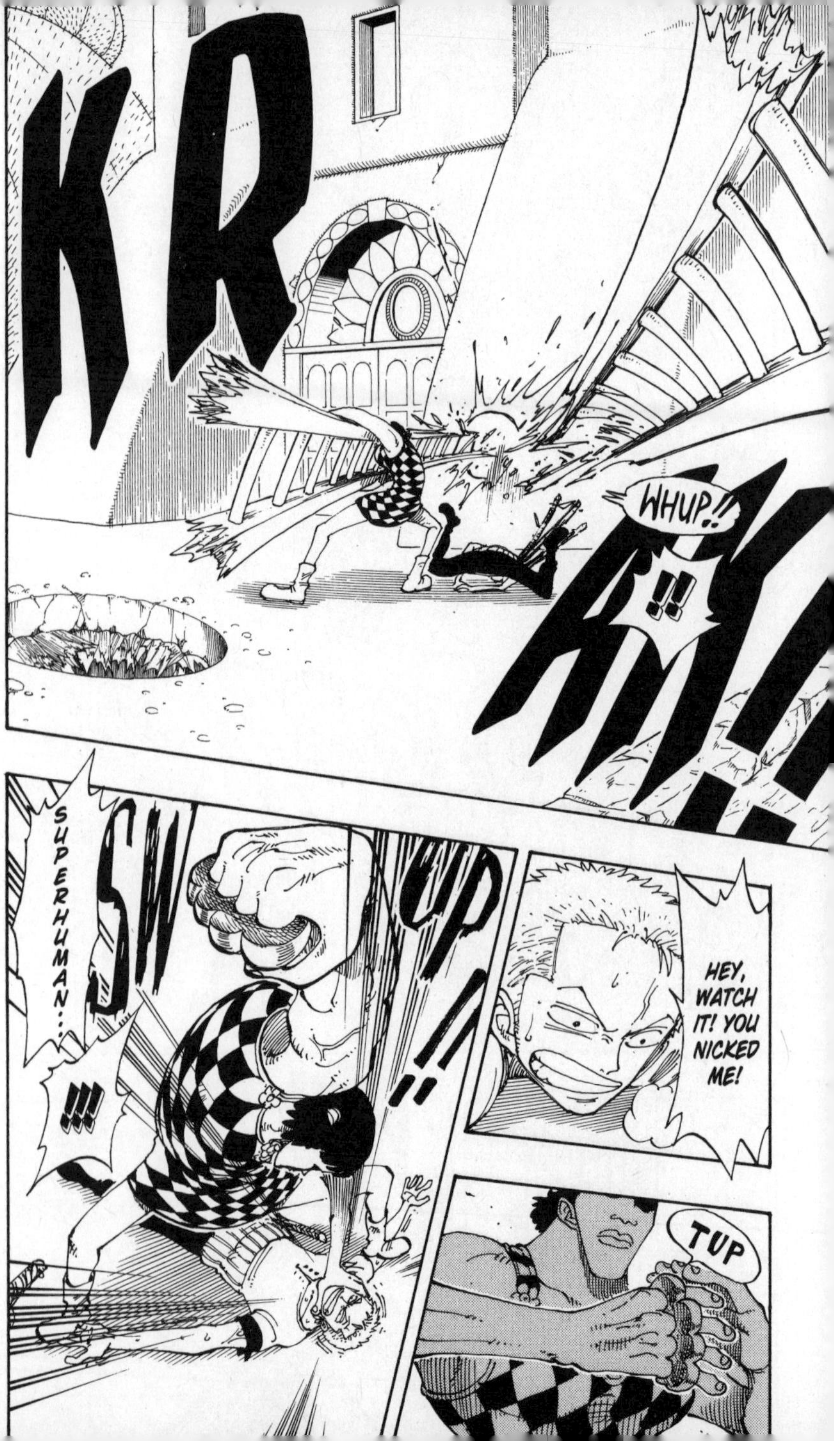
KR
WHUP!!
!!
HEY, WATCH IT! YOU NICKED ME!
TUP
SUPERHUMAN...
!!!

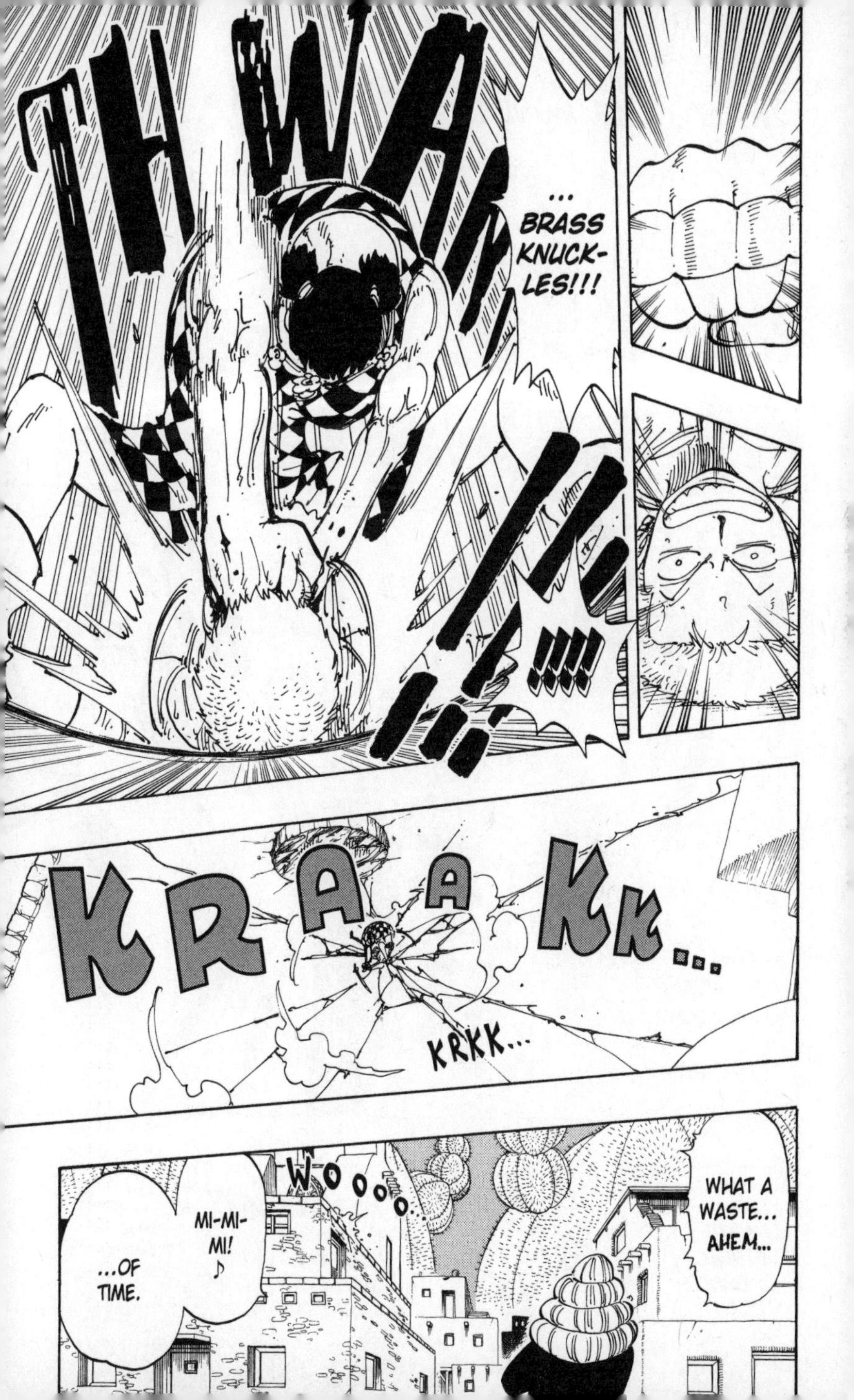
... BRASS KNUCK-LES!!!
THWAK!!!!
KRAAKK...
KRKK...
WHAT A WASTE... AHEM...
WOOOO...
MI-MI-MI! ♪
...OF TIME.

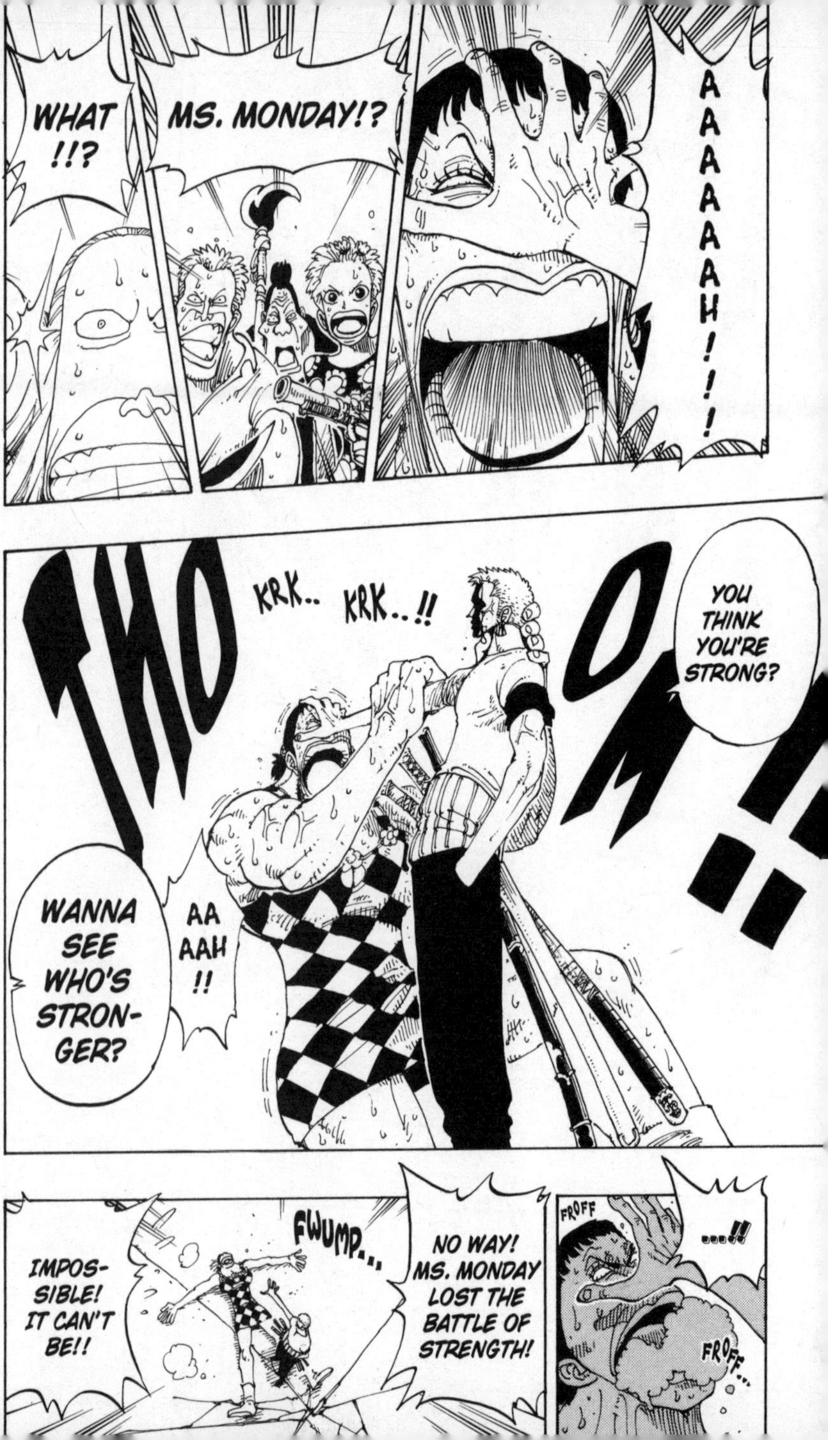
AAAAAAAH!!!
MS. MONDAY!?
WHAT !!?
YOU THINK YOU'RE STRONG?
THOOM!!
KRK.. KRK..!!
AA AAH !!
WANNA SEE WHO'S STRON-GER?
FROFF
...!!
FROFF...
NO WAY! MS. MONDAY LOST THE BATTLE OF STRENGTH!
FWUMP...
IMPOS-SIBLE! IT CAN'T BE!!

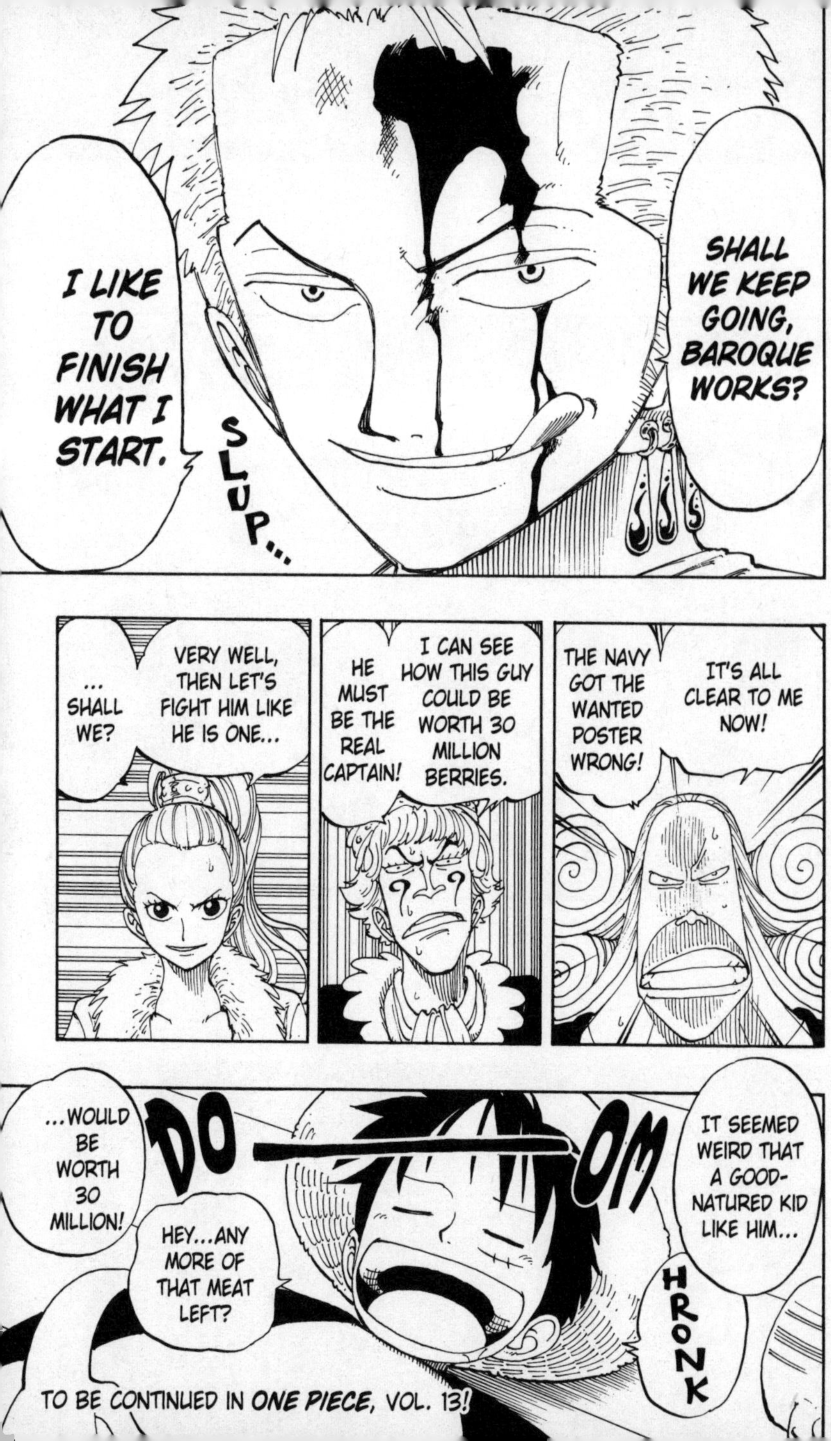
SHALL WE KEEP GOING, BAROQUE WORKS?
I LIKE TO FINISH WHAT I START.
SLUP...
IT'S ALL CLEAR TO ME NOW!
THE NAVY GOT THE WANTED POSTER WRONG!
I CAN SEE HOW THIS GUY COULD BE WORTH 30 MILLION BERRIES.
HE MUST BE THE REAL CAPTAIN!
VERY WELL, THEN LET'S FIGHT HIM LIKE HE IS ONE...
... SHALL WE?
IT SEEMED WEIRD THAT A GOOD-NATURED KID LIKE HIM...
...WOULD BE WORTH 30 MILLION!
DO—OM
HRONK
HEY...ANY MORE OF THAT MEAT LEFT?

TO BE CONTINUED IN *ONE PIECE*, VOL. 13!

COMING NEXT VOLUME:

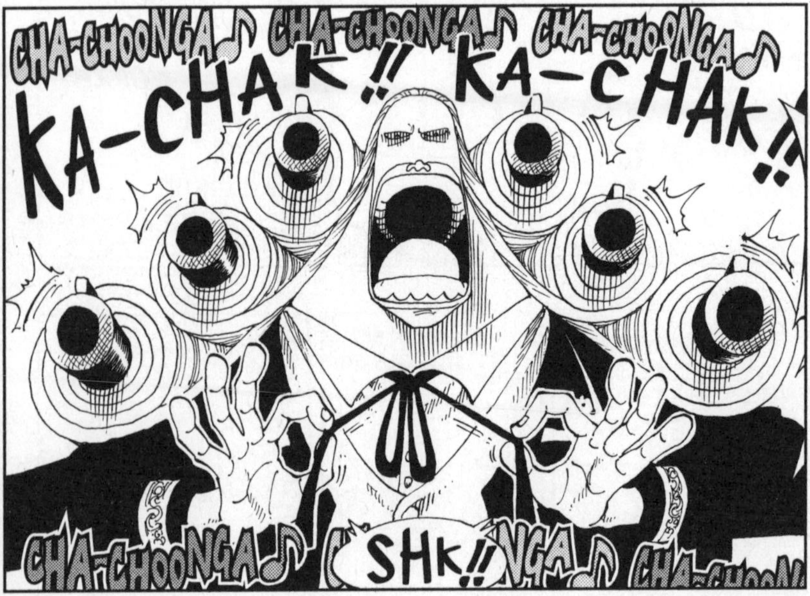
CHA-CHOONGA♪
CHA-CHOONGA♪
CHA-CHOONGA♪
KA-CHAK!!
KA-CHAK!!
CHA-CHOONGA♪
SHK!!

The reward for the capture of the Straw Hat Pirates has made them irresistible to bounty hunters for miles around, including the mysterious agents of Baroque Works. While his crewmates sleep off their night of revelry, Zolo takes on the agents in a battle that reveals a few surprises, including a lethal hairdo armed with multiple cannons!

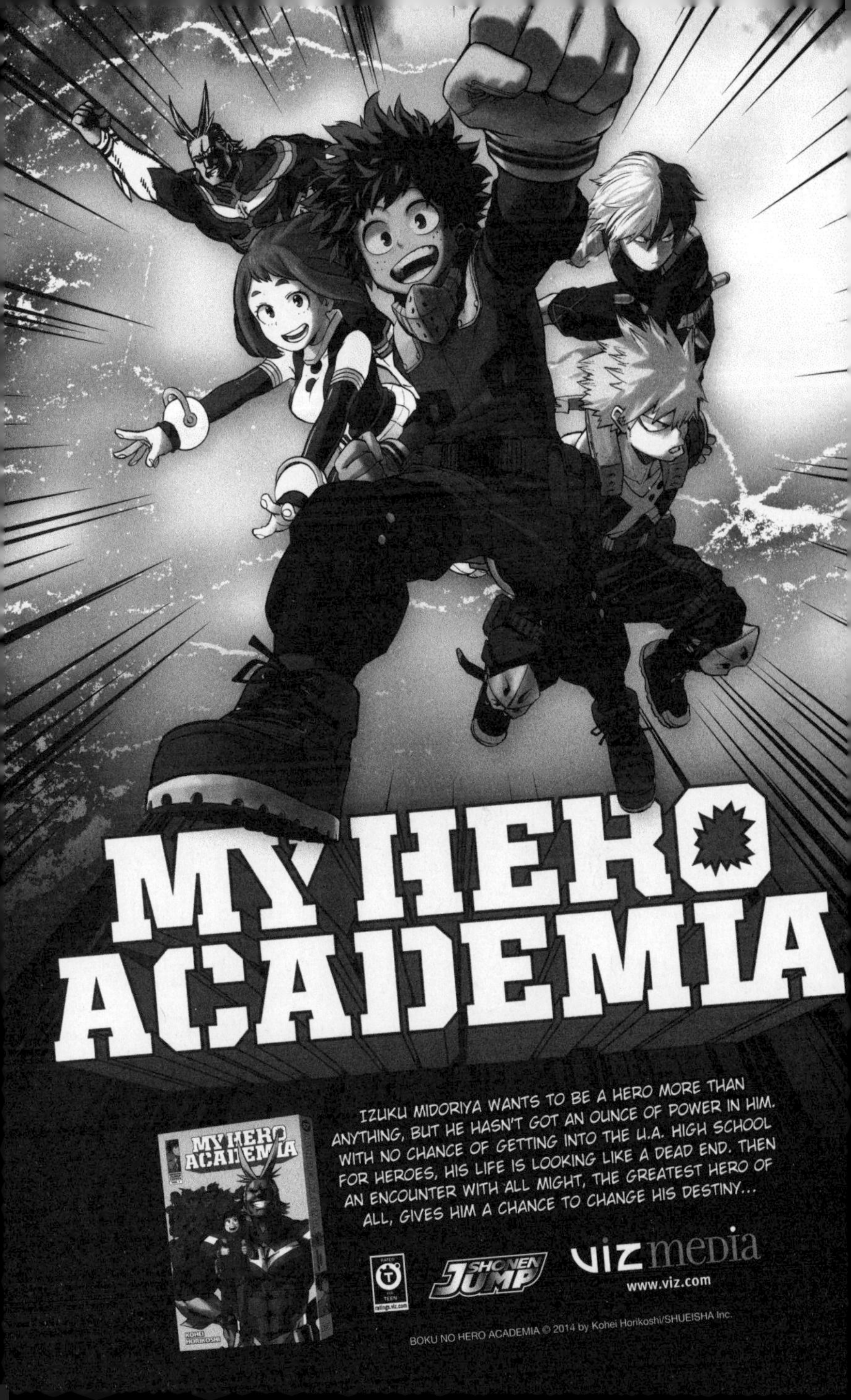
MY HERO ACADEMIA
IZUKU MIDORIYA WANTS TO BE A HERO MORE THAN ANYTHING, BUT HE HASN'T GOT AN OUNCE OF POWER IN HIM. WITH NO CHANCE OF GETTING INTO THE U.A. HIGH SCHOOL FOR HEROES, HIS LIFE IS LOOKING LIKE A DEAD END. THEN AN ENCOUNTER WITH ALL MIGHT, THE GREATEST HERO OF ALL, GIVES HIM A CHANCE TO CHANGE HIS DESTINY...
MY HERO ACADEMIA
KOHEI HORIKOSHI
TEEN
SHONEN JUMP
viz media
www.viz.com
BOKU NO HERO ACADEMIA © 2014 by Kohei Horikoshi/SHUEISHA Inc.

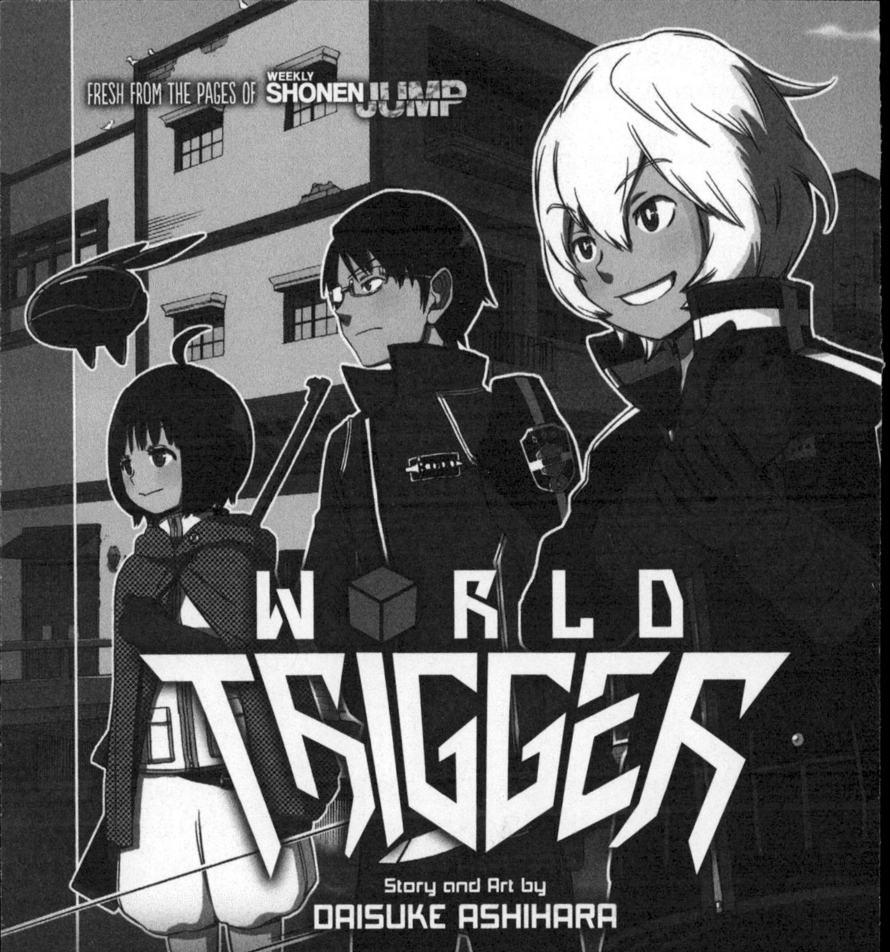
FRESH FROM THE PAGES OF WEEKLY SHONEN JUMP
WORLD TRIGGER
Story and Art by
DAISUKE ASHIHARA

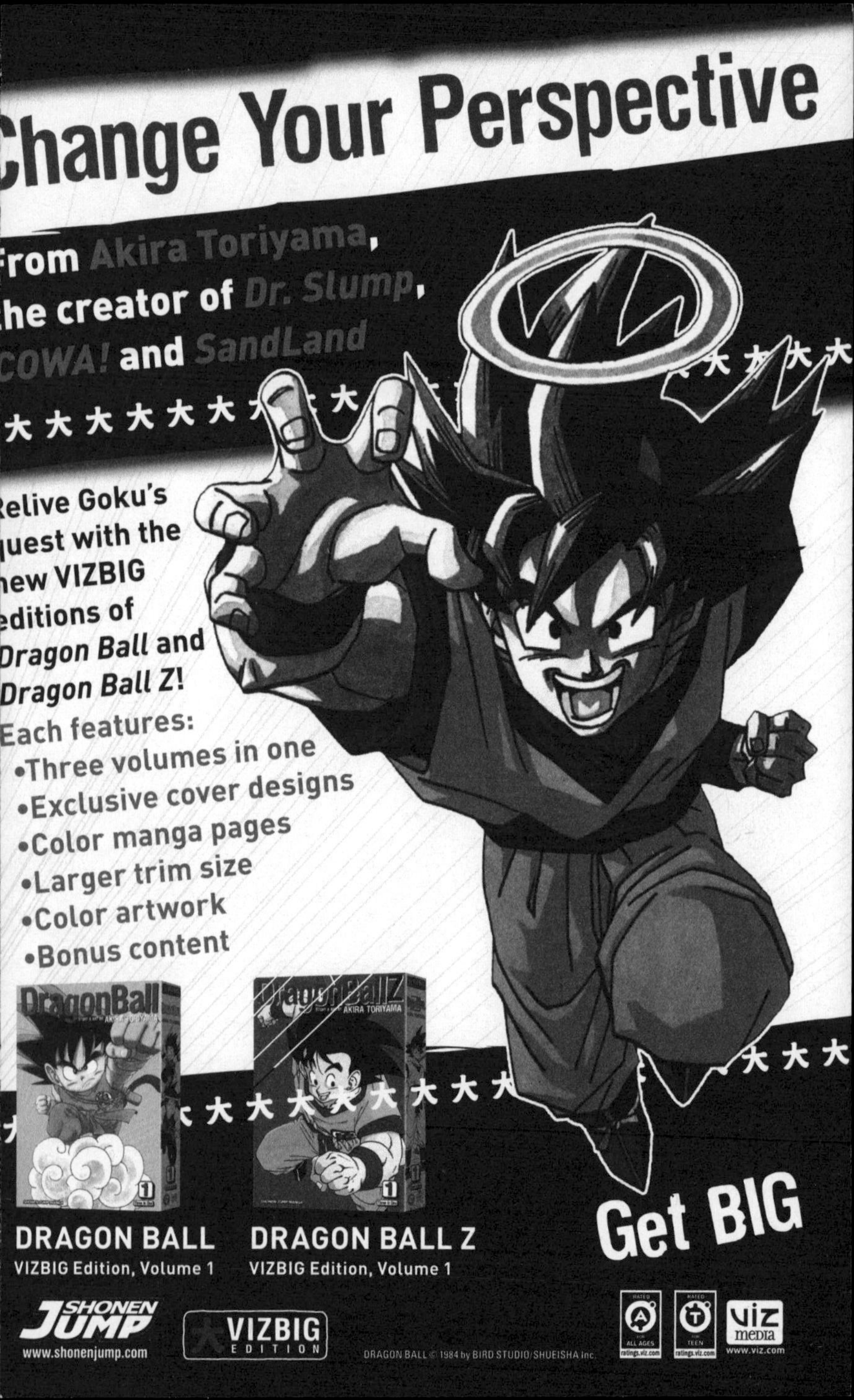
Change Your Perspective
From Akira Toriyama,
the creator of Dr. Slump,
COWA! and SandLand
Relive Goku's quest with the new VIZBIG editions of Dragon Ball and Dragon Ball Z!
Each features:
•Three volumes in one
•Exclusive cover designs
•Color manga pages
•Larger trim size
•Color artwork
•Bonus content
DRAGON BALL
VIZBIG Edition, Volume 1
DRAGON BALL Z
VIZBIG Edition, Volume 1
Get BIG
SHONEN JUMP
www.shonenjump.com
VIZBIG EDITION
DRAGON BALL © 1984 by BIRD STUDIO/SHUEISHA Inc.
www.viz.com

Black ✤ Clover

STORY & ART BY YUKI TABATA

Asta is a young boy who dreams of becoming the greatest mage in the kingdom. Only one problem—he can't use any magic! Luckily for Asta, he receives the incredibly rare five-leaf clover grimoire that gives him the power of anti-magic. Can someone who can't use magic really become the Wizard King? One thing's for sure—Asta will never give up!

www.viz.com

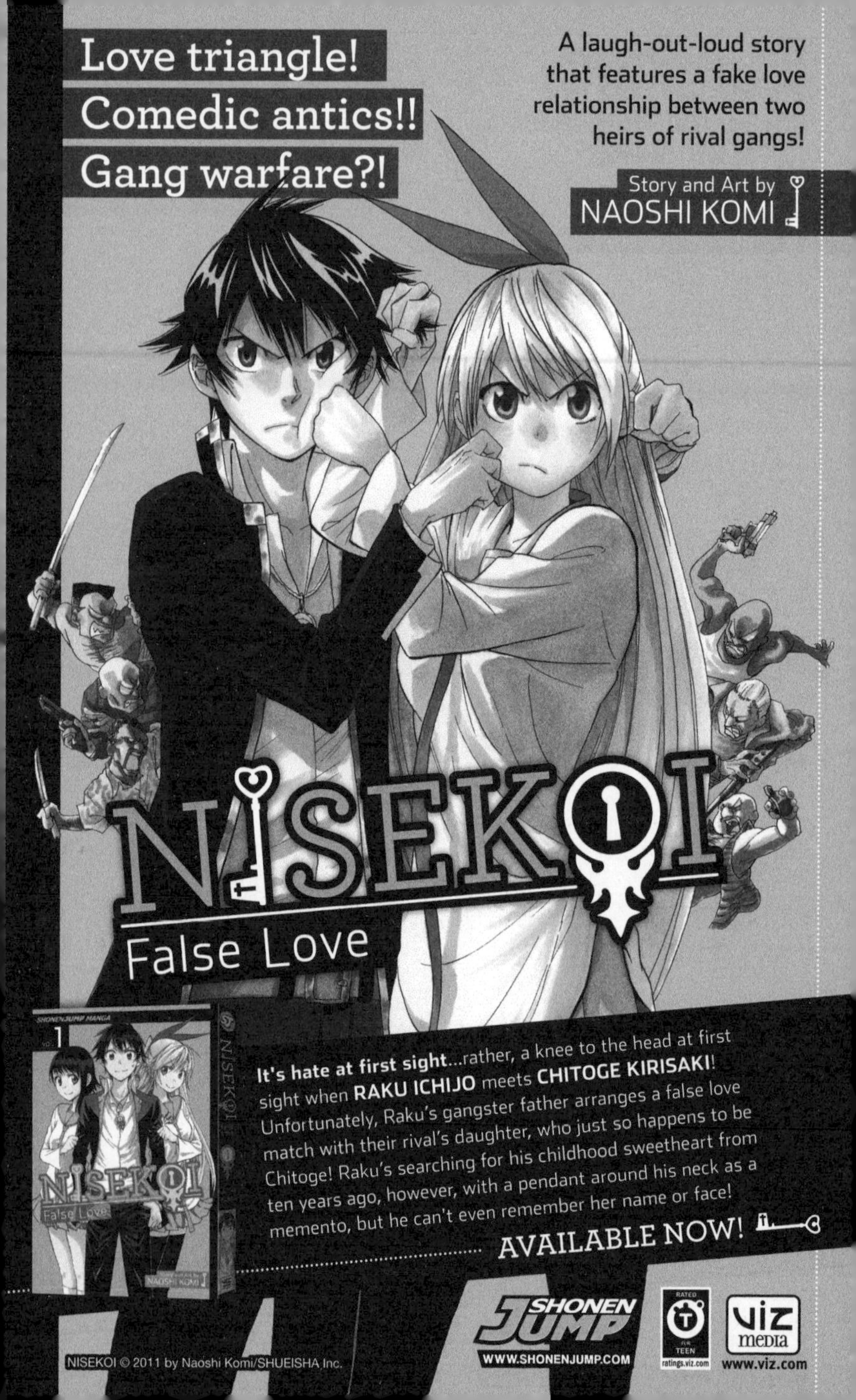
Love triangle!
Comedic antics!!
Gang warfare?!
A laugh-out-loud story that features a fake love relationship between two heirs of rival gangs!
Story and Art by
NAOSHI KOMI
NISEKOI
False Love
SHONEN JUMP MANGA
1
NISEKOI
False Love
NAOSHI KOMI
It's hate at first sight...rather, a knee to the head at first sight when RAKU ICHIJO meets CHITOGE KIRISAKI! Unfortunately, Raku's gangster father arranges a false love match with their rival's daughter, who just so happens to be Chitoge! Raku's searching for his childhood sweetheart from ten years ago, however, with a pendant around his neck as a memento, but he can't even remember her name or face!
AVAILABLE NOW!
SHONEN JUMP
WWW.SHONENJUMP.COM
RATED T FOR TEEN
ratings.viz.com
VIZ media
www.viz.com
NISEKOI © 2011 by Naoshi Komi/SHUEISHA Inc.

You're Reading in the Wrong Direction!!

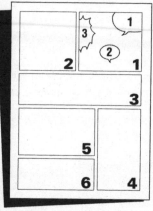

Whoops! Guess what? You're starting at the wrong end of the comic!

...It's true! In keeping with the original Japanese format, **One Piece** is meant to be read from right to left, starting in the upper-right corner.

Unlike English, which is read from left to right, Japanese is read from right to left, meaning that action, sound effects and word-balloon order are completely reversed... something which can make readers unfamiliar with Japanese feel pretty backwards themselves. For this reason, manga or Japanese comics published in the U.S. in English have sometimes been published "flopped"— that is, printed in exact reverse order, as though seen from the other side of a mirror.

By flopping pages, U.S. publishers can avoid confusing readers, but the compromise is not without its downside. For one thing, a character in a flopped manga series who once wore in the original Japanese version a T-shirt emblazoned with "M A Y" (as in "the merry month of") now wears one which reads "Y A M"! Additionally, many manga creators in Japan are themselves unhappy with the process, as some feel the mirror-imaging of their art skews their original intentions.

We are proud to bring you Eiichiro Oda's **One Piece** in the original unflopped format. For now, though, turn to the other side of the book and let the journey begin...!

—Editor

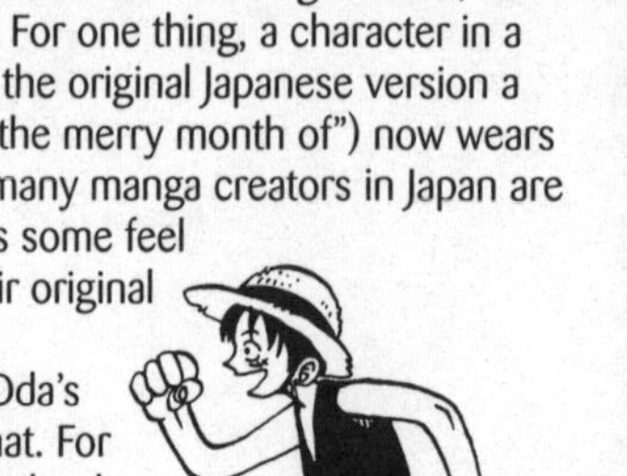